Lecture Notes in Computer Science   **10049**

Commenced Publication in 1973
Founding and Former Series Editors:
Gerhard Goos, Juris Hartmanis, and Jan van Leeuwen

Jesus Carretero et al. (Eds.)

Algorithms and Architectures for Parallel Processing

ICA3PP 2016 Collocated Workshops:
SCDT, TAPEMS, BigTrust, UCER, DLMCS
Granada, Spain, December 14–16, 2016
Proceedings

 Springer

Editors

see next page

ISSN 0302-9743   ISSN 1611-3349   (electronic)
Lecture Notes in Computer Science
ISBN 978-3-319-49955-0   ISBN 978-3-319-49956-7   (eBook)
DOI 10.1007/978-3-319-49956-7

Library of Congress Control Number: 2016959169

LNCS Sublibrary: SL1 – Theoretical Computer Science and General Issues

Printed on acid-free paper

This Springer imprint is published by Springer Nature
The registered company is Springer International Publishing AG
The registered company address is: Gewerbestrasse 11, 6330 Cham, Switzerland

Volume Editors

Jesus Carretero
University Carlos III of Madrid
Getafe, Spain

Javier Garcia-Blas
University Carlos III of Madrid
Getafe
Spain

Victor Gergel
Mathematical Support for Computers
N. I. Lobachevsky State University
   of Nizhny Novgorod
Nizhny Novgorod
Russia

Vladimir Voevodin
Research Computing Center (RCC)
Moscow State University
Moscow
Russia

Iosif Meyerov
Research Computing Center (RCC)
Moscow State University
Moscow
Russia

Juan A. Rico-Gallego
E.U. Politécnica
Universidad de Extremaddura
Cáceres
Spain

Juan C. Díaz-Martín
Ingenieria de Sistemas Informáticos
Universidad de Extremaddura
Cáceres
Spain

Pedro Alonso
Universitat Politécnica de València
Valencia
Spain

Juan Durillo
Distributed and Parallel Systems Group
Institute for Computer Science
Innsbruck
Austria

José Daniel Garcia Sánchez
Universidad Carlos III de Madrid
Getafe
Spain

Alexey L. Lastovetsky
UCD School of Computer Science
University College Dublin
Dublin
Ireland

Fabrizio Marozzo
University of Calabria
Rende (CS)
Italy

Qin Liu
Information Science and Engineering
Central South University
Changsha, Hunan
China

Zakirul Alam Bhuiyan
Information Science and Engineering
Central South University
Changsha, Hunan
China

Karl Fürlinger
Ludwig Maximilian University of Munich
Munich
Germany

Josef Weidendorfer
Informatik 10 - Rechnertechnik
Technische Universität München
Munich
Germany

José Gracia
High Performance Computing Center
(HLRS)
Stuttgart
Germany

Welcome Message from the ICA3PP 2016 General and Program Chairs

Welcome to the workshop proceedings of the 16th International Conference on Algorithms and Architectures for Parallel Processing (ICA3PP 2016), which was organized by the University of Madrid Carlos III and the University of Granada.

It was our great pleasure to organize the ICA3PP 2016 conference in Granada, Spain, during December 14–16, 2016. On behalf of the Organizing Committee of the conference, we would like to express our cordial gratitude to all participants who attended the conference.

ICA3PP 2016 was the 16th event in the series of conferences started in 1995 that is devoted to algorithms and architectures for parallel processing. ICA3PP is now recognized as the main regular international event that covers many dimensions of parallel algorithms and architectures, encompassing fundamental theoretical approaches, practical experimental projects, and commercial components and systems. The conference provides a forum for academics and practitioners from around the world to exchange ideas for improving the efficiency, performance, reliability, security, and interoperability of computing systems and applications. ICA3PP 2016 attracted high-quality research papers highlighting the foundational work that strives to push beyond the limits of existing technologies, including experimental efforts, innovative systems, and investigations that identify weaknesses in existing parallel processing technology.

ICA3PP 2016 consisted of the main conference and five international workshops. Many individuals contributed to the success of the conference. We would like to express our special appreciation to Prof. Yang Xiang, Prof. Weijia Jia, Prof. Laurence T. Yang, Prof. Yi Pan, and Prof. Wanlei Zhou, the Steering Committee chairs, for giving us the opportunity to host this prestigious conference and for their guidance with the conference organization. Special thanks to the program chairs, Dr. Peter Muller, Dr. Ryan K.L. Ko, and Dr. Javier García Blas, for their outstanding work on the technical program. Thanks also to the workshop chairs, Dr. Atsushi Hori, Dr. Ryan K.L. Ko, and Dr. Florin Isaila, for their excellent work in organizing attractive symposia and workshops. Thanks also to the local arrangements chair, Prof. Julio Ortega. We would like to give our thanks to all the members of the Organizing Committee and Program Committee as well as the external reviewers for their efforts and support. We would also like to give our thanks to the keynote speakers, Prof. Vladimir Voevodin, Dr. Rafael Asenjo, and Prof. Pedro José Marrón, for offering insightful and enlightening talks. Last but not least, we would like to thank all the authors who submitted their papers to conference associated workshops.

The five workshops were in the ICA3PP 2016 edition were:

- Supercomputing Co-Design Technology Workshop (SCDT).
- International Workshop in Theoretical Approaches to Performance Evaluation, Modeling and Simulation (TAPEMS).

- The First International Workshop on Trust, Security and Privacy for Big Data (BigTrust 2016).
- Ultrascale Computing for Early Researchers (UCER 2016).
- First International Workshop on Data Locality in Modern Computing Systems (DLMCS 2016).

We would like to thank the workshop organizers for their effort, dedication, and contribution to the conference success.

Jesus Carretero
Javier Garcia-Blas

Welcome Message from the SCDT 2016 General Chairs

On behalf of the Program Committee we are pleased to present the proceedings of the First Workshop on Supercomputing Co-Design Technology (SCDT-2016) organized in conjunction with the 16th International Conference on Algorithms and Architectures for Parallel Processing (ICA3PP 2016). The workshop addresses the urgent need for theoretical and practical technologies of an accurate and efficient design of high-performance computing systems, highly parallel methods, and extreme-scale applications to be able to solve large problems using the current and prospective generations of high-performance computing systems. The most essential concept behind these technologies is co-design. Supercomputing co-design is a very close partnership or interrelationship between all the layers involved in the process of solving these problems on high-performance computing systems: mathematical methods, algorithms, applications, programming technologies, runtime systems, layers of system software and hardware.

The Workshop on Supercomputing Co-Design Technology consists of talks from individuals or teams from academia, industry, and other educational and research institutes on topics highlighting various aspects of the tight interrelationship between algorithms and computer architectures, parallel programming technologies and runtime systems, and between all these layers for a wide spectrum of computer architectures. The most interesting and important topics for discussion at the workshop are enabling co-design technologies for high-performance computing, future-generation application-aware supercomputer architectures, extreme-scale concepts including exascale, parallel programming models, interfaces, languages, libraries, and tools, supercomputer hardware-aware applications and algorithms, scalable runtime systems, methods and tools for holistic performance, scalability and efficiency analysis, education and supercomputing co-design technology, best education practices, and others.

The workshop covered a wide range of hot topics. Several papers are related to methods and tools for performance and scalability analysis that is very important for increasing the efficiency of utilization of modern and future supercomputers. A few papers consider state-of-the-art problems of computational sciences. The authors employ co-design technologies for high-performance computing in astrophysics, plasma physics, and heart simulation on traditional and heterogeneous supercomputers. The other topics featured at the workshop included parallel pattern processing using cellular automata, distributed algorithms on large graphs, and educational software for parallel computing. And of course, we are very grateful to professor Thomas Sterling, who kindly accepted our invitation to give a keynote talk at the workshop.

December 2016

Victor Gergel
Vladimir Voevodin

Welcome Message from the TAPEMS 2016 Program Chairs

On behalf of the Program Committee of the First International Workshop on Theoretical Approaches to Performance Evaluation, Modeling and Simulation (TAPEMS 2016), we would like to welcome you to the proceedings of the event, which was held in Granada, Spain, during December 14–16, 2016.

The TAPEMS workshop aims at bringing together researchers who are working on modeling performance issues of parallel computing. The workshop features technical presentations covering various aspects including performance modeling and evaluation, modeling energy efficiency of communication runtimes, and heterogeneous computing systems. Our intention was for this edition of TAPEMS to be the first of a series of successful workshops on theoretically biased performance analysis of current computer system. The TAPEMS 2016 workshop collected a bunch of interesting papers from all around the world. We would like to give our thanks to the researchers who submitted their manuscripts, and to the Program Committee and the external reviewers, who contributed their valuable time and expertise to provide professional reviews. We believe that the TAPEMS meeting will provide a good opportunity for participants to know themselves, learn from each other, and hopefully design joint strategies.

Juan Antonio Rico Gallego
Juan Carlos Díaz Martín
José Daniel García Sánchez
Alexey L. Lastovetsky

Welcome Messages from the BigTrust 2016 General Chairs

On behalf of the Program Committee of the First International Workshop on Trust, Security and Privacy for Big Data (BigTrust 2016), we would like to express our gratitude to all the participants who attended the workshop in Granada, Spain, during December 14–16, 2016.

BigTrust 2016 aims at bringing together people from both academia and industry to present their most recent work related to trust, security, and privacy issues in big data, and exchange ideas and thoughts in order to identify emerging research topics and define the future of big data.

BigTrust 2016 was the first event in a series of workshops on trust, security and privacy for big data (BigTrust). This international workshop collected research papers on the aforementioned research issues from all around the world. Each paper was reviewed by at least three experts in the field. We feel very proud of the high number of submissions, and it was difficult to collect the best papers from all those received.

Many individuals contributed to the success of this high-caliber international workshop. We would like to express our special appreciation to the program chairs, Prof. Peter Mueller, Prof. Ryan K.L. Ko, and Prof. Javier Garcia-Blas, for giving us the opportunity to hold this workshop and for their guidance on the symposium organization. In particular, we would like to thank all researchers and practitioners who submitted their manuscripts, and the Program Committee members and the additional reviews for their tremendous efforts and timely reviews.

We hope you enjoy the proceedings of BigTrust 2016.

Qin Liu
Md Zakirul Alam Bhuiyan

Welcome Messages from the UCER 2016 General Chairs

Welcome to the proceedings of the first edition of the workshop on Ultrascale Computing for Early Researchers (UCER 2016), which took place in Granada, Spain, on December 15, 2016.

The aim of this workshop is to give the opportunity to early-stage researchers (PhD students or recent PhD graduates) to show their work related to ultrascale computing. Although a future technology, currently many systems are designed with the goal of being used in ultrascale systems. Many different subtopics are related in the exploration of system software and applications for enabling a sustainable development of future high-scale computing platforms. The tasks involved range from the analysis of the current state of the art on sustainability in large-scale systems to the proposition of new tools that aim to improve computations on these systems. The topics addressed are, among others, HPC, distributed systems, and big data communities in cross-cutting aspects such as programmability, scalability, resilience, energy efficiency, and data management.

Six Papers Were Accepted For Presentation At The Workshop After A Peer-Review Process.

We hope that UCER will become a reference event for early-stage researchers attending future ICA3PP conferences.

Pedro Alonso
Juan Durillo
Fabrizio Marozzo

Welcome Messages from the DLMCS 2016 General Chairs

On behalf of the Program Committee of the First International Workshop on Data Locality in Modern Computing Systems (DLMCS 2016), we welcome you to the proceedings of the workshop, which was held in Granada, Spain, during December 14–16, 2016.

The cost of moving data is becoming a dominant factor for performance and energy efficiency in high-performance computing systems. To minimize data movement, applications have to consider initial data placement and to optimize both vertical data movement in the memory hierarchy and horizontal data transfer between processing units.

The DLMCS workshop aims to present the most recent works, both from academia and industry, related to mechanisms to be used in computing systems for increasing data locality including hardware, software, and co-design approaches. Topics such as programming abstractions for data locality, multilevel locality, task-based data locality, hardware mechanisms for exploiting locality, and data locality in large-scale HPC systems were addressed in this workshop.

This international workshop collected research papers on the aforementioned research issues from all around the world. Each paper was peer reviewed by at least three experts in the field, thus ensuring the high quality of the workshop.

Karl Fürlinger
Josef Weidendorfer
José Gracia

Organization

Supercomputing Co-design Technology Workshop (SCDT)

Victor Gergel, Co-chair	Lobachevsky State University of Nizhni Novgorod, Russia
Vladimir Voevodin, Co-chair	Moscow State University, Russia
Arndt Bode	Leibniz Supercomputing Centre, Germany
Alexander Boukhanovsky	ITMO University, Russia
Yuefan Deng	Stony Brook University, USA
Florent de Dinechin	INSA Lyon, France
Torsten Hoefler	Swiss Federal Institute of Technology, Switzerland
Thomas Ludwig	German Climate Computing Center, Germany
Iosif Meyerov, Scientific secretary	Lobachevsky State University of Nizhni Novgorod, Russia
Marek Michalewicz	A*STAR Computational Resource Centre, Singapore
Bernd Mohr	Jülich Supercomputing Centre, Germany
Mikhail Moshkov	King Abdullah University of Science and Technology, Saudi Arabia
Sergey Orlov	Transport and Telecommunication Institute, Latvia
Nina Popova	Moscow State University, Russia
Arnold Rosenberg	Northeastern University, USA
Ahmed Seffah	Lappeenranta University of Technology, Finland
Yaroslav Sergeyev	University of Calabria, Italy
Andrey Sozykin	Ural Federal University, Russia
Roman Wyrzykowski	Czestochowa University of Technology, Poland

International Workshop on Theoretical Approaches to Performance Evaluation, Modeling, and Simulation (TAPEMS)

Marco Aldinucci	University of Torino, Italy
Pedro Alonso Jordá	Polytechnic University of Valencia, Spain
Damián Álvarez Mallón	Jülich Supercomputing Center, Germany
Hrachya Astsatryan	National Academy of Sciences, Republic of Armenia
María Barreda	Jaume I University, Spain
Silvina Caíno Lores	Carlos III University, Spain
Miguel Cárdenas Montes	Ciemat, Spain
Sandra Catalán	Jaume I University, Spain
Georges Da Costa	IRIT/Toulouse, France
Manuel F. Dolz	Carlos III University, Spain

Juan L. García-Zapata	University of Extremadura, Spain
Ester Martin Garzón	University of Almería, Spain
Arturo Gonzalez-Escribano	University of Valladolid, Spain
José L. González	CenitS Supercomputing Center, Spain
José Gracia	HLRS, Germany
Khalid Hasanov	IBM, Ireland
Atanas Hristov	University of Information Science and Technology, Macedonia
Cristoph Kessler	University of Linköping, Sweden
Algirdas Lancinskas	University of Vilnius, Lithuania
Rafael Mayo Gual	Jaume I University, Spain
Konstantina Mitropoulou	University of Cambridge, UK
Benoit Parrein	University of Nantes, France
Abel Paz Gallardo	CETA-Ciemat, Spain
Dana Petcu	West University of Timisoara, Romania
Félix R. Rodríguez	University of Extremadura, Spain
Ravi Reddy	University College Dublin, Ireland
Daniel Rubio	HLRS, Germany
Luis M. Sánchez	Carlos III University, Spain
David E. Singh	Carlos III University, Spain
Didem Unat	Lawrence Berkeley National Laboratory, USA
Beat Wolf	School of Engineering of Fribourg, Switzerland

Ultrascale Computing for Early Researchers (UCER 2016)

Sergio Nesmachnow	Universidad de la República, Uruguay
Biagio Cosenza	TU Berlin, Germany
Grégoire Danoy	University of Luxembourg
Juan Antonio Rico	University of Extremadura
Eugenio Cesario	ICAR-CNR, Italy
Gábor Kecskeméti	MTA SZTAKI, Institute for Computer Science and Control, Hungarian Academy of Sciences, Hungary
Daniele Lezzi	BSC, Spain
Hugo Daniel Meyer	BSC, Spain
Manuel F. Dolz	University Carlos III of Madrid, Spain
José Ranilla	University of Oviedo, Spain
Krzysztof Rojek	Czestochowa University of Technology, Poland

First International Workshop on Trust, Security, and Privacy for Big Data (BigTrust 2016)

Habtamu Abie	Norwegian Computing Center/Norsk Regnesentral, Norway
Yan Bai	University of Washington Tacoma, USA
Saad Bani-Mohammad	Al al-Bayt University, Jordan

Salima Benbernou	Université Paris Descartes, France
Christian Callegari	The University of Pisa, Italy
Sudip Chakraborty	Valdosta State University, USA
Anupam Chattopadhyay	Nanyang Technological University, Singapore
John A. Clark	University of York, UK
Alfredo Cuzzocrea	University of Trieste and ICAR-CNR, Italy
Sabrina De Capitani di Vimercati	Università degli Studi di Milano, Italy
Zhihui Du	Tsinghua University, China
Yucong Duan	Hainan University, China
Saurabh Kumar Garg	University of Tasmania, Australia
Dieter Gollmann	Hamburg University of Technology, Germany
Sheikh M. Habib	Technical University of Darmstadt, Germany
Ching-Hsien Hsu	Chung Hua University, Taiwan
Xinyi Huang	Fujian Normal University, China
Young-Sik Jeong	Dongguk University, Korea
Hai Jiang	Arkansas State University, USA
Vana Kalogeraki	Athens University of Economics, Greece
Ryan Ko	University of Waikato, New Zealand
Yingjiu Li	Singapore Management University, Singapore
Xin Liao	Hunan University, China
Giovanni Livraga	Università degli Studi di Milano, Italy
Rongxing Lu	Nanyang Technological University, Singapore
Haibing Lu	Santa Clara University, USA
David Naccache	École normale supérieure, France
Günther Pernul	University of Regensburg, Germany
Roberto Di Pietro	Nokia Bell Labs, France
Vincenzo Piuri	Università degli Studi di Milano, Italy
Imed Romdhani	Edinburgh Napier University, UK
Bimal Roy	Indian Statistical Institute, India
Jun Shen	University of Wollongong, Australia
Dimitris E. Simos	SBA Research, Austria
Chao Song	University of Electronic Science and Technology of China, China
Chunhua Su	Advanced Institute of Science and Technology, Japan
Chang-Ai Sun	University of Science and Technology Beijing, China
Luis Javier García Villalba	Universidad Complutense de Madrid, Spain
Yunsheng Wang	Kettering University, USA
Mingzhong Wang	University of the Sunshine Coast, Australia
Yongdong Wu	Institute for Infocomm Research, Singapore
Hejun Wu	Sun Yat-Sen University, China
Muneer Masadeh Bani Yassein	Jordan University of Science and Technology, Jordan
Baoliu Ye	Nanjing University, China
Shucheng Yu	University of Arkansas at Little Rock, USA

Hua Yu	Huazhong University of Science and Technology, China
Sherali Zeadally	University of Kentucky, USA
Yun-Wei Zhao	Tilburg University, Netherlands
Ruggero Donida Labati	Università degli Studi di Milano, Italy

First International Workshop on Data Locality in Modern Computing Systems (DLMCS 2016)

Marco Aldinucci	University of Torino, Italy
Michael Bader	Technische Universität München, Germany
Rosa Badia	Barcelona Supercomputing Center, Spain
Denis Barthou	Inria Bordeaux, France
Lars Bauer	Karlsruhe Institute of Technology, Germany
Kristof Beyls	ARM Ltd., UK
Tobias Fuchs	Ludwig-Maximilians-Universität München, Germany
Karl Fürlinger	Ludwig-Maximilians-Universität München, Germany
Jose Gracia	HLRS Stuttgart, Germany
Armin Größlinger	University Passau, Germany
Frank Hannig	University of Erlangen, Germany
Costin Iancu	Lawrence Berkeley National Laboratory, USA
Paul Kelly	Imperial College London, UK
Andreas Knüpfer	TU Dresden, Germany
Jakub Kurzak	Innovative Computing Laboratory, UTK, USA
Hatem Ltaief	KAUST, Saudi Arabia
Peter Luszek	Innovative Computing Laboratory, UTK, USA
Sven-Bodo Scholz	Heriot-Watt University, Edinburgh, UK
Martin Schulz	Lawrence Livermore National Laboratory, USA
John Shalf	Lawrence Berkeley National Laboratory, USA
Didem Unat	Koc University, Turkey
Josef Weidendorfer	TU München, Germany

Contents

First International Workshop on Data Locality in Modern Computing Systems (DLMCS 2016)

Ultrascale Computing for Early Researchers (UCER 2016)

SCDT-2016: Supercomputing Co-Design Technology Workshop

TAPEMS 2016: International Workshop in Theoretical Approaches to Performance Evaluation, Modeling and Simulation

OTFX: An In-memory Event Tracing Extension to the Open Trace Format 2

Michael Wagner[1,2]([⊠]), Andreas Knüpfer[2], and Wolfgang E. Nagel[2]

[1] Barcelona Supercomputing Center, 08034 Barcelona, Spain
michael.wagner@bsc.es
[2] Center for Information Services and HPC (ZIH), 01062 Dresden, Germany

Abstract. In event-based performance analysis the amount of collected data is one of the most urgent challenges. It can massively slow down application execution, overwhelm the underlying file system and introduce significant measurement bias due to intermediate memory buffer flushes. To address these issues we propose an in-memory event tracing approach that dynamically adapts the volume of application events to an amount that is guaranteed to fit into a single memory buffer, and therefore, avoiding file interaction entirely. These concepts include runtime filtering, enhanced encoding techniques, and novel strategies for runtime event reduction. The concepts further include the hierarchical memory buffer a multi-dimensional, hierarchical data structure allowing to realize these concepts with minimal overhead. We demonstrate the capabilities of our concepts with a prototype implementation called OTFX, based on the Open Trace Format 2, a state-of-the-art open source tracing library used by the performance analyzers Vampir, Scalasca, and Tau.

Keywords: Performance analysis · Tracing · Tools · OTFX · OTF2

1 Introduction

High performance computing (HPC) systems provide enormous computational resources. But the increasing performance introduces more and more complexity, as well. Current leading edge HPC systems consist of millions of heterogeneous processing elements [17]. They require consideration of parallel execution, network, system topology, and hardware accelerators as well as a variety of different parallel programming models such as message passing (MPI), threading and tasking (OpenMP), one-sided communication (PGAS), and architecture specific models to incorporate hardware accelerators such as GPUs. As a result, appropriate support tools have become inevitable in the development process.

Performance analysis tools assist developers not only in identifying performance issues within their applications but also in understanding their complex parallel behavior. The two main approaches in performance analysis are profiling and event tracing. While profiling gathers aggregated information about different performance metrics, event tracing records runtime events together with a

© Springer International Publishing AG 2016
J. Carretero et al. (Eds.): ICA3PP 2016 Workshops, LNCS 10049, pp. 3–17, 2016.
DOI: 10.1007/978-3-319-49956-7_1

precise time stamp and further event specific metrics. Profiling with its nature of summarization decreases the amount of data that needs to be stored during runtime. However, profiles may lack essential information and hide dynamically occurring effects. In contrast, event tracing records each event of an application in detail. Thus, it allows capturing the dynamic interaction between concurrent processing elements and enables the identification of outliers from the regular behavior. Moreover, event tracing records inter-process dependencies thus allowing a detailed communication analysis.

While single events are small, event-based tracing frequently results in huge data volumes. In fact, the large amount of collected data, in particular, for massively parallel or long running applications is one of the most urgent challenges in event-based performance analysis. Large amounts of collected data can massively slow down application execution and overwhelm the file system. In the context of a correct analysis of inter-process dependencies, e.g. MPI communication, there is another critical impact of the large recorded data volumes. Whenever an event collecting memory buffer is exhausted, data is flushed to the file system, which leads to a noticeable interrupt of application execution. Since each process collects different events or at least events with different parameters (e.g. time stamps), the parallel processes are interrupted at different times. As a result, they bias the recorded program behavior and potentially create or conceal critical performance issues [21].

In this paper we focus on the issues arising from recording high data volumes: application slow down, overwhelming the underlying file system and measurement bias. We propose an in-memory event tracing approach that automatically adapts the volume of application events to an amount that is guaranteed to fit into a single memory buffer. This way, file system interaction in the monitoring tool can even be avoided entirely. Our prototype implementation *OTFX* realizes this approach and allows utilizing an in-memory event tracing workflow within existing tools. It is based on the Open Trace Format 2 (OTF2) [2,18], a state-of-the-art Open Source event trace library used by the performance analysis tools Vampir, Scalasca, and Tau [3,6,16].

In the following section we distinguish our work from other approaches. After that, we detail the concepts for in-memory event tracing in Sect. 3 and the hierarchical memory buffer data structure in Sect. 4. Finally, in Sect. 5 we evaluate the overhead, trace size reduction, and trace analysis capabilities of our prototype and summarize the presented work.

2   Related Work

The Open Trace Format 2 (OTF2) [2] is an event tracing format and access library used by the monitoring environment Score-P [8,18] and by the trace analyzers Vampir [6], Scalasca [3], and Tau [16]. It is the starting point for the OTFX in-memory extension to OTF2 and, therefore, has many similarities with our OTFX prototype, e.g., similar interfaces and event definitions.

Today's event tracing monitors provide different strategies to reduce the amount of collected data. Score-P can filter function calls based on their occurrence, i.e., the user can specify a value n so that all calls to a function are filtered after this function is called n times [8]. This approach, however, is less accurate than the duration filter presented in this paper, since it does not keep outliers that are particularly interesting for performance analysis. In addition, if the n is too small in long-running applications even main routines might get filtered. Score-P also supports a rewind feature that allows to statically filter complete program phases, e.g., single iteration steps [8]. Scalasca offers a static code analysis prior to the source code instrumentation to exclude functions with a short source code length [12]. Paraver's monitoring tool Extrae uses cluster and spectral analysis to reduce the number of events in traces and, thus, the traces sizes during runtime [10]. This approach relies on global synchronization points to pause the application recording, forward performance data and analyze it on a front-end. The results are broadcasted back to the monitoring nodes, which use the information to selectively record further events.

All of the above approaches differ in two ways from our proposed prototype. First, while all approaches can reduce the resulting trace size, they cannot adapt the trace size dynamically to fit into a single fixed-size memory buffer. As a result, for larger traces the internal measurement memory buffers get exhausted and trace data is stored at the file system, leading to the above described bias on the recorded behavior. Second, none of the above approaches distinguishes MPI events for filtering; although, some have the potential to distinguish them. Consequently, MPI events are filtered just like all other events leading to a possible failure of the communication analysis [20].

Next to these filter methods, compressed complete call graphs CCCG [7], a study of reduction techniques [11], and ScalaTrace [13] use pattern recognition to accumulate recurring patterns to minimize trace data. While these techniques are capable of reducing the trace data to a nearly constant trace size (depending on the granularity of the aggregation), they are very time consuming and, thus, not applicable during runtime. Only CCCG [7] provides overhead results but for the others similar overheads can be expected.

3   Concepts for In-memory Event Tracing

The OTFX tracing library is designed to support in-memory event tracing by drastically reducing the amount of tracing data during runtime. To clearly characterize the target and contribution of this paper and to avoid misconceptions, the term *in-memory event tracing*, as it is used in the context of this work, is defined as a method in performance analysis where runtime events are recorded and stored individually in a trace that remains in main memory (or caches and registers but not the file system) for the entire measurement workflow.

Consequently, the main challenge for an in-memory event tracing workflow is to keep events of an entire measurement within a single fixed-sized memory buffer. Therefore, an in-memory workflow must apply methods to reduce the amount of data in the memory buffer by reducing the number of events and the amount of memory per event during the measurement runtime.

Additional constraints are that, first, these methods introduce minimal overhead to avoid additional measurement perturbation, second, the measurement can contain an arbitrary but finite amount of events, and, third, the memory buffer can be of arbitrary but fixed size. In other words, keeping an event trace of arbitrary size within main memory cannot be achieved by increasing the size of the memory buffer accordingly. Furthermore, the size of the memory buffer is usually small (about one to ten percent of main memory) since most of main memory is left to the observed application to minimize measurement bias. Otherwise, an application that runs out of memory due to a too large memory buffer would render the measurement useless [24].

3.1   Non-intrusive Runtime Filtering

Today, automatic instrumentation techniques like compiler instrumentation are the default in most monitoring tools [3, 8, 16]. However, in most cases automatic instrumentation includes also short-running functions such as small helper functions or get and set class methods. If they are heavily called they might overwhelm the capacity of the recording memory buffer while at the same time contribute very little to the overall application behavior.

Methods to filter functions depending on their number of occurrences, e.g., filter all calls after a function is recorded n times, already exist [8]. While this method is easy to realize, it includes three critical disadvantages. First, there is no heuristic to determine a general number n of function calls after which all further calls are filtered. If it is too high, a lot of unimportant function calls are recorded; if it is too low important function calls might get filtered. Second, the first n calls to an unimportant highly frequent function are still stored. Especially, if there are multiple of these high-frequency functions, this might already exhaust the recording memory buffer. Third and last, with the method of keeping a maximum of n calls to each function, possible outliers of this function after n calls that actually have an impact on the application behavior are not recorded and, thus, cannot be identified.

In contrast, OTFX implements a filter that only relies on the actual duration of each individual function call. This approach identifies function calls whose duration is shorter than a predefined threshold and eliminates them. Hence, it effectively detects and removes all short function calls while keeping outliers that have an potential impact on the application behavior. Consequently, this technique overcomes the above mentioned disadvantages of existing filters based on the number of occurrences [19].

3.2   Enhanced Encoding Techniques

OTFX introduces five enhanced encoding techniques to reduce memory allocation [22] based on the Open Trace Format 2 [2]. These techniques include, first, the splitting of timing information and event data to omit the redundant storage of timing information of events with identical time stamp. Second, the elimination of leading zero bytes. Since the memory reserved for each attribute of an event record is usually determined by the largest value the element theoretically represents, the majority of values, which are much smaller, contain a number of leading zero bytes (or trailing zero bytes for Little Endian encoding). Omitting these zero bytes can reduce the resulting memory allocation for the vast majority of event records. Third, storing only the difference (delta) to the previous value leads to much smaller values to store, especially for monotonic increasing values starting with a high offset like time stamps or hardware performance counters. In combination with the leading zero elimination this results in less memory allocation for the stored value. Fourth, small numbers can be encoded directly into the token byte of each event to further reduced memory allocation. OTFX provides an encoding where small IDs of function calls are encoded directly into the token byte resulting in event sizes of only a single byte (plus timing) for the most frequent functions [22].

3.3 Event Reduction

While filtering and encoding can achieve a remarkable reduction of the stored data, they lack the capability to reduce the data to a fixed size – the size of the memory buffer. In other words, they fail the by far most important criterion for an in-memory workflow: they cannot guarantee that event data of an arbitrary measurement fits into a single memory buffer of fixed size. Without a guarantee to keep the event data within a single memory buffer, however, an in-memory event tracing workflow is impossible.

Consequently, event reduction follows a completely different approach. Event reduction is triggered only when the memory buffer is exhausted; typically this is the point where the memory buffer is either flushed to a file or the measurement is aborted. The crucial point is making memory space available again by reducing the number of events already stored within the memory buffer while at the same time introducing minimal overhead.

Each event reduction operation selects events by dynamic criteria and discards them from the memory buffer. Such a selection follows similar heuristics as the selection and filter methods in the first step; the main difference is that events matching a criterion are not filtered in any case but only if a reduction is inevitable, i.e., the memory buffer is exhausted. In addition, the criteria for event reduction are not static but adapt to previous event reduction operations, allowing an incremental reduction of events.

OTFX introduces four strategies for event reduction: a reduction by the order of occurrence of the events, by their event type, by the current calling depth, and by the duration of function calls. The main focus of the comparison of these methods is based on two criteria. First, the quality of the remaining information. Whether or not it allows to still understand the behavior of the application and detect occurring performance issues. Second, the granularity of the individual event reduction operation. In this respect, granularity means the amount of data that is discarded in a single event reduction operation. If the reduction steps are too large, information might unnecessarily be discarded.

The first strategy is to reduce events by their order of occurrence. This means that events are either discarded or kept depending on the time they occurred. If the memory buffer is capable to store n events, there are three different ways this method can be applied: First, store the first n events, i.e., recording is stopped once the memory buffer is exhausted. Second, store the last n events. This method requires a cyclic buffer that starts overwriting events in the front of the buffer whenever the end of the buffer is reached. Third, store either the first or last n events within a specific application phase. This strategy provides the complete application behavior within the recorded interval; either at the beginning, at the end, or somewhere in the middle of an application, depending on which method is chosen. Thus, a performance analysis based on this strategy allows a good understanding about the recorded interval of the application but cannot provide any information about the part that was discarded. The same applies for the ability to detect performance issues. An event reduction by the order of occurrence is the most basic of the four event reduction strategies. In particular, the first method with a fixed starting point is not too different from a measurement abortion but with the difference that all recorded events are kept for analysis instead of being dismissed. However, due to their very high granularity and their easy application these methods serve well as a fallback if all other event reduction operations fail.

The second and third strategy are similar; both sort events in groups and start event reduction with the least important group. The second strategy, a reduction by event type, categorizes events into different classes of events, e.g., entering and leaving a function, point-to-point or collective communication, performance metrics like hardware performance counters, or I/O operations. Naturally, not all of these different event classes are of same importance when analyzing an application. For instance, for an analysis of the communication behavior, obviously, communication events are very important while specific hardware performance counters, like cache misses, are less important. For an analysis of single thread performance it is the other way around.

The third strategy, a reduction by calling depth, groups events based on their position in the call stack and starts reduction with the deepest call stack level. It is based on the assumption that events on the deepest call stack level usually contribute less to the overall analysis of the application behavior than those on higher levels. Still, these events may be the source for a performance issue. This strategy allows a partial performance analysis for the entire application interval similar to an event reduction by event class. Similar to the second strategy, the behavior and potential performance issues can only be fully reconstructed with the events in the remaining call stack levels. However, while the first two strategies completely discard the information with the events that carry them, this strategy allows to obtain parts of the information from higher call stack levels. In particular, when reducing the call stack level that contains the events that mark a performance issue, the actual cause of the performance issue is lost.

Yet, a performance analysis might still allow to recognize the impact of this performance issue in the remaining call stack levels.

The fourth and last strategy uses the duration of function calls as criterion for event reduction. Having in mind that enter/leave events are the most dominant event class next to performance metrics if they are recorded, the removal of less important function calls bears great potential for an event reduction. This strategy is quite similar to the duration filter mentioned above. Instead of a single threshold (as with the filter), this strategy groups function calls depending on their duration and starts event reduction with those function calls that fall in the group of the shortest calls. However, our experience showed that for many applications the number of highly frequent function calls is so tremendous, that this strategy delivers similar results to the aforementioned duration filter. Since the duration filter operates with less overhead while providing similar results, OTFX prefers the duration filter over this strategy.

4   The Hierarchical Memory Buffer

This section introduces the hierarchical memory buffer, a novel data structure that allows to perform the aforementioned event reduction operations with minimal overhead. The presented event reduction strategies require an efficient identification and elimination of events that are already stored in the memory buffer. However, currently none of the existing event tracing tools and libraries supports such an efficient elimination of events. They all use a flat continuous memory buffer that, although, allowing the elimination of events already stored in the memory buffer, introduces an enormous overhead when engaged.

A flat continuous memory buffer stores the recorded events in the order they occurred until the memory buffer is exhausted (see Fig. 1(a)). When the memory buffer is exhausted the event reduction is triggered. Since all events that are supposed to be reduced are scattered over the memory buffer, the entire memory buffer needs to be scanned to find all events that match the criterion for reduction, e.g., all events of the deepest call stack level for a reduction based on the calling depth. When all events matching the reduction criteria are found, they are discarded and the according memory sections are marked as free. Since events occur at a high frequency and are typically only a few bytes small, there are plenty of small free sections scattered over the whole memory buffer. This leaves a highly fragmented memory buffer that cannot be used for writing further events. Thus, all non-free memory sections need to be moved to collapse the fragmented memory buffer to a single continuous memory segment that leaves a continuous free memory section at the end to store further events. The computational complexity of the reduction operation is in $\mathcal{O}(n)$, with n being the number of stored events. Since a memory buffer, depending on its size, can contain several million events such a reduction operation introduces a remarkable overhead when using a traditional flat continuous memory representation.

In contrast to a flat continuous memory buffer, the hierarchical memory buffer is organized as a multi-dimensional array, where each *hierarchy dimension*

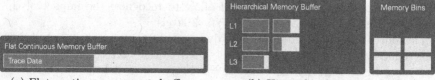

(a) Flat continuous memory buffer.   (b) Hierarchical memory buffer

Fig. 1. Comparison of the event representation in a flat continuous memory buffer and in the hierarchical memory buffer.

represents one possible hierarchical order with a flexible number of different values within that hierarchical order, called *hierarchy levels* (see Fig. 1(b)).

In the context of event reduction, for instance, one dimension can represent the calling depth and another the event class. Instead of one huge memory chunk, the total memory allocation for the according memory buffer is divided in plenty of small memory sections, called *memory bins*. These memory bins can be dynamically distributed to any hierarchy level in each dimension. Whenever an event needs to be stored at a certain hierarchy level and there is either no memory bin assigned or the current memory bin is exhausted, a free memory bin is distributed to this hierarchy level.

The following paragraph highlights the event reduction with such a hierarchical memory buffer. Again, for simplification this example considers at first only one reduction criterion, e.g., the calling depth. Thus, the according memory buffer's layout is an one-dimensional array. When the first event needs to be stored, usually on call stack level $L1$, no memory bin has been assigned to this hierarchy level, so far. Thus, the memory buffer checks if there is a free memory bin available, which is true in this case, and one memory bin is assigned to the hierarchy level $L1$, so, the event can be stored. If an event needs to be stored on a different hierarchy level, a free memory bin is assigned the same way. The same applies when on any hierarchy level the current memory bin is exhausted. After some time, this leads to a situation like in Fig. 1(b): Five of the memory bins are assigned to the hierarchy levels $L1$–$L3$ and four free memory bins are available. Hence, four additional memory bins can be assigned to the hierarchy levels. After that, all memory bins are assigned and there are no free memory bins available anymore. If a further event needs to be stored at a filled hierarchy level but there are no free memory bins available, the event reduction is triggered and all events of a certain hierarchy level are discarded, for instance, all events of the deepest call stack level, in this case, level $L3$. Since all events are already sorted by their call stack level the event reduction operation can be done with minimal costs. The event reduction just revokes all memory bins assigned to the hierarchy level $L3$ and adds them again to the pool of free memory bins. In addition, the hierarchy level $L3$ is marked as closed, so, all future events on this hierarchy level are discarded right away. One of the newly freed memory bins can be assigned to the hierarchy level that triggered the event reduction and the according event can be stored.

This way, the computational complexity of the reduction operation is reduced to be in $\mathcal{O}(b)$, with b being the number of memory bins to revoke. Next to the layout as one-dimensional array as for the example above, the hierarchical memory buffer event representation can be organized as a multi-dimensional array, as well. In that case, the event reduction can be applied on a complete row or column within the multi-dimensional array. This way, a hierarchical memory representation is able to support all event reduction techniques simultaneously.

The hierarchical memory buffer data structure and its construction, as well as the application of event reduction with the hierarchical memory buffer and the adaption of common analysis techniques are discussed in more detail in a dissertation thesis, Chapters 4.2–4.5 [24].

5   Evaluation

We use the OTFX prototype containing the above described methods to demonstrate the resulting trace size reduction and to examine the introduced overhead for the event tracing library. In addition, we evaluate the usefulness of the resulting traces for performance analysis.

5.1   Methodology and Target Applications

Event tracing libraries are usually closely coupled with the monitoring tools who use them. This makes it virtually impossible to distinguish effects caused by the monitoring tool from those caused by the event tracing library. In addition, many parameters, e.g., function durations, deviate in each measurement run. Therefore, we do not use the OTF2 and OTFX libraries directly for the measurement. Instead, we generate an OTF2 trace with Score-P [8] and use this trace as a baseline. For the comparison run with OTFX, we replay each application from its baseline trace. This method ensures, that both traces (OTF2 and OTFX) use exactly the same input data and, thus, eliminates the effect of runtime deviations.

We use Taurus a Linux cluster at ZIH for trace generation and an Intel Core i7 system for the overhead measurements. The evaluation is based on traces of the molecular dynamics package *Gromacs* [4], the cloud simulation model system *COSMO-SPECS+FD4* [9], the computational fluid dynamics solver *Nek5000* (*3dbox, pipe*) [1], and the molecular dynamics simulator *LAMMPS* (*colloid, lennard-jones, rigid*) [14,15].

5.2   Runtime Overhead

To determine the runtime overhead introduced by our prototype we applied the trace replay described above for all target applications. For the trace replay both tracing libraries were modified to use up to 2 GiB of memory to keep the entire trace data in main memory to eliminate all effects of file interaction in OTF2 and event reduction in OTFX, respectively.

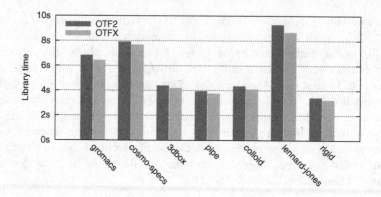

Fig. 2. Runtime of OTF2 and OTFX.

Figure 2 shows the runtime of OTF2, Score-P's standard tracing library, in comparison to our OTFX prototype for the target applications. In comparison to OTF2, OTFX was in average 5.1 % faster. In total, the library times of OTFX account for 7.8 % of the overall runtime in average. This demonstrates that our prototype suffices our requirement to not introduce additional overhead in the measurement process.

5.3   Trace Size Reduction

To evaluate the trace size reduction of our prototype we again applied the trace replay but this time with enabled duration filtering. We choose a minimum duration of 1 µs for the duration filter, i.e., all function calls shorter than 1 µs are filtered. This way, all short-running functions are eliminated while important routines remain in the trace.

Table 1 shows the results for the target applications. It contains the resulting trace sizes of OTF2, OTFX without any duration filtering or event reduction (compression), OTFX with duration filtering (comp + filter), and solely for comparison the size of a trace keeping only MPI events (MPI-only). From Table 1 can be inferred, first, the traces of all applications are much larger than a normal-sized memory buffer of 50 to 200 MiB [5]. As a result, application execution would be frequently interrupted by intermediate buffer flushes and disturb the original application behavior. Second, an MPI-only trace would fit into a normal sized buffer for all applications. These two values, the size of the complete trace and the size of the MPI-only trace set the boundaries for a trace size reduction with our prototype. While MPI events can be filtered as well, ideally they are kept to allow an undisturbed communication analysis. Thus, the MPI-only column indicates also the limits of OTFX if all MPI events are kept. Third, the memory allocation of our prototype without duration filtering and event reduction (OTFX) is already 2.8 to 3.5 times smaller than OTF2. Fourth, the duration filter eliminates short-running functions and reduces the trace size by additional 82 %, on average, which results in trace sizes of 0.2 to 12.6 % of the original trace

Table 1. Trace sizes of OTF2, OTFX with and without filter and MPI only.

Application	Trace size (per process)			
	OTF2	OTFX Compression	OTFX Comp + filter	MPI-only
Gromacs	1.7 GB	603 MB	127 MB	9.8 MB
Cosmo-specs	1.5 GB	514 MB	21 MB	80 kB
3dbox	919 MB	297 MB	116 MB	8.8 MB
Pipe	817 MB	267 MB	88 MB	8.5 MB
Colloid	900 MB	266 MB	40 MB	12 MB
Lennard-Jones	1.8 GB	546 MB	4.1 MB	690 kB
Rigid	709 MB	203 MB	23 MB	680 kB

size in OTF2. The duration filter is particularly effective on applications with highly-frequent short-running function calls, common in C++ applications, e.g., COSMO-SPECS+FD4 and the Lennard-Jones example from LAMMPS. Fifth, for all applications, except Gromacs and both examples from Nek5000, the duration filter suffices to keep the trace within a single memory buffer of 50 MiB and avoid intermediate memory buffer flushes. For Graomas and Nek5000, the event reduction is triggered whenever the internal memory buffer is exhausted. This leads to a reduction of the recorded calling depth from 14 to 8, 19 to 10, and 19 to 13 for Gromacs, 3dbox, and pipe, respectively. However, all MPI events that occur up to the original calling depth of 14 and 19 are kept. The resulting trace size is 30, 42, and 46 MiB for Gromacs, 3dbox, and pipe, respectively.

5.4 Trace Analysis

The previous two sections show that OTFX allows a remarkable reduction of the trace size without addition overhead. However, it is inevitable to answer the question about the usefulness of the remaining events and, thus, the usability of the event reduction in general.

While it is impossible to answer this question for each and any application, the following example showcases the analysis capabilities for a more extreme situation. The example includes Gromacs in a more realistic production setting. In that case, the sheer amount of trace data triggered OTFX's event reduction to reduce the trace size to about 0.1 % of the original size. To achieve this, MPI events had to be reduced as well, since already their volume would have been too large. It is obvious, that an extreme reduction like this cannot deliver the same level of detail as an unreduced trace. The question is if the remaining coarse trace can still contribute to a meaningful performance analysis, help to better understand the application behavior and identify performance issues.

Figure 3 shows a comparison of the full trace with the reduced OTFX trace that is 1,000 times smaller. It shows a screen shot of a visual performance analysis

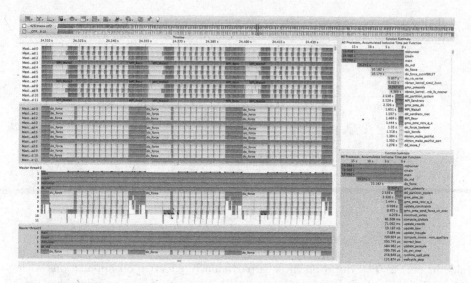

Fig. 3. Event trace visualization with Vampir without (top, white background) and with event reduction (bottom, blue background) zoomed to three iterations. (Color figure online)

with Vampir of Gromacs without (top, white background) and with event reduction (bottom, blue background) zoomed to a small section of approximately three iterations. The screen shot contains a timeline view of the first twelve processes with the application behavior over time on the horizontal axis and the processes on the vertical axis (top, left), a detailed call stack of process zero (bottom, left) and a function summary showing the inclusive function time (right). The figure visualizes the prominent functions on calling depth five *do_force* and *gmx_pme_do* in yellow (for better visibility nested functions of *do_force*, except MPI communication, are marked yellow, too) and blue, respectively, the rest of the application in green, and MPI communication in red.

It can be seen, that the remaining events of the reduced version equal exactly the complete version, i.e., the filtering and reduction do not alter the program behavior. And, while the reduced trace contains considerably lower detail, it clearly identifies the overall program behavior. It illustrates the function decomposition within each group of four processes and the iterative blocks of the application. It also still allows to identify the load imbalance in the function decomposition between three out of four process that compute the particle-particle interaction (PP) and the other that computes the Particle Mesh Ewald method (PME).

Of course, this screen shot provides only limited insight into the analysis process of this use case; not mentioning the analysis process of applications in general. Nonetheless, it demonstrates that a reduced trace resulting from the proposed in-memory event tracing workflow still allows a meaningful performance analysis even in such an extreme case. This way it becomes possible to record and analyze an entire production run of real-life applications, such as Gromacs.

6   Conclusion

In this paper we focus on the impact of high data volumes in event trace recording, namely, application slow down, overwhelming the underlying file system and measurement bias. We propose an in-memory event tracing approach that automatically adapts the remaining application events to an amount that fits into a single memory buffer. Furthermore, we present the underlying concepts for an in-memory event tracing workflow: runtime filtering, enhanced encoding techniques, novel strategies for runtime event reduction, and the hierarchical memory buffer data structure, which incorporates a multi-dimensional, hierarchical ordering of events allowing to realize these concepts with minimal overhead. We evaluate the capabilities of our approach with the OTFX prototype implementation on the basis of seven application traces from different scientific domains. In comparison to the state-of-the-art tracing library OTF2, OTFX introduces in average 5.1 % less overhead and reduces the trace size up to three orders of magnitude. Most importantly, with OTFX the bias caused by uncoordinated intermediate memory buffer flushes is completely eliminated. This way, OTFX reduces the resulting trace size, measurement slow down, and bias, which allows a feasible performance analysis of applications that previously had been impossible.

References

1. Argonne National Laboratories. Nek5000 website (2016). http://nek5000.mcs.anl. gov
2. Eschweiler, D., Wagner, M., Geimer, M., Knüpfer, A., Nagel, W.E., Wolf, F.: Open trace format 2: the next generation of scalable trace formats and support libraries. In: Applications, Tools and Techniques on the Road to Exascale Computing, vol. 22 of Advances in Parallel Computing, pp. 481–490 (2012)
3. Geimer, M., Wolf, F., Wylie, B.J., Ábrahám, E., Becker, D., Mohr, B.: The scalasca performance toolset architecture. Concurrency Comput. Pract. Exp. **22**(6), 702–719 (2010)
4. Hess, B., Kutzner, C., van der Spoel, D., Lindahl, E.: GROMACS 4: algorithms for highly efficient, load-balanced, and scalable molecular simulation. J. Chem. Theor. Comput. **4**(3), 435–447 (2008)
5. Ilsche, T., Schuchart, J., Cope, J., Kimpe, D., Jones, T., Knüpfer, A., Iskra, K., Ross, R., Nagel, W.E., Poole, S.: Enabling event tracing at leadership-class scale through I/O forwarding middleware. In: Proceedings of the 21th International Symposium on High Performance Distributed Computing (HPDC 2012), pp. 49–60. ACM, June 2012
6. Knüpfer, A., Brunst, H., Doleschal, J., Jurenz, M., Lieber, M., Mickler, H., Müller, M.S., Nagel, W.E.: The vampir performance analysis tool-set. In: Resch, M., Keller, R., Himmler, V., Krammer, B., Schulz, A. (eds.) Tools for High Performance Computing, pp. 139–155. Springer, Heidelberg (2008). doi:10.1007/978-3-540-68564-7_9

7. Knüpfer, A., Nagel, W.E.: Compressible memory data structures for event-based trace analysis. Future Gener. Comput. Syst. **22**(3), 359–368 (2006)
8. Knüpfer, A., Rössel, C., Mey, D., Biersdorff, S., Diethelm, K., Eschweiler, D., Geimer, M., Gerndt, M., Lorenz, D., Malony, A., Nagel, W.E., Oleynik, Y., Philippen, P., Saviankou, P., Schmidl, D., Shende, S., Tschüter, R., Wagner, M., Wesarg, B., Wolf, F.: Score-P: a joint performance measurement run-time infrastructure for periscope, scalasca, TAU, and vampir. In: Brunst, H., Müller, M.S., Nagel, W.E., Resch, M.M. (eds.) Tools for High Performance Computing 2011, pp. 79–91. Springer, Heidelberg (2012)
9. Lieber, M., Grützun, V., Wolke, R., Müller, M.S., Nagel, W.E.: Highly scalable dynamic load balancing in the atmospheric modeling system COSMO-SPECS+FD4. In: Jónasson, K. (ed.) PARA 2010. LNCS, vol. 7133, pp. 131–141. Springer, Heidelberg (2012). doi:10.1007/978-3-642-28151-8_13
10. Llort, G., Gonzalez, J., Servat, H., Gimenez, J., Labarta, J.: On-line detection of large-scale parallel application's structure. In: 2010 IEEE International Symposium on Parallel Distributed Processing (IPDPS), pp. 1–10 (2010)
11. Mohror, K., Karavanic, K.L.: Evaluating similarity-based trace reduction techniques for scalable performance analysis. In: Proceedings of the Conference on High Performance Computing Networking, Storage and Analysis (SC 2009), pp. 55:1–55:12 (2009)
12. Mußler, J., Lorenz, D., Wolf, F.: Reducing the overhead of direct application instrumentation using prior static analysis. In: Jeannot, E., Namyst, R., Roman, J. (eds.) Euro-Par 2011. LNCS, vol. 6852, pp. 65–76. Springer, Heidelberg (2011). doi:10.1007/978-3-642-23400-2_7
13. Noeth, M., Ratn, P., Mueller, F., Schulz, M., de Supinski, B.R.: ScalaTrace: scalable compression and replay of communication traces for high-performance computing. J. Parallel Distrib. Comput. **69**(8), 696–710 (2009)
14. Plimpton, S.: Fast parallel algorithms for short-range molecular dynamics. J. Comput. Phys. **117**(1), 1–19 (1995)
15. Sandia National Laboratories. Lammps website (2016). http://lammps.sandia.gov
16. Shende, S.S., Malony, A.D.: The tau parallel performance system. Int. J. High Perform. Comput. Appl. **20**(2), 287–311 (2006)
17. Top500. Top 500 supercomputer sites (2015). http://www.top500.org
18. Virtual Institute – High Productivity Supercomputing (VI-HPS). Score-P and OTF2 website and download page (2016). http://www.vi-hps.org/projects/score-p
19. Wagner, M., Doleschal, J., Knüpfer, A., Nagel, W.E., Monitoring, S.R.: Nonintrusive elimination of high-frequency functions. In: Proceedings of the International Conference on High Performance Computing & Simulation (HPCS), pp. 295–302 (2014)
20. Wagner, M., Doleschal, J., Knüpfer, A., Nagel, W.E.: Runtime message uniquification for accurate communication analysis on incomplete MPI event traces. In: Proceedings of the 20th European MPI Users' Group Meeting (EuroMPI 2013), pp. 123–128 (2013)
21. Wagner, M., Doleschal, J., Knüpfer, A.: MPI-focused tracing with OTFX: an MPI-aware in-memory event tracing extension to the open trace format 2. In: Proceedings of the 22th European MPI Users' Group Meeting (EuroMPI 2015), pp. 7: 1–7: 8 (2015)

22. Wagner, M., Knüpfer, A., Nagel, W.E.: Enhanced encoding techniques for the open trace format 2. Proc. Comput. Sci. **9**, 1979–1987 (2012)
23. Wagner, M., Knüpfer, A., Nagel, W.E.: Hierarchical memory buffering techniques for an in-memory event tracing extension to the open trace format 2. In: 2013 42nd International Conference on Parallel Processing (ICPP), pp. 970–976 (2013)
24. Wagner, M.: Concepts for In-memory Event Tracing: Runtime Event Reduction with Hierarchical Memory Buffers. Doctoral thesis (2015)

Tuning the Blocksize for Dense Linear Algebra Factorization Routines with the Roofline Model

Peter Benner[3], Pablo Ezzatti[1], Enrique S. Quintana-Ortí[2], Alfredo Remón[3(✉)], and Juan P. Silva[1]

[1] Instituto de Computación, Universidad de la República,
11300 Montevideo, Uruguay
{pezzatti,jpsilva}@fing.edu.uy
[2] Dep. de Ingeniería y Ciencia de la Computación, Universidad Jaime I,
12701 Castellón, Spain
quintana@icc.uji.es
[3] Max Planck Institute for Dynamics of Complex Technical Systems,
39106 Magdeburg, Germany
{benner,remon}@mpi-magdeburg.mpg.de

Abstract. The optimization of dense linear algebra operations is a fundamental task in the solution of many scientific computing applications. The *Roofline Model* is a tool that provides an estimation of the performance that a computational kernel can attain on a hardware platform. Therefore, the RM can be used to investigate whether a computational kernel can be further accelerated. We present an approach, based on the RM, to optimize the algorithmic parameters of dense linear algebra kernels. In particular, we perform a basic analysis to identify the optimal values for the kernel parameters. As a proof-of-concept, we apply this technique to optimize a blocked algorithm for matrix inversion via Gauss-Jordan elimination. In addition, we extend this technique to multiblock computational kernels. An experimental evaluation validates the method and shows its convenience. We remark that the results obtained can be extended to other computational kernels similar to Gauss-Jordan elimination such as, e.g., matrix factorizations and the solution of linear least squares problems.

Keywords: Roofline model · Dense linear algebra · Gauss-Jordan elimination

1 Introduction

Dense numerical linear algebra operations are crucial for the solution of a vast number of scientific computing applications. In response to this, highly tuned

All researchers acknowledge the support from the EHFARS project funded by the German Ministry of Education and Research BMBF.

E.S. Quintana-Ortí—Supported by the CICYT project TIN2014-53495-R of the *Ministerio de Economía y Competitividad* and FEDER.

© Springer International Publishing AG 2016
J. Carretero et al. (Eds.): ICA3PP 2016 Workshops, LNCS 10049, pp. 18–29, 2016.
DOI: 10.1007/978-3-319-49956-7_2

basic numerical linear algebra subroutines (BLAS) [5], as well as more complex routines as those defined in LAPACK [1], have been developed and integrated into high performance libraries. There are several implementations of BLAS and/or LAPACK, usually specialized and maintained for different types of architectures by the processor manufacturer, such as IBM ESSL, Intel MKL or NVIDIA CUBLAS.

The *Roofline model* (RM) [16] is a graphical tool that can be leveraged to investigate the performance as well as identify the limiting factors of a computational kernel, including e.g. those in BLAS and LAPACK, executed in a given hardware architecture. Concretely, the RM consists of a two-dimensional chart that displays the (theoretical) peak memory bandwidth and performance of a platform, and relates these bounds to the *arithmetic intensity* (AI) of a computational kernel, defined as the ratio between floating-point arithmetic operations (flops) and memory accesses (memops) of the implementation.

In this paper we analyze the effect that AI exerts on the practical performance of blocked algorithms for dense matrix factorizations, such as those in LAPACK, making the following concrete contributions:

- We introduce a simple theoretical analysis to determine the *algorithmic blocksize* that reduces memops, optimizing AI and in general performance, of a blocked algorithm for matrix inversion via Gauss-Jordan elimination (GJE) [6].
- We extend this simple model to deal with more complex multi-block variants that improve AI for the inversion procedure.
- We provide a compact experimental analysis on a quadcore Intel processor to validate our findings.
- Finally, we remark that our study carries over, among others, to several other matrix factorization algorithms for the solution of linear systems and linear least squares problems [6].

The rest of the paper is structured as follows. In Sect. 2, we offer a brief review of the RM. Next, in Sect. 3 we revisit matrix inversion via GJE; and in Sect. 4 we introduce the analysis to compute the optimal algorithmic blocksize from the perspective of AI. Additionally, in that section we extend our study to a multi-block variant, which is a conventional technique to improve the performance of dense linear algebra factorization algorithms. In Sect. 5, we outline the experimental impact of the blocksizes previously, on a practical implementation. Finally, in Sect. 6 we summarize the results and emphasize a few concluding remarks derived from our work.

2   The Roofline Model

The RM separates the memory-bound and compute-bound "spaces" of an architecture as a function of AI. In particular, the model provides a two-dimensional easy-to-read chart that illustrates the crossover threshold between the peak

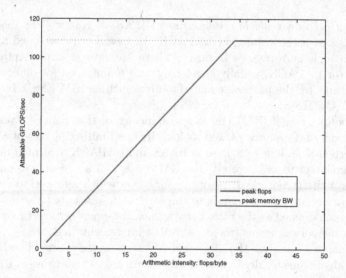

Fig. 1. The RM for an Intel Core i7-4770. The intersection between the red and blue lines identify the threshold between memory bandwidth (BW)-bound and compute-bound areas, as a function of the operation's AI. (Color figure online)

memory bandwidth and performance (in terms of flops per second) of the hardware platform, showing the relation between the maximum performance attainable by the hardware and the AI of the computational kernel.

To create the model, the peak performance and memory bandwidth of the target system are needed. These figures are typically obtained from the hardware manufacturer, though it is also possible to use benchmarks to experimentally replace them with more realistic/practical values, see e.g. [14]. To illustrate this, Fig. 1 presents the RM for the hardware platform employed in the experimental evaluation in Sect. 5.

In order to position a computational kernel with respect to the bounds defined by the RM, it is necessary to determine the kernel's AI. This can be computed from (estimations for) the total flops and memory accesses performed by the kernel. It should be noted that the RM is platform-specific, but can be re-used for any computational kernel executed in that system.

To summarize, the RM provides a helpful means to understand how the memory bandwidth constrains the performance, for memory-bounded algorithms, and/or identify how much an application can be accelerated (as the gap between the real and the attainable performance reported by the model). More details on the RM can be found in [8, 10, 15].

3   Matrix Inversion via GJE

Our general goal for this work is to exploit the principles underlying RM to improve the performance of dense linear algebra operations. As a proof-of-concept,

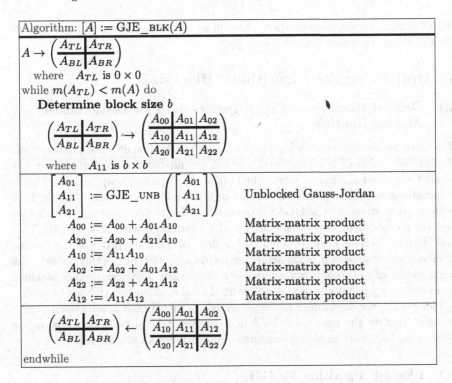

Fig. 2. Blocked algorithm for matrix inversion via GJE without pivoting.

we perform our study on the blocked algorithm for matrix inversion, based on GJE, described in this section.

GJE is an appealing method for matrix inversion, with a computational cost and numerical properties analogous to those of the conventional approach based on the LU factorization [9], but superior performance on a variety of architectures, from clusters [13] to general-purpose multicore processors and GPUs [3].

Figure 2 shows a blocked version of GJE for matrix inversion using the FLAME notation. There, $m(A)$ stands for the number of rows of the matrix A. More details on the notation can be found in [4,7]. For a detailed description of the algorithm and the unblocked version of GJE, invoked from inside the blocked routine, see [2,13]. For simplicity, we do not include the application of pivoting during the factorization, but details can be found there as well. Given a square (nonsingular) matrix of size $n = m(A)$, the cost of matrix inversion using this algorithm is $2n^3$ flops. Furthermore, the inversion is carried out in-place so that, upon completion, the entries of A are overwritten with those of its inverse.

At this point, we emphasize that the blocked algorithm in Fig. 2 casts most of its operations in terms of matrix-matrix products and other BLAS (inside the unblocked routine for GJE). Therefore, the conclusions from our intensity-performance analysis via RM in the next section can be also extended to several other dense linear algebra operations, such as the solution of linear systems via the LU and Cholesky factorizations, as well as least-squares computations using the QR decomposition, among others [6].

4   Optimizing the Algorithmic Blocksize

4.1   General Discussion of High Performance for Dense Linear Algebra Routines

The usual approach to attain high performance for the execution of a dense linear algebra operation in a current architecture formulates the computation in the form of a blocked algorithm, where the bulk of the flops are computed via BLAS-3 operations such as, e.g., matrix-matrix products. This is motivated by the high performance offered by the BLAS-3 operations, due to their intrinsic parallelism and their convenient flops-to-memops ratio. Compared with this, the BLAS-1 and BLAS-2 kernels perform a number of flops of the same order as the volume of memory accesses, in general achieving a small fraction of the theoretical peak performance of a current general-purpose architecture. The performance attained by blocked algorithms strongly depends on the value of the algorithmic blocksize, b. This parameter determines how operations are distributed among the different kernels. Identify the best value for b is a complex task since it depends on the underlying hardware as well as on the computational kernel [11,12].

4.2   Blocked Algorithm for GJE

In the particular case of the GJE, the use of a large algorithmic blocksize b concentrates most of the flops inside subroutine GJE_UNB, which is rich in BLAS-1 and BLAS-2 kernels. Consequently, the performance provided by the unblocked stages in GJE_UNB will dictate the performance of the whole algorithm. At the opposite extreme, the selection of a very small value for b transforms the BLAS-3 operations in GJE_BLK into quasi-BLAS-2 kernels (due to the reduced number of columns in the blocks of the form A_{x1}). Our aim is therefore to identify the value of b that maximizes the use of BLAS-3 operations, and thus minimizes the volume of memory accesses. Given an algorithm with a fixed computational cost, reducing the memops factor improves its AI (as the ratio between flops and memops), and generally the attained performance.

The main loop of GJE_BLK requires a total of n/b iterations (see Fig. 2), with each step requiring the computation of BLAS-3, BLAS-1/BLAS-2 kernels. Note that in general, BLAS-3 are compute-bound while BLAS-1/BLAS-2 are memory-bound. Concretely, the flops of each iteration are distributed as follows:

– BLAS-1 and BLAS-2: $2\,n\,b^2$ flops to factorize the panel, i.e. $[A_{01}; A_{11}; A_{21}]$.
– BLAS-3: $2\,n\,(n-b)\,b$ flops to update the rest of the matrix.

Now, assuming that BLAS-1 and BLAS-2 kernels perform $O(1)$ flops per memop while BLAS-3 kernels perform $O(b)$ flops per memop, the total number of memory accesses needed by GJE is approximately:

$$n/b\,(2\,n\,(n-b) + 2\,n\,b^2),\tag{1}$$

which can be simplified into:

$$2n^2 \left(n/b - 1 + b\right) \text{ memops.} \tag{2}$$

If we consider communication (memops) as overhead, finding the optimal blocksize b^{opt} is then equivalent to minimizing the number of memops given by (2). Therefore, we just need to find the root(s) of the derivative function of (2) with respect to b in order to obtain $b^{opt} = \sqrt{n}$.

Moreover, the arithmetic intensity of the GJE_BLK is then given by

$$\frac{2n^3}{2n^2 \left(n/b^{opt} - 1 + b^{opt}\right)} \text{ flops-per-memop} \tag{3}$$

and, as $b^{opt} = \sqrt{n}$, the "best" arithmetic intensity we can attain with our blocked algorithm for matrix inversion via GJE_BLK is

$$\frac{n}{2\sqrt{n} - 1} \approx \frac{\sqrt{n}}{2} \text{ flops-per-memop.} \tag{4}$$

4.3   Multi-block Variant of GJE

In this section we describe a multi-block strategy to accelerate GJE, and how to extend the analysis based on the RM/AI in order to identify the optimal blocksizes for this variant.

The Multi-block GJE partly casts the operations involved by the panel factorization in terms of BLAS-3 kernels, in order to further increase the number of flops performed using this type of kernels in the algorithm. For this purpose, in the multi-block version of the algorithm, subroutine GJE_UNB is replaced by a slightly modified version of GJE_BLK that can operate with rectangular matrices. As a result, the multi-block variant of GJE is parametrized by two blocksizes: the outer blocksize b, applied during the execution of the blocked algorithm, and the inner blocksize c, employed during the factorization of the panel. For simplicity, hereafter we will assume that b is an integer multiple of c.

Leveraging RM to Select the Optimal Blocksizes. Using a similar strategy to that presented in Sect. 4.1, we can infer the optimal values for both blocksizes and use them to establish the best arithmetic intensity attainable by the multi-block variant of the GJE algorithm.

In this case, the flops performed during an iteration of the main loop can be decomposed into the following three terms:

- BLAS-1 and BLAS-2: $2 n c^2$ flops to factorize the panel (note that this factorization itself requires b/c steps).
- BLAS-3: $2 n (b - c) c$ flops to update the elements within the panel.
- BLAS-3: $2 n (n - b) b$ flops to update the rest of the matrix.

Let us assume that c offers a rough measure of the relation between the flops and memory accesses for the BLAS-3 operations executed inside the panel, and let b be its counterpart for the BLAS-3 operations to update the elements placed out of the panel. Consider again that the BLAS-1 and BLAS-2 kernels perform $O(1)$ flops per memory access, while the ratio for the BLAS-3 is $O(b)$. Then, the outer loop is executed n/b times, while the inner loop b/c times per step of the outer loop; and the total number of memops of the multi-block variant is

$$n/b\left(b/c\left(2\,n\,c+2\,n\left(b-c\right)\right)+2\,n\left(n-b\right)\right), \tag{5}$$

which can be simplified to

$$2n^2\left(c+b/c+n/b-2\right) \text{ memops.} \tag{6}$$

Differentiating the previous expression with respect to c, and finding the roots of the result, we obtain that the value of the inner blocksize that minimizes the number of memory accesses is $c^{opt}=\sqrt{b}$. This is natural as the computation performed by the inner loop is analogous to the application of a "rectangular" version of the blocked algorithm for GJE to a matrix of dimension $n\times b$.

Replacing c by its optimal value c^{opt}, in Eq. (6), we then obtain:

$$2n^2\left(n/b-2+2\sqrt{b}\right) \text{ memops.} \tag{7}$$

Similarly, if we derive Eq. (7) with respect to b, and equate the result to zero, we obtain the value of b that minimizes the number of memory accesses as $b^{opt}=\left(\sqrt[3]{n}\right)^2$.

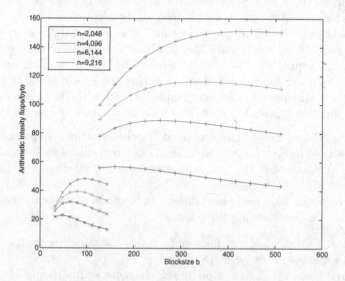

Fig. 3. Effect of the external blocksize b on AI. Lines with marks "$\times$" and "$+$" represent the AI for the blocked and the multi-block algorithm respectively. For the multi-block algorithm, $c=c^{opt}=\sqrt{b}$.

Finally, the arithmetic intensity of the multi-block variant of GJE is given by

$$\frac{2n^3}{2n^2\left(n/b - 2 + b/c + c\right)} \text{ flops-per-memop,} \tag{8}$$

and, in the case of b^{opt} and c^{opt},

$$\frac{n}{n/b - 2 + 2\sqrt{b}} = \frac{n}{3\sqrt[3]{n} - 2} \approx \frac{(\sqrt[3]{n})^2}{3} \text{ flops-per-memop.} \tag{9}$$

To close this section, Fig. 3 illustrates the effect of the (external) blocksize b on the AI of the blocked GJE-algorithm for matrix inversion and its multi-block version, clearly identifying the existence of optimal values for both algorithms, and the much higher AI of the multi-level variant.

5   Experimental Evaluation

The experiments in this section were performed on an Intel-based server equipped with an Intel Core i7-4770 processor (4 cores operating at 3.40 GHz) using double precision (DP) floating-point arithmetic. The (theoretical) peak floating-point rate of this hardware platform is 108.8 DP GFLOPS (billions of flops/sec) and the (theoretical) peak bandwidth is 25.5 GB/s (i.e., 3.18 millions of DP numbers per second). All the implementations rely on the multi-threaded implementation of BLAS provided by Intel MKL 11.1, and the experiments are configured to exploit all 4 cores in the platform by spawning 4 threads during the execution of the BLAS.

We first carry out an experiment that aims to empirically assess the impact of the blocksize on the performance of the blocked implementation of the GJE method to invert matrices of four dimensions. To avoid variations due to cache dimensions and associativity, we select $n = 2,048$, $4,096$, $6,144$ and $9,216$. For brevity, and to better exploit the processor's vector units, we only experiment with "spaced" values of b that are integer multiples of $s = 32$ (except for the 2,048 case, where we use integer multiples of $s = 16$). For each matrix dimension, the theoretical optimal blocksize b^{opt} is computed as described in Sect. 4.1. We then test three different values for b, corresponding to the two integer multiples of s closer to b^{opt} above it (i.e., $(\lfloor b^{opt}/s \rfloor + 1)s$ and $(\lfloor b^{opt}/s \rfloor + 2)s$) as well as the closest integer multiple below this value ($\lfloor b^{opt}/s \rfloor s$).

Table 1 displays the results obtained for this initial study, showing the value of b^{opt} for each matrix dimension and the performance (in GFLOPS) attained using the three values selected for b. The best performance is always observed for the value of b closest to b^{opt}, validating our formula to determine the optimal blocksize setting.

In addition, the performance observed for the implementation of GJE_BLK grows with the dimension of the matrix, a result that is also aligned with the theoretical study, as the computational intensity is proportional to b and larger matrices demand larger blocksizes.

Table 1. Performance (in GFLOPS) of GJE_BLK to invert matrices of different dimensions using several blocksizes b.

Matrix dimension	b^{opt}	b	GFLOPS
2,048	45	32	38
		48	40
		64	40
4,096	64	32	45
		64	52
		96	51
6,144	78	64	62
		96	76
		128	75
9,216	96	64	78
		96	102
		128	98

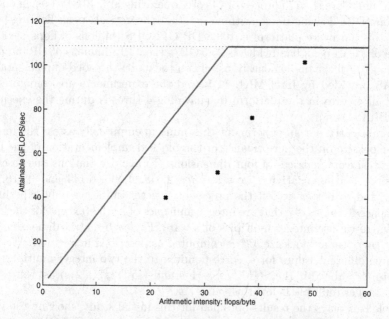

Fig. 4. RM applied to the inversion of matrices via GJE on an Intel Core i7-4770. (Color figure online)

Figure 4 relates performance/AI of the GJE kernel with the parameters of RM for the target architecture. The position in the x-axis is calculated using Eq. (3), and the black dots show the performance attained with the optimal value of b for each problem dimension.

Table 2. Performance (in GFLOPS) reported by the multi–block GJE variant.

Matrix dimension n	$b^{opt} - c^{opt}$	$b - c$	GFLOPS	Arithmetic intensity
2,048	161–12	160–16	62	56
4,096	256–16	256–16	69	89
6,144	335–18	320–16	82	115
9,216	406–20	384–16	94	149

Considering the results in the figure, we point out that the increment in AI is accompanied with improvements in the actual performance. However, the values calculated for AI seem to be overestimated, as the line connecting the black dots shows a gradient similar to that of the bandwidth limit (red line), but shifted in the x-axis.

We next evaluate the multi-block version of GJE, described in Sect. 4.3, to identify the optimal value for the two blocksizes: b and c. Table 2 presents the theoretical optimal values for these parameters, the actual values tested for the blocksizes, the performance attained (in GFLOPS), and the AI according to Eq. (8).

An inspection of the results in the table reveals that the use of a multi-block technique is especially effective for the inversion of matrices of moderate dimension. Concretely, the multi-block algorithm increases the performance by 50% for the smallest problem but it is slightly slower for the largest problem. This is because this technique aims to reduce the impact of the memory-bound operations, a hazard that has a stronger effect for small- to moderate-size problems. In particular, when $n = 9,216$, the computation is not memory-bound and, therefore, the multi-block technique does not yield any gain. Additionally, the blocked algorithm employs the optimal blocksize while suboptimal blocksizes are employed by the multi-block algorithm (due to the multiple of 32 restriction).

In practice, even though the AI factors show that the performance should be limited by the peak performance of the system, in practice it is limited by the memory bandwidth. This is a sign that the theoretical model overestimates the actual AI.

6   Concluding Remarks and Future Work

The Roofline model offers a measure of the optimization potential of a computational routine, relating its AI to the theoretical peak memory bandwidth and peak performance of the target architecture. For dense linear algebra factorization methods, blocked algorithms aim to improve performance by casting a significant fraction of its computations in terms of efficient, compute-bound BLAS-3 kernels that are only constrained by the processor's peak GFLOPS rate. A key parameter to optimize these algorithms is the blocksize, which determines the fraction of the flops that are computed as BLAS-3 vs. BLAS-1/2 kernels and, therefore, governs the performance of the global algorithm.

In this paper we have presented simple yet accurate models to determine the blocksize that optimizes AI for a blocked matrix inversion algorithm based on GJE. Furthermore, we have extended the formulation to a multi-level variant that delivers even higher rates of AI. Our experimental results in an Intel processor with four cores validates the approach, showing that the increases in AI actually result in a performance improvement for both the original blocked algorithm and its multi-level counterpart.

In the future we plan to apply the same techniques to other dense linear algebra algorithms and platforms. We also intend to obtain more precise formulas for the arithmetic intensity.

References

1. Anderson, E., Bai, Z., Demmel, J., Dongarra, J.E., DuCroz, J., Greenbaum, A., Hammarling, S., McKenney, A.E., Ostrouchov, S., Sorensen, D.: LAPACK Users' Guide. SIAM, Philadelphia (1992)
2. Benner, P., Ezzatti, P., Quintana-Ortí, E.S., Remón, A.: Unleashing CPU-GPU acceleration for control theory applications. In: Caragiannis, I., et al. (eds.) Euro-Par 2012. LNCS, vol. 7640, pp. 102–111. Springer, Heidelberg (2013). doi:10.1007/978-3-642-36949-0_13
3. Benner, P., Ezzatti, P., Quintana-Ortí, E.S., Remón, A.: Matrix inversion on CPU-GPU platforms with applications in control theory. Concurrency Comput. Pract. Exp. **25**(8), 1170–1182 (2013)
4. Bientinesi, P., Gunnels, J.A., Myers, M.E., Quintana-Ortí, E.S., van de Geijn, R.A.: The science of deriving dense linear algebra algorithms. ACM Trans. Math. Softw. **31**(1), 1–26 (2005)
5. Dongarra, J.J., Du Croz, J., Hammarling, S., Duff, I.: A set of level 3 basic linear algebra subprograms. ACM Trans. Math. Softw. **16**(1), 1–17 (1990)
6. Golub, G.H., Van Loan, C.F.: Matrix Computations, 3rd edn. The Johns Hopkins University Press, Baltimore (1996)
7. Gunnels, J.A., Gustavson, F.G., Henry, G.M., van de Geijn, R.A.: FLAME: formal linear algebra methods environment. ACM Trans. Math. Softw. **27**(4), 422–455 (2001)
8. Hennessy, J.L., Patterson, D.A.: Computer Architecture: A Quantitative Approach. Elsevier, London (2011)
9. Higham, N.J.: Accuracy and Stability of Numerical Algorithms, 2nd edn. Society for Industrial and Applied Mathematics, Philadelphia (2002)
10. Lo, Y.J., Williams, S., Straalen, B., Ligocki, T.J., Cordery, M.J., Wright, N.J., Hall, M.W., Oliker, L.: Roofline model toolkit: a practical tool for architectural and program analysis. In: Jarvis, S.A., Wright, S.A., Hammond, S.D. (eds.) PMBS 2014. LNCS, vol. 8966, pp. 129–148. Springer, Heidelberg (2015). doi:10.1007/978-3-319-17248-4_7
11. Mehta, S., Garg, R., Trivedi, N., Yew, P.: TurboTiling: leveraging prefetching to boost performance of tiled codes. In: Proceedings of the 2016 International Conference on Supercomputing, ICS 2016, New York, NY, USA, pp. 38:1–38:12. ACM (2016)
12. The ELAPS framework: http://hpac.rwth-aachen.de/~peise/elaps. High Performance and Automatic Computing group at RWTH-Aachen University

13. Quintana-Ortí, E.S., Quintana-Ortí, G., Sun, X., van de Geijn, R.A.: A note on parallel matrix inversion. SIAM J. Sci. Comput. **22**, 1762–1771 (2001)
14. Talagala, N., Arpaci-Dusseau, R.H., Patterson, D.A.: Micro-benchmark based extraction of local and global disk characteristics. Citeseer (1999)
15. Unat, D., Chan, C., Zhang, W., Williams, S., Bachan, J., Bell, J., Shalf, J.: ExaSAT: an exascale co-design tool for performance modeling. Int. J. High Perform. Comput. Appl. **29**(2), 209–232 (2015)
16. Williams, S., Waterman, A., Patterson, D.: Roofline: an insightful visual performance model for multicore architectures. Commun. ACM **52**(4), 65–76 (2009)

Network-Aware Optimization of MPDATA on Homogeneous Multi-core Clusters with Heterogeneous Network

Tania Malik[1]([⊠]), Lukasz Szustak[2]([⊠]), Roman Wyrzykowski[2], and Alexey Lastovetsky[1]

[1] School of Computer Science, University College Dublin, Belfield, Dublin 4, Ireland
tania.malik@ucdconnect.ie, Alexey.Lastovetsky@ucd.ie
[2] Czestochowa University of Technology,
Dabrowskiego 69, 42-201 Czestochowa, Poland
{lszustak,roman}@icis.pcz.pl

Abstract. The communication layer of modern HPC platforms is getting increasingly heterogeneous and hierarchical. As a result, even on platforms with homogeneous processors, the communication cost of many parallel applications will significantly vary depending on the mapping of their processes to the processors of the platform. The optimal mapping, minimizing the communication cost of the application, will strongly depend on the network structure and performance as well as the logical communication flow of the application. In our previous work, we proposed a general approach and two approximate heuristic algorithms aimed at minimization of the communication cost of data parallel applications which have two-dimensional symmetric communication pattern on heterogeneous hierarchical networks, and tested these algorithms in the context of the parallel matrix multiplication application. In this paper, we develop a new algorithm that is built on top of one of these heuristic approaches in the context of a real-life application, MPDATA, which is one of the major parts of the EULAG geophysical model. We carefully study the communication flow of MPDATA and discover that even under the assumption of a perfectly homogeneous communication network, the logical communication links of this application will have different bandwidths, which makes the optimization of its communication cost particularly challenging. We propose a new algorithm that is based on cost functions of one of our general heuristic algorithms and apply it to optimization of the communication cost of MPDATA, which has asymmetric heterogeneous communication pattern. We also present experimental results demonstrating performance gains due to this optimization.

A. Lastovetsky—This publication has emanated from research conducted with the financial support of Science Foundation Ireland (SFI) under Grant Number 14/IA/2474. This research was conducted with the financial support of NCN under grants no. UMO-2015/17/D/ST6/04059. This work is partially supported by EU under the COST Program Action IC1305: Network for Sustainable Ultrascale Computing (NESUS). Experiments were carried out on Grid'5000 developed under the INRIA ALADDIN development action with support from CNRS, RENATER and several Universities as well as other funding bodies (see https://www.grid5000.fr).

J. Carretero et al. (Eds.): ICA3PP 2016 Workshops, LNCS 10049, pp. 30–42, 2016.
DOI: 10.1007/978-3-319-49956-7_3

Keywords: Heterogeneous computing · Communication optimization · Topology-aware optimization · Performance-aware optimization · Data partitioning · MPDATA

1   Introduction

Modern high performance computing (HPC) platforms are becoming increasingly complex, heterogeneous and hierarchical. Heterogeneity appears not only in the computing devices but also in networks. Even with homogeneous processors, efficient execution of data-parallel applications is a big challenge due to ever increasing heterogeneity and complexity of the underlying networks. Optimization of data-parallel applications on such platforms is typically achieved by minimizing the cost of data movement between the processors. In this work, we consider the network heterogeneity rather than the processor heterogeneity. Thus, the target platform comprises homogeneous processors connected with a heterogeneous network. Assuming that the workload is balanced among the processors, we propose a mapping approach that optimizes the overall communication performance of a parallel computational fluid dynamics (CFD) application on such a platform.

We target HPC platforms with heterogeneous networks having two levels of hierarchy, such as interconnected compute nodes and clusters. These networks are very common in the computing world. Popular examples include Grid and Cloud infrastructures. Even supercomputers with thousand of nodes are also examples of heterogeneous network where the communication cost is different on different hierarchical levels e.g. intra-node vs inter-node communication. In data-intensive parallel applications, data transfer between different hierarchical levels is a primary cause of the execution delay. Application scalability has been highly hampered from this data transfer communication overhead. Communication cost can significantly vary depending on mapping of the application processes to the processors of the platform, and the optimal solution minimizing the communication cost strongly depends both on the structure and performance characteristics of the network and on the logical communication flow of the application. In our previous work [1], we proposed a general approach and two heuristic algorithms aimed at minimization of the communication cost of data parallel applications which have symmetrical two-dimensional communication pattern on heterogeneous hierarchical networks, and tested these algorithms in the context of the parallel matrix multiplication application. In this work, we propose a new algorithm that is built on top of cost functions and heuristics of one of our previously proposed algorithms. This algorithm reduces overall message hops and increases data throughput for a wider range of applications, and we apply it to a real-life CFD application.

The CFD application we consider in this work is the multidimensional positive definite advection transport algorithm (MPDATA), which is one of the major parts of the dynamic core of the EULAG geophysical model [2,3]. This geophysical model can be used for simulating thermo-fluid flows across a wide range of scales and physical scenarios, including the numerical weather prediction. The MPDATA belongs to the group of non-oscillatory forward-in-time algorithms, and performs a sequence of stencil computations. The original version of MPDATA has been implemented in FORTRAN 77 and parallelized using MPI library. In our previous work [4] we proposed to rewrite the MPDATA code and replace conventional HPC systems with modern homogeneous and heterogeneous multi- and many-core based platforms. In particular, we have successfully developed a new version of MPDATA that allowed us to much better exploit the available computational features of novel processors and Intel Xeon Phi coprocessors.

However, the communication cost of MPDATA on modern HPC clusters has not been properly optimized. The current approach to mapping of the partitions of the MPDATA computational domain onto computing resources take into account neither the actual properties of the MPDATA communication flow nor the heterogeneity, hierarchy and performance of the communication network.

In this work, we first study and analyse the communication pattern of the MPDATA application. The analysis reveals that MPDATA is very sensitive to the choice of logical topology of processes as the cost per byte of horizontal communications is higher than that of vertical communications even for homogeneous communication networks. This property of MPDATA further complicates the task of partitioning of the MPDATA computational domain and mapping of the sub-domains to the processors in a way that minimizes the cost of communications between different levels of the network hierarchy. In general, finding the optimal arrangement of processors in a 2-D grid is an NP-complete combinatorial optimization problem [5] but it can be approximately solved by using heuristics [6]. For MPDATA, we propose a new heuristic algorithm based on one of our general heuristic approach presented in [1] and apply it to optimization of the communication cost of MPDATA. This algorithm is non-intrusive to the source code of the application and, compared to [1], is not application specific. Our previous algorithms deal with two-dimensional symmetric communication patterns that is why we tested these algorithms in the context of the parallel matrix multiplication application. With this new algorithm, any data-parallel application with two-dimensional homogeneous computational domain and asymmetric heterogeneous communication pattern can benefit. We demonstrate the accuracy and efficiency of the proposed solution using experiments on two-level hierarchical networks, namely, interconnected nodes (intra- and inter-node communication levels) and interconnected clusters (intra- and inter-cluster communication levels).

The rest of the paper is organized as follows. In Sect. 2, we introduce MPDATA and overview existing approaches to topology-aware optimization of communications for MPI applications. In Sect. 3, we analyze the communication pattern of MPDATA and describe its implementation in a cluster environment. In Sect. 4, we present the proposed approach to finding the optimal configuration of MPDATA. In Sect. 5, we give experimental results demonstrating performance gains due to this optimization.

2 Related Work

In this section, we describe MPDATA and its modifications over time. We also overview related work on topology-aware optimization of communications.

2.1 MPDATA

The MPDATA application is used to solve the advection equation on a moving grid according to the subsequent time steps [7]. This real-life application offers several advanced options that allow for modeling a wide range of complex geophysical flows. Depending on the type of modeled phenomena, this application can demand a high computing performance of HPC clusters. Therefore, the configurable code of MPDATA was developed and delivered over the years [2,7,8]. This code was implemented in FORTRAN 77 and parallelized using MPI library, however, without taking into account of the features of todays computing architectures.

The MPI parallelization of the MPDATA computations on x86-based clusters as a part of the EULAG model was thoroughly studied in [8], using tens of thousands of cores, or even more than 100 K cores in the case of IBM Blue Gene/Q. The parallelization strategy of this implementation is based on 3D domain decomposition, and executes computations according to the distributed memory model where each core is assigned to a single MPI_rank. This approach ignores the advantages of shared memory systems available in modern multi-core platforms. Moreover, it also does not take into account the network-aware partitioning of communications across computing resources.

The MPDATA code has been recently re-written and optimized for execution on modern CPU and Intel co-processors based high-performance computing platforms. The new C++ implementation proposed in [4] allows for more efficient distribution of computational tasks on the available resources. It makes use of the (3+1)D decomposition strategy for the stencils computation, that transfers the data traffic from the main memory to cache hierarchy by proper reusing of the cache memory. Additionally, to improve the computational efficiency the algorithm groups the cores (threads) into independent work teams in order to reduce inter-cache communication overheads due to the communications between neighbouring threads/cores, and synchronizations.

2.2 Communication Optimization for Parallel Applications

Communication optimization is a very broad field that comprises a number of different approaches. The goal of all such optimization approaches is to reduce the overall runtime of the communication operations. Communication optimization on heterogeneous HPC platform is comprehensively covered in [9], where all the existing approaches were classified as performance or topology-aware. The increasing complexity of HPC platforms has made topology awareness a critical component of HPC application optimization. A number of topology-aware approaches have been proposed in [10,11]. The main idea behind the topology-aware optimizations is to reduce communication traffic and contention by taking into account the network topology so that most of the communication occurs between nearby processors. Whereas, in performance-aware optimizations, network properties are reconstructed with performance measurements by using communication benchmarks. This approach is used in the absence of topology information.

Topology information has been used in developing a number of topology-aware implementations of MPI collectives for optimal scheduling of messages on heterogeneous HPC platforms [12–15]. In [12], the optimization of the MPICH broadcast algorithm was proposed for efficient execution of broadcast on interconnected clusters. Interconnected clusters are presented as two-level communication graphs, inter- and intra-cluster ones. Clusters communicate via selected nodes, coordinators, which form the inter-cluster communicator. Within a cluster all nodes communicate with the cluster coordinator, forming the intra-cluster communicator. This topology-aware implementation of broadcast algorithm aims to minimize the amount of data sent over the slow wide-area links and results in significant improvement.

Further performance improvement is realized in [13] and [16], where collective operations were optimized by adopting multilevel hierarchical heterogeneous networks and Grid. Pipelining and offloading techniques were used to overlap the inter- and intra-node communications in multi-core clusters. [11] has shown that topology-aware collectives can be used to reduce the communication cost on homogeneous supercomputers which have complex network topologies, like BlueGene and Cray.

Many existing MPI applications can be executed efficiently on hierarchical heterogeneous HPC platforms by using topology-aware collectives and does not require to modify application source code. However, it is applicable to collective operations only and does not affect the applications that are based on point-to-point exchanges. In this case, the communication cost can be reduced by placing frequently communicating tasks on physically nearby processors. This closeness is application-specific and depends on the logical communication flow of the application.

In [10,17], the problem of topology-aware optimization of point-to-point communications is solved by introducing a graph, which represents the logical communication flow of the application and is mapped onto the network topology. [17] applied this approach to the mesh and graph virtual MPI topologies and SMP clusters. In [10], it was applied to the mesh topology on BlueGene/L.

3   MPDATA on Clusters

One of the common methods for exploiting the multicore clusters is to employ the hybrid programming model, that allows for efficient usage of the distributed and shared memory hierarchies of these systems. This implies to combine different programming paradigms, such as MPI and OpenMP. Such a mixture is successfully utilized for the MPDATA computation, where a single MPI_rank is

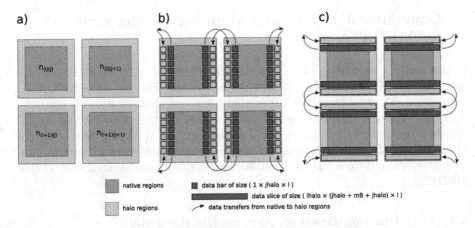

Fig. 1. Data flow between nodes for the MPDATA application: (a) 2D domain decomposition between computing nodes: $n_{ij}, n_{ij+1}, ...$, (b) the communication pattern for the horizontal direction, (c) the communication pattern for the vertical direction

assigned to every multicore node while OpenMP threads are employed to utilize the multicore computational resources.

The 3D $n \times m \times l$ MPDATA domain is firstly partitioned in two dimensions n and m into equal sub-domains that are further one-to-one mapped to adequate nodes of the homogeneous clusters. Every sub-domain of size $nB \times mB \times l$ is decomposed according to the (3+1)D decomposition proposed in our previous works [4]. This strategy contributes to ease the main-memory and communications bounds, that characterize MPDATA, and to better exploit modern computational resources such as cores and vector units.

Since the (3+1)D strategy allows for independent calculation of every sub-domain for a single time step, the inter-node communications and synchronization points have to take place only between subsequent time steps in order to exchange the required partial outcomes. The exchanged data corresponds to the halo regions determined by data dependencies of MPDATA computations. These regions take place on the border of the MPDATA domain partitioning. As a result, the data traffic is generated only between nodes that are mapped onto adjacent sub-domains in both directions: vertical and horizontal. Figure 1 illustrates the data flow between nodes of MPDATA application.

After every time step each node has to send/receive in horizontal direction the adequate halo regions to/from adjacent nodes placed on the left and right sides (Fig. 1b). Since the necessary halo regions for this direction are periodically placed in the main memory, each node exchanges nB data bar of size $1 \times jhalo \times l$ to the left node, and to the right one. Then, the same node is responsible for sending/receiving in vertical direction the adequate halo regions to/from adjacent nodes placed on the top and bottom sides (Fig. 1c). Transferred data in this communication path is placed in the contiguous memory areas, thus this node moves the data slices of size $ihalo \times (jhalo + mB + jhalo) \times l$ to/from the top and bottom nodes.

4   Communication-Optimal Mapping Arrangement for MPDATA

In this section, we first propose an extension of the network-bandwidth-based cost function [1] to accurately measure the communication cost of the MPDATA application. Then we formulate the heuristic solution that efficiently constructs a near-optimal arrangement for MPDATA based on the extended cost function by using information about network topology and the application communication flow. This heuristic solution reduces the search space of sub-domain arrangements and finds the one that minimizes the communication cost of the MPDATA.

4.1   Cost Function Based on Asymmetric Bandwidth

In our previous work [1], we defined the cost function based on network bandwidth. The main idea was to estimate the communication cost accurately by using information about the network topology and the application communication flow. That cost function proved to work well with applications having symmetric communication patterns. However, MPDATA has asymmetric communication behavior, namely, even in the case of a homogeneous communication layer the effective bandwidth of horizontal communications is higher than that of the vertical ones. One of the reasons behind this phenomenon is that data communicated vertically is stored in a contiguous region of memory while the data communicated horizontally is not. As a result, this cost function fails to accurately characterize the communication cost of MPDATA. Therefore, we propose to extend this bandwidth-based cost function to account for applications with asymmetric communication patterns. The proposed extension characterizes the communication time, using the asymmetric bandwidths properties. We call it a cost function based on asymmetric bandwidth in the rest of the paper. The function takes into account two bandwidth values, one for horizontal communication and the other is for vertical one. The problem of finding the communication-optimal arrangement can be formulated as minimization of the sum of the horizontal and vertical communication costs.

Assuming that the data is equally partitioned among the processors, so that the size of each sub-domain is same, we define the asymmetric cost function for horizontal communication as follows:

$$cost_H = \sum_{i=1}^{r} \left(h \times \sum_{j=1}^{c} \frac{1}{b_H(Q_{ij}, Q_{i,(j+1)\%c})} \right), \tag{1}$$

where i iterates over the rows and j iterates over the partitioned sub-domains in each row. h is the height of a row (in bytes) that is same for each row because data is equally partitioned. Function $b_H(X, Y)$ returns the horizontal bandwidth (in bytes per second) between processors X and Y, and Q_{ij} designates the processor holding the j-th sub-domain in row i. Thus, this cost function estimates the communication time in seconds. The inner sum represents sending a part of the pivot column in a row. The outer sum represents the upper bound on the communication time required to send the whole pivot column to all rows. We use the upper bound because the bandwidth of some links may be divided between multiple communications corresponding to different rows.

We define the asymmetric cost function for vertical communication in a similar way:

$$cost_V = \sum_{j=1}^{c} \left(w \times \sum_{i=1}^{r} \frac{1}{b_V(Q_{ij}, Q_{i,(j+1)\%r})} \right), \tag{2}$$

Here j iterates over the columns, and i iterates over the partitioned sub-domains in each column. w is the width of a column (in bytes) that is same for each column because data is equally partitioned. Function $b_V(X, Y)$ returns the vertical bandwidth (in bytes per second) between processors X and Y.

The communication cost associated with arrangement A is represented by two values $(cost_H(A), cost_V(A))$. The problem of finding the communication-optimal arrangement can be formulated as minimization of their sum:

$$cost_H(A) + cost_V(A) \rightarrow \min. \tag{3}$$

4.2 Heuristic Based on Asymmetric Bandwidth Cost Function

The heuristic algorithm using the asymmetric bandwidth cost function for estimating the volume of communications is built on top of the bandwidth-based heuristic presented in [1]. It assumes that the target platform consists of p interconnected homogeneous processors. The processors are naturally partitioned into a number of groups based on their communication proximity, which reflects the two-level hierarchy of the communication layer. If processors x_0, x_1, y_0 and y_1 belong to the same group then $b_H(x_0, y_0) = b_H(x_1, y_1)$ and $b_V(x_0, y_0) = b_V(x_1, y_1)$.

The algorithm starts with any initial arrangement $P_1, P_2, \ldots, P_p$ of the processors such that processors from the same group will follow one other in this linear arrangement. Note, the orders naturally determined by application configuration files typically satisfy this assumption. Alternatively, a simple clustering algorithm guided by functions $b_H(x, y)$ and $b_V(x, y)$ can be applied to re-order the original arrangement if it does not satisfy this assumption.

The algorithm then repeatedly executes the following two steps. The first step finds the optimal two-dimensional arrangement of the processors, $m \times n$, which preserves their linear order as follows. For each factor pair $r \times c = p$, the processors are arranged column-wise and row-wise into r rows and c columns forming arrangement A. The cost of these arrangements are estimated as $cost(P_1, \ldots, P_p, r, c) = cost_H(A) + cost_V(A)$, and the optimal pair $m \times n$ is found as the one that minimizes this cost, $cost(P_1, \ldots, P_p, m, n) = \min_{r,c} cost(P_1, \ldots, P_p, r, c)$.

The second step applies the bandwidth-based algorithm from [1] slightly modified by the use of the asymmetric cost function to this 2D arrangement. This step may changes the linear order of the processors within the arrangement in order to reduce its communication cost while preserving the shape of the arrangement, $m \times n$. The reordering is guided by the 2D partitioning of the computational domain induced by the 2D processor arrangement and uses the fact that within each column of the domain, sub-domains held by processors from the same group will also make a group of adjacent sub-domains. In brief, we first try permutations of the groups in the first column and pick the one that minimizes the vertical communication cost for this column. Then, for each following column $k = 2, \ldots, n$, we try permutations of the groups in this column and pick the one that minimizes the sum of vertical and horizontal costs for first k columns. This guarantees that while improving communications horizontally, we will not deteriorate the vertical routes. Permutation of groups rather than individual processors in a column will significantly reduce the solution space that otherwise would be $p!$. Finally, we try all permutations of whole columns and pick the one that minimizes the sum of horizontal and vertical communication costs for the whole domain.

This step can change our original linear arrangement of the processors. If this is the case, we will feed the new arrangement to the first step of next iteration of our heuristic algorithm that will find the optimal $m \times n$ arrangement for this new order. Then, this 2D arrangement will be re-arranged by the second step of this iteration. This procedure continues until we find a fixed point of the transformation performed by one iteration of the algorithm.

The presented iterative algorithm does not require to run the application or any benchmarks to compare the communication cost of the application for different arrangements. Instead, it uses information about the network topology and the application communication flow. This heuristic is efficient for applications having 2D communication pattern on heterogeneous networks. Not only it reduces unnecessary exchanges between the sub-networks but also employs the fastest routes between them.

5   Experimental Results

In this section, we demonstrate that the communication performance of MPDATA can be significantly improved due to optimization proposed by the asymmetric bandwidth heuristic not only for heterogeneous but also for a perfectly homogeneous communication network.

We perform experiments on the Grid'5000 infrastructure, which is a large scale distributed platform. It consists of a number of clusters distributed between 10 sites in France and connected via the Renater network. Each site hosts several clusters of identical nodes. For our experiments, we choose two clusters, Grisou and Grimoire, from the Nancy site and the other two, Paravance and Parasilo, from the Rennes site. All clusters have identical Intel Xeon E5-2630 v3 processors with 8 cores per node. To demonstrate performance gains, we first perform two types of experiments on interconnected clusters. These interconnected clusters form a two-level hierarchy, with very heterogeneous inter-cluster links. Then, we conduct experiments on a single fully homogeneous cluster, with homogeneous processors and a homogeneous communication network. We have a priori information about the network topology and asymmetric bandwidths of MPDATA. We have tried ten different initial mappings as an input and our experiment shows that all of these mappings converges to the optimal solutions have same communication cost after applying asymmetric bandwidth heuristic. It has been noted that there is more than one optimal solutions exist. However, the communication cost and execution time of all optimal solutions are same. To make sure the experimental results are reliable, the application is repeatedly executed until the sample mean lies in the 95% confidence interval and a precision of 0.025 (2.5%) has been achieved and results follows the normal distribution. We also make sure the nodes are fully reserved and dedicated to our experiments.

5.1 Inter-cluster Experiments

In these experiments, we use four clusters with 12 nodes in total: Grimoire(3), Parasilo(4), Grisou(2), Paravance(3). We spawn one MPI process per node. Because logical communication links of MPDATA has different bandwidths, we have two bandwidth values for each link. Horizontal and vertical bandwidths are shown in Table 1. MPDATA is configured with problem size $512 \times 512 \times 64$.

Table 1. Horizontal/Vertical bandwidths of communicating links(GB/sec)

	Grimoire	Parasilo	Grisou	Paravance
Grimoire	0.03963/0.48068	0.00007/0.00056	0.03889/0.49341	0.00007/0.00056
Parasilo	0.00007/0.00056	0.03876/0.48858	0.00007/0.00056	0.03732/0.45943
Grisou	0.03889/0.49341	0.00007/0.00056	0.03834/0.48916	0.00007/0.00056
Paravance	0.00007/0.00056	0.03732/0.45943	0.00007/0.00056	0.03920/0.46808

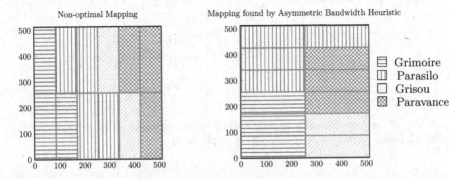

Fig. 2. One of the non-optimal mappings and the mapping returned by the asymmetric bandwidth heuristic for the heterogeneous platform.

Table 2. Inter-cluster experimental results

Nodes	Cost		Ratio	Exec. time (sec)		Ratio
	Non-optimal	Heuristic		Non-optimal	Heuristic	
12	22424946	2143978	10.46	994.02	154.20	6.44

Figure 2 shows one of the considered default initial mappings and the optimal mapping found by the asymmetric bandwidth heuristic. Table 2 shows the communication cost of these mappings, calculated using the cost function, and the measured total execution time of MPDATA. To find the optimal mapping, the asymmetric bandwidth heuristic took 1.130000e-03 s. The mapping found by the asymmetric bandwidth heuristic is more then 6 times faster then the non-optimal case mapping.

5.2　Intra-cluster Experiments

We also perform experiments on a homogeneous multi-core cluster to check the effect of asymmetric bandwidth of MPDATA on the communication performance with a perfectly homogeneous network. We use 12 nodes from the Grisou cluster. MPDATA is configured with problem size $512 \times 512 \times 64$.

Figure 3 shows one of the non-optimal mappings and the mapping returned by the asymmetric bandwidth heuristic. Table 3 shows the calculated communication cost of both mappings and the measured total execution time of MPDATA. The mapping found by the asymmetric bandwidth heuristic is 3 times faster then the non-optimal mapping. Asymmetric bandwidth heuristic took 3.730000e-04 s to find this optimal mapping.

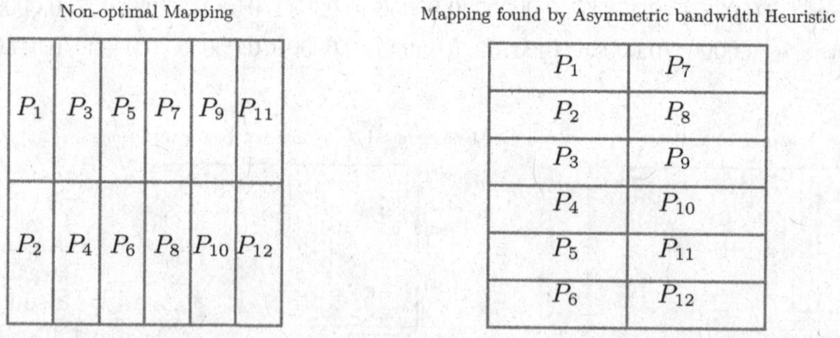

Non-optimal Mapping

Mapping found by Asymmetric bandwidth Heuristic

P_1	P_3	P_5	P_7	P_9	P_{11}
P_2	P_4	P_6	P_8	P_{10}	P_{12}

P_1	P_7
P_2	P_8
P_3	P_9
P_4	P_{10}
P_5	P_{11}
P_6	P_{12}

Fig. 3. One of the non-optimal mappings and the mapping returned by the asymmetric bandwidth heuristic for the fully homogeneous platform.

Table 3. Intra-cluster experimental results

Nodes	Cost		Ratio	Exec. time (sec)		Ratio
	Non-optimal	Heuristic		Non-optimal	Heuristic	
12	65658	18535	3.5	3.86	1.32	3.0

6   Conclusions

In this paper, we have applied an approach aimed to minimize the communication cost of a parallel CFD application using information about the network topology/performance and application communication flow. We have also demonstrated that the proposed solution provides significant performance gains.

References

1. Malik, T., Rychkov, V., Lastovetsky, A.: Network-aware optimization of communications for parallel matrix multiplication on hierarchical hpc platforms. Concurrency Comput. Pract. Experience **28**, 02–821 (2016). cpe.3609
2. Wyrzykowski, R., Szustak, L., Rojek, K.: Parallelization of 2D MPDATA EULAG algorithm on hybrid architectures with GPU accelerators. parallel Comput. **40**, 425–447 (2014)
3. Wyrzykowski, R., Szustak, L., Rojek, K., Tomas, A.: Towards efficient decomposition and parallelization of MPDATA on hybrid CPU-GPU cluster. In: Lirkov, I., Margenov, S., Waśniewski, J. (eds.) LSSC 2013. LNCS, vol. 8353, pp. 457–464. Springer, Heidelberg (2014). doi:10.1007/978-3-662-43880-0_52
4. Szustak, L., Rojek, K., Wyrzykowski, R., Gepner, P.: Toward efficient distribution of mpdata stencil computation on intel mic architecture. In: Proceedings of the 1st International Workshop on High-Performance Stencil Computations, pp. 51–56 (2014)
5. Beaumont, O., Boudet, V., Legrand, A., Rastello, F., Robert, Y.: Heterogeneous matrix-matrix multiplication or partitioning a square into rectangles: Np-completeness and approximation algorithms. In: Proceedings of the Ninth Euromicro Workshop on Parallel and Distributed Processing, pp. 298–305 (2001)
6. Lastovetsky, A., Dongarra, J.: High Performance Heterogeneous Computing. Wiley (2009)
7. Smolarkiewicz, P.: Multidimensional positive definite advection transport algorithm: an overview. Int. J. Numer. Meth. Fluids **50**, 1123–1144 (2006)
8. Piotrowski, Z., Wyszogrodzki, A., Smolarkiewicz, P.: Towards petascale simulation of atmospheric circulations with soundproof equations. Acta Geophys. **59**, 1294–1311 (2011)
9. Dichev, K., Lastovetsky, A.: Optimization of collective communication for heterogeneous hpc platforms. Wiley-Interscience (2013)
10. Agarwal, T., Sharma, A., Laxmikant, A., Kale, L.: Topology-aware task mapping for reducing communication contention on large parallel machines. In: IPDPS 2006, p. 10 (2006)
11. Solomonik, E., Bhatele, A., Demmel, J.: Improving communication performance in dense linear algebra via topology aware collectives. In: SC 2011, pp. 77: 1–77: 11. ACM, New York (2011)

12. Kielmann, T., Hofman, R.F., Bal, H.E., Plaat, A., Bhoedjang, R.A.: MagPIe: MPI's collective communication operations for clustered wide area systems. In: ACM Sigplan Notices, vol. 34, pp. 131–140. ACM (1999)

13. Karonis, N., De Supinski, B., Foster, I., Gropp, W., Lusk, E., Bresnahan, J.: Exploiting hierarchy in parallel computer networks to optimize collective operation performance. IPDPS **2000**, 377–384 (2000)

14. Ma, T., Bosilca, G., Bouteiller, A., Dongarra, J.: HierKNEM: an adaptive framework for kernel-assisted and topology-aware collective communications on manycore clusters. In: IPDPS 2012, pp. 970–982 (2012)

15. Kandalla, K., Subramoni, H., Vishnu, A., Panda, D.K.: Designing topology-aware collective communication algorithms for large scale infiniband clusters: case studies with scatter and gather. In: 2010 IEEE International Symposium on Parallel Distributed Processing, Workshops and Phd Forum (IPDPSW), pp. 1–8(2010)

16. Coti, C., Herault, T., Cappello, F.: MPI applications on grids: a topology aware approach. In: Sips, H., Epema, D., Lin, H.-X. (eds.) Euro-Par 2009. LNCS, vol. 5704, pp. 466–477. Springer, Heidelberg (2009). doi:10.1007/978-3-642-03869-3_45

17. Traff, J.: Implementing the MPI process topology mechanism. In: Supercomputing 2002, pp. 1–23 (2002)

Formalizing Data Locality in Task Parallel Applications

Germán Ceballos$^{(\boxtimes)}$, Erik Hagersten$^{(\boxtimes)}$, and David Black-Schaffer$^{(\boxtimes)}$

Department of Information Technology, Uppsala University, Uppsala, Sweden
{german.ceballos,erik.hagersten,david.black-schaffer}@it.uu.se

Abstract. Task-based programming provides programmers with an intuitive abstraction to express parallelism, and runtimes with the flexibility to adapt the schedule and load-balancing to the hardware. Although many profiling tools have been developed to understand these characteristics, the interplay between task scheduling and data reuse in the cache hierarchy has not been explored. These interactions are particularly intriguing due to the flexibility task-based runtimes have in scheduling tasks, which may allow them to improve cache behavior.

This work presents StatTask, a novel statistical cache model that can predict cache behavior for arbitrary task schedules and cache sizes from a single execution, without programmer annotations. StatTask enables fast and accurate modeling of data locality in task-based applications for the first time. We demonstrate the potential of this new analysis to scheduling by examining applications from the BOTS benchmarks suite, and identifying several important opportunities for reuse-aware scheduling.

Keywords: Task-based · Cache modeling · Performance model

1 Introduction

Multicore architectures bring new levels of performance, but at the cost of more complex development and performance analysis, particularly with regards to shared memory system resources, such as caches. Multicores have traditionally been used with multi-program or thread-based workloads, and many tools exist for analyzing their performance.

Recently, task-based programming has become popular as tasks are simple to program and move the complexity of parallel scheduling and load balancing to a runtime, instead of requiring explicit user-directed threading. As a result, task-based programs can more easily take advantage of available resources. These strengths have led to the development of many production-quality frameworks, including OpenMP tasks [18], Intel's TBB and StarPU [3].

This work was supported by the Swedish Foundation for Strategic Research project FFL12-0051, the Swedish Research Council Linnaeus UPMARC centre of excellence.

J. Carretero et al. (Eds.): ICA3PP 2016 Workshops, LNCS 10049, pp. 43–61, 2016.
DOI: 10.1007/978-3-319-49956-7_4

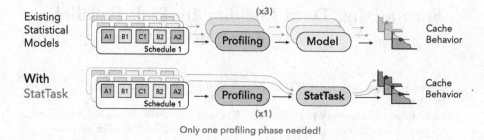

Fig. 1. StatTask allows us to re-order profiled reuse pairs to obtain the profile for an arbitrary schedule without having to execute and profile the schedule explicitly.

However, understanding performance of these systems has become harder due to shared resources, demanding new analyses. Existing tools analyze scheduling and load-balancing [10, 16, 19], but have largely ignored *shared data reuse between tasks*. This is a substantial omission as data locality (through caches) is one of the key factors for performance on today's multicore processors. Understanding the reuse of shared data between tasks is critical for optimizing cache locality and memory behavior.

For serial or thread-based applications, there has been an extensive work on characterizing data reuse, including instrumentation [20] and statistical modeling [4, 13]. However, these methods only provide insight into the memory behavior of the *observed execution* of the program. Yet a key strength of task-based programs is that they have great flexibility in how they schedule work (tasks), as they can do better load balancing and parallelism exploitation. However, this affects the actual data reuse.

This paper presents a novel statistical cache model (StatTask) that enables analysis of cache behavior. The model captures the interaction of shared data between (and within) tasks and is capable of estimating how data reuse and locality is affected by scheduling. With this, it can predict cache behavior for *different execution schedules* from the analysis of a *single* run.

Figure 1 illustrates the potential of having such a model. While typical statistical cache modeling approaches would require one profiling phase per application schedule, StatTask allows us to model any arbitrary schedule from a single profiling run.

To understand the potential of task-based data reuse analysis, we first analyze the overall data reuse in the BOTS task benchmark suite (Sect. 2). We then look at sparseLU in detail, by connecting its reuse profile and schedule. With that background, we introduce a detailed formal description of the underlying data representation for statistical cache frameworks (Sect. 3), and our contributions to handle tasks and schedules (Sect. 4). Finally we describe the details of our implementation and analyze the results obtained when applying it to multiple benchmarks of the BOTS suite with different input data sets and schedules (Sect. 5). In addition, we discuss this work in relation to existing profiling tools (Sect. 6), addressing future work and limitations.

2   Motivation: Task Data Reuse

Optimizing a program for data reuse through the cache is essential for performance on modern systems: cache latency is between 4 to 30 cycles, while main memory can easily have a latency over 100 cycles. However, caches are much smaller, so data placement has to be done carefully. For task-based programs, data is initially brought into the cache by a task, and, if it is reused, it can either be from the same task (private reuse) or by a later task (shared reuse). Tasks that execute between tasks with shared reuses also bring data into the cache, which may evict the shared data, thereby turning cache hits into misses, and hurting performance.

Following this intuition, we classify accesses in task-based applications into three types, depending on who originates the access, and whether they are in the cache:

- *DRAM Accesses*: accesses that miss in the cache and must be brought in from DRAM, such as the first accesses to data.
- *Private Reuses*: accesses to data previously loaded by the *same* task. These will hit in the cache if it is large enough to hold the task's entire data set.
- *Shared Reuses*: accesses to data previously loaded by *another* task. These will hit in the cache if it is large enough to hold the data sets of both sharing tasks, and the data is not evicted between the two tasks that share the reuse.

A scheduler that understands how its decisions affect the amount of shared reuses that hit in the cache can intelligently make a trade-off between cache behavior and other metrics. The potential for such optimizations varies across applications (depending on the amount of shared reuses and the scheduling flexibility) and architectures (depending on the sizes and configurations of the caches). To illustrate this, we analyzed a range of task-based applications from the BOTS benchmarks suite [11].

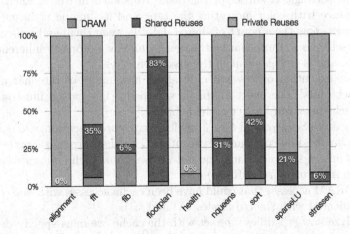

Fig. 2. Shared vs Private Reuses in the BOTS benchmarks. Shared reuses can help performance if the tasks can be scheduled to ensure the data remains in the cache.

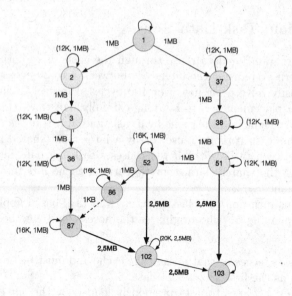

Fig. 3. SparseLU Reuse Graph, showing inter- and intra-task accesses. (Color figure online)

Figure 2 shows the breakdown of the accesses types. This data is schedule-agnostic, and shows the maximum *potential* shared reuse across all tasks. The benchmarks demonstrate significant diversity, with `sort`, `fft`, `sparseLU` and `nqueens` exhibiting over 30% shared reuses on average, and `floorplan` reaching nearly 80%. As the portion of shared reuses increases, the potential benefits of scheduling to ensure that those reuses are present in the cache increases as well.

If we look more closely at the `sparseLU` benchmark, we can see that it has a complex internal task structure, generating over 40.000 tasks when running with default settings. A subset of the tasks are shown in Fig. 3. Each node is a task instance with color indicating the type and its unique *id* inside. Edges between tasks show the amount of shared data between them and self-edges the amount of self reuses. Importantly, this *reuse graph* is a property inherent to the application, and is *independent* of the execution.

Different execution orders will only affect how many of the shared reuses become cache hits. The effect of this is shown in Fig. 4 which illustrates how execution schedules can impact cache behavior.

The schedules S_{GOOD_1} and S_{BAD_1} are for single-core execution, while S_{GOOD_2} and S_{BAD_2} are for dual-core parallel execution. The black arrows show the shared reuses that hit in the cache and the red arrows show cache misses when data comes from main memory (DRAM).

Some DRAM accesses that could have been cache accesses with better schedules are indicated with the red circles (A) and (B).

To analyze how schedules interact with the cache, we must specify the cache size to know how much data it can hold. For this examples, we assume a 1MB

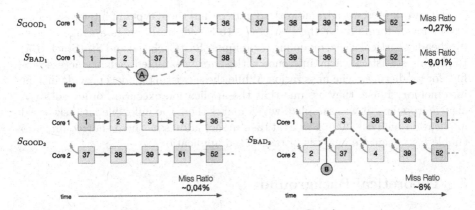

Fig. 4. Different schedules for `sparseLU`: reuses that successfully hit in the cache are shown as black arrows indicating the source of the reused data. Reuses that are not in the cache due to poor scheduling are shown in red. (Color figure online)

private cache for each core. Note that in Fig. 3 the green tasks (2 through 36) and the blue tasks (37 to 52) share data, but the red and green datasets are independent from each other.

If we look at the bad single core schedule (S_{BAD_1}), task 1 will bring 1MB of data from DRAM and store it in the cache. When it finishes, task 2 will reuse all of task 1's data from the cache and generate 1MB of output data that will be stored in the cache. However, when task 37 is executed next according to the schedule, it will bring 1MB of its own data into the cache, evicting all of task 2's output data. When task 3 executes after task 37, it will not find task 2's output data in the cache, and will instead be forced to reload it from DRAM, thereby evicting all of task 37's data. This schedule is far from optimal as task it evicts task 1's output data from the cache that otherwise could have been reused by task 3. S_{GOOD_1} avoids these unnecessary cache evictions by executing first tasks 2 through 36 and then 37 through 52, thereby maximizing the shared reuses between tasks through the cache.

These two schedules have significantly different cache miss ratios due to the execution order of the tasks. S_{BAD_1} will miss approximately 1 K times between tasks 1 and 52, while each task has around 12 K self reuses that will hit in the cache, giving a miss ratio around 8.0%. S_{GOOD_1}'s better schedule, however, results in a cache miss ratio of only 0.3%.

The optimization potential is even clearer for multicore execution. S_{BAD_2} shows the analogous scenario for parallel execution across multiple cores with private caches. S_{BAD_2} executes the first schedulable task as soon as a core is ready. While this approach helps load balance across cores, it provides poor data locality, causing constant evictions and misses. S_{GOOD_2} demonstrates a better schedule that preserves locality by executing tasks locally to the core that spawned them, and thereby reducing cache misses by 200x from 8% to 0.04%.

This work presents a framework to understand these types of inter-task memory behavior formally for the first time. To do so, we leverage a range of low-overhead statistical cache modeling techniques (StatCache [4] and StatStack [13]) to provide statistical cache inference with sparsely-sampled memory access profiles for predicting cache miss ratios. While these existing models provide insight into memory reuse, they assume that the application execution order does not change from how it was sampled, which makes them too inflexible for task-based application analysis. Our new StatTask model addresses these shortcomings to enable fast, accurate analysis of task-based applications.

3   Theoretical Background

Existing statistical cache models [4,5] model the execution of an application as a sequence of memory accesses. Although this is a widely-used formalization, it is not expressive enough to identify the tasks executing those memory accesses. To address this, we present an extended representation, which models the execution of an application as a sequence of tasks. This enables us to model different schedules from one particular set of profiled data. To explain this representation, we present the first formal description of existing statistical cache modeling and extend it to support parallel tasks.

3.1   Sequential Memory Access Execution Model

For statistical cache models, the execution of an application P is captured as a sequence of n memory accesses $E = x_1 x_2 \ldots x_n$ (the *access trace of P*). Formally, a memory access x is an m-tuple $x = (a, p_1, \ldots, p_{m-1})$ with a the memory address accessed, and each p_j a different property of the access. Many previous works have used a 4-tuple $x = (a, t, p, o)$ with t the time of the access, p the instruction pointer and o the type of operation (read, write, read-write). We will denote the address of an access x_i with a^i.

The set of accesses of an execution E will be given by $A_E = \bigcup_{i=1}^n \{x_i\}$. We will assume that the applications are deterministic for the inputs, making this set an inherent property (i.e. schedule and cache hierarchy independent). Note that we evaluate this assumption's effects for different inputs in Sect. 5.

3.2   Distances and Reuses

The *access distance* between two accesses x_j and x_k is given by $\delta(x_j, x_k) = |j - k|$. Intuitively, a memory address accessed throughout an execution is *reused* when it is accessed several times. An address is *reused within the cache* only if there are few enough unique accesses in between the reuse such that is not evicted from the cache before it can be reused. The set of reuses for an execution E of an application P will be denoted $\tilde{\mathcal{R}}_P^E$. If a reuse is *consecutive*, it implies that all addresses accessed in-between are different from the one being reused. The subset of *consecutive reuses* is formally defined as

$$\mathcal{R}_P^E = \{(x_j, x_k) \in \tilde{\mathcal{R}}_P^E \mid \forall x_s \in E, \ k < s < j, \ a^s \neq a^k\},$$

and it is the basic information used by existing statistical cache models to understand locality properties of an application[2]. In this context, the *reuse distance* will be the distance $\delta_{\mathcal{R}^E}$ of the consecutive reuses.

The global set of reuses of an application $(\tilde{\mathcal{R}}^E)$ is almost execution-independent: for any execution, the global set of reuses will be the same, except for the order of the pairs (tuples). This property is expressed formally and proven in the Appendix.

3.3 Task Execution Model

In task-based programming, applications are structured as small functional units of code called `task`. Each of these units will define a different task *type*, and during execution, many instances of each type may be spawned to operate on different pieces of the data and submitted to a runtime system for scheduling. Thus, from the runtime system's point of view, an execution of a task-based application P can be seen as a *task-schedule* (or a set of task-schedule, one per core), which is a sequence of m task instances $S = T_1 T_2 \ldots T_m$.

Each task instance T_i has a type associated given by $t(T_i)$. The set of all tasks instances that appear when executing P will be denoted by $\mathcal{T}_P$. The number of task types of P is commonly known as the *task diversity* of the application.

3.4 Equivalence Between Schedules and Memory Accesses

It is possible to show that both models (execution of an application as a sequence memory accesses vs as a sequence of tasks) presented in Sects. 3.1 and 3.3 are equivalent for the same schedule. That is, whether we track memory reuses via tasks or as part of the application, the results are the same.

The equivalence becomes a key property for this work, as it enables the following feature: If we have the sequence of memory accesses E of a task-based application, we can infer the schedule S, and therefore the respective execution sequence for each task T in S, E_T. Conversely, if we know the task-schedule of an application and their execution sequences E_T, we can infer the execution sequence of the entire application. *This enables us to compute the sequential memory accesses for an arbitrary schedule, which allows us to use statistical modeling to analyze cache behavior for arbitrary schedules from a single profiling run.*

To show this equivalence, we first show how to get a mapping from the execution of a task T_i in a schedule S[3] to a sequence of memory accesses

---

[2] Note that these properties have never been formally described.

[3] For a particular input data set.

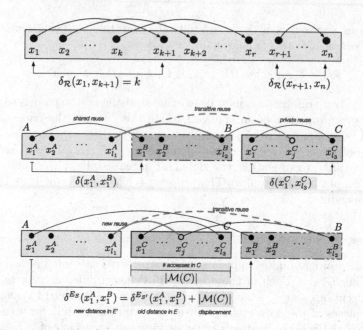

Fig. 5. Reuse Pairs: The same reuse pairs are shown for traditional sequential access models and our new task-based model. Note how the reuses change as the tasks are rescheduled between 5b and c.

$E_{T_i} = x_1^{T_i} \dots x_{l_i}^{T_i}$ with l_i the last memory access index of task i, $\forall i$. This is done by defining the linear operator $\mathcal{M}$ which gives the sequence of memory accesses per task by

$$\mathcal{M}(T_i) = E_{T_i} = x_1^{T_i} \dots x_{l_i}^{T_i} = [x_1^{T_i}, x_{l_i}^{T_i}] \ \forall i.$$

Then, we use this operator to obtain the memory access sequence of an application P with schedule $S = T_1 \dots T_m$ by observing that

$$E_S = \mathcal{M}(S) = \mathcal{M}(T_1)\mathcal{M}(T_2)\dots\mathcal{M}(T_m)$$
$$= E_{T_1} E_{T_2} \dots E_{T_m} = x_1^{T_1} \dots x_{l_1}^{T_1} x_1^{T_2} \dots x_{l_2}^{T_2} \dots x_1^{T_m} \dots x_{l_m}^{T_m}$$

By doing this, we have used the operator $\mathcal{M}$ to reconstruct the execution trace E from the task-schedule S, which shows that if we have an arbitrary task schedule, we can now reconstruct the sequential execution trace.

To complete the equivalence between both models, it is necessary to show the counterpart, where from a memory access trace, the task schedule is inferred. For this, it is necessary to know which task is executing each memory accesses. To do so, the task information is saved along with each memory access. This new definition allow us to prove the equivalence as shown in the Appendix.

4   Statistical Cache Modeling with Task Support

4.1   Existing Statistical Cache Models

In this section we present the main contribution of this paper: a formal model to predict cache behavior for different schedules from a single execution profile. This model is a solid source of insight and analysis for data-locality related bottlenecks that can leverage the performance of task-parallel applications. We will do so by first introducing the theory behind existing statistical cache models and its limitations for the task based applications, and then extend it to support task-based programs.

Figure 5a shows how existing statistical cache models represent the memory accesses (execution) of a serial application, displaying reuses between memory accesses as arcs. For instance, (x_1, x_{k+1}) is a reuse with reuse distance $\delta_{\mathcal{R}}(x_1, x_{k+1}) = k$.

To estimate an application's miss ratio for different cache configurations, cache models such as StatCache (more details in [4]) first looks at the *reuse distance distribution* by defining a reuse distance histogram with bins $H(i)$ mapped to the number of reuse pairs with distance i. Then a linear equation is solved for the bins in H and a probability function which estimates the cache misses for a fixed size cache with random replacement policy. The result is an estimation for the application's global miss ratio for a given cache size. The probability function is tied to the replacement policy of the cache, its size and associativity.

Implementations of these techniques are fast and have a low-overhead for data collection. Their performance is largely due to sparse data sampling and a very fast modeling step that allows the miss ratio to be calculated for any cache size quickly. Their input information is a (sampled) subset of the reuse pairs in $\mathcal{R}_P^E$. Since time (instruction order) is also kept for each access, the distances between accesses are straightforward to calculate, which makes it easy to build the histogram H.

However, existing models assume that the order of the memory accesses is the same for different sequential executions. In Fig. 4, it is shown that a change in task scheduling can affect an application's cache miss ratio. Figure 5b and c show the effect on the reused data from a change in schedule, because different task schedules lead to a different sequence of memory accesses.

The same memory access sequence from Fig. 5a is depicted in Fig. 5b, but for a task-based program. Each box represents a task (A, B, C). In this case, the distances between the pairs from A to B, (x_1^A, x_1^B), are increased by C's accesses, which may evict some of task A's thereby causing task B to miss in the cache if it is not large enough. This displacement is shown as $|\mathcal{M}(C)|$, which is the length of the sequence of accesses of task C.

Formally, each task-schedule S generates a particular memory access sequence E_S, and therefore a different set of consecutive reuses $\mathcal{R}^{E_S}$. These define a particular *schedule-dependent reuse distance operator* $\delta_{\mathcal{R}^{E_S}}$. Reuse distances, and consequently their distributions H, are now dependent on the schedule chosen.

Existing statistical cache models do not take this into account: two different schedules will be considered as two different applications giving misleading information about the application's data locality and preventing the analysis of schedules that have not been profiled.

4.2   The StatTask Model

Figure 1 compares traditional statistical cache modeling and the StatTask model. It shows how the StatTask model can use a single profiling run to re-order the reuse pairs, generating the memory access stream that would have been seen in the execution of another schedule. From these new reuse pairs, existing statistical cache models can be used without having to re-profile the actual execution.

To estimate the miss ratio under an arbitrary schedule S for a task-based program P, existing statistical cache models require a profiling execution such that $\mathcal{R}^{E_S}$ is captured. If we are interested in modeling a different schedule, S', the same process needs to be repeated increasing the overhead significantly. StatTask allows us to evaluate arbitrary schedules S' from a profile of schedule S by:

1. Profiling the execution of *any* particular task-schedule S, and saving the information about consecutive reuses.
2. Calculating the reuse distances for each reuse pair.
3. Rebuilding the set of reuses that would have appeared if another schedule S' would have been executed, based on the already profiled reuse pairs.
4. Calculating the reuses distances of the new reuse pairs for S', which can then be used with existing statistical cache models to estimate miss ratio of different schedules and cache sizes

4.3   Methodology of the StatTask Model

To show how the model works, we first analyze how different types of reuses change as we change the task schedule. As mentioned in Sect. 2 reuses can be *private* or *shared*. When the schedule changes, the distances of *private* reuses are offset *relatively* to the start of the task. This means that the reuse distance of private reuses is the same across all execution schedules, as the task schedule does not change the sequence of accesses *within* the task. An example of this is shown in Figs. 5b and c with $(x_1^C, x_{l_3}^C)$. On the other hand, *shared* reuse distances may change with the schedule, as happens in the same figures with (x_1^A, x_1^B).

In order to classify reuses as *private* or *shared*, we will use the *task* property (T) of the memory accesses. These identifiers enable the characterization of the reuse pairs (x_j, x_k). If a reuse is private, then both accesses x_j and x_k will be generated by the same task, thus making $T(x_j) = T(x_k)$. Otherwise it is a *shared reuse*. This classification is used to calculate the set of reuses of a new schedule without executing it.

Calculating the Reuse Pairs. This section shows how the reuse pairs are generated for a new schedule $S' = T_1 \dots T_{m_1}$. From the information we already have from profiling schedule S, we can make the following observations about what we expect under the schedule S':

1. The private reuses of each task in S will appear *unmodified* in S', since they are relatively offset and not affected.
2. Some shared reuses between different tasks T and T' that appear in schedule S, can also appear when executing S'.
3. Some shared reuses between different tasks T and T' may appear in S', but were not captured in the profile of S. These need to be created from the *global set of reuses* of the application.

Formally, StatTask defines a particular set Q, and it is proven that this set is actually the set of reuses that will be observed if the new schedule is executed (i.e. $Q = \mathcal{R}^{E_{S'}}$, proof in the Appendix).

The definition of Q is based on several smaller sets, as follows, where for each $T, T' \in \mathcal{T}_P$ we have:

$$Q_{T,T} = (T \to T)_S$$
$$Q_{T,T'} = \{(x_k, x_j) \in \mathcal{C}_S(T, T') \mid \forall T_q \in S' : T(x_k) < T_q < T(x_j) \Rightarrow a^j \notin a(T_q)\}$$
$$Q = \bigcup_{\forall T, T' \in S'} Q_{T,T'}.$$

$(T \to T)_S$ denotes the set of private reuse pairs of task T in schedule S and $\mathcal{C}$ denotes the transitive closure operator.

Calculating the Reuse Distances. Finally, we show how to predict the reuse distances of schedule S' from the distances profiled from schedule S. We expect the following from the distances of the reuses in S': In a *private reuse*, its distance is the same in any schedule. However, *shared reuses* can either carry over to the new schedule S' (kept from the profiled execution) or appear/disappear due to the new schedule via StatTask's analysis.

If the reuse pair is carried over, computing the reuse distance in the new schedule must account (add or subtract) for the number of independent memory access corresponding to each task in-between the new schedule. On the other hand, if the reuse pair is generated transitively by StatTask, its reuse distance is computed in terms of all the distances for the pairs used to obtain the reuse.

Formally, StatTask defines a function γ over the reuses for the new schedule S', and we prove that this function is in fact the reuse distance function that would be observed if S' is executed (i.e. $\gamma = \delta_{\mathcal{R}^{E_{S'}}}$, proof in the Appendix).

The function γ is given by

$$(x_j, x_k) \in (T \to T)_{S'} \Rightarrow \gamma(x_j, x_k) = \delta_{\mathcal{R}^{E_S}}(x_j, x_k).$$
$$(x_j, x_k) \in (T \to T')_{S'} \Rightarrow \gamma(x_j, x_k) = \delta_{\tilde{\mathcal{R}}^{E_S}}(x_j, x_k) - \nu_S(T, T') + \nu_{S'}(T, T').$$

The operator ν_S, when applied to two tasks, will give the number of accesses of the tasks exactly between T and T' in schedule S ($\delta_{\tilde{R}}$ over a pair (x_j, x_k) gives the distance within the set of global reuses).

StatTask opens the door to a new category of tools and predictive analyses, as metrics such as cache miss ratios for arbitrary cache sizes can be obtained for arbitrary task schedules, without additional profiling and execution.

5   Evaluation

To evaluate StatTask, we implemented it using the Pin [17] binary instrumentation tool to profile applications, and compared StatTask's ability to predict cache miss ratios for different schedules across the BOTS benchmark suite. Our tool generates a profile by sampling 1/1000 of the memory accesses (randomly selected, exponentially distributed) and collecting the corresponding address, reuse distance, task *id*, program counter, and instruction count. Our sampling approach follows the one described in [4], yielding a 20% sampling overhead. By using Pin for dynamic binary instrumentation we avoid the need to modify the applications' source code, being transparent to the programmer and runtime, and enabling the same methodology to be applied in other task-based frameworks such as StarPU, Intel's Cilk, Intel's TBB and OmpSs. Despite the data collection is done in a single threaded execution, StatTask allows to model multicore executions based on the per-task reuses. The resulting profile is consistent with both formalisms presented in Sects. 3.1 and 3.3.

After profiling, the StatTask model is run with the desired schedule and cache size as inputs. StatTask rebuilds the reuse pairs and their reuse distances according to the desired schedule, and uses this information to calculate the cache miss ratio for the given cache size with the StatStack [13] statistical model. Reference results are obtained by measuring the L3 miss ratio via hardware performance counters for a single-threaded execution of the specific schedule on a machine with the modeled cache size. To avoid calculating expensive transitive closures (Sect. 4.3), we implemented *reuse unfolding*, wherein the reuses are annotated with starting and ending accesses in a time-ordered table for rapid analysis.

Figure 6 shows StatTask's accuracy across the BOTS benchmarks for different schedules and input sizes. Each benchmark was sampled when run with multiple different schedules (S1, S2, S3) and we present results for StatTask's prediction for the same schedules compared to measured results for each schedule.

StatTask's modeled cache miss ratios (dark green bars) show an 8,7% average error (max 19%) with respect to the measured cache miss ratios (light green bars). The inaccuracies are a result of our 1-in-1000 memory access sampling rate, and can be reduced by increasing the sampling rate at a cost of increased overhead. These results demonstrate that StatTask is able to accurately predict the cache miss ratio for a variety of schedules.

To evaluate StatTask's ability to model arbitrary schedules from a single input, we gathered profile data for schedules S1 and S2 and used StatTask to predict for all possible combinations: S1→S1, S1→S2, S2→S1, S2→S2. Figure 7 shows StatTask's accuracy across these different schedule/modeling combinations, and demonstrates that StatTask can accurately predict the miss ratio for schedules other than the one used in sampling.

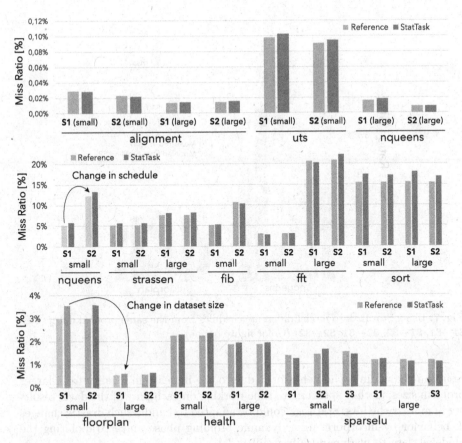

Fig. 6. Comparison of measured cache miss ratios (light) against StatTask's predictions (dark), for two arbitrary schedules (S1 and S) for each of the BOTS benchmarks. (Color figure online)

To evaluate StatTask's sensitivity to changes in input data, we compared several of the benchmarks (`sparselu`, `strassen`, `sort`, `floorplan`, `nqueens`) with varying inputs: three different small and large datasets (blue bars) across multiple schedules[1]. Figure 8 shows that several of the benchmarks see little change in behavior with varying input data, as the per-task execution and the overall distribution of tasks varies little with the input data. For these applications StatTask can accurately predict schedule behavior even in the presence of data set changes.

However, several applications show large changes in cache miss behavior as the *size* of their data sets change. Figure 6 highlights how the behavior of `floorplan` and `nqueens` changes as their data set sizes are increased by 4× and 3×, respectively, resulting in 40× and 120× increases in execution time. The

---

[1] The *sizes* of the inputs were all within 5%.

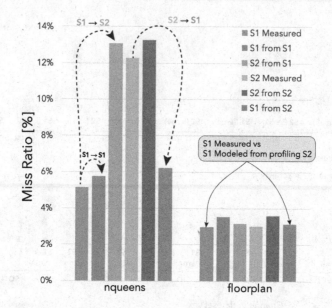

Fig. 7. Using StatTask to model different schedules from the same profiled data. (e.g., S1→S1, S1→S2, S2→S1, S2→S2) (Color figure online)

resulting change in cache behavior is due to the increase in locality from larger problem sizes, as they spend more time working on each part of the data, resulting in more cache hits. StatTask could be adapted to handle such drastic changes in behavior by incorporating a dynamic profiling phase and extrapolating the modeled data to fit dynamically profiled data.

Our implementation and evaluation of StatTask across the BOTS benchmarks demonstrates that this technique is both capable accurately predicting the cache behavior of task-based programs and flexible enough to predict the behavior of different schedules from the originally profiled one.

6   Related Work

There are three categories of related work: existing profiling tools that identify bottlenecks of task-based applications, task-scheduling optimization techniques, and finally techniques to analyze and understand data locality properties of applications.

Many tools exist to profile scheduling and load-balancing of tasks. Ding et al. [10] presented a generic and accessible tool for task monitoring, independent of any program or library and able to acquire rich information with very low overhead, targeting load balancing and scheduling problems unrelated to data reuse. Lorenz et al. developed [16], a library for identifying performance problems inherent to tasking with OpenMP through direct instrumentation. Schmidl et al. [19]

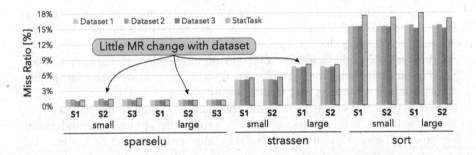

Fig. 8. Sensitivity to different input data sets of the same size.

surveyed different techniques to analyze data delivered by instrumentation of task-based programs in order to integrate parallel performance modeling to the automation of load-balancing. Ghosh et al. [14] have proposed OpenMP extensions to support dependence-based synchronization; Brinkmann et al. presented a graphical debugging tool for task parallel programming that works with most of the production frameworks. Weng and Chapman [21] looked at the task graph for OpenMP applications to optimize load balance.

In the second category, work has been done on improving scheduling strategies. The standard work-stealing approach was carefully analyzed by Blumofe and Leiserson in [7] and [2]. Strategies accounting for the tasks types were presented by Wimmer et al. Recently, important work on cache-aware task stealing was carried out in [9] by Chen et al. Qian Cao et al. [8] proposed a hybrid scheduling policy for heterogeneous multicores using breadth-first over the available task-pool.

None of these approaches for task-based profiling have incorporated a general method for understanding the data reuse implications of the tasks and schedules. In this category, characterization of data reuse has been done theoretically in [1] by Frigo. Practically, this can be done through instrumentation based techniques as presented by Aamer et al. in [15] and Weidendorfer in [20].

Statistical cache modeling, first introduced in [4], is another widely used way to characterize data locality. This work has been extended to other cache replacement policies by Eklov in [13], and to support thread-based or multicore shared caches in [6,12].

7   Conclusion and Future Work

This work addresses the interplay between task scheduling and shared data reuse through caches. We have presented StatTask, a new statistical model that can sample a single, serial run of a task-based application build reuse graphs, reuse sets, and distance metrics. From these, StatTask can accurately predict cache behavior for arbitrary schedules of the tasks and cache sizes on multicore parallel systems. We have implemented a tool, which requires no programmer annotation, code or runtime changes, analyzed a range of benchmarks and shown that there is a potential to share an average of 35% of the memory accesses between tasks (up to 80%), while demonstrated how this analysis can be used to better understand the sharing characteristics.

With StatTask we have a new ability to rapidly explore the impact of task scheduling on cache behavior, which opens up a range of possibilities for intelligent, reuse-aware schedulers and better performance.

We see several ways to move forward, the main one being to incorporate this technique within a task runtime system to profile the applications and tasks being executed, create profiles, and use this information during future runs to identify reuse patterns, predict miss ratios and modify task placement.

Regarding tools to analyze data reuse and provide insight to developers, several optimizations can be done to achieve better analysis modeling performance, as well as more intelligent sampling by, for instance, phase-guided sampling to avoid collecting redundant information for private reuses while getting more dense samples on shared ones.

A   Appendix: Proofs

Lemma. Let E and E' be execution traces such that they share the exact same set of accesses, but in different order. Then

$$(x_j, x_k) \in \tilde{\mathcal{R}}^E \Rightarrow (x_j, x_k) \in \tilde{\mathcal{R}}^{E'} \lor (x_k, x_j) \in \tilde{\mathcal{R}}^{E'}.$$

Proof. Let (x_j, x_k) be an element of $\tilde{\mathcal{R}}^E$. By definition, $a^j = a^k$. Since E and E' share the same set of accesses, there exist x_0 and x_1 in E' such that $x_j = x_0$ and $x_k = x_1$. Lets assume $x_0 < x_1$, since $a^j = a^k$ then $(x_0, x_1) \in \tilde{\mathcal{R}}^{E'}$. If $x_1 < x_0$ then $(x_0, x_1) \in \tilde{\mathcal{R}}^{E'}$

Lemma. $\mathcal{M}^{-1}$ and $\mathcal{M}$ are inverses.

Proof. Let T be a task, such that $E_T = x_1 \dots x_r$. We can see that

$$\mathcal{M}(\mathcal{M}^{-1}(x_1 \dots x_r)) = \mathcal{M}(T(x_1)) = \mathcal{M}(T) = E_T = x_1 \dots x_r$$

Conversely,

$$\mathcal{M}^{-1}(\mathcal{M}(T)) = \mathcal{M}^{-1}(E_T) = \mathcal{M}^{-1}(x_1 \dots x_r) = T(x_1) = T$$

Theorem. $Q = \mathcal{R}^{E_{S'}}$

Proof. It is straightforward to prove that $Q \subseteq \mathcal{R}^{E_{S'}}$. It is enough to observe that $\mathcal{C}_S(T, T')$ gives al the pairs in $\tilde{\mathcal{R}}^{E_S}$ that start in T and end in T'. Since this set is execution independent, those pairs are also in $\tilde{\mathcal{R}}^{E_S}$. The condition $\forall T_q \in S'$ such that $T(x_k) < T_q < T(x_j) \Rightarrow a^j \notin a(T_q)$ filters out the non-consecutive reuses. Therefore, all the elements of Q are consecutive reuses.

We will now show an outline for the proof that $R^{E_{S'}} \subseteq Q$. If $(x_j, x_{j+d}) \in (T_0 \rightarrow T_0)_{S'}$, then $T(x_j) = T(x_{j+d}) = T_0$. As S and S' use the same task universe, $\exists T_r \in S$ such that $T_0^S = T_r^{S'}$. By Lemma 1, $E_{T_0} = E_{T_r}$. Therefore, $\exists x_p \in E_{T_r}$ such that $x_p = x_j$ and $x_{p+d} = x_{j+d}$, as private reuses are relatively offset. Then $(x_j, x_{j+d}) \in (T_r \rightarrow T_r)_S \in Q_{T_r, T_r} \subseteq Q$.

Let's now consider the case $(x_j, x_{j+d}) \in (T_n \rightarrow T_m)_{S'}$. The tasks T_n and T_m also occur in S. We will assume that $T_n < T_m$. Let $T_1, \ldots, T_k$ such that $T_n < T_1 < \cdots < T_k < T_m$. The proof is by induction on k.

When $k = 0$, then the sequence $T_n T_m$ occur in S. Therefore, it exists x_r in E_S such that $[x_j, x_j + d] = [x_r, x_r + d]$. Since $x_r = x_j$ and $(x_j, x_{j+d}) \in \mathcal{R}^{E_{S'}}$, we know that $\forall x_r < x_s < x_{r+d}, a^r \neq a^s$. Therefore $(x_j, x_{j+d}) = (x_r, x_{r+d}) \in (T_n \rightarrow T_m)^0 \subseteq Q_{T_n, T_m} \subseteq Q$.

When $k = 1$, then $T_n T_{n+1} T_m \in S$. Lets assume that $a(T_{n+1}) \neq a(T_n)$, thus, $\forall x_s$ such that $x_j < x_s < x_j + d \Rightarrow a^s \neq a^j$. Therefore $(x_j, x_{j+d}) \in (T_n \rightarrow T_m) \subseteq Q_{T_n, T_m}$.

If that does not happen, it is enough to assume that there are unique $x_1, \ldots, x_q$ such that $x_j < x_1 < \cdots < x_q < x_{j+d}$ and that $a^j = a^1 = \cdots = a^q = a^{j+d}$, with all the accesses in between with different addresses. This means that the pairs $(x_j, x_1), (x_1, x_2), \ldots, (x_q, x_{j+d})$ are elements of $\mathcal{R}^{E_S}$. Therefore, by definition of $\mathcal{C}$, this means that $(x_j, x_{j+d}) \in \mathcal{C}(T_n, T_m) \subseteq Q_{T_n, T_m} \subseteq Q$.

The final case is $k \Rightarrow k+1$. Let $T_n T_1 \ldots T_{k+1} T_m \in S$. Two cases are necessary to prove. The first one, where the set of addresses are of tasks $T_1, \ldots, T_k$ are disjoint from T_n, T_m. If that happens, then the only thing left to check is the set of addresses of T_k, which is analogous to the case $k = 1$ for T_{k+1}. Otherwise, a unique number of accesses with the same address appear in $T_1, \ldots, T_k$, which by inductive hypothesis can be used transitively to obtain a pair in Q.

The proof for when $T_m < T_n$ is analogous.

Theorem. $\gamma = \delta_{\mathcal{R}^{E_{S'}}}$

Proof. Let $(x_j, x_k) \in \mathcal{R}^{E_{S'}}$, and let $T_{x_j} = T(x_j)$ and $T_{x_k} = T(x_k)$. Let $T_{n_1}, \ldots, T_{n_r}$ be such that $T_{x_j} T_{n_1} \ldots T_{n_r} T_{x_k} \in S'$. These are the tasks scheduled between the starting and ending tasks causing the reuse in S'. Lets also assume $T_{m_1}, \ldots, T_{m_s}$ such that $T_{x_j} T_{m_1} \ldots T_{m_s} T_{x_k} \in S$, thus representing the tasks between the starting and ending tasks of the reuse in S. It is easy to see the following memory access sequence when S' is executed:

$$x_j \ldots x_l^{T_{x_j}} x_1^{T_{n_1}} \ldots x_l^{T_{n_1}} \ldots x_1^{T_{n_r}} \ldots x_l^{T_{n_r}} x_1^{T_{x_k}} \ldots x_k = x_j \ldots x_l^{T_{x_j}} E_{T_{n_1}} \ldots E_{T_{n_r}} x_1^{T_{x_k}} \ldots x_k.$$

Therefore, the since the *access distance* is linear, we can see that

$$\delta_{\mathcal{R}^{E_{S'}}}(x_j, x_k) = \delta_{\tilde{\mathcal{R}}^{E_{S'}}}(x_j, x_l^{T_{x_j}}) + |E_{T_{n_1}}| + \cdots + |E_{T_{n_r}}| + \delta_{\tilde{\mathcal{R}}^{E_{S'}}}(x_1^{T_{x_k}}, x_k)$$

$$= \delta_{\tilde{\mathcal{R}}^{E_{S'}}}(x_j, x_l^{T_{x_j}}) + |\mathcal{M}(T_{n_1})| + \cdots + |\mathcal{M}(T_{n_r})| + \delta_{\tilde{\mathcal{R}}^{E_{S'}}}(x_1^{T_{x_k}}, x_k)$$

$$= \delta_{\tilde{\mathcal{R}}^{E_{S'}}}(x_j, x_l^{T_{x_j}}) + \nu_{S'}(T_{x_j}, T x_k) + \delta_{\tilde{\mathcal{R}}^{E_{S'}}}(x_1^{T_{x_k}}, x_k)$$

On the other hand, we can also see the following sequence when S is executed:

$$x_j \ldots x_l^{T_{x_j}} x_1^{T_{m_1}} \ldots x_l^{T_{m_1}} \ldots x_1^{T_{m_s}} \ldots x_l^{T_{m_s}} x_1^{T_{x_k}} \ldots x_k,$$

analogously, see that $\delta_{\mathcal{R}^{E_S}}(x_j, x_k) = \delta_{\tilde{\mathcal{R}}^{E_S}}(x_j, x_l^{T_{x_j}}) + \nu_S(T_{x_j}, T_{x_k}) + \delta_{\tilde{\mathcal{R}}^{E_S}}(x_1^{T_{x_k}}, x_k)$, and therefore, $\delta_{\mathcal{R}^{E_S}}(x_j, x_l^{T_{x_j}}) + \delta_{\tilde{\mathcal{R}}^{E_S}}(x_1^{T_{x_k}}, x_k) = \delta_{\tilde{\mathcal{R}}^{E_S}}(x_j, x_k) - \nu_S(T_{x_j}, T_{x_k})$. Since the sequence $x_j \ldots x_l^{T_{x_j}}$ is identical both in E_S and $E_{S'}$ then $\delta_{\tilde{\mathcal{R}}^{E_S}}(x_j, x_l^{T_{x_j}}) = \delta_{\tilde{\mathcal{R}}^{E_{S'}}}(x_j, x_l^{T_{x_j}})$. The same holds for $x_1^{T_{x_k}} \ldots x_k$. Then,

$$\begin{aligned}
\delta_{\mathcal{R}^{E_{S'}}}(x_j, x_k) &= \delta_{\tilde{\mathcal{R}}^{E_{S'}}}(x_j, x_l^{T_{x_j}}) + \nu_{S'}(T_{x_j}, Tx_k) + \delta_{\tilde{\mathcal{R}}^{E_{S'}}}(x_1^{T_{x_k}}, x_k) \\
&= \delta_{\tilde{\mathcal{R}}^{E_{S'}}}(x_j, x_l^{T_{x_j}}) + \delta_{\tilde{\mathcal{R}}^{E_{S'}}}(x_1^{T_{x_k}}, x_k) + \nu_{S'}(T_{x_j}, Tx_k) \\
&= \delta_{\tilde{\mathcal{R}}^{E_S}}(x_j, x_k) - \nu_S(T_{x_j}, T_{x_k}) + \nu_{S'}(T_{x_j}, T_{x_k}) \\
&= \gamma(x_j, x_k)
\end{aligned}$$

References

1. The cache complexity of multithreaded cache oblivious algorithms. Theory of Computing Systems **45**(2) (2009)
2. Acar, U., Blelloch, G., Blumofe, R.: The data locality of work stealing. Theory Comput. Syst. **35**(3), 321–347 (2002)
3. Augonnet, C., Thibault, S., Namyst, R., Wacrenier, P.: StarPU: a unified platform for task scheduling on heterogeneous multicore architectures. Concurr. Comput. Pract. Exper. **23**(2), 187–198 (2011)
4. Berg, E., Hagersten, E.: Statcache: a probabilistic approach to efficient and accurate data locality analysis. In: Proceedings of the 2004 IEEE International Symposium on Performance Analysis of Systems and Software (2004)
5. Berg, E., Hagersten, E.: Fast data-locality profiling of native execution. SIGMETRICS Perform. Eval. Rev. **33**(1), 169–180 (2005)
6. Berg, E., Zeffer, H., Hagersten, E.: A statistical multiprocessor cache model. In: IEEE International Symposium on Performance Analysis of Systems and Software, pp. 89–99, March 2006
7. Blumofe, R.D., Leiserson, C.E.: Scheduling multithreaded computations by work stealing. J. ACM **46**(5), 720–748 (1999)
8. Cao, Q., Zuo, M.: A scheduling strategy supporting OpenMP task on heterogeneous multicore. In: 26th IEEE International Parallel and Distributed Processing Symposium Workshops & PhD Forum, IPDPS 2012, Shanghai, China, 21–25 May 2012, pp. 2077–2084 (2012)
9. Chen, Q., Guo, M., Huang, Z.: Cats: cache aware task-stealing based on online profiling in multi-socket multi-core architectures. In: Proceedings of the 26th ACM International Conference on Supercomputing, ICS 2012, pp. 163–172 (2012)
10. Ding, Y., Hu, K., Zhao, Z.: Performance monitoring and analysis of task-based OpenMP (2013)
11. Duran, A., Teruel, X., Ferrer, R., Martorell, X., Ayguade, E.: Barcelona OpenMP tasks suite: a set of benchmarks targeting the exploitation of task parallelism in OpenMP. In: International Conference on Parallel Processing, ICPP 2009, pp. 124–131, September 2009

12. Eklov, D., Black-Schaffer, D., Hagersten, E.: StatCC: a statistical cache contention model. In: Proceedings of the 19th International Conference on Parallel Architectures and Compilation Techniques, PACT 2010, pp. 551–552 (2010)

13. Eklöv, D., Hagersten, E.: StatStack: efficient modeling of LRU caches. In: Proceeding International Symposium on Performance Analysis of Systems and Software: ISPASS 2010, pp. 55–65. IEEE (2010)

14. Ghosh, P., Yan, Y., Eachempati, D., Chapman, B.: A prototype implementation of OpenMP task dependency support. In: Rendell, A.P., Chapman, B.M., Müller, M.S. (eds.) IWOMP 2013. LNCS, vol. 8122, pp. 128–140. Springer, Heidelberg (2013). doi:10.1007/978-3-642-40698-0_10

15. Jaleel, A., Cohn, R.S., keung Luk, C., Jacob, B.: Cmp$im: a pin-based on-the-fly multi-core cache simulator. In: The Fourth Annual Workshop on Modeling, Benchmarking and Simulation (MoBS), Co-located with ISCA 2008 (2008)

16. Lorenz, D., Philippen, P., Schmidl, D., Wolf, F.: Profiling of OpenMP tasks with Score-P. In: 41st International Conference on Parallel Processing Workshops, ICPPW 2012, Pittsburgh, PA, USA, 10–13 September 2012, pp. 444–453 (2012)

17. Luk, C.-K., Cohn, R., Muth, R., Patil, H., Klauser, A., Lowney, G., Wallace, S., Reddi, V.J., Hazelwood, K.: Pin: building customized program analysis tools with dynamic instrumentation. In: Proceedings of the 2005 ACM SIGPLAN Conference on Programming Language Design and Implementation, PLDI 2005, pp. 190–200 (2005)

18. OpenMP Architecture Review Board. OpenMP application program interface version 3.0 (2008)

19. Schmidl, D., Philippen, P., Lorenz, D., Rössel, C., Geimer, M., Mey, D., Mohr, B., Wolf, F.: Performance analysis techniques for task-based OpenMP applications. In: Chapman, B.M., Massaioli, F., Müller, M.S., Rorro, M. (eds.) IWOMP 2012. LNCS, vol. 7312, pp. 196–209. Springer, Heidelberg (2012). doi:10.1007/978-3-642-30961-8_15

20. Weidendorfer, J., Kowarschik, M., Trinitis, C.: A tool suite for simulation based analysis of memory access behavior. In: Bubak, M., Albada, G.D., Sloot, P.M.A., Dongarra, J. (eds.) ICCS 2004. LNCS, vol. 3038, pp. 440–447. Springer, Heidelberg (2004). doi:10.1007/978-3-540-24688-6_58

21. Weng, T., Chapman, B.: Towards optimisation of openmp codes for synchronisation and data reuse. Int. J. High Perform. Comput. Netw. 1(1–3), 43–54 (2004)

Improving the Energy Efficiency of Evolutionary Multi-objective Algorithms

J.J. Moreno[1], G. Ortega[1(✉)], E. Filatovas[2], J.A. Martínez[1], and E.M. Garzón[1]

[1] Informatics Department, University of Almería, Agrifood Campus of Int. Excell., ceiA3, 04120 Almería, Spain
jrm069@inlumine.ual.es, {gloriaortega,jmartine,gmartin}@ual.es
[2] Institute of Mathematics and Informatics, Vilnius University, Vilnius, Lithuania
Ernest.Filatov@gmail.com

Abstract. Problems for which many objective functions have to be simultaneously optimized can be easily found in many fields of science and industry. Solving this kind of problems in a reasonable amount of time while taking into account the energy efficiency is still a relevant task. Most of the evolutionary multi-objective optimization algorithms based on parallel computing are focused only on performance. In this paper, we propose a parallel implementation of the most time consuming parts of the Evolutionary Multi-Objective algorithms with major attention to energy consumption. Specifically, we focus on the most computationally expensive part of the state-of-the-art evolutionary NSGA-II algorithm – the Non-Dominated Sorting (NDS) procedure. GPU platforms have been considered due to their high acceleration capacity and energy efficiency. A new version of NDS procedure is proposed (referred to as EFNDS). A made-to-measure data structure to store the dominance information has been designed to take advantage of the GPU architecture. NSGA-II based on EFNDS is comparatively evaluated with another state-of-art GPU version, and also with a widely used sequential version. In the evaluation we adopt a benchmark that is scalable in the number of objectives as well as decision variables (the DTLZ test suite) using a large number of individuals (from 500 up to 30000). The results clearly indicate that our proposal achieves the best performance and energy efficiency for solving large scale multi-objective optimization problems on GPU.

1 Introduction

Many real-world problems attempt to satisfy multiple conflicting objectives at once. It is obviously impossible to find a single optimal solution which would

This work has been partially supported by the Spanish Ministry of Science throughout projects TIN2015-66680 and CAPAP-H5 network TIN2014-53522, by J. Andalucía through projects P12-TIC-301 and P11-TIC7176, and by the European Regional Development Fund (ERDF). Ernestas Filatovas has been partially granted by the European COST Action IC1305: Network for sustainable Ultrascale computing (NESUS).

© Springer International Publishing AG 2016
J. Carretero et al. (Eds.): ICA3PP 2016 Workshops, LNCS 10049, pp. 62–75, 2016.
DOI: 10.1007/978-3-319-49956-7_5

be the best by all objectives. The main goal of Multi-Objective Optimization (MOO) is to provide the set of compromising solutions called Pareto set. However, for some problems it is impossible to identify the exact Pareto front due to reasons such as continuity of the front, non-existence of analytical expression or complexity of the problem being solved. On the other hand, in many real-world applications there is no need to find the whole Pareto front, but rather an approximation.

The most popular approach to solve MOO problems is Evolutionary Multi-Objective Optimization (EMO). Some well-known EMO algorithms to approximate the Pareto front are: NSGA-II [4], PAES [18], MOAE/D [30], IBEA [32], SPEA2 [33], etc. Several phases can be identified in most of them: evaluation of an objective function; Pareto dominance ranking, or Non Dominated Sorting (NDS) and genetic operations. Examples of EMO approaches based on Pareto dominance ranking are: PESA-II [2], NSGA-II [4], R-NSGA-II [5], Synchronous R-NSGA-II [11], etc. Usually, the computational requirements of the EMO algorithms are very relevant. Therefore, their High Performance implementations are of great interest.

Nowadays, processors usually include accelerators such as Graphics Processing Units (GPUs), that provide a considerable computational power to the desktop, laptop and mobile platforms [14]. They are referred to as heterogeneous platforms. GPUs are widely used in the High Performance Computing (HPC) field due to their performance/cost ratio. In the last few years, the use of GPUs in general purpose applications has greatly increased thanks to the availability of application programming interfaces, such as Compute Unified Device Architecture (CUDA)[1] and OpenCL [24]. GPUs have hundreds of cores that can collectively run thousands of computing GPU-threads. Previous works have shown the high energy efficiency of the GPU platforms for software when they are appropriately exploited [15].

In this work, NSGA-II is taken as an example of EMO algorithm to be adapted and evaluated on modern heterogeneous platforms. Some parallel versions of NSGA-II have been developed: in [7–9] parallel versions of NSGA-II algorithm based on master-slave paradigm are presented, where population is distributed among the workers in order to speed-up the process of functions evaluation; in [19] several parallel strategies where the Pareto ranking is parallelized in NSGA-II are proposed, and are experimentally investigated when solving the competitive facility location problem in [20].

Usually, the cost of the evaluation of the objective function in EMO approaches is not very high in the sense of computation time. Hence, most of the computation time is spent on the NDS phase. The procedure referred to as 'Fast Non-Dominated Sorting' was proposed by Deb *et al.* in [4] to compute it. In such proposal, the dominance information of every individual consists of: the number of dominator individuals, the number and the list of dominated individuals. Then, the Pareto dominance ranking is computed from this dominance information. If N is the number of individuals of the population and M the

---

[1] https://developer.nvidia.com/cuda-toolkit.

number of objectives, then, the complexity order of this process is $O(MN^2)$ and it requires a storage of $O(N^2)$. Previous proposals of NDS have a high complexity $O(MN^3)$, and a high number of redundant comparisons between pairs of individuals, but as a counterpart their storage requirements grow up as $O(N)$. The reduction of the complexity order of the NDS has been a focus of interest for researchers [10,17,21,28,31]. Some improvements were implemented by developing more efficient sorting strategies, however, computational burden of the NDS procedure has a complexity $O(MN^2)$ in the worst case for all the approaches. Summarizing, two kinds of approaches to compute NDS can be distinguished: FNDS with a previous dominance computation which has few redundant comparisons and an intensive memory use; and NDS with redundant comparisons to evaluate the dominance without additional memory requirements.

Due to the fact that NDS consumes most of the NSGA-II runtime, the acceleration of this procedure is mandatory to speed up NSGA-II, as it is justified in [12,23,27,29]. Thus, parallel strategies should be considered to accelerate the computation of the procedure. Recently, a novel NSGA-II parallel implementation on a GPU, which is focused on the FNDS procedure, has been proposed in [12]. The NDS version of complexity $O(MN^3)$ is accelerated on GPU with every thread computing the dominance of every individual without writing in auxiliary structures. Therefore, it is a parallel NDS version on GPU with more redundant dominance comparisons (hereinafter this version is referred to as Gupta-NDS). Moreover, an efficient parallel version of the FNDS procedure has been formally presented in [29], but its experimental analysis is very limited. Both works are very related to our proposal, since it is based on the acceleration of the NDS procedure on GPU platforms. However, none of them consider and evaluate the energy efficiency of their proposal.

Most of current approaches of parallel EMO algorithms do not consider energy consumption and savings, and they are related to development of more effective algorithms considering the execution time as main criterion. However, nowadays the energy costs represent a relevant share of the total costs of High Performance Computing (HPC) systems. As consequence, the energy efficiency is a target for the HPC implementations of EMO algorithms.

In this paper we propose a GPU implementation of NDS which defines a new data structure to store the dominance information to efficiently compute the sets of non dominated individuals (fronts) on the GPU. This proposal is referred to as Efficient Fast Non-Dominated Sorting (EFNDS). It is integrated in NSGA-II and comparatively evaluated with the recent Gupta's proposal to compute NDS on GPU [12] from the perspectives of both performance and power/energy efficiency. They are assessed on a NVIDIA K80, as prototype of a modern GPU architecture. Results have shown that EFNDS achieves the best performance and consumes less energy, thus having better energy efficiency than the other proposal.

In summary, the major contribution of our paper is the proposal of an energy efficient NDS procedure on GPU, a representative procedure included in the

EMO algorithms. Therefore, it is of great interest for developing energy efficiency aware applications based on Multi-Objective Optimization.

The rest of this paper is organized as follows. In Sect. 2, the definition of the multi-objective problem is provided. In Sect. 3, the Efficient Fast Non-Dominated Sorting Procedure (EFNDS) as well as its parallel implementations on GPU are described. A comparative evaluation of NSGA-II based on EFNDS and NDS on GPU is carried out in Sect. 4. It is analysed in terms of performance, power and energy. Finally, Sect. 5 shows the conclusions of this work.

2 Description of the Problem

A multi-objective minimization problem is formulated as follows [22]:

$$\min_{\mathbf{x} \in S} \mathbf{f}(\mathbf{x}) = [f_1(\mathbf{x}), f_2(\mathbf{x}), \dots, f_M(\mathbf{x})]^T \qquad (1)$$

where $\mathbf{z} = \mathbf{f}(\mathbf{x})$ is an *objective vector*, defining the values for all objective functions $f_1(\mathbf{x})$, $f_2(\mathbf{x})$, ..., $f_M(\mathbf{x})$, $f_i \colon \mathbb{R}^V \to \mathbb{R}$, $i \in \{1, 2, \dots, M\}$, where $M \geq 2$ is the number of objective functions; and $\mathbf{x} = (x_1, x_2, \dots, x_V)$ is a vector of variables (*decision vector*) and V is the number of variables $\mathbf{S} \subset \mathbb{R}^V$ is *search space*, which defines all feasible decision vectors.

A decision vector $\mathbf{x}' \in \mathbf{S}$ is a *Pareto optimal solution* if $f_i(\mathbf{x}') \leqslant f_i(\mathbf{x})$ for all $\mathbf{x} \in \mathbf{S}$ and $f_j(\mathbf{x}') < f_j(\mathbf{x})$ for at most one j. Objective vectors are defined as optimal if none of their elements can be improved without worsen at least one of the other elements. An objective vector $\mathbf{f}(\mathbf{x}')$ is Pareto optimal if the corresponding decision vector $\mathbf{x}'$ is Pareto optimal. The set of all the Pareto optimal decision vectors is called the *Pareto set*. The region defined by all the objective function values for the Pareto set points is called the *Pareto front*.

For two objective vectors $\mathbf{z}$ and $\mathbf{z}'$, $\mathbf{z}'$ *dominates* $\mathbf{z}$ (or $z' \succ z$) if $z_i' \leqslant z_i$ for all $i = 1, \dots, M$ and there exists at most one j such that $z_j' < z_j$. In EMO algorithms, the subset of solutions in a population whose objective vectors are not dominated by any other objective vector is called the *non-dominated set*, and the objective vectors are called the *non-dominated objective vectors*. The main aim of the EMO algorithms is to generate well-distributed non-dominated objective vectors as close as possible to the Pareto front.

NSGA-II [4] is the most widely-used and well-known EMO algorithm for approximating the Pareto front that is based on NDS. Thus, it is selected to analyse the energy efficiency of EMO algorithms when different number of CPU cores and/or GPU cards are exploited. The steps of NSGA-II are described in Algorithm 1.

The Step 2 of the Algorithm 1 is devoted to computing the FNDS procedure which is the most computationally expensive in the NSGA-II.

3 Efficient Fast Non-Dominated Sort on GPU

CUDA (Compute Unified Device Architecture) is the parallel interface introduced by NVIDIA to help develop parallel codes using C or C++ language.

Algorithm 1. NSGA-II

Step 1: Generate a random initial population P_0 of size N.

Step 2: Sort the population to different non-domination levels (fronts) and assign each individual a fitness equal to its non-domination level (1 is the best level).

Step 3: Create an offspring population of size N using binary tournament selection, recombination and mutation operations (parents with larger crowding distance are preferred if their non-domination levels are the same).

Step 4: Combine the parent and the offspring populations and create a population of $2N$ individuals.

Step 5: Reduce the size of population to N: sort the initial population into different non-dominated fronts; select individuals from the best non-dominated fronts until the size of P is equal to N; if all the individuals in a front cannot be picked fully, calculate a crowding distance and add individuals with the largest distances into the population.

Step 6: Check if the termination criterion is satisfied. If yes, go to Step 7, else return to Step 2.

Step 7: Stop.

CUDA provides some abstraction to the GPU hardware, and it provides the SIMT (Single Instruction, Multiple Threads) programming model to exploit the GPU [26]. However, the programmer has to take into account several features of the architecture, such as the topology of the multiprocessors and the management of the memory hierarchy. For the execution of the program, the CPU (called host in CUDA) performs a succession of parallel routines (kernels) invocations to the device. The input/output data to/from the GPU kernels are communicated between the CPU and the 'global' GPU memories. GPUs have hundreds of cores which can collectively run thousands of computing threads. Each core, called Scalar Processor (SP), belongs to a set of multiprocessors units called Streaming Multiprocessors (SM). The SMs are composed by 192 (or 128) SPs on Kepler (or Maxwell) GPU architectures [13,25,26]. This way, the GPU device consists of a set of SMs and each kernel is executed as a batch of threads organized as a grid of thread blocks [1].

In this work, a new approach to compute and store the dominance information is proposed. The corresponding FNDS procedure is described in Algorithm 2 and referred to as Efficient FNDS (EFNDS). It selects N individuals as 'Elite population' from the initial population P_0 with $2N$ individuals (step 5 of Algorithm 1). Algorithm 2 includes two phases. The Phase 1 computes the dominance matrix, D, of dimensions $2N \times 2N$, for the initial population and the Phase 2 selects the individuals of the first fronts until half of them are selected in the 'elite' set. The structure of the Phase 2 is well known. However, it is based on a new way to store the dominance information. Our proposal is based on the previous computation of a dominance matrix D whose elements, $D_{i,j}$, store if the individual P_i is dominated by P_j. That is, $D_{i,j} = 1$ if P_j dominates P_i and $D_{i,j} = 0$ in other case.

This way, the idea for checking if P_i is dominated by the population P (line 14 of Algorithm 2) is based on the computation of the number of individuals of

Algorithm 2. Outline of the Efficient Fast Non-Dominated Sorting procedure (EFNDS) to compute Step 5 of Algorithm 1

Require: P_0: population M: number of objective functions
    Phase 1: Compute the information of dominance
1: $2N \leftarrow |P_0|$
2: **for** $i \leftarrow 1$ **to** $2N$ **do**
3:     **for** $j \leftarrow 1$ **to** $2N$ **do**
4:         **for** $l \leftarrow 1$ **to** M **do**
5:             Check dominance between individuals P_i and P_j for the objective l
6:         $D_{i,j} = 0$
7:         **if** P_j dominates P_i **then**
8:             $D_{i,j} = 1$
    Phase 2 Compute fronts from the dominance information of Phase 1
9: $P = P_0;$ $Elite \leftarrow \emptyset;$ $rank = 0$
10: **while** $|Elite| < N$ **do**
11:     $rank = rank + 1$
12:     $F_{Rank} \leftarrow \emptyset$
13:     **for** each $P_i \in P$ **do** (Check if P_i dominates P from the matrix D)
14:         $d = \sum_{P_j \in P} D_{ij}$
15:         **if** $d = 0$ (i.e. P_i is a dominator of P) **then**
16:             $P \leftarrow P \backslash \{P_i\}$
17:             $F_{Rank} \leftarrow F_{Rank} \cup \{P_i\}$
18:     **if** $|Elite| + |F_{Rank}| > N$ **then**
19:         $F_{Rank} \leftarrow N - |Elite|$ individuals of F_{Rank} with higher crowding distance
20:     $Elite \leftarrow Elite \cup F_{Rank}$
21: **return** $Elite$

P which dominate P_i as $d_i = |\{D_{i,j} = 1; \quad \forall P_j \in P\}|$, so if $d_i = 0$ then P_i is not dominated by P and it belongs to the new front. Therefore, the computation of d_i can be carried out reading the corresponding values $D_{i,j}$ on the i-th row of D. This new approach to identify the individuals into every new front is very appropriate to efficiently exploit the GPU architecture.

It is relevant to underline that the computation of dominance consumes most of the runtime of FNDS procedures when it is executed in sequential [12,29]. Our approach to compute D with a high level of parallelism, can efficiently compute the dominance information on the GPU architecture. Moreover, the fronts computation can also be accelerated on GPU by the use of the fast shuffled reductions of CUDA. This way, our parallel EFNDS version efficiently computes D and the corresponding fronts on GPU.

Algorithm 3 shows the host pseudocode to compute EFNDS on GPU. It is based on two kernels: *CuDominance* (line 3) which computes the matrix D and *CuFronts* (line 8) which computes one front from the dominance information stored in D. *CuDominance* is executed once and *CuFronts* is iteratively computed until a *Elite* population of N individuals is classified. In order to fit the classified population to N individuals a subset of last front is selected according to the crowding distance on CPU.

Algorithm 3. Host pseudocode to compute EFNDS on GPU based on the kernels $CuDominance$ and $CuFronts$

Require: P_0: population M: number of objective functions

    Phase 1: Compute the information of dominance

1: $2N \leftarrow |P_0|$
2: Communicate input population P_0 from CPU memory to the GPU device memory
3: $D = CuDominance()$ (**Algorithm 4 is computed on GPU**)

    Phase 2 Compute fronts from the dominance information of Phase 1

4: $P = P_0$; $Elite \leftarrow \emptyset$; $rank = 0$
5: **while** $|Elite| < N$ **do**
6:     $rank = rank + 1$
7:     $F_{Rank} \leftarrow \emptyset$
8:     $F_{Rank} = CuFronts()$ (**Algorithm 5 is computed on GPU**)
9:     Communicate new F_{Rank} from GPU device memory to the host memory
10:     **if** $|Elite| + |F_{Rank}| > N$ **then**
11:         Arrange F_{Rank} in increasing order according to crowding distance
12:         $F_{Rank} \leftarrow$ Selection of $N - |Elite|$ individuals of the ordered F_{Rank}
13:     $Elite \leftarrow Elite \cup F_{Rank}$
14: **return** $Elite$

Algorithm 4. $CuDominance$ kernel to compute the dominance matrix of EFNDS on GPU

Require: P_0: population M: number of objective functions

    CuDominance Kernel

1: $2N \leftarrow |P_0|$
2: **if** $idx < 2N \times 2N$ **then**
3:     $i = \lfloor idx/2N \rfloor$; $j = idx\%2N$
4:     **for** $l \leftarrow 1$ **to** M **do**
5:         Check dominance between individuals P_i and P_j for the objective l
6:         $D_{i,j} = 0$
7:         **if** P_j dominates P_i **then**
8:             $D_{i,j} = 1$

Algorithm 4 shows the procedure to compute the dominance matrix on GPU, $CuDominance$. The input is the population of $2N$ individuals. This way, $4N^2$ threads are activated to check concurrently the dominance between all pairs of individuals and update the elements of D without any synchronization among them.

When $CuDominance$ finishes, the matrix D is on memory and the fronts can be computed by successive executions of $CuFronts$. Algorithm 5 describes the procedure to compute one front on GPU. One thread block is activated for every individual. Therefore, the threads of every block compute the reduction of a particular row of D and a fast reduction scheme based on shuffled functions is applied [2]. The shuffled functions enable a thread to directly reads a register from

---

[2] https://devblogs.nvidia.com/parallelforall/faster-parallel-reductions-kepler/.

Algorithm 5. *CuFronts* kernel to compute the set of fronts of EFNDS on GPU

1: $idB = blockIdx.x$; Cuda block identification
2: $idx = threadIdx.x$; Cuda thread identification
3: $BlockSize = blockDim.x$; number of threads in every Cuda block
4: **if** $idx < 2N \times BlockSize$ AND $P_{idB} \in P$ **then**
        Check if P_{idB} dominates the population P from the matrix D
5:      **for** $i = 0$; $i < 2N$; $i = i + BlockSize$ **do**
6:          **if** $P_i \in P$ **then**
7:              $d = d + D_{idB,i}$
8:          $d_{idB} = BlockReduceSum(d)$ (Fast Shuffled Reduction into Threads Blocks)
9: **if** $d_{idB} = 0$ (i.e. P_{idB} is a dominator of P) **then**
10:     **if** $idx == idB \times BlockSize$ (First Thread in every Cuda Block) **then**
11:         $P \leftarrow P \backslash \{P_i\}$
12:         $F_{Rank} \leftarrow F_{Rank} \cup \{P_i\}$
13: **return** F_{Rank}

another thread in the same warp, therefore, threads can compute fast reductions avoiding memory accesses.

It is noteworthy that the output of *CuFronts* is written in a vector F of dimension $2N$, where every element F_i stores the front number for the individual i. So, when *CuFronts* is executed, a new selection of individuals is classified in the new front. Additionally, F defines the set of individuals in the population P since if $F_i = 0$ then the individual i has not classified and it is a potential individual of posterior fronts, i.e. $i \in P$. Posterior fronts classifications will be computed only for the individuals with $F_i = 0$. Therefore, F also defines the population P to compute a new front. Figure 1 illustrates the computation of

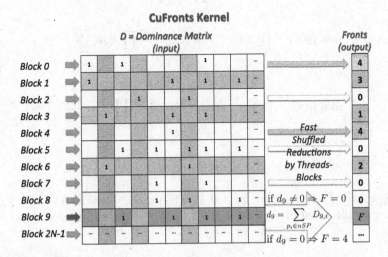

Fig. 1. Computation of the fourth front from D matrix when *CuFronts* kernel is executed on GPU

the fourth front on the GPU. It shows the data structures and their threads mapping involved in the computation of a front.

4   Experimental Evaluation

In this section, we evaluate two GPU versions of NSGA-II based on: (1) the EFNDS algorithm above described and (2) the version of NDS proposed by Gupta in [12]. Additionally, the sequential NSGA-II version 1.1.6 of K. Deb [3] is also evaluated.

We have executed these algorithms on a Bull R421-E4 node. This platform features an Intel Xeon E5-2620 v3 CPU at 2.40 GHz and a NVIDIA Tesla K80 accelerator, which contains two independent NVIDIA Tesla GK210 GPUs. The implementations evaluated in this work only employ one of these GPUs. The node runs Ubuntu 14.04.3 LTS with CUDA Toolkit 7.5. The programs have been compiled using gcc 4.8.4 and nvcc 7.5.17 with optimization flags O3 for GPU architecture 3.5.

For the acquisition of energy measurement data, we have developed a tool that collects this information from various hardware counters. For Intel, it uses the Running Average Power Limit (RAPL) interface. For NVIDIA, it uses the NVIDIA Management Library (NVML) API.

As test problems, we consider DTLZ2 and DTLZ7. The family of DTLZ problems was specially designed for evaluating multi-objective algorithms. They also allow to define an arbitrary number of objective functions [6, 16].

The formulation of DTLZ2 is as follows:

$$\min f_1(\mathbf{x}) = (1 + g(x)) \prod_{i=1}^{M-1} cos(\frac{x_i \pi}{2})$$

$$\min f_2(\mathbf{x}) = (1 + g(x))sin(\frac{x_{M-1}\pi}{2}) \prod_{i=1}^{M-2} cos(\frac{x_i \pi}{2})$$

$$\cdots \tag{2}$$

$$\min f_l(\mathbf{x}) = (1 + g(x))sin(\frac{x_{M-l+1}\pi}{2}) \prod_{i=1}^{M-l} cos(\frac{x_i \pi}{2})$$

$$\cdots$$

$$\min f_M(\mathbf{x}) = (1 + g(x))sin(\frac{x_1 \pi}{2})$$

where $g(\mathbf{x}) = \sum_{i=M}^{n}(x_i - 0.5)^2$, $x_i \in [0, 1]$. The number of variables V is selected according to the equation $V = M + k - 1$, with a suggested value of $k = 10$.

The formulation of DTLZ7 is as follows:

$$\min \quad f_1(\mathbf{x}) = x_1$$
$$\min \quad f_2(\mathbf{x}) = x_2$$
$$\cdots$$

$$\min \quad f_{M-1}(\mathbf{x}) = x_{M-1}$$
$$\min \quad f_M(\mathbf{x}) = (1 + g(x_M))h(f_1, f_2, \ldots, f_{M-1}, g)$$

$$\text{where} \quad g(x_M) = 1 + \frac{9}{|x_M|} \sum_{x_i \in x_M} x_i$$

(3)

$$h(f_1, f_2, \ldots, f_{M-1}, g) = M - \sum_{i=1}^{M-1} \left[\frac{f_1}{1+g} (1 + \sin(3\pi f_i)) \right]$$

subject to $0 \leq x_1 \leq 1$, for $i = 1, 2, \ldots, n$

This test problem has 2^{M-1} disconnected Pareto-optimal regions. The function g requires $k = |x_M|$ decision variables and the total number of variables is $V = M + k - 1$. The original author suggests $k = 20$.

Both DTLZ2 and DTLZ7 have been evaluated with $M = 5, 10, 15$ objective functions and varying population sizes. The results for test problem DTLZ7 are displayed in Tables 1, 2 and 3. In order to clarify the analysis, no results for DTLZ2 are shown, as our experiments suggest that both problems behave similarly on all the tests performed.

Table 1. Runtime and power dissipated by the evaluated algorithms for 50 NSGA-II generations with test problem DTLZ7 and 5 objectives.

2N	Time (s)			Average power (W)		
	Deb[3]	Gupta [12]	EFNDS	Deb [3]	Gupta [12]	EFNDS
1000	0.91	0.76	0.63	58.03	88.19	89.21
2000	2.60	1.34	1.06	65.47	88.41	89.53
5000	12.49	3.11	2.53	61.57	91.85	91.75
10000	43.67	6.04	5.36	61.04	104.77	99.58
20000	154.27	14.38	12.90	61.07	120.23	112.46
30000	327.44	33.20	23.06	61.13	125.14	122.99
40000	563.71	47.12	34.98	61.30	133.89	129.94
50000	870.68	61.33	50.30	61.16	142.58	132.36
60000	1251.48	94.57	69.40	61.14	144.12	133.69

These tables report mean time spent in seconds and average power dissipated in watts for each algorithm, when 50 generations are computed with varying population sizes. The power dissipated is the aggregate of CPU and GPU power

Table 2. Runtime and power dissipated by the evaluated algorithms for 50 NSGA-II generations with test problem DTLZ7 and 10 objectives.

2N	Time (s)			Average power (W)		
	Deb[3]	Gupta[12]	EFNDS	Deb [3]	Gupta [12]	EFNDS
1000	1.68	1.00	0.81	58.98	87.47	86.32
2000	5.50	1.76	1.45	59.64	88.63	87.10
5000	29.11	4.24	3.69	59.90	90.46	90.37
10000	106.02	8.81	8.27	60.34	93.99	95.20
20000	402.42	19.82	19.49	60.41	115.64	118.54
30000	874.49	41.87	36.04	60.56	128.40	125.62
40000	1550.48	62.13	57.00	60.61	128.08	126.77
50000	2511.14	85.04	80.25	60.66	140.70	135.70
60000	3822.55	123.65	111.56	60.74	142.52	140.87

Table 3. Runtime and power dissipated by the evaluated algorithms for 50 NSGA-II generations with test problem DTLZ7 and 15 objectives.

2N	Time (s)			Average power (W)		
	Deb[3]	Gupta[12]	EFNDS	Deb [3]	Gupta [12]	EFNDS
1000	2.39	1.22	0.95	58.73	87.90	86.95
2000	7.95	2.25	1.77	59.59	89.13	87.79
5000	43.78	5.45	4.61	59.95	91.89	91.93
10000	166.14	11.83	10.94	60.13	95.45	96.70
20000	642.53	30.62	26.29	60.21	129.03	125.24
30000	1436.45	63.10	51.03	60.21	130.38	126.20
40000	2635.97	93.59	80.24	60.37	137.41	133.95
50000	4385.16	139.06	120.07	60.53	144.76	138.36
60000	6589.02	205.64	170.95	60.54	143.00	142.56

reported by our measuring tool. Each test has been executed ten times using an unique seed for the random procedures of NSGA-II. This way we assert than every run has the same computational load and the only variances in the experimental measures come from the behavior of the hardware. The statistical analysis of the results shows a precision of at least 5% with a confidence level of 95%. Also, CPU-GPU communications time has been evaluated for all tests. The experimental results have shown that they consume less than 0.1% of the total execution times.

If we compare the two GPU implementations (Gupta and EFNDS), we observe that EFNDS is faster, with sightly lesser power dissipation. As described in [12], the algorithm proposed by Gupta does not store any data in device memory, instead opting to recalculate all dominance information between individuals each time it has to compute a front. This strategy works best when the number of fronts is low.

In our experimentation, we also measured the number of fronts needed to generate the parent population for each generation. We found that problems with high number of objectives have fewer starting fronts, and need fewer generations to get parent populations where all individuals are in the same front. Even in these situations, our implementation is faster than Gupta on the test platform. The way EFNDS stores partial dominance results takes advantage of the computing capabilities of the platform, allowing for parallel reductions and re-usage of information without being excessively penalized by memory operations.

If we compare EFNDS against the sequential implementation (called Deb in the tables), we can observe that EFNDS is faster, regardless of problem size and number of objectives. This speed offsets the additional energy consumed by the GPU, making our proposal the most energy efficient between the evaluated algorithms. Finally, comparing the three tables, we can note that our proposal scales well when increasing the population, providing respectable speedups against the sequential version.

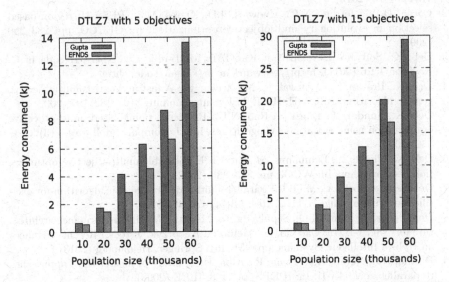

Fig. 2. Energy consumption in kilojoules of the two GPU implementations, for DTLZ7 with $M = 5, 15$ and varying population sizes.

Figure 2 exhibits the energy consumed by Gupta and EFNDS versions while solving test problem DTLZ7 for 5 and 15 objectives. As mentioned above, the advantages of EFNDS over Gupta are most notable when the number of objectives is low, since those are the cases where we have multiple fronts per generation.

5   Conclusions and Future Works

In this paper we have proposed a GPU implementation of NDS (referred to as EFNDS) which defines a new data structure to store the dominance informa-tion to efficiently compute the sets of non-dominated individuals (fronts) on the GPU. It has been integrated in NSGA-II algorithm and comparatively evaluated with the recent Gupta's proposal to compute NDS on GPU from the perspec-tives of both performance and power/energy efficiency. Results have shown that EFNDS achieves the best performance and consumes less energy, thus having better energy efficiency than the other proposal. Therefore, it is of great inter-est for developing energy efficiency aware applications based on Multi-Objective Optimization.

References

1. Brodtkorb, A.R., Trond, R.H., Sætra, M.L.: Graphics processing unit (GPU) pro-gramming strategies and trends in GPU computing. J. Parallel Distrib. Comput. **73**(1), 4–13 (2013)
2. Corne, D.W., Jerram, N.R., Knowles, J.D., Oates, M.J.: PESA-II: region-based selection in evolutionary multiobjective optimization. In: GECCO, pp. 283–290 (2001)
3. Deb, K.: Software Developed at KanGAL: Multi-objective NSGA-II code in C. Revision 1.1.6 (2011). http://www.iitk.ac.in/kangal/codes.shtml
4. Deb, K., Pratap, A., Agarwal, S., Meyarivan, T.: A fast and elitist multiobjective genetic algorithm: NSGA-II. IEEE T. Evolut. Comput. **6**(2), 182–197 (2002)
5. Deb, K., Sundar, J., Bhaskara Rao, N.U.: Reference point based multi-objective optimization using evolutionary algorithms. Int. J. Comput. Intell. Res. **2**(3), 273–286 (2006)
6. Deb, K., Thiele, L., Laumanns, M., Zitzler, E.: Scalable multi-objective optimiza-tion test problems. In: WCCI, pp. 825–830 (2002)
7. Dehuri, S., Ghosh, A., Mall, R.: Parallel multi-objective genetic algorithm for clas-sification rule mining. IETE J. Res. **53**(5), 475–483 (2007)
8. Domínguez, J., Montiel, O., Sepúlveda, R., Medina, N.: High performance architec-ture for NSGA-II. In: Castillo, O., Melin, P., Kacprzyk, J. (eds.) Recent Advances on Hybrid Intelligent Systems, pp. 451–461. Springer, Heidelberg (2013)
9. Durillo, J.J., Nebro, A.J., Luna, F., Alba, E.: A study of master-slave approaches to parallelize NSGA-II. In: IPDPS, pp. 1–8. IEEE (2008)
10. Fang, H., Wang, Q., Tu, Y., Horstemeyer, M.F.: An efficient non-dominated sorting method for evolutionary algorithms. Evol. Comput. **16**(3), 355–384 (2008)
11. Filatovas, E., Kurasova, O., Sindhya, K.: Reference point based multi-objective optimization using evolutionary algorithms. Informatica **26**(1), 33–50 (2015)
12. Gupta, S., Tan, G.: A scalable parallel implementation of evolutionary algorithms for multi-objective optimization on GPUs. In: CEC, pp. 1567–1574. IEEE (2015)
13. Harris, M.: Maxwell: the most advanced CUDA GPU ever made (2014)
14. Hennessy, J.L., Patterson, D.A.: Computer Architecture - A Quantitative App-roach, 5th edn. Morgan Kaufmann, San Francisco (2012)
15. Huang, S., Xiao, S., Feng, W.: On the energy efficiency of graphics processing units for scientific computing. In: IEEE IPDPS 2009, pp. 1–8 (2009)

16. Huband, S., Hingston, P., Barone, L., While, L.: A review of multiobjective test problems and a scalable test problem toolkit. IEEE T. Evolut. Comput. **10**(5), 477–506 (2006)
17. Jensen, M.T.: Reducing the run-time complexity of multiobjective EAs: The NSGA-II and other algorithms. IEEE T. Evolut. Comput. **7**(5), 503–515 (2003)
18. Knowles, J.D., Corne, D.W.: Approximating the non-dominated front using the Pareto archived evolution strategy. Evol. Comput. **8**(2), 149–172 (2000)
19. Lančinskas, A., Žilinskas, J.: Approaches to parallelize pareto ranking in NSGA-II algorithm. In: Wyrzykowski, R., Dongarra, J., Karczewski, K., Waśniewski, J. (eds.) PPAM 2011. LNCS, vol. 7204, pp. 371–380. Springer, Heidelberg (2012). doi:10.1007/978-3-642-31500-8_38
20. Lančinskas, A., Žilinskas, J.: Solution of multi-objective competitive facility location problems using parallel NSGA-II on large scale computing systems. In: Manninen, P., Öster, P. (eds.) PARA 2012. LNCS, vol. 7782, pp. 422–433. Springer, Heidelberg (2013). doi:10.1007/978-3-642-36803-5_31
21. McClymont, K., Keedwell, E.: Deductive sort and climbing sort: new methods for non-dominated sorting. Evol. Comput. **20**(1), 1–26 (2012)
22. Miettinen, K.: Nonlinear Multiobjective Optimization. Springer, Heidelberg (1999)
23. Moreno, J.J., Ortega, G., Filatovas, E., Martínez, J.A., Garzón, E.M.: Using low-power platforms for evolutionary multi-objective optimization algorithms. J. Supercomput (2016). doi:10.1007/s11227-016-1862-0
24. Munshi, A., Gaster, B., Mattson, T.G., Fung, J., Ginsburg, D.: OpenCL Programming Guide, 1st edn. Addison-Wesley Professional, Boston (2011)
25. NVIDIA. NVIDIA's next generation CUDA compute architecture: Kepler GK110 (2012)
26. NVIDIA. CUDA C programming guide. version 7.0 (2015)
27. Ortega, G., Filatovas, E., Garzón, E.M., Casado, L.G.: Non-dominated sorting procedure for pareto dominance ranking on multicore CPU and/or GPU. J. Global Optim. (2016). doi:10.1007/s10898-016-0468-7
28. Shi, C., Chen, M., Shi, Z.: A fast nondominated sorting algorithm. In: ICNN, vol. 3, pp. 1605–1610. IEEE (2005)
29. Smutnicki, C., Rudy, J., Żelazny, D.: Very fast non-dominated sorting. Decision Making Manufact. Serv. **8**(1–2), 13–23 (2014)
30. Zhang, Q., Li, H.: MOEA/D: a multiobjective evolutionary algorithm based on decomposition. IEEE T. Evolut. Comput. **11**(6), 712–731 (2007)
31. Zhang, X., Ye, T., Cheng, R., Jin, Y.: An efficient approach to non-dominated sorting for evolutionary multi-objective optimization. IEEE T. Evolut. Comput. **19**(2), 201–213 (2015)
32. Zitzler, E., Künzli, S.: Indicator-based selection in multiobjective search. In: Yao, X., Burke, E.K., Lozano, J.A., Smith, J., Merelo-Guervós, J.J., Bullinaria, J.A., Rowe, J.E., Tiño, P., Kabán, A., Schwefel, H.-P. (eds.) PPSN 2004. LNCS, vol. 3242, pp. 832–842. Springer, Heidelberg (2004). doi:10.1007/978-3-540-30217-9_84
33. Zitzler, E., Laumanns, M., Thiele, L.: SPEA2: improving the strength pareto evolutionary algorithm. Technical Report 103, Computer Engineering and Networks Laboratory (TIK), ETH Zurich, Zurich, Switzerland (2001)

A Parallel Model for Heterogeneous Cluster

Thiago Marques Soares, Rodrigo Weber dos Santos, and Marcelo Lobosco[✉]

Graduate Program in Computational Modelling,
Federal University of Juiz de Fora, Juiz de Fora, Brazil
thiagomarquesmg@gmail.com, {marcelo.lobosco,rodrigo.weber}@ufjf.edu.br

Abstract. The LogP model was used to measure the effects of latency, occupancy and bandwidth on distributed memory multiprocessors. The idea was to characterize distributed memory multiprocessor using these key parameters, studying their impacts on performance in simulation environments. This work proposes a new model, based on LogP, that describes the impacts on performance of applications executing on a heterogeneous cluster. This model can be used, in a near future, to help choose the best way to split a parallel application to be executed on this architecture. The model considers that a heterogeneous cluster is composed by distinct types of processors, accelerators and networks.

Keywords: Performance modeling · Parallel architectures · Heterogeneous clusters · Scheduling

1   Introduction

Large scale scientific applications demand the use of parallel environments, such as a cluster of computers, in order to execute their tasks. Clusters are becoming more heterogeneous, mixing, in a single system, distinct processors, accelerators, such as GPUs, and network connections. To explore all the resources available in such a heterogeneous platform, a data-parallel application must divide its data across multiple devices. This is not an easy task due to the distinct processing power of devices and the distinct latencies of the networks, which can lead to unbalance in the computation and delays in process synchronization.

The goal of this paper is to present a parallel model that estimates the execution time of applications running on heterogeneous clusters. The proposed model extends some characteristics of the LogP [4] model in a similar way that Lastovetsky et al. [8] did, but considering that processing units may have distinct computational power as well as they are interconnected by connections with distinct latencies. The idea is to use the results of this estimation, in future works, to predict the best data division to be used in a heterogeneous cluster, taking into account not only the processing power of each processor and accelerator, but also the communication and synchronization costs. In order to present an initial

The authors would like to thank UFJF, FAPEMIG, CAPES, and CNPq.

J. Carretero et al. (Eds.): ICA3PP 2016 Workshops, LNCS 10049, pp. 76–90, 2016.
DOI: 10.1007/978-3-319-49956-7_6

evaluation of the model, we also present the estimated and real computation, communication and total execution time for distinct applications.

The remaining of this work is organized as follows. Section 2 briefly reviews the LogP model and Sect. 3 presents related works. Section 4 presents the new model. The experimental results are presented in Sect. 5. Finally, Sect. 6 presents our conclusions and plans for future works.

2   The LogP Model

LogP [4] model measures the effects of latency, occupancy and bandwidth on distributed memory multiprocessors. On these type of machine, processors communicate using point-to-point messages using a network infrastructure. The main parameters used in the LogP model are the following: (a) **L**, that represents an upper bound on the communication latency due to the use of point-to-point messages; (b) **o**, that represents the overhead, i.e., the time that a processor spends in the transmission or reception of each message and that cannot be used to execute other instructions; (c) **g**, the gap, that represents the minimum time interval between consecutive message transmissions/receptions by a processor; and **P**, the number of processor/memory modules. Observe that the reciprocal of the **g** parameter represents the communication bandwidth.

The model assumes an asynchronous computation model, with processors working in an independent way. In this model, the latency experienced by any application message is unpredictable, but the model imposes the upper limit **L** to it. The model also considers that the network has a finite capacity of sending messages, so that at most $\lceil L/g \rceil$ messages can be in transit from any pair of processors at any time. If a processor tries to send a message while the network capacity is full, it stalls until the message can be sent without exceeding the network capacity. Also, the original model assumes that all messages are of the same small size.

3   Related Works

One of the first works to propose a model for parallel computing was the bulk-synchronous parallel model (BSP) [15]. It considers that the computation on the processing units can occur independently and communication and computation does not have to follow a specific time order. The model imposes, at each timestep (called superstep), the use of a barrier for synchronization purposes, which is a restriction of the model.

Other works have proposed models to characterize the effects of communication and overheads on the performance of applications. The LogP model works well with fixed-sized short messages, but when large messages are considered, the model does not predict the communication costs with the same precision. Trying to solve this issue, Alexandrov et al. [1] proposed the LogGP model. This model extended the LogP model with a simple linear model for long messages, by introducing a new parameter G that represents the gap per byte for long messages. Using this approach, the authors argue that the model can capture the behavior of both long and short messages. Another model that took into account the message size was proposed by Kielmann *et al.* [7]. The PLogP model defines five parameters, two of which, the latency and the number of processors, with the same role of the LogP model. The other three parameters are the following: (a) the send overhead ($o_s(m)$), (b) the receive overhead ($o_r(m)$), and (c) the gap ($g(m)$). These three parameters are functions of the message size. A method to measure the parameters, implemented as a MPI application that adapts itself to the network characteristics and does not saturate the network, was also suggested by the authors. Other works focused on studying the impacts of communication on performance. Holt *et al.* [6] used a wide range of applications in order to evaluate the effects of some parameters of the LogP model on a distributed shared memory (DSM) machine. The results of these experiments have shown that the occupancy of the communication controller is critical to achieve good performance in this type of machine. The authors argue that despite of the impacts caused by contention, it is difficult to model contention analytically, especially for applications that try to hide latency. For this reason, our proposed model does not use a specific parameter to describe the effects of contention in computation; the effect caused by it is captured indirectly by the overhead parameter. Although applications show strong sensitivity to the overhead, as Martin *et al.* [11] have shown, we decided to keep the model as simple as possible, as described in the next section.

In order to deal with heterogeneous processors interconnected by an Ethernet-based network, Lastovetsky *et al.* [8] extended the LogP model with the main goal of predicting the impact of communication into the total execution time of an application. The model tries to represent accurately the communication behavior of applications using distinct communication patterns: point to point, one to many, many to one and many to many. Later, Lastovetsky *et al.* proposed a technique for estimating the parameters of their model [9]. This work not only predicts the communication time, but also the total execution time of parallel applications.

All previous models are not suited to deal with: (a) a heterogeneous cluster, that mixes distinct CPUs and accelerators on the same environment, and (b) heterogeneous networks. A parallel model that takes into account the execution time and capture the characteristics of a heterogeneous environment is the HLoGP model [3]. The HLoGP is a very accurate model, but the large number of parameters is an issue, specially when dealing with large clusters that include accelerators. This work proposes a simpler model that predicts the execution time of parallel applications, regardless of the computational environment used, homogeneous or heterogeneous one.

4   The New Model

The LogP model has been used to guide parallel algorithm design, since it could predict the behavior of applications in a distributed memory, homogeneous processor environment. This work proposes to extend LogP in order to deal with modern heterogeneous environments, composed by distinct processors, accelerators and networks. The main parameters used in the new model are the same used in the LogP model, but considering a heterogeneous environment: (a) $\mathbf{L}_d$, that represents an upper bound on the communication latency of a device d; (b) $\mathbf{o}_d$, that represents the overhead in device d, i.e., the time that a processor spends in the transmission or reception of each message and that cannot be used to execute other instructions; (c) $\mathbf{g}_d$, the gap, that represents the minimum time interval between consecutive message transmissions/receptions by a processor in a device d; and (d) $\mathbf{R_P}$, the relative computing power of a processing unit.

There are two ways to measure $R_{\mathbf{p}}$: (a) running a benchmark on each processing unit to collect a metric, such as the processing units per time step, or (b) using the average computation time that a processing unit takes to run one iteration of an application. In the first case, given the size of the problem (**size**) and the number of processing units per time step a device can execute ($\mathbf{R_p}$), the computation time is given by: size/R_p. In the second case, the computation time can be obtained multiplying $R_{\mathbf{p}}$ by the total number of iterations. If the application does not scale linearly with the problem size, the first way to measure the computation time can lead to a wrong estimation. The second alternative solves this issue since the problem size is considered implicitly.

The values of $\mathbf{L}_d$ and $\mathbf{g}_d$ are also obtained prior to the execution of the application. A network benchmark is used for this purpose. The benchmark is executed for each type d of network that is available in the cluster. The benchmark collects the values of $\mathbf{L}_d$ and $\mathbf{g}_d$ for distinct message sizes, ranging from 0 to 4MB. Each message size modeled by our model uses their corresponding $\mathbf{L}_d$ and $\mathbf{g}_d$ values found by the benchmark.

The value of $\mathbf{o}_d$ is computed using a benchmark [5]. This benchmark considers that the overhead varies with the message size. The total overhead in a point-to-point communication operations is given by: $o_{\mathbf{d}} = o_{\mathbf{s}} + o_{\mathbf{r}}$, where $o_{\mathbf{s}}$ and $o_{\mathbf{r}}$ are respectively the send and the receive overheads. Again, each message size modeled by our model uses its corresponding $\mathbf{o}_d$ value found by the benchmark.

The use of benchmarks to collect the communication costs, overheads, as well as the relative performance of the processors and accelerators, can be executed only once, or each time a new hardware or network is included in the system.

We decided to keep the model as simple as possible, resisting the temptation to provide a more detailed model, such as (a) including separate intra-node communication and synchronizations costs (that could occur, for example, if a GPU and a CPU exchange data), (b) considering the network topology. If the intra-node communication costs are representative, they can be included in the model using $\mathbf{L}_d$, $\mathbf{o}_d$ and $\mathbf{g}_d$, where the device is the GPU and its associated latency, overhead and bandwidth. The network topology was not considered because: (a) algorithms usually are not attached to a particular network topology, although the communication protocol can use this information in order to optimize collective communication; and (b) the network topology is reflected in the $\mathbf{L}_n$ and $\mathbf{g}_n$ parameters.

5 Model Evaluation

Two kernels (EP and FT) and one application (SP) from the NAS benchmark [2] were used to validate the model. Since these benchmarks were developed to execute in a CPU environment, another application, HIS, was chosen to evaluate the model on a GPU environment. The HIS application simulates some components of the human immune system [14]. The goal is to evaluate the model with applications that have distinct computation and communication characteristics and observe whether the model can capture them.

Some considerations were made when estimating the execution time: (a) all benchmarks compute during several iterations, so the communication cost described in Sect. 4 was multiplied not only by the number of communication operations that occur at each iteration ($\mathbf{N_{op}}$), but also by the total number of interactions ($\boldsymbol{I}$); (b) the Maximum Transmission Unit (MTU) size was used to estimate the values of $\mathbf{L}_n$ and $\mathbf{g}_n$; (c) a simple load balancing was used to distribute the data size that each processing unit receives to compute: for example, if CPU_a is twice faster than CPU_b, then CPU_a receives twice the data size of CPU_b.

5.1 Benchmarks

EP. The Embarrassingly Parallel kernel (EP) [2] generate pairs of Gaussian pseudorandom deviates and tabulate the number of pairs in successive square annuli, a typical problem of many Monte Carlo based applications. The communication occurs only at the end of the computation: a collective MPI routine is used to combine the suns generate from all processors. The class C problem set was used in the evaluation.

Algorithm 1 gives an overview of the EP kernel.

Algorithm 1. Pseudocode of the EP kernel

2: **main**
    ... generate the seed for each process ...
4:
    ... calculate counts and sums in each process ...
6:
    ... Use MPI_Allreduce to send parameter to all processes ...
8:
    end-main

FT. A 3-D fast-Fourier transform kernel (FT) [2] is used to numerically solve partial differential equation (PDE) using forward and inverse FFTs. This kernel tests the long-distance communication performance, considering that the 3-D FFT steps require considerable communication for operations such as array transpositions. Such communication operations are implemented using all-to-all exchange. In order to predict the communication time for this kernel, only the global transpose operations were considered because the amount of data they exchanged is higher than the amount exchanged by other transpose operations. The class B problem set was used in the evaluation.

Algorithm 2 presents the pseudocode of the FT kernel.

Algorithm 2. Pseudocode of the FT kernel

```
     main
2:
        for t from 1 to number of iterations do
4:
            ... evolve u0 to u1 (t time steps) in fourier space ...
6:
            ... calls the fft subroutine ...
8:
            ... transpose operations in each process ...
10:
            ... use MPI_Alltoall to exchange the transpose results ...
12:
            ... call checksum ...
14:
        end-for
16:
     end-main
```

SP. Scalar Penta-Diagonal solver (SP) solves multiple, independent systems of nondiagonally-dominant, scalar pentadiagonal equations using a multi-partition scheme. The multi-partition scheme uses a coarse grained communication. The class B problem set was used in the evaluation.

Algorithm 3 presents the pseudocode of the SP application.

Algorithm 3. Pseudocode of the SP application

```
     main
2:
        for t from 1 to number of iterations do
4:
            ... performs the block-diagonal matrix vector multiplicator ...
6:
            ... use MPI_Isend to send the buffer ...
8:
            ... use MPI_Ireceive to receive the buffer ...
10:
            ... performs aproximate factorization in the x-plane ...
12:
            ... use MPI_Isend to send the buffer ...
14:
            ... use MPI_Ireceive to receive the buffer ...
16:
            ... performs aproximate factorization in the y-plane ...
18:
            ... use MPI_Isend to send the buffer ...
20:
            ... use MPI_Ireceive to receive the buffer ...
22:
            ... performs aproximate factorization in the z-plane ...
24:
            ... use MPI_Isend to send the buffer ...
26:
            ... use MPI_Ireceive to receive the buffer ...
28:
            ... add the u vector ...
30:
        end-for
32:
     end-main
```

HIS. A three dimensional simulator of the Human Immune System (HIS) [14] was used in the model evaluation. The simulator implements a mathematical model that uses a set of eight Partial Differential Equations (PDEs) to describe how some cells and molecules involved in the innate immune response react to a pathogen. A detailed discussion about the model can be found in [12–14]. The implementation is based on the Finite Difference Method [10] for the spatial discretization and the explicit Euler method for the time evolution. The code was implemented in C and uses CUDA to solve the PDEs in GPUs. One or more GPUs can be used simultaneously to solve the PDEs for a piece of a mesh. The CPU is responsible for the communication, due to border exchange between GPUs, using MPI for this purpose. Border exchange occurs at the end of each iteration. Two mesh sizes were used in the evaluation of the model: $150 \times 150 \times 150$ and $200 \times 200 \times 200$. For this application, the communication between CPU and GPU was not considered.

Algorithm 4 gives an overview of the GPU implementation of the HIS simulator.

Algorithm 4. GPU implementation of the HIS simulator

```
   main
2:
      ... define the mesh slice to be computed by each GPU ...
4:
      ... initialize submeshes according to their initial conditions ...
6:
      for t from 0 to final time do
8:
         ... call the kernels that computes the points ...
10:
         ... use MPI_Isend and MPI_Receive to exchange boundaries between distinct machines ...
12:
         ... synchronize all machines ...
14:
      end-for
16:
   end-main
```

5.2   Computational Platform

The experiments were executed on a small cluster with 16 machines. Half of these machines have two Intel Xeon $E5620$ processors with 16 GB of main memory, six of these have two Tesla C1060 GPUs (240 CUDA cores and 4 GB of global memory each) and the other two have two Tesla M2050 GPUs (448 CUDA cores and 3 GB of global memory). The other eight machines have two AMD 6272 processors, with 32 GB of main memory, two Tesla M2075 GPUs, each one with 448 CUDA cores and 6 GB of global memory. Linux 2.6.32, CUDA driver version 6.0, OpenMPI version 1.6.2, nvcc release 6.0 and gcc version 4.4.7 were used to run and compile all codes. Two distinct networks cards are available in the cluster: Intel 82576 Gigabit Ethernet and InfiniBand Mellanox MT26428 with a QDR of 40 Gb/s. The Intel machines are connected by the Gigabit Ethernet card, while the AMD machines are connected by both cards. Both cards have the full-duplex mode, so data can be transmitted and received simultaneously. For this reason, the model for each application considers only half of the number of messages exchanged since they occur in parallel. Although the total number of cores available in each machine is equal to 32 for AMD (2×16) and 8 for Intel (2×4), in all experiments reported in the next section only one process was used per machine.

Two distinct environments were used in the experiments. A homogeneous environment that uses only one type of CPU and a heterogeneous one, that mixes distinct types of CPUs. In the homogeneous environment, composed by AMD processors, we also used distinct types of network cards (Ethernet and Infiniband). In the heterogeneous environment, half of the processors are AMD and half are Intel. The only exception is the SP benchmark running with 9 processors, in which 5 Intel and 4 AMD CPUs were used. Also, we evaluated our model on a homogeneous and a heterogeneous GPU environment. The homogeneous environment is composed only by M2075 GPUs, while the heterogeneous one mixes C1060, M2050 and M2075 GPUs.

5.3   Results

This section presents, for each benchmark, the estimations obtained by our model for the computation time, communication time and total execution time. The computation time for EP, FT and SP was estimated for the execution on the CPU, and the computation time for HIS was estimated for execution on the GPU. The estimated execution time is compared with the real one and the error in the estimation is presented. Each benchmark was executed 5 times for each configuration in order to minimize the standard deviation.

EP. The EP benchmark is modeled using the following equation:

$$T_{total} = \frac{size}{R_p} + I \times N_{op} \times \log_2 P \times (L_d + \frac{M}{B_d} + o_d), \qquad (1)$$

where $size$ is the size of the problem, R_p is the relative computing power, I is the number of iterations, N_{op} is the number of communication operations per iteration, L_d is the latency, o_d is the overhead, P is the number of processors used in the experiments and M is the message size. Recall that B_d is the reciprocal of the g parameter. The first part of the equation describes the execution time, and the remaining the communication time. For this problem we used the first way to compute R_p because the execution is composed by a unique iteration. Also, $size = 8,589,934.592$ units, $R_p^{AMD} = 14,518,343.266$ units/s, $R_p^{Intel} = 24,350,979.353$ units/s (both multiplied by the number of processors of each type - AMD and Intel - used), $I = 1$ and two messages ($N_{op} = 2$) with $M = 8 \times 10^{-6}$ MB and one ($N_{op} = 1$) with $M = 8 \times 10^{-5}$ MB. The MTU size, 1.5 Kbytes, defines the values used for the latency and bandwidth, which are equal to (a) $L_{eth} = 6.9 \times 10^{-5}$ s and $B_{eth} = 93.4$ MB/s for Ethernet and (b) $L_{inf} = 5.1 \times 10^{-6}$ s and $B_{inf} = 1,030.3$ MB/s for Infiniband. The main communication

Table 1. Results for the EP kernel using 2 AMD processors. All times are in seconds.

EP	Ethernet		Infiniband	
	Real	Estimated	Real	Estimated
Computation Time	295.6	295.8	297.2	295.8
Standard Deviation	0.6%	-	1%	-
Error	-	0.1%	-	0.5%
Communication Time	2.0×10^{-4}	2.1×10^{-4}	1.3×10^{-5}	1.6×10^{-5}
Standard Deviation	22.3%	-	29.7%	-
Error	-	6.4%	-	14.5%
Total Execution Time	295.6	295.8	297.2	295.8
Standard Deviation	0.6%	-	1%	-
Error	-	0.1%	-	0.5%
Overhead	2.2×10^{-6}	-	3.5×10^{-7}	-

Table 2. Results for the EP kernel using 4, 8 and 16 heterogeneous nodes. All times are in seconds.

EP	4 Nodes		8 Nodes		16 Nodes	
	Real	Estimated	Real	Estimated	Real	Estimated
Computation Time	118.0	110.5	52.0	55.2	28.5	28.5
Standard Deviation	0.1%	-	0.2%	-	2.8%	-
Error	-	6.4%	-	6.3%	-	0.0%
Communication Time	4.5×10^{-4}	4.2×10^{-4}	7.6×10^{-4}	6.3×10^{-4}	8.8×10^{-4}	8.4×10^{-4}
Standard Deviation	14.8%	-	10.4%	-	8.2%	-
Error	-	6.3%	-	17.3%	-	4.6%
Total Execution Time	118.0	110.5	52.0	55.2	28.6	28.6
Standard Deviation	0.1%	-	0.2%	-	2.8%	-
Error	-	6.4%	-	6.3%	-	0.0%
Overhead	8.6×10^{-6}	-	1.7×10^{-5}	-	3.4×10^{-5}	-

operation used in this kernel are the MPI_Allreduce() using the binomial tree algorithm. Table 1 presents the estimated and real computation, communication and total execution time for EP when running on the homogeneous environment. In all tables, the overhead represents the sum of the overheads found for each message size.

Table 2 presents the results obtained by EP when running on a heterogeneous environment composed by 4, 8 and 16 processors. Each configuration mixes Intel and AMD CPUs. For example, the configuration that uses 4 processors uses 2 AMD and 2 Intel CPUs.

Tables 1 and 2 show that the model estimates precisely the computation, communication and total execution time of the benchmark. The computation time has the biggest contributiThe other parameters are $size = 4,251,528$ unitson on the total execution time, while the communication time has almost no influence. The standard deviation and the error for computation time were both below 1% in Table 1, and below 6.5% in Table 2. In contrast, in both tables the communication time presented a high standard deviation and error. This occurred because both real and estimated communication time are tiny, and any fluctuations on these values imposes an increase on the deviation and error. Nevertheless, one can observe that the error was less than the standard deviation for all estimations, except the estimation with 8 nodes in the heterogeneous environment.

FT. The FT benchmark is modeled using the following equation:

$$T_{total} = I \times (R_p + N_{op} \times (P - 1) \times (L_d + \frac{M}{B_d} + o_d)). \tag{2}$$

For this and the remaining benchmarks, we used the second way to compute R_p because they do not scale linearly with the number of processors. For this benchmark, $R_p^{AMD} = 3.341\,s$, $I = 20$, $N_{op} = 2$, $P = 2$ and $M = 67.1$ MB for the first way to compute R_p. The main communication operation used in this kernel is the MPI_AlltoAll() using the pair-wise exchange algorithm. Table 3 presents the estimated and real computation, communication and total execution time for FT using the homogeneous environment.

Table 3. Results for the FT kernel using 2 AMD processors. All times are in seconds.

FT	Ethernet		Infiniband	
	Real	Estimated	Real	Estimated
Computation Time	64.6	66.8	63.4	66.8
Standard Deviation	1.2%	-	1.5%	-
Error	-	3.4%	-	5.3%
Communication Time	30.4	28.7	2.6	2.5
Standard Deviation	2.3%	-	7.1%	-
Error	-	5.4%	-	0.2%
Total Execution Time	95.0	96.3	66.1	69.4
Standard Deviation	1.4%	-	1.2%	-
Error	-	1.5%	-	5.0%
Overhead	1.0	-	0.1	-

As shown in Table 3, the errors between the real and the estimated computation and communication time were lower for this benchmark, with values below 5.4%. The error in the prediction of the total execution time was kept low, below 5%. Also, the model accurately predicts the communication time when using the Infiniband network.

Table 4. Results for FT kernel using 4, 8 and 16 heterogeneous nodes. All times are in seconds.

FT	4 Nodes		8 Nodes		16 Nodes	
	Real	Estimated	Real	Estimated	Real	Estimated
Computation Time	24.7	26.7	14.3	16.2	7.8	8.7
Standard Deviation	2.5%	-	3.1%	-	4.2%	-
Error	-	8.1%	-	13.4%	-	12.0%
Communication Time	46.7	43.1	52.7	50.3	58.0	54.0
Standard Deviation	3.6%	-	2.2%	-	0.7%	-
Error	-	8.0%	-	4.4%	-	7.0%
Total Execution Time	71.4	72.0	67.0	68.1	65.8	64.1
Standard Deviation	2.6%	-	1.9%	-	2.0%	-
Error	-	0.9%	-	1.8%	-	2.7%
Overhead	2.2	-	1.6	-	1.4	-

Table 4 presents the results for FT running on a heterogeneous environment. The values of R_p were 1.331 s, 0.811 s, and 0.434 s respectively for $P = 4$, 8 and 16 nodes. The values of M are 33.5 MB, 16.8 MB, and 8.3 MB respectively for $P = 4$, 8 and 16 nodes. All other parameters values were kept. As one can observe, the values estimated for the computation time were worst than those estimated for the homogeneous experiment with 2 nodes, although the error on the estimation of the total execution time were kept low, below 3%.

SP. The SP benchmark is modeled using the following equation:

$$T_{total} = I \times (R_p + N_{op} \times (L_d + \frac{M}{B_d} + o_d)). \tag{3}$$

The number of processors used for this application must be a square (1, 4, 9, 16, ...). In this benchmark, we used the second way to compute R_p.

For this experiment, the parameters change depending on the number of nodes used. For the experiments with 4 nodes, the messages size are: one message of length 0.1 MB and $N_{op} = 1$; one message of length 0.5 MB and $N_{op} = 3$; and one message of length 0.1 MB and $N_{op} = 3$. The R_p value is 1.052 s. For 9 nodes, the values are: one message of length 0.5 MB and $N_{op} = 1$; three messages of length 0.5 MB and $N_{op} = 6$; and three messages of length 0.2 MB and $N_{op} = 3$. The R_p value is 0.473 s. Finally, for 16 nodes the message sizes are the following: one of length 0.3 MB and $N_{op} = 1$; five of length 0.0.35 MB and $N_{op} = 10$; six of length 0.4 MB and $N_{op} = 10$; and one of length 0.1 MB and $N_{op} = 10$. The R_p value used for 16 nodes is 0.359 s and $I = 400$. The main communication operation used in this kernel is the MPI_Isend() and MPI_Ireceive(). Due to the lack of space, for this application we do not shown the results for the homogeneous configuration, only for the heterogeneous one (Table 4).

The large number of messages exchanged is probably responsible for the error values observed in the estimation of the communication time. However, the values estimated for the total execution time are very close to the real values, with all errors below 1% (Table 5).

Table 5. Results for SP kernel using 4, 9 and 16 heterogeneous nodes. All times are in seconds.

SP	4 Nodes		9 Nodes		16 Nodes	
	Real	Estimated	Real	Estimated	Real	Estimated
Computation Time	414.3	420.8	181.4	189.2	130.7	143.6
Standard Deviation	0.2%	-	0.1%	-	3.1%	-
Error	-	1.5%	-	4.2%	-	10.3%
Communication Time	28.0	24.0	83.5	74.0	213.0	188.8
Standard Deviation	3.1%	-	0.3%	-	0.7%	-
Error	-	14.1%	-	11.4%	-	11.4%
Total Execution Time	442.3	445.7	265.9	267.7	343.7	345.4
Standard Deviation	0.3%	-	0.1%	-	1.0%	-
Error	-	0.6%	-	1.0%	-	0.51%
Overhead	0.9	-	4.5	-	13.0	-

HIS. The HIS benchmark is modeled using the following equation:

$$T_{total} = I \times (R_p + T_{ij}), \tag{4}$$

where i represents the current GPU and j the GPU whose identification number is equal to the value of i plus one. As can be observed, this equation uses the second way to compute R_p. T_{ij} represents the border exchange time between these two GPU and is defined by Eq. 5.

$$T_{ij} = (L_d + \frac{M}{B_d} + o_d). \tag{5}$$

For a mesh of size equal to $150 \times 150 \times 150$, the values used in our model are $M = 1.08$ MB and $R_p = 9.8 \times 10^{-3}$ s.

Table 6 illustrates that the model successfully predicted, in a homogeneous environment, the total execution time for both networks. All the errors stayed below 6%. Again, the biggest error occurs in the estimation of the communication time in Infiniband, about 10%, but in absolute values the error was low, about 1 s.

A second experiment used three distinct GPUs models: C1060, M2050 and M2075. Since these hardware present distinct characteristics, a simple load balancing was used to divide data among all GPUs, in the way described in Sect. 4.

Table 6. Results for the HIS application using 2 M2075 GPUs and a mesh of size $150 \times 150 \times 150$. All times are in seconds.

HIS	Ethernet		Infiniband	
	Real	Estimated	Real	Estimated
Computation Time	91.4	98	91.1	98
Standard Deviation	1.6%	-	1.9%	-
Error	-	7.2%	-	7.6%
Communication Time	122.0	116.3	11.6	10.5
Standard Deviation	2.2%	-	3.1%	-
Error	-	4.7%	-	9.4%
Total Execution Time	213.4	219.1	102.7	109
Standard Deviation	1.9%	-	1.7%	-
Error	-	2.7%	-	6.1%
Overhead	4.8	-	0.5	-

The GPUs with more relative power (M2075 and M2050) received the biggest chunk of data, while the other GPU (C1060) received the smallest one. The parameters used in this experiment are: a grid of size $200 \times 200 \times 200$ ($size = 80,000,000$ units), $R_p = 1.1 \times 10^{-2}$ (for 4 nodes) and $R_p = 1.0 \times 10^{-2}$ s (for 8 nodes), $I = 10,000$ and $M = 1.9$ MB. The main communication operations considered for this application were the MPI_Isend() and MPI_Receive(). Table 7 presents the results. As can be observed, the error in the estimation of the total

Table 7. Results for the HIS application using 4 GPUs (2 M2075, 1 C1060 and 1 M2050) and 8 GPUs (4 M2075, 2 C1060 and 2 M2050) and a mesh of size $200 \times 200 \times 200$. All times are in seconds.

HIS	4 Nodes		8 Nodes	
	Real	Estimated	Real	Estimated
Computation Time	95.0	108.0	86.1	99
Standard Deviation	0.3%	-	0.7%	-
Error	-	14.0%	-	15.0%
Communication Time	684.6	618.7	1298,1	1443.7
Standard Deviation	0.1%	-	0.3%	-
Error	-	9.6%	-	11.2%
Total Execution Time	779.6	761.0	1384.2	1611.3
Standard Deviation	0.1%	-	0.3%	-
Error	-	2.4%	-	16.4%
Overhead	34.3	-	68.6	-

execution time for the configuration with 4 nodes was below 2.5%, but the error for the configuration with 8 nodes was high, about 16%.

6   Conclusion and Future Works

This paper described a new model that generalizes the LogP model in order to deal with heterogeneous parallel environments. The model is general and can be used to describe the computation and communication characteristics of a parallel application. While the original LogP model were used to guide parallel algorithm design, the model proposed in this work will be used to find the best combination of computing units available (accelerators and CPUs) in order to minimize the execution time of a parallel application. The results have shown that the model can predict the total computation time of applications with distinct characteristics, running on distinct devices and interconnected by different network types. The error found during the estimation of the total execution time stayed below 6% in all experiments, except for the HIS simulator, where the error was about 16% when 8 nodes were used in the simulation. As future work, we plan to better understand the causes of this error. In addition, we plan to: (a) evaluate the model with more applications, especially those that mix the use of distinct devices during their computation; and (b) use the model to choose the data partition and work assignment that minimizes the execution time of an application.

References

1. Alexandrov, A., Ionescu, M.F., Schauser, K.E., Scheiman, C.: LogGP: incorporating long messages into the logP model one step closer towards a realistic model for parallel computation. In: Proceedings of the seventh annual ACM symposium on Parallel algorithms and architectures, pp. 95–105. ACM (1995)
2. Bailey, D.H., Barszcz, E., Barton, J.T., Browning, D.S., Carter, R.L., Dagum, L., Fatoohi, R.A., Frederickson, P.O., Lasinski, T.A., Schreiber, R.S., et al.: The NAS parallel benchmarks. Int. J. High Perform. Comput. Appl. 5(3), 63–73 (1991)
3. Bosque, J.L., Pastor, L.: A parallel computational model for heterogeneous clusters. IEEE Trans. Parallel Distrib. Syst. 17(12), 1390 (2006)
4. Culler, D., Karp, R., Patterson, D., Sahay, A., Schauser, K.E., Santos, E., Subramonian, R., Von Eicken, T.: LogP: towards a realistic model of parallel computation, vol. 28. ACM (1993)
5. Doerfler, D., Brightwell, R.: Measuring MPI send and receive overhead and application availability in high performance network interfaces. In: Mohr, B., Träff, J.L., Worringen, J., Dongarra, J. (eds.) EuroPVM/MPI 2006. LNCS, vol. 4192, pp. 331–338. Springer, Heidelberg (2006). doi:10.1007/11846802_46
6. Holt, C., Heinrich, M., Singh, J.P., Rothberg, E., Hennessy, J.: The effects of latency, occupancy, and bandwidth in distributed shared memory multiprocessors. Stanford University, Computer Systems Laboratory (1995)
7. Kielmann, T., Bal, H.E., Verstoep, K.: Fast measurement of LogP parameters for message passing platforms. In: Rolim, J. (ed.) IPDPS 2000. LNCS, vol. 1800, pp. 1176–1183. Springer, Heidelberg (2000). doi:10.1007/3-540-45591-4_162

8. Lastovetsky, A., Mkwawa, I.H., O'Flynn, M.: An accurate communication model of a heterogeneous cluster based on a switch-enabled ethernet network. In: 12th International Conference on Parallel and Distributed Systems, ICPADS 2006, vol. 2, p. 6. IEEE (2006)

9. Lastovetsky, A., Rychkov, V.: Building the communication performance model of heterogeneous clusters based on a switched network. In: IEEE International Conference on Cluster Computing, 2007, pp. 568–575. IEEE (2007)

10. LeVeque, R.: Finite Difference Methods for Ordinary and Partial Differential Equations: Steady-State and Time-Dependent Problems (Classics in Applied Mathematics Classics in Applied Mathemat). Society for Industrial and Applied Mathematics, Philadelphia, PA, USA (2007)

11. Martin, R.P., Vahdat, A.M., Culler, D.E., Anderson, T.E.: Effects of communication latency, overhead, and bandwidth in a cluster architecture, vol. 25. ACM (1997)

12. Pigozzo, A.B., Macedo, G.C., Santos, R.W., Lobosco, M.: On the computational modeling of the innate immune system. BMC Bioinform. **14**(Suppl 6), S7 (2007)

13. Rocha, P.A.F., Xavier, M.P., Pigozzo, A.B., M. Quintela, B., Macedo, G.C., Santos, R.W., Lobosco, M.: A three-dimensional computational model of the innate immune system. In: Murgante, B., Gervasi, O., Misra, S., Nedjah, N., Rocha, A.M.A.C., Taniar, D., Apduhan, B.O. (eds.) ICCSA 2012. LNCS, vol. 7333, pp. 691–706. Springer, Heidelberg (2012). doi:10.1007/978-3-642-31125-3_52

14. Soares, T.M., Xavier, M.P., Pigozzo, A.B., Campos, R.S., Santos, R.W., Lobosco, M.: Performance evaluation of a human immune system simulator on a GPU cluster. In: Malyshkin, V. (ed.) PaCT 2015. LNCS, vol. 9251, pp. 458–468. Springer, Heidelberg (2015). doi:10.1007/978-3-319-21909-7_44

15. Valiant, L.G.: A bridging model for parallel computation. Commun. ACM **33**(8), 103–111 (1990)

Comparative Analysis of OpenACC Compilers

Daniel Barba$^{(\boxtimes)}$, Arturo Gonzalez-Escribano, and Diego R. Llanos

Departamento de Informatica, Universidad de Valladolid, Valladolid, Spain
{daniel,arturo,diego}@infor.uva.es

Abstract. OpenACC has been on development for a few years now. The OpenACC 2.5 specification was recently made public and there are some initiatives for developing full implementations of the standard to make use of accelerator capabilities. There is much to be done yet, but currently, OpenACC for GPUs is reaching a good maturity level in various implementations of the standard, using CUDA and OpenCL as backends. Nvidia is investing in this project and they have released an OpenACC Toolkit, including the PGI Compiler. There are, however, more developments out there. In this work, we analyze different available OpenACC compilers that have been developed by companies or universities during the last years. We check their performance and maturity, keeping in mind that OpenACC is designed to be used without extensive knowledge about parallel programming. Our results show that the compilers are on their way to a reasonable maturity, presenting different strengths and weaknesses.

1 Introduction

OpenACC is an open standard which defines a collection of compiler directives or pragmas for execution of code blocks on accelerators like GPUs or Xeon Phi coprocessors. OpenACC aims to reduce both the required learning time and the parallelization of sequential code in a portable way [1]. OpenACC specification is currently on its 2.5 version [2], which has been released recently.

OpenACC was founded by Nvidia, CRAY, CAPS and PGI, but now there is a large list of consortium members, both from the industry and academy, including the Oak Ridge National Laboratory, the University of Houston, AMD, and the Edinburgh Parallel Computing Centre (EPCC), among others. The Corporate Officers are, at the time of writing this paper, from Nvidia, Oak Ridge National Laboratory, CRAY and AMD. Academic memberships are available to interested institutions.

There are several compilers supporting OpenACC. The PGI Compiler (from the Portland Group, which is a subsidiary of Nvidia for some time now) is being

---

This research has been partially supported by MICINN (Spain) and ERDF program of the European Union: HomProg-HetSys project (TIN2014-58876-P), CAPAP-H5 network (TIN2014-53522-REDT), and COST Program Action IC1305: Network for Sustainable Ultrascale Computing (NESUS). Thanks also to Dr. Hector Ortega and Dr. Javier Fresno for their thoughtful comments, help, and encouragement.

© Springer International Publishing AG 2016
J. Carretero et al. (Eds.): ICA3PP 2016 Workshops, LNCS 10049, pp. 91–104, 2016.
DOI: 10.1007/978-3-319-49956-7_7

distributed as part of the Nvidia OpenACC Toolkit, under a free 90-day trial license, a free annual academic license, or a commercial license. The PGI Compiler uses CUDA or OpenCL as backend. CAPS enterprise, a provider of software and services for the High Performance Computing community, also developed a compiler which supports CUDA and OpenCL. However, the company is no longer in business and its development is not available anymore. CRAY Inc. has its own OpenACC compiler, available with their computers. It is reported to be one of the most mature commercial compilers. However, they have not yet offered an academic or trial license for the purposes of studies like this one. Pathscale Inc., a compiler and multicore software developer, also made an OpenACC implementation on their ENZO compiler. Unfortunately, after private communications they were reluctant to allow us to use their compiler for this study.

There are also several academic attempts of developing an OpenACC compiler. In particular, OpenUH [3] developed at the University of Houston, and accULL [4] from Universidad de La Laguna (Spain). Both of them are available for free to anyone interested.

This work presents a study about the level of support of OpenACC in the available compilers, examining their strengths and weaknesses, and giving insights on their performance.

We analyze the level of maturity of each compiler, in terms of their *completeness in the support of the standard* and *robustness*, using each compiler's documentation to check what parts of the specification have been implemented. We check the support of OpenACC compiler directives with the help of a benchmark suite, developed by the Edinburgh Parallel Computing Centre, which will be described later.

Another aspect to test is the *relative performance* of the generated code. For this, we would want to run more complex applications and measure the differences between the performance of the executable code generated by each compiler. The ideal situation would be to test applications as close to real world problems as possible, avoiding synthetic code fragments. Since the use of OpenACC is not common yet, we have to rely on existing benchmarks. At this point, comparing the results from OpenACC code with CUDA or OpenCL direct implementations might seem appropriate, but porting the different benchmarks to these languages makes the result dependent on human interference, as the developer's ability for CUDA programming impacts on the performance.

The experiments conducted in this work were carried out using several benchmarks. First, the EPCC benchmark suite which contains a group of 13 kernels ported to OpenACC, called "Level 1" benchmarks. This benchmark suite also contains three real applications called "Himeno", "27stencil", and "le_core" [5]. We have also used the Pathscale port of the Rodinia benchmark [6]. We also wanted to use the OpenACC Validation Testsuite [7] developed by the University of Houston, but at this moment that tool is only available for OpenACC members.

Our conclusion is that the different compilers are on their way to a reasonable maturity. However, there is a number of features not fully implemented yet by some of the compilers.

The rest of this paper is organized as follows. Section 2 describes the selected compilers. Section 3 shows the characteristics of the benchmark suites chosen, enumerating some problems encountered when compiling them with the compilers selected. Section 4 contains the result of our analysis, in terms of completeness of the OpenACC features supported, robustness of compiler implementations, and relative performance of the generated code. Finally, Sect. 5 concludes our paper.

2   Available Compilers

In the introduction we mentioned several compilers. In this section we describe with more detail the compilers we were able to obtain and use for this study, and we will discuss their installation particularities on our Linux based platform.

2.1   PGI Compiler

The PGI Compiler [8] is being developed by The Portland Group, being owned by Nvidia. This compiler is widely used in webinars, workshops, and conferences.

The PGI Compiler is, at the time of writing this paper, available for download as part of the OpenACC Toolkit from Nvidia. This toolkit includes a 90-day free trial, the possibility of acquiring an academic license for a whole year, or buying a commercial license.

2.2   accULL

The accULL [4] compiler developed by Universidad of La Laguna (Spain) is an open source initiative. accULL consists on a structure of two layers containing YaCF [9] (Yet another Compiler Framework) and Frangollo [10], a runtime library. YaCF acts as a source-to-source translator while Frangollo works as an interface providing the most common operations found in accelerators.

2.3   OpenUH

The OpenUH [3] compiler, developed by the University of Houston (USA) is another open source initiative. It makes use of Open64, a discontinued opensource optimizing compiler.

3   Benchmark Description

This section describes the different benchmarks used in our work, enumerating the main characteristics that make them interesting for this study, and any issue detected during their compilation with the three compilers studied.

3.1   EPCC OpenACC Benchmarks

This benchmark suite [11] has been developed by the Edinburgh Parallel Computing Centre (EPCC). The benchmarks are divided in three categories: "Level 0", "Level 1" and "Applications". The compiled program launches all the benchmarks in the suite sequentially. By default, the number of repetitions is ten, and the result is the average for each benchmark. Time is measured in microseconds in double precision, using the OpenMP function omp_get_wtime(). We describe briefly the benchmarks included bellow:

Level 0. Level 0 includes a collection of small benchmarks that execute single host and accelerator operations, such as memory transfers.

Level 1. Level 1 benchmarks [12] consist on a series of BLAS-type kernels. They are based on Polybench [13] and Polybench/GPU kernels. They measure the performance of executing those codes. These benchmarks are run on the CPU first in order to have results to compare those obtained on the GPU.

A brief description of the different issues found while running this suite for these compilers follows.

OpenUH: The following benchmarks cannot be compiled due to unsupported pragmas present in their code:

kernels_if: Problems using #pragma kernels if(0).
parallel_private: Problems declaring params as private.
parallel_firstprivate: Problems declaring params as firstprivate.
le_core: Problems with non scalar pointers.
himeno: Problems with non scalar pointers.

accULL: There is a problem related to a function pointer in the host program. The compiler, during the source to source translation modifies the syntax of the function pointer. A double (*test)(void) is converted to a double *(test(void)). This was solved by manually correcting this change in the intermediate C code generated, re-compiling the object file and copying it to the main directory to link all the object files again. No warning from any of the pragmas was detected so we were able to run all the benchmarks.

3.2   Rodinia OpenACC

Rodinia is a benchmark suite for heterogeneous computing [14,15]. It includes applications and kernels for multicore CPU or GPU applications.

There is an effort to port existing Rodinia benchmarks for OpenACC. Pathscale [6] is working on this. We have tested their Rodinia version committed to GitHub on April 25, 2014. Most of the suite works with PGI, but OpenUH and accULL have many problems to compile most of the tests. We have been able to successfully compile the following benchmarks contained in the suite with two or more compilers: gaussian, nw, lud, cfd, hotspot, pathfinder, and srad2.

4 Evaluation

In this section we analyze the OpenACC compilers, using both documentation and experimentation. We use each compiler's documentation to check the *completeness of OpenACC features supported*. Then we use the EPCC benchmarks to check both *robustness* and *relative performance*. Finally we check *thread-block size sensibility*, measuring the impact on performance of different geometries.

4.1 Experimental Setup

We used a Nvidia GTX Titan Black to run the experiments. This GPU contains 2880 CUDA cores with a clock rate of 980 Mhz and 15 SMs. It has 6 GB of RAM, and Compute Capability 3.5. The host is a Xeon E5-2690v3 with 12 cores at a clock rate of 1.9 GHz, and 64 GB in four 12 GB modules.

The PGI compiler is the one contained in the Nvidia OpenACC Toolkit, version 15.7-0, published in Jul 13, 2015. We used OpenUH version 3.1.0 (published in November 4, 2015), based on Open64 version 5.0 and using GCC 4.2.0, prebuilt, downloaded from the High Performance Computing Tools group website [16]. accULL is version 0.4alpha (published in November 28, 2013), downloaded from Universidad de La Laguna's research group "Computación de Altas Prestaciones" [17].

4.2 Completeness of OpenACC Features Supported

From each compiler documentation we get some insight on the completeness of the OpenACC features supported. From this information, we can conclude that the OpenACC standard is not fully implemented yet by any of the available compilers. There is work to be done, but the three compilers are at a respectable maturity level.

4.3 Robustness and Pragma Implementation

The EPCC Benchmark suite contains several benchmarks for testing OpenACC directives. These benchmarks are contained in the "Level 0" group, which has been described in the previous section. Table 1 contains the results obtained for the three compilers. In this section we enumerate the problems with each benchmark and we explain the results obtained, including the overhead of the different pragma implementations.

Except for *Update_host*, *Kernels_Invoc.*, and *Parallel_Invoc.*, the time shown is the difference between executing and not executing each pragma. When the overhead is zero (or the pragma is not implemented), the times are very similar, with minimal stochastic variation. These variations may produce a very small negative result when calculating the difference. When differences in time are on the order of tens of microseconds (positive or negative), it can be assumed that there is no difference in time between the different versions tested in that benchmark.

Table 1. EPCC level 0: directive's overhead (in μsec), 1 MB dataset

EPCC L0	PGI	OpenUH	accULL
Kernels_if	−37.50	Fail	4.54
Parallel_if	−30.76	−0.48	1237.02
Parallel_private	−21.94	Fail	51.09
Parallel_1stpriv	Fail	Fail	−213.83
Kernels_comb.	−1.67	−108.43	−127.17
Parallel_comb.	−0.05	−2.74	33.38
Update_host	478.63	373.22	548.77
Kernels_Invoc.	Fail	12.76	2398.20
Parallel_Invoc.	31.81	13.47	1377.88
Parallel_reduct.	−14.85	−164.41	−2168.12
Kernels_reduct	−8.49	−172.31	−2009.11

PGI. There was a problem with the "Kernels_Invocation" benchmark: It returned an incorrect result. The code was not being parallelized and the pragmas were ignored because it wasn't specifically stated that the iterations were independent. This could be solved adding the keyword restrict to the pointer or the clause independent to the pragma.

The "kernels_if" and "parallel_if" results are very similar, and in both cases the results indicate that the code with the pragma is slightly faster than the one without it, even though both are being run on the host. In [5] it was stated that this could be because of optimizations done by the compiler while or after processing the pragmas.

The "parallel_private" benchmark shows that the creation of private variables for each thread running the loop is slightly faster than the allocation of device memory.

"Kernels_combined" shows a very small difference of time between writing two pragmas instead of a combined one, the former being slightly faster than the latter although the difference is almost negligible. The same occurs for the "parallel_combined" benchmark, the difference being smaller in this case.

Finally "Parallel_reduction" and "Kernels_reduction" show that PGI has very little overhead for the reduction clause. In [5] it is stated that the PGI compiler does the reduction even if it is not annotated. This could explain the very small difference in both benchmarks.

OpenUH. We got some errors during compilation of the "Kernels_if", "Parallel_private" and "Parallel_1stprivate" benchmarks so they are ignored in this analysis. However, the "Parallel_if" directive is supported and the difference between using the pragma to run code on the host or running it directly is almost negligible.

"Kernels-combined" shows an overhead of the combined pragma versus the separated version. However, this is not the case for the "Parallel-combined" benchmark, where the difference is much smaller. The invocation of kernels and parallel directives are very similar. And for both of them, the reduction adds a similar overhead. This might be related to OpenUH assuming loops to be independent inside kernels regions.

accULL. No errors were shown while compiling or running the benchmarks with accULL. There is a big difference between the two versions contained in the "Kernels-if" and the "Parallel-if" benchmarks, where the kernels directive version has a very small overhead compared to the non-annotated code. This overhead is very large in the parallel directive version. This is explained by the accULL developers in [5] where they say that the absence of a loop clause in the parallel directive is causing the loop to be executed sequentially in each thread. Therefore, this clause is not correctly supported, as we understand from the OpenACC Specification that the loop should be executed only on the host.

Robustness Summary. The overall results indicate that some of the clauses are not implemented yet, but the three compilers are in their way to a reasonable maturity level and, since the most used directives are working, they can actually be used for code parallelization using OpenACC.

4.4   Relative Performance of Generated Code

In this section we analyze the performance of the generated code describing the impact of pragmas overhead in accULL. Performance measurement is divided into *data movement*, where we analyze the results of the data movement benchmarks in Level 0 of EPCC OpenACC Benchmark Suite, and *execution performance*, using Level 1 and Application Level of EPCC OpenACC Benchmark Suite, and selected benchmarks from Rodinia.

Effect of Pragmas Overhead in accULL. Some results from the Level 0 of the EPCC Benchmark Suite show a performance impact introduced by some clauses and directives in the accULL generated code.

Kernels and Parallel invocations in accULL have a higher overhead than other compilers. This is due to the runtime calls and it is specially noticeable in the reduction clause. These overheads accumulation does not have a significant impact for complex kernels, or launching the same kernel over and over again. However, this could be a problem when running simple kernels or many different small kernels. This is the main reason behind the overall results showing a worse performance of the accULL compiler in this analysis.

Data Movement. Data movement performance can be measured in four benchmarks from the Level 0 of the EPCC OpenACC benchmark suite. We have

Table 2. EPCC data movement results (in μsec), 1 kB dataset. White cells highlight the best results. *norm.* is the normalized result using PGI as reference.

Data Mvmnt	PGI		OpenUH		accULL	
10reps, 1kB	time	norm.	time	norm.	time	norm.
ContigH2D	30.827	1.0	322.699	10.47	338.218	10.97
ContigD2H	14.686	1.0	323.319	22.01	343.919	23.42
SlicedH2D	12.087	1.0	310.897	25.72	315.914	26.13
SlicedD2H	14.948	1.0	324.010	21.67	327.714	21.92
			GeoMean	18.93	GeoMean	19.58

Table 3. EPCC data movement results (in μsec), 1 MB dataset. White cells highlight the best results. *norm.* is the normalized result using PGI as reference.

Data Mvmnt	PGI		OpenUH		accULL	
10reps, 1MB	time	norm.	time	norm.	time	norm.
ContigH2D	484.347	1.0	950.789	1.96	727.839	1.50
ContigD2H	461.936	1.0	632.691	1.37	792.761	1.72
SlicedH2D	17.094	1.0	267.982	15.68	274.462	16.06
SlicedD2H	36.335	1.0	254.702	7.01	285.685	7.86
			GeoMean	4.14	GeoMean	4.24

Table 4. EPCC data movement results (in μsec), 10 MB dataset. White cells highlight the best results. *norm.* is the normalized result using PGI as reference.

Data Mvmnt	PGI		OpenUH		accULL	
10reps, 10MB	time	norm.	time	norm.	time	norm.
ContigH2D	4141.402	1.0	6887.984	1.66	3354.666	0.81
ContigD2H	5876.088	1.0	2043.747	0.35	4396.052	0.74
SlicedH2D	27.322	1.0	404.214	14.79	427.203	15.64
SlicedD2H	48.017	1.0	269.818	5.62	280.203	5.84
			GeoMean	2.64	GeoMean	2.72

Table 5. EPCC data movement results (in μsec), 1 GB dataset. White cells highlight the best results. *norm.* is the normalized result using PGI as reference.

Data Mvmnt	PGI		OpenUH		accULL	
10reps, 1GB	time	norm.	time	norm.	time	norm.
ContigH2D	32310.009	1.0	788945.913	24.42	296340.991	9.17
ContigD2H	55179.119	1.0	553282.976	10.03	347280.359	6.29
SlicedH2D	400.066	1.0	535.011	1.34	533.943	1.34
SlicedD2H	158.071	1.0	2818.100	17.83	4294.407	27.17
			GeoMean	8.75	GeoMean	6.76

launched 10 repetitions of those benchmarks with datasizes of 1 kB, 1 MB, 10 MB, and 1 GB. The results can be seen in Tables 2, 3, 4, and 5.

In [5] it was stated that PGI used pinned memory and that it was causing issues in smaller datasets. It seems that PGI has solved this issue since then and, looking at the documentation, it is now possible to specify the type of memory access we want with a compilation flag. When using large datasets, OpenUH and accULL do not show the expected results according to the evolution shown in Tables 2, 3, and 4. We guess that this is related to the usage of pinned memory by the PGI Compiler, allowing it to obtain better results when datasets are big enough.

Table 6. EPCC execution results (in μsec), 1 kB dataset. White cells highlight the best results.

Exec. time	PGI		OpenUH		accULL	
10reps, 1kB	time	norm.	time	norm.	time	norm.
2MM	99.087	1.0	522.304	5.27	2799.229	28.25
3MM	80.204	1.0	380.683	4.75	3799.048	47.37
ATAX	58.103	1.0	327.110	5.63	2564.702	44.14
BICG	72.408	1.0	350.380	4.84	2628.499	36.30
MVT	80.037	1.0	354.743	4.43	2665.299	33.30
SYRK	68.426	1.0	289.512	4.23	2394.803	35.00
COV	87.261	1.0	314.617	3.61	3795.372	43.49
COR	104.976	1.0	337.362	3.21	5208.668	49.62
SYR2K	73.290	1.0	317.574	4.33	2469.765	33.70
GESUMMV	65.613	1.0	312.996	4.77	1500.021	22.86
GEMM	49.710	1.0	323.725	6.51	1237.473	24.89
2DCONV	46.444	1.0	286.174	6.16	1207.528	26.00
3DCONV	45.514	1.0	285.792	6.28	1202.494	26.42
27S	335.884	1.0	432.801	1.29	3273.728	9.75
LE2D	6842374	1.0	*	*	*	*
HIMENO	547939	1.0	*	*	*	*
			GeoMean	4.39	GeoMean	24.38

Execution Performance, EPCC Benchmarks. In this section we will analyze the performance of the code generated by the PGI, OpenUH, and accULL compilers with the benchmarks contained in the EPCC Level 1 and Application level. We use three different datasets: 1 kB, 1 MB, and 10 MB. This choice is based on the fact that bigger datasets result in an out of memory error due to how the benchmarks try to allocate memory on the device. We suspect the memory allocation is being done in each thread inside the generated kernels, using more memory than expected. In summary, PGI code obtains better results in almost every benchmark. However, the differences shorten when using bigger datasets.

For datasets of 1kB the results can be seen in Table 6. Benchmarks that fail to execute with a specific compiler are shown with an asterisk in the table. PGI code shows a very good performance, followed by the OpenUH code, which also behaves quite good. accULL is showing slightly worse results because it is paying a high price in overhead for loading kernels in memory for the first time while this operation is not required for subsequent kernel calls, or it is less noticeable on complex kernels where computation is more time consuming. This situation makes it very hard to compete with other compilers for such small and simple problems. This issue is less noticeable with bigger datasets.

When using the default dataset size of 1 MB, we can see in Table 7 that the differences between PGI and the rest are smaller than when a dataset of 1 kB was used. The increment of time due to the increment of dataset size for these benchmarks is more noticeable for the PGI compiler and, to a lesser extent, for

Table 7. EPCC execution results (in μsec), 1 MB dataset. White cells highlight the best results.

Exec. time	PGI		OpenUH		accULL	
10reps, 1MB	time	norm.	time	norm.	time	norm.
2MM	2305.698	1.0	3467.703	1.50	4002.412	1.74
3MM	705.409	1.0	1453.137	2.06	5265.778	7.46
ATAX	484.204	1.0	1222.420	2.52	4212.914	8.70
BICG	502.849	1.0	1256.871	2.50	4229.466	8.41
MVT	538.135	1.0	*	*	4355.322	8.09
SYRK	1374.769	1.0	2543.616	1.85	4000.674	2.91
COV	3681.660	1.0	4251.957	1.15	23969.443	6.51
COR	3863.096	1.0	4318.953	1.12	25732.814	6.66
SYR2K	1968.789	1.0	2532.029	1.29	4586.741	2.37
GESUMMV	406.623	1.0	1195.669	2.94	2709.591	6.66
GEMM	1041.651	1.0	23642.850	22.70	3595.218	3.45
2DCONV	1637.363	1.0	1912.236	1.17	2991.542	1.83
3DCONV	9388.137	1.0	9670.520	1.03	10058.497	1.07
27S	2179.599	1.0	2224.064	1.02	8342.865	3.83
LE2D	6861089	1.0	*	*	*	*
HIMENO	540513	1.0	*	*	*	*
			GeoMean	1.92	GeoMean	4.11

OpenUH. accULL results are very similar to the results obtained with the first dataset of 1 kB. Notice the results obtained for the GEMM benchmark with OpenUH, which is probably being executed sequentially.

For datasets of 10 MB, the results can be seen in Table 8. Some benchmarks, for example "2MM" and "GEMM", need unexpected amounts of time. Running the accULL generated code for 2MM requires one third of the time required by PGI and OpenUH codes. The GEMM benchmark shows a huge execution time, probably for the reason described in the previous paragraph.

The 27 stencil application is the only benchmark in the application level that compiles and runs successfully with all the compilers. It is a representative application of stencil codes that uses a three-dimensional neighbour synchronization pattern. Thus, it is a good representative of a well-known class of applications. In Fig. 1a we show the execution times obtained for this application in the chosen platform. The results show that one of the compilers cannot produce an efficient implementation. However, as it is shown in Fig. 1b, all compilers can derive similar solutions for simpler 3-dimensional stencil codes, as the 3DCONV benchmark of level one.

Execution Performance, Rodinia. Regarding Rodinia, We should remark that the compilation presented some problems and there was a very limited amount of compiled benchmarks to choose from. The performance results can be seen in Tables 9 and 10. Only the Gaussian benchmark reports results for

Table 8. EPCC execution results (in msec), 10 MB dataset. White cells highlight the best results.

Exec. time	PGI		OpenUH		accULL	
10reps, 10MB	time	norm.	time	norm.	time	norm.
2MM	64.407	1.0	64.336	0.99	20.476	0.32
3MM	11.610	1.0	21.113	1.82	30.009	2.58
ATAX	4.345	1.0	7.415	1.71	7.659	1.76
BICG	4.385	1.0	7.397	1.69	7.689	1.75
MVT	4.406	1.0	*	*	7.945	1.80
SYRK	26.537	1.0	57.242	2.16	42.834	1.61
COV	117.757	1.0	134.047	1.14	230.241	1.96
COR	120.612	1.0	122.814	1.02	223.836	1.86
SYR2K	23.450	1.0	27.939	1.16	30.062	1.28
GESUMMV	3.567	1.0	7.191	2.02	6.297	1.77
GEMM	17.788	1.0	239.713	13.48	48.567	2.73
2DCONV	7.848	1.0	7.725	0.98	8.687	1.11
3DCONV	40.551	1.0	40.235	0.99	43.729	1.08
27S	9.243	1.0	9.254	1.00	42.389	4.59
LE2D	6863	1.0	*	*	*	*
HIMENO	528	1.0	*	*	*	*
			GeoMean	1.59	GeoMean	1.63

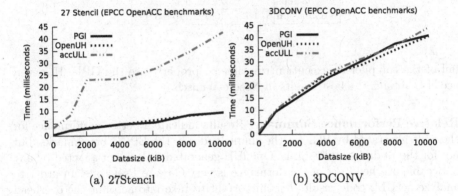

(a) 27Stencil   (b) 3DCONV

Fig. 1. Execution results (in msec).

execution time including and not including memory transfers. Benchmarks that fail to compile with specific compilers are shown with an asterisk in the table.

Here we can see how the code produced by PGI is not behaving as we would expect from the results obtained from the EPCC benchmark suite. PGI code is taking a lot of time in data transfer operations, while OpenUH code is not expending so much time in those operations. We discovered that the EPCC Benchmark Suite runs a function which contains an OpenACC pragma in order to make sure that the accelerator device is awake when the real benchmarks are run. This does not happen in Rodinia where the first OpenACC section is the data movement pragma. PGI generated code needs more than two seconds to set up the accelerator device, whereas OpenUH and accULL don't need that time. Beside this, accULL code is having some trouble running Gaussian as the time is not being spent in data transfer operations, but inside the generated kernels. We suspect that they might be executing sequential code in the host, due to a

Table 9. Rodinia execution time results including memory transfers. Total time (in msec). White cells highlight the best results.

Exec. time 3 reps	PGI	OpenUH	accULL
gaussian	2440.206	52.491	15422.944
nw	2640.497	652.180	322.101
lud	3803.756	1723.576	*
cfd	2677.387	0.846	*
hotspot	2386.325	53.219	*
pathfinder	5137.865	34.738	*
srad2	2488.895	692.063	*

Table 10. Rodinia execution results. Kernel time (in msec) not including memory transfers. White cells highlight the best results.

Kernel time 3 reps	PGI	OpenUH	accULL
Gaussian	57.345	36.092	15415.992

fail of the compiler or execution run-time to properly use the GPU. However, accULL obtains the best results in Needle-Wunsch.

Relative Performance Summary. Results indicate a better performance for the code generated by PGI for the simple codes in the EPCC benchmarks, but not for the Rodinia applications. OpenUH generated code is not affected by any noticeable overhead and its performance is very close to PGI code. In order to analyze accULL code results it is important to take into account the overhead produced by kernel loading operations. If a bigger input set was used, results could be much better, but due to limitations on benchmark implementation this was not possible at this time.

5   Conclusions

During this work, we have realized that both the OpenACC standard and its compiler implementations are in their way to a reasonable maturity level. Although many details are still not completely developed, the efforts to arrive at a solid implementation are promising. Nvidia and PGI are devoting many resources to this project, and this results in a very competitive and solid compiler. However, open-source alternatives are also on a good position. OpenUH and accULL, being academic implementations, are also very interesting and show a huge amount of work done by their creators.

Regarding completeness of OpenACC features, according to each compiler's documentation, we find that none of them fully support the standard. This was expected as all of them are still not totally mature.

Speaking about robustness and pragma implementation, PGI shows the best behaviour, as the errors detected were related to implementation issues of the benchmark codes instead of a compiler problem. Compared to the others, the overhead of the implementation is smaller and it even includes some optimizations when processing pragmas that are going to be executed in the host.

Finally, the performance comparison we have made shows better results for PGI, but the other alternatives have also shown their strengths. It would also be interesting to run this performance analysis on several machines and different GPUs in order to also observe the differences of the execution of the generated code in different hardware, and this is part of our future work. The lack of OpenACC benchmark suites makes it very difficult to try different problems or datasizes. Our work shows that there is a need for real application codes annotated with OpenACC pragmas to test the actual potential of the current compiler implementation, as many articles before [5,18,19] have stated. This is part of our current and future work.

References

1. OpenACC-standard.org, About OpenACC
2. OpenACC-Standard.org, The OpenACC application programming interface version 2.5, October 2015
3. Tian, X., Xu, R., Yan, Y., Yun, Z., Chandrasekaran, S., Chapman, B.: Compiling a high-level directive-based programming model for GPGPUs. In: Caşcaval, C., Montesinos, P. (eds.) LCPC 2013. LNCS, vol. 8664, pp. 105–120. Springer, Heidelberg (2014). doi:10.1007/978-3-319-09967-5_6
4. Reyes, R., López-Rodríguez, I., Fumero, J.J., Sande, F.: accULL: an OpenACC implementation with CUDA and OpenCL support. In: Kaklamanis, C., Papatheodorou, T., Spirakis, P.G. (eds.) Euro-Par 2012. LNCS, vol. 7484, pp. 871–882. Springer, Heidelberg (2012). doi:10.1007/978-3-642-32820-6_86
5. Grillo, L., de Sande, F., Reyes, R.: Performance evaluation of OpenACC compilers. In: 2014 22nd Euromicro International Conference on Parallel, Distributed and Network-Based Processing (PDP), pp. 656–663, February 2014
6. Pathscale, Rodinia benchmark suite 2.1 with OpenACC port, April 2014. https://github.com/pathscale/rodinia
7. Wang, C., Xu, R., Chandrasekaran, S., Chapman, B., Hernandez, O.: A validation testsuite for OpenACC 1.0. In: 2014 IEEE International Parallel Distributed Processing Symposium Workshops (IPDPSW), pp. 1407–1416, May 2014
8. PGI, Pgi accelerator compilers with OpenACC directives. https://www.pgroup.com/resources/accel.htm, November 2015
9. Universidad de La Laguna: YaCF, November 2015. https://bitbucket.org/ruyman/llcomp
10. Universidad de La Laguna: Frangollo, November 2015. https://bitbucket.org/ruyman/frangollo
11. EPCC, Epcc OpenACC benchmark suite, September 2013. https://github.com/EPCCed/epcc-openacc-benchmarks
12. Grauer-Gray, S., Xu, L., Searles, R., Ayalasomayajula, S., Cavazos, J.: Auto-tuning a high-level language targeted to GPU codes. In: 2012 Innovative Parallel Computing (InPar), pp. 1–10. IEEE (2012)

13. Pouchet, L.-N.: Polybench: the polyhedral benchmark suite, July 2012. http://www.cs.ucla.edu/~pouchet/software/polybench/

14. Che, S., Boyer, M., Meng, J., Tarjan, D., Sheaffer, J.W., Lee, S.-H., Skadron, K.: Rodinia: a benchmark suite for heterogeneous computing. In: 2009 IEEE International Symposium on Workload Characterization (IISWC 2009), pp. 44–54. IEEE (2009)

15. Che, S., Sheaffer, J.W., Boyer, M., Szafaryn, L.G., Wang, L., Skadron, K.: A characterization of the Rodinia benchmark suite with comparison to contemporary CMP workloads. In: 2010 IEEE International Symposium on Workload Characterization (IISWC), pp. 1–11. IEEE (2010)

16. University of Houston, Open-source UH compiler, November 2015. http://web.cs.uh.edu/~openuh/download/

17. Universidad de La Laguna, accULL, November 2015. http://cap.pcg.ull.es/es/accULL

18. Wienke, S., Springer, P., Terboven, C., Mey, D.: OpenACC — first experiences with real-world applications. In: Kaklamanis, C., Papatheodorou, T., Spirakis, P.G. (eds.) Euro-Par 2012. LNCS, vol. 7484, pp. 859–870. Springer, Heidelberg (2012). doi:10.1007/978-3-642-32820-6_85

19. Hart, A., Ansaloni, R., Gray, A.: Porting and scaling OpenACC applications on massively-parallel, GPU-accelerated supercomputers. Eur. Phys. J. Spec. Top. **210**(1), 5–16 (2012)

BigTrust 2016: The 1st International Workshop on Trust, Security and Privacy for Big Data

The Research of Recommendation System Based on User-Trust Mechanism and Matrix Decomposition

PanPan Zhang[✉] and Bin Jiang

College of Computer Science and Engineering,
Hunan University, Changsha, China
994771093@qq.com, jiangbin@hnu.edu.cn

Abstract. Recommendation system is a tool that can help users quickly and effectively obtain useful resources in the face of the large amounts of information. Collaborative filtering is a widely used recommendation technology which recommends source for users through similar neighbors' scores, but is faced with the problem of data sparseness and "cold start". Although recommendation system based on trust model can solve the above problems to some extent, but still need further improvement to its coverage. To solve these problems, the paper proposes a matrix decomposition algorithm mixed with user trust mechanism (hereinafter referred to as UTMF), The algorithm uses matrix decomposition to fill the score matrix, and combine trust rating information of users in the filling process. According to the results of experiment using the E-opinions Data set, UTMF algorithm can improve the precision of the recommended, effectively ease the cold start problem.

Keywords: Cold start · Data sparseness · UTMF · Trust mechanism

1 Introduction

With the development of Internet information technology, recommendation system of information filtering is becoming more and more important and attractive. It is a specific type of information filtering technology, try to recommend items that users might be interested in to them, including movies, books, music, news, web pages, images, etc. The typical filtering recommendation system is base on coordination algorithm which can recommend by analyzing the similar users and items. Although recommendation system has been widely studied, many problems still block its development, such as cold start and data sparseness. Traditional recommendation system ignores the trust relationship between users, in fact, users are more likely to focus on their friends' choose, so the traditional recommendation system is not able to fully excavate the information of the user-item matrix, and will not produce realistic recommend results.

© Springer International Publishing AG 2016
J. Carretero et al. (Eds.): ICA3PP 2016 Workshops, LNCS 10049, pp. 107–114, 2016.
DOI: 10.1007/978-3-319-49956-7_8

2   Related Literature

With the rapid development of Internet technology, the recommendation system [1] is widely used in the online network platform. Collaborative filtering [2] is one of the most widely used recommendation technology, whose method just depends on the user history score, to calculate users' similarity and then predict every item's rating according to their nearest neighbors, to generate user's target recommendation. In recent years, in order to improve the performance of this algorithm, Zhou [3, 4] using the knowledge of the physical dynamics, put forward recommendation algorithm based on substance diffusion. LIU [5] also introduced the concept of material diffusion dynamics into the collaborative filtering algorithm. The accuracy of these kinds of algorithm is much better than the classical collaborative filtering algorithms; hence significantly improving the accuracy of recommendation results. However, these methods encounter date sparsity, cold start and other issues.

In order to make up for the inadequacy of previously developed algorithms, recommendation system [6, 7] based on the trust model arose. At present, the implementation of trust mechanisms in recommendation systems is still under further research. TidalTrust [8] used a modified breadth-first method to calculate trust between users. Other literature introduced by MoleTrust [9], which is similar to TidalTrust algorithm but calculates trust propagation distance from the source user to target users first. This kind of algorithm makes recommendation through calculating the trust value between source user and target users in the user trust network. These approaches can explain recommendation more reasonable, plays an important role in overcoming the data sparsity and easing the cold start problem and improve the accuracy. However, the method still needs further improvement.

In fact, in the recommendation system based on trust, the source user and the neighbors they trust tend to share their interests. The researchers found that trust relationship among has a strong positive correlation with the user's preference, this method can effectively reduce the the error of the recommendation. RAY and Mahanti [10] put forward that, deleting neighbors whose trust value is below the present threshold and getting a new trust network can improve the recommendation accuracy, but at the expense of the coverage. According to the above problem in previous methods, this paper proposes a new recommendation algorithm based on trust mechanism-UserTrust matrix decomposition algorithm (UTMF).

3   The UTMF Method

3.1   Matrix Decomposition

Matrix decomposition is a way that decompose a matrix into two or more matrix, then multiply them into a new matrix. It can effectively relieve the data sparseness.

$$R_{m \times n} \approx U_{m \times k} \cdot I_{k \times n} = R'_{m \times n} \tag{1}$$

R represents User-Item matrix, U represents User-Factor matrix, I represents Factor-Item matrix and R' represents new predict matrix.

Different values of k makes a different prediction of score matrix and different error with real matrix.

3.2   Loss Function

This is needed to calculate the differences between R and matrix UV, and also minimize the difference.

$$E = \min\left(\sum_{i=1}^{m}\sum_{j=1}^{n}(R_{ij} - U_i^T V_j)^2\right) \tag{2}$$

3.3   The Introduction of the Regularization

The method function experiences a problem when decomposing our matrix whereby the sparsity of the original score matrix is too big, making it difficult to resist the excessive fitting problem i.e. accommodating some wrong remote values lead to the entire model's error. Therefore, through adding a regularization in the objective function to avoid over fitting problem i.e., in the objective function, using a factor vector.

$$L = \sum_{i=1}^{n}\sum_{j=1}^{m}(R_{ij} - U_i^T V_j)^2 + \lambda_1||U_i||^2 + \lambda_2||V_j||^2 \tag{3}$$

λ_1 is the user factor regularization parameter vector, λ_2 is the project factor regularization parameter vector.

3.4   The Regularization Parameters

When the data error level is unknown, the function can determine the regular parameter according to the proposed optimum criterion. The basic idea is: make the regular parameters and the solution of the rate of change of the parameters and stability level as small as possible; using the quasi optimum method for calculating the principles as follows:

$$\alpha_{opt} = \min_{\alpha > 0}\left\{\left\|\alpha\frac{dx^\alpha}{d\alpha}\right\|\right\} \tag{4}$$

The calculation method of λ_1 and λ_2 is same to α_{opt}.

3.5   Into the User's Trust Mechanism

In order to minimize the loss function, we introduce the trust mechanism based on the vector and trust of users in the collection project score vector error analysis.

Finally, after plus penalty factor into the basis of loss function, form new loss measurement strategy. The benefit is that the method procedure fully considers the influence of similar users in the iterative process method, and while reducing the influence of non-affiliated users. This means it can improve the speed and accuracy of matrix decomposition to a certain extent.

Therefore, the new loss function is as follows:

$$L = \sum_{i=1}^{n} \sum_{j=1}^{m} (R_{ij} - U_i^T V_j)^2 + \lambda_1 ||U_i||^2 + \lambda_2 ||V_j||^2 + \sum_{d \in S^i} \beta T_{id}(U_i - U_d)^2 \qquad (5)$$

β is penalty factor, S^i is the trusted collection of user, and T_{id} is the user's trust value.

3.6 Iterative Optimization

We use gradient descent algorithm to optimize iterations, whereby the negative gradient direction is used to decide the direction of each iteration, so that each iteration can be made to optimize the objective function through gradual reductions.

$$\Delta U_i = \frac{\partial L}{\partial U_i}, \ \Delta V_j = \frac{\partial L}{\partial V_j} \qquad (6)$$

$$U_i^{t+1} = U_i^t - \alpha \Delta U, \ V_j^{t+1} = V_j^t - \alpha \Delta V \qquad (7)$$

t represents iteration times.

4 The Experimental Simulation and Analysis

In order to verify the algorithm proposed in this paper, experiment(s) are conducted with a E-opinions real data sets; subdivided into 80% training and 20% testing respectively. The main components of each experiment include: (1) The determination of the number of potential factors in matrix decomposition; (2) UTMF algorithm results; (3) Comparison with other algorithms performance.

4.1 Experimental Data Set

This experiment used data from a real data in the E-opinions. The data represents users expression of their opinions from a website environment whereby, the site allows users to comment on products such as movies, books, software, etc. In the website, users can rate products with scores ranging from 1 to 5 points and also at the same time, they can also make trust rating to other users i.e. trust is 1 and converse is 0. The data set includes 49,290 users against 39,738 different products; at least having a score. A total of 664,824 grades were done, and users trust between scores being 487,181.

4.2   The Experimental Setup and Results

Determination of the number of hidden factor in matrix decomposition:

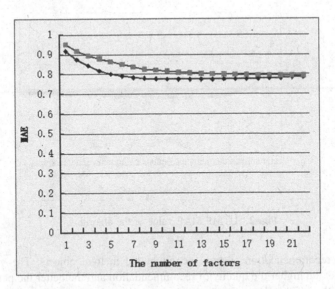

Fig. 1. MAE changes along with the potential factors

In collaborative filtering we usually assume that some users, or some items belongs to a type, and then use type to recommend. Here, we can also assume that class, or factor. We assume that the user has a certain degree of 'being fond of' to a particular factor, and items has certain degrees of 'contains' to a particular factor. The analysis diagram showing the results suggest that, with the increase in the number of potential factors, the MAE value is fast falling down to a minimum value and then rise again; The minimum value of potential factor is different according to different datasets. This is because the potential factors which influence the users' choice are fixed. When decomposition dimension is too small, it leads to smaller prediction precision. When Matrix decomposition dimension is too large, the uncorrelated noise was introduced, making the prediction accuracy smaller (Fig. 1).

When the number of iterations nears 30, the MAE's value is lowest which is between 0.772 to 0.775. Otherwise, when the number of iterations more than 40, it begins to show over-fitting phenomenon (Fig. 2).

4.3   UTMF Algorithm's Performances

Below is a table showing performances of UTMF algorithm and other algorithms performance comparison under the E-opinions datasets. It shows the values of MAE and the RC (Rate of Coverage) values of UTMF algorithm. The smaller MAE value shows that the algorithm accuracy is higher; and the RC value indicates the proportion

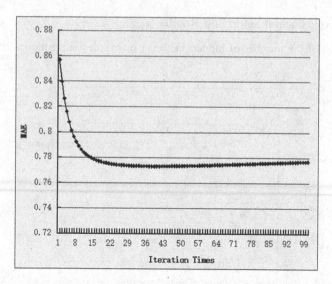

Fig. 2. UTMF MAE value of the algorithm

that objects recommendation system recommended in total objects. The greater the coverage rate, the higher the quality of recommendation and the better the performance of our algorithm (Table 1).

From the experimental results, it can be concluded that the collaborative filtering algorithm based on substance diffusion has greatly improved accuracy than collaborative filtering algorithm.

Algorithm based on user trust relationship solves the problem of cold start when it improves the algorithm's accuracy to some extent. Therefore, the trust mechanism in the decomposition of matrix can make use of the user's trust rating information to enrich the available data and also improve the reliability of recommendation system, which can further improve the system ability to alleviate cold start problems. Comparison experiments' results shows that the UTMF algorithm's performance for all users and cold start users' accuracy rate is 7.0% and 5.0% higher than the MT3 algorithm. Also, the coverage to all users and cold start users increased by 13.0%, 36.3% than the MT3.

Table 1. E-opinions the experimental results of RC and MAE.

Algorithm	MAE		RC	
	All Users	Cold Users	All Users	Cold Users
UCF	0.860	1.063	51.26	3.22
MD-UCF	0.765	0.946	52.35	3.86
MT1	0.839	0.853	27.34	8.81
MT2	0.849	0.886	59.06	23.54
MT3	0.831	0.829	73.03	41.72
UTMF	0.773	0.788	82.55	56.87

4.4   Main Program Code

```
for m = 1:iter
        for n = 1:length(Xtraining)
            i = Xtraining(n,1) ;
            j = Xtraining(n,2) ;
            r = Xtraining(n,3) ;
            i_trust_set =
trust(find(trust(:,1)==i),2);
            i_trusted_set =
trust(find(trust(:,2)==i),1);
            h = globalBias + userBias(i) +
itemBias(j) + U(i,:) * V(j,:)';

            resid = h - r;
            if(isempty(i_trust_set))
                U(i,:) = U(i,:)-alpha*(resid.*
V(j,:) + lambda_U.* U(i,:));
            else
                U(i,:) = U(i,:)-alpha*(resid.*
V(j,:) + lambda_U.* U(i,:)...

+(size(i_trust_set,1).*(beta).*U(i,:)
(beta).*sum(U(i_trust_set,:))));
            end
            userBias(i) = userBias(i) - alpha
* resid;
            itemBias(j) = itemBias(j) - alpha
* resid;
            globalBias = globalBias - alpha *
resid;
        end
        train_predictions = predict(globalBias,
Xtraining(:,1), Xtraining(:,2), U, V, userBias,
itemBias);
        test_predictions = predict(globalBias,
Xtest(:,1), Xtest(:,2), U, V, userBias,
itemBias);
        train_rmse(m) = rmse(train_predictions,
Xtraining(:,3));
        test_rmse(m) = rmse(test_predictions,
Xtest(:,3));
        resBetaTrain(t,m) =    train_rmse(m);
        resBetaTest(t,m) =    test_rmse(m);
        fprintf('iteration %d, train rmse =
%.4f, validation rmse = %.4f\n', m,
train_rmse(m), test_rmse(m));
        end
```

5 Conclusion and Future Suggestions

In this paper, the study focused into the concept of modeling trust mechanism based on the users, through the introduction of trusted users rating information, to improve prediction accuracy of matrix decomposition and the coverage of cold start users.

Based on real data sets on E-opinions, experimental results showed that UTMF algorithm achieved higher performances in terms of accuracy and coverage metrics as compared to other algorithms. Additionally, the proposed algorithmic method solves the problem of data sparseness and cold start, hence also proving that this algorithm can give impressive results.

This work focused just on the E-opinions dataset, without fully considering the larger data sets, and just considered the fusion from user trust mechanism. As a further study, the next step is focusing on project label similarity which can be merged into the field of matrix decomposition. Also using a larger data set, the study aims to analyze and introduced parallel algorithms, which could be able, to a certain extent, improve the performance of the algorithm.

References

1. Lv, L.Y., Chi, H.Y., Matus, M., et al.: Recommend systems. Phys. Rep. **519**(1), 1–49 (2012)
2. Su, X.Y., Khoshgoftaar, M.T.: A survey of collaborative filtering techniques. J. Adv. Artif. Intell. **2009**, 421425 (2009)
3. Zhou, T., Ren, J., Medo, M.: Bipartite network projection and personal recommendation. Phys Rev E **76**(4), 046115 (2007)
4. Zhou, T.: Effect of initial configuration on network-based recommendation. Europhy. Lett. **81**(5), 58004 (2008)
5. Liu, J.G., Wang, B.H.: Improved collaborative filtering algorithm via information transformation. Int. J. Mod. Phys. C **20**(2), 285–293 (2009)
6. Massa, P., Averani, P.: Trust-aware recommend systems. In: The ACM Conference on Recommend Systems, pp. 17–24. ACM Press, Minneapolis (2007)
7. Jamali, M., Ester, M.: Using a trust network to improve top-n recommendation. In: The third ACM Conference on Recommend Systems, pp. 181–188. ACM, New York (2009)
8. Golbeck, J.: Computing and Applying Trust in Web-based Social Networks. University of Maryland, Washington D.C. (2005)
9. Massa, P., Averani, P.: Trust metrics on controversial users: balancing between tyranny of the majority and echo chambers. Int. J. Semantic Web Inf. Syst. **3**(1), 39–64 (2007)
10. Ray, S., Mahanti, A.: Improving prediction accuracy in trust-aware recommend systems. In: The 43rd Hawaii International Conference on System Sciences, pp. 1–9. IEEE Press Hawaii (2010)

Traffic Sign Recognition Based on Parameter-Free Detector and Multi-modal Representation

Gu Mingqin[1](✉), Chen Xiaohua[1], Zhang Shaoyong[1], and Ren Xiaoping[2]

[1] BAIC Group New Technology Institute,
101300 Beijing, People's Republic of China
gu_mingqin@hotmail.com,
{chenxiaohua, zhangshaoyong}@baicgroup.com.cn
[2] National Institute of Metrology,
100029 Beijing, People's Republic of China
renxp@nim.ac.cn

Abstract. For the traffic sign that is difficult to detect in traffic environment, a traffic sign detection and recognition is proposed in this paper. First, the color characteristics of the traffic sign are segmented, and region of interest is expanded and extracts edge. Then edge is roughly divided by linear drawing and miscellaneous points removing. Turing angle curvature is computed according to the relations between the curvature of the vertices, vertices type is classified. The standard shapes such as circular, triangle, rectangle, etch are detected by parameter-free detector. For improving recognition accuracy, two different methods were presented to classify the detected candidate regions of traffic sign. The one method was dual-tree complex wavelet transform (DT-CWT) and 2D independent component analysis (2DICA) that represented candidate regions on grayscale image and reduced feature dimension, then a nearest neighbor classifier was employed to classify traffic sign image and reject noise regions. The other method was template matching based on intra pictograms of traffic sign. The obtained different recognition results were fused by some decision rules. The experimental results show that the detection and recognition rate of the proposed algorithm is higher for conditions such as traffic signs obscured, uneven illumination, color distortion, and it can achieve the effect of real-time processing.

Keywords: Parameter-free detector · Curvature · Shape classification · Multi-modal representation · Traffic sign recognition

1 Introduction

Automatic detection and recognition of road traffic signs is an essential task for regulating the traffic, guiding and warning drivers or pedestrians. Traffic sign recognition had attracted a great attention in automatic vehicular technology for their complexity of detection and recognition from background. Generally, this system mainly can be

J. Carretero et al. (Eds.): ICA3PP 2016 Workshops, LNCS 10049, pp. 115–124, 2016.
DOI: 10.1007/978-3-319-49956-7_9

divided in two parts. First, the algorithms tried to extract all regions with possible traffic sign candidates, termed as detection phase. Second, the previous detected regions were classified or recognized by special classifier, referred to as classification phase.

The detection phase can be divided in three approaches. Some authors preferred to detect traffic sign edges information in grayscale image, as they did not consider obviously reliable color segmentation due to its sensitivity to various factors. A fast histogram of oriented gradient features [1] was used to detect pedestrian and sign. Edge image was resulted by edge detection methods such as Sobel [2], Canny [3] operator on grayscale image and looked for candidate regions of traffic sign. R. Belaroussi et al. [4] built a geometric model of the image gradient orientation to detect triangular signs. Nevertheless, these methods were mainly focused on shape analysis and sensitive to noise. Other approaches analyzed clustering and intelligent feature for extracting regions of interest(RoI). Features such as Haar, orientation correction [5] and classifiers such as Adaboost were employed to detect traffic sign in input images. However, the algorithms expressed a bias against the weak classifier families.

After the initial detection for traffic sign, several RoIs were sent to classification stage. Typical classification method was template matching [6]. RoIs should be previously normalized in same size, and matched traffic sign templates in a collected database by cross correlation. The approach was vulnerable to imperfect traffic sign regions since the result of the normalized cross correlation was strongly dependent on the similarity of template and RoIs. The other commonly methods of the classification were neural network. Lim King Hann et al. [7] applied principle component analysis (PCA) and Fisher's linear discriminant (FLD) to extract pictogram discriminant features, and proposed RBFNN (Radial Basis Function Neural Networks) based on Lyapunov stability theory to train and classify features. Neural networks can cope with large variances, however input data had to be normalized and their time complexity was high. The same drawback was existed in Support Vector Machine [8]. Other approaches developed special classification methods, The above methods were either difficult to recognize traffic sign in urban environments or had high computing complexity. Due to drawbacks of above methods, a novel algorithm was proposed in this paper.

2 Traffic Sign Detection

In China, traffic signs were designed in standard geometrical shapes such as circle, octagon, triangle, rectangle, and square with distinctive colors (red, blue, yellow etc.) Traffic signs in urban and highway scenes carried mass of useful messages for drivers. ·

2.1 Color Segmentation of Traffic Signs

For obtaining a well segmentation result, each pixel value $v = [v_R, v_G, v_B]$ in RGB color space was converted by following formulas:

$$\begin{cases} Color_{red}(x,y) = \min((v_R - v_G)/S, (v_R - v_G)/S) \\ Color_{blue}(x,y) = \min((v_B - v_R)/S, (v_B - v_G)/S) \\ Color_{yellow}(x,y) = \min((v_G - v_B)/S, (v_R - v_B)/S) \end{cases} \quad (1)$$

where, $S = v_R + v_G + v_B$, (x,y) was pixel coordinates. Through this transformation, each distinctive color can be separated from background with only one threshold, i.e.:

$$Binary_c(x,y) = \begin{cases} 1, Color_c(x,y) > threshold_c \\ 0, Color_c(x,y) \leq threshold_c \end{cases} \quad (2)$$

where, $c \in \{red, blue, yellow\}$ $threshold_c$ was taken $\{0.1, 0.1, 0.15\}$ along different color here. The interested regions of traffic sign were obtained by fixed threshold segmentation. According to the area and shape, the suitable connected areas of each binary image were retained.

2.2 Interested Regional Extension and Edge Detection

In order to obtain complete regions of traffic signs, the upper left corner and lower right corner coordinates of retained regions $R_{i,c}$ were $(x_{il,c}, y_{il,c})$ and $(x_{ir,c}, y_{ir,c})$ respectively. Then the height and width of $R_{i,c}$ are extended to contain complete regions of traffic signs. The height and width of the original image were set as H, W, respectively. The top and bottom of $R_{i,c}$ were extended to $H_{i,c}/4$, and left and right were extended to $W_{i,c}/4$.

Then the color image of the extended region was cut from the original image. The edge of this region was detected by Canny algorithm. Then the outer contour edge of traffic sign interested region was obtained (Fig. 1).

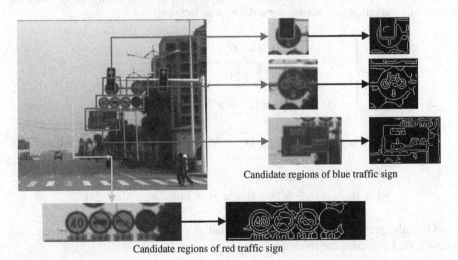

Candidate regions of blue traffic sign

Candidate regions of red traffic sign

Fig. 1. Interest of Region and edge extracting of traffic sign (Color figure online)

2.3   Specific Shape Judgment and Classification

The shape of traffic signs in China included the regular shape such as circle, triangle, and rectangle. So the traffic sign shapes were detected by curvature and angle of edge pixels.

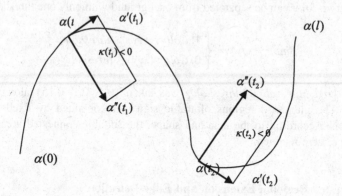

Fig. 2. Demonstration of curvature of curve

Parameter-free Detector. In the geometric analysis, curvature is composed of curve derivative, can be calculated by the following formula:

$$\kappa(t) = \frac{\dot{x}(t)\ddot{y}(t) - \ddot{x}(t)\dot{y}(t)}{\left[\dot{x}^2(t) + \dot{y}^2(t)\right]^{3/2}} \tag{3}$$

Defined $\alpha'(t) = (x'(t), y'(t))$, $\alpha''(t) = (x''(t), y''(t))$, as showed in Fig. 2. Then the directional curvature and values were defined as followed:

$$\begin{cases} \kappa_\alpha(t) = sign \dfrac{2\left|\angle\left(\vec{G}_i, \vec{G}_{i+1}\right)\right|}{\left\|\vec{G}_i\right\| + \left\|\vec{G}_{i+1}\right\|} = \dfrac{\alpha(t) - \alpha(t-\varepsilon)}{\|t - (t-\varepsilon)\|} \\ \kappa_d(t) = \left(\alpha'(t)_x \alpha''(t)_y - \alpha''(t)_x \alpha'(t)_y\right) \Big/ \|\alpha'(t)\|^3 \end{cases} \tag{4}$$

v_x and v_y were components of x, y in $v \in R^2$ respectively. Their differentials were:

$$\begin{cases} \alpha'(t) = \alpha(t) - \alpha(t-\varepsilon) \\ \alpha''(t) = \alpha'(t) - \alpha'(t-\varepsilon) = \alpha(t) - 2\alpha(t-\varepsilon) + \alpha(t-2\varepsilon) \end{cases} \tag{5}$$

Once the previous and next points (P_p and P_n) were determined, we obtain two vectors V_1, V_2 to compute the angle α:

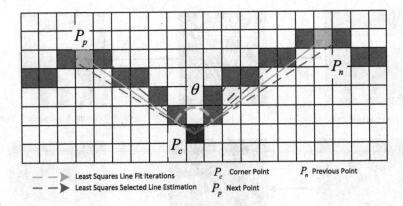

Fig. 3. Illustration of corner validation algorithm

$$V_1 = P_c - P_p, V_2 = P_c - P_n \tag{6}$$

$$\theta = \tan^{-1}\left(\frac{V_1 \cdot V_2}{\|V_1\| \cdot \|V_2\|}\right) \tag{7}$$

Firstly, edges were split and divided into the corresponding edge. Then the edges were sorted. Calculate the two edge angle α, and judge turning angle type (Fig. 3):

(1) If turning angle $\theta \in [110°, 130°]$, this point was a vertex of triangle.
(2) If turning angle $\theta \in [80°, 100°]$, this point was a vertex of rectangle.
(3) If turning angle $\theta \in [0°, 60°]$, two edges were fitting straight line of a circle.

Therefore, the shape type can be judged by turning angle value between two straight, the length of near straight, and vertices location. The final results were showed in Figs. 4 and 5.

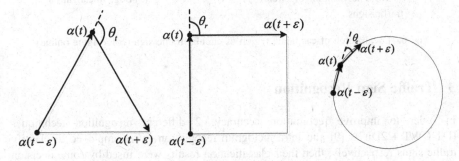

Fig. 4. Turning angle curvature of standard geometry

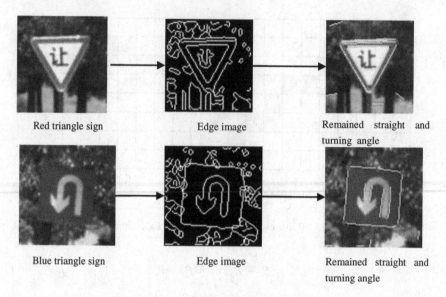

Red triangle sign   Edge image   Remained straight and
                                               turning angle

Blue triangle sign   Edge image   Remained straight and
                                                turning angle

Fig. 5. Turning angle curvature of traffic signs

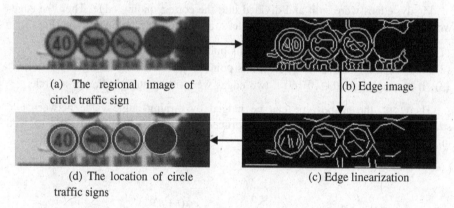

(a) The regional image of   (b) Edge image
circle traffic sign

(d) The location of circle   (c) Edge linearization
traffic signs

Fig. 6. Localization of candidate region of circular traffic sign (color figure online)

3 Traffic Sign Recognition

In order to improve recognition accuracy, 2 different recognition techniques (DT-CWT + 2DICA [9] and intra pictogram recognition) were employed to classify traffic signs respectively, then their classification results were fused by some decision rules.

3.1   DT-CWT + 2DICA

Due to directional advantage, less computation requirement and nearest shift and rotation invariance, DT-CWT was suitable for traffic sign representation. In order to obtain the same number of DT-CWT image feature, candidate image of traffic sign was converted into grayscale image from RGB, and normalized to 64×64 pixels in advance. Two trees were used for the rows of the image and two trees for the columns in a quad-tree structure with 4:1 redundancy. The four quad-tree components of each DT-CWT coefficient were combined by simple arithmetic sum and difference operations to yield a pair of complex coefficients. This produced six directionally selective subbands for each scale of the two-dimensional DT-CWT at approximately $\pm 15°$, $\pm 45°$ and $\pm 75°$. Synthesis filters were used to dual-tree complex wavelet transform for obtaining $O_i, i = 1, \cdots, 4$ represented synthesis filtering result of six directional selective subbands. Each O_i had been normalized to unit variance before matrix concatenation $\chi = (O_1, \cdots, O_4)^T$.

To reduce the computational complexity, feature matrix χ was interlaced sampling previously. Then a 2DICA algorithm described in [19] was used to reduce dimension and eliminate redundancy of traffic sign sample feature. The nearest neighbor classifier was adopted to classify the category of traffic sign.

3.2   Intra Pictogram Extraction and Matching

For extracting intra pictogram, color image $CI_{i,c}$ and binary image $BI_{i,c}$ of candidate region were processed simultaneously. For prohibition, speed limit or yield signs, pictogram extractions were affected by red border, since red pixels had approximate value with black in gray image. Then red border of traffic sign candidate were set 0 in advance. Assume $row \times col$ was size of $BI_{i,c}$, and $IntraI$ was zero image with same size of $BI_{i,c}$. Non-zero elements of each row in binary image $BI_{i,c}$ were found and denoted their ordinates as $y_k = \{y_{k,1}, y_{k,2}, \cdots, y_{k,N}\}$, $k = 1, 2, \cdots, row$, N was the number of non-zero elements. Let $D_{j-1} = y_{k,j} - y_{k,j-1}$, the following rule was adopted to achieve inner regions of candidate.

$$IntraI(k, y_{k,j-1} : y_{k,j}) = \begin{cases} 1, D_{j-1} > 0 \\ 0, otherwise \end{cases} \qquad (8)$$

Region with maximum area in $IntraI$ was labeled and showed in Fig. 6. Then it was cropped from $CI_{i,c}$ and converted into gray image $G_{i,c}$.

Warning, information or direction signs were made up of 2 different representative colors generally. So $CI_{i,c}$ was only directly converted into grayscale image $G_{i,c}$ from RGB color space at preprocessing stage.

Histogram that fell into 256 bins was counted gray value of the intra region. To obtain the threshold $Level_{i,c}$ of segmentation, Otsu's method was employed to automatically perform histogram shape-based image thresholding. Supposed that (x, y) was the coordinate of inner pixel in candidate region. Since letters or pictograms of red and yellow traffic sign were generally black, whereas letters or pictograms of blue traffic sign were white, for red and yellow traffic sign, if $G_{i,c}(x, y) < L_{i,c}$, then $In_{i,c}(x, y) = 1$, else $In_{i,c}(x,y) = 0$. Otherwise, for blue traffic sign, if $G_{i,c}(x,y) > L_{i,c}$, then $In_{i,c}(x,y) = 1$, else $In_{i,c}(x,y) = 0$.

Erosion and dilation by same structuring element were used to eliminate noise pixels in binary image $InB_{i,c}$. The following steps performed pictograms extracting:

(1) If one row or column of $InB_{i,c}$ was all 0, then it was removed from $InB_{i,c}$.
(2) If $InB_{i,c}$ was empty or null, then its output result was labeled as 0, else, go to (3).
(3) Send $InB_{i,c}$ to classifier of template matching, decide whether it belonged to classes of traffic sign or not and label its corresponding result (class number or 0).

3.3   Fusion of Classification Results

Assumed that the two classification results of three consecutive frames by DT-CWT + 2DICA and intra pictogram +template matching were $\{Dre_1, Dre_2, Dre_3\}$, $\{Ire_1, Ire_2, Ire_3\}$, respectively. The following decision rules were used to decision-making:

(1)
$$OutR_1 = \begin{cases} Dre, \text{more than 2 values } Dre \text{ in } \{Dre_1, Dre_2, Dre_3\} \\ 0, otherwise \end{cases}$$

(2)
$$OutR_2 = \begin{cases} Ire, \text{more than 2 values } Ire \text{ in } \{Ire_1, Ire_2, Ire_3\} \\ 0, otherwise \end{cases}$$

(3)
$$Out = \begin{cases} OutR_1, OutR_1 = OutR_2 \cap OutR_1 \neq 0 \cap OutR_2 \neq 0 \\ 0, otherwise \end{cases}$$

If Out was 0, then this candidate was not a traffic sign, else the traffic sign's category $OutR_1$ will be sent to control center to make decision according to traffic sign's category.

4   Experiment and Analysis

4.1   Experiment Data

To evaluate traffic sign recognition system, a camera which equipped with a 12 mm fixed mega-pixel lens with $38.3 \times 26.2°$ field of view was used to face straight ahead and mounted to the front of car roof. Its resolution and frame rate were 1040×1392, 25 fps respectively. Since detection algorithm depended primarily on color, the gain and shutter speeds were fixed to avoid saturation of the traffic signs, particularly mirror reflection of sign's smooth surface.

4.2 Overall Performance

Figure 7 showed some results of traffic sign recognition using the proposed algorithm. Detected traffic sign regions were enclosed by yellow boundaries and their recognition results were demonstrated with small standard pictures below the image.

Table 1. Algorithm performance (%)

Database	Video number	True detection rate	False negative rate	False recognition rate	Recognition rate
Test1	131	97.23	2.77	3.21	96.57
Test2	145	98.42	1.58	2.93	97.55
Test3	119	96.51	3.49	4.85	95.96
Test4	121	98.26	1.74	2.13	95.29
Test5	132	95.24	4.76	2.37	95.813

Fig. 7. Detection and recognition results of traffic sign in different traffic scenes (Color figure online)

To test overall performance of algorithm, 5 group video sequences captured from road scenes in a city were input the proposed recognition system. Table 1 illustrated their detection and recognition rate, and it showed that overall recognition rate of proposed algorithm was up to 95.24% at the peak. Experimental results indicated that the proposed recognition method was robust, effective for classifying traffic signs. False positive cases were validly reduced because color and shape of traffic sign were considered in detection stage. At same time, false negative rate slightly decreased with fusion of different recognition algorithm: DT-CWT + 2DICA and intra pictogram + template matching. However, the total recognition rate slightly dropped.

5 Conclusion

This paper introduces a novel algorithm for traffic signs recognition. In detection stage, the color feature was used to segment the image. Then the interesting regions were extracted by binarization and geometrical characteristic of regions. The parameter-free detector can search the given shapes such as circle, triangle, and rectangle in the extended interesting region. In recognition stage, two different methods are used to classify the detected traffic sign candidate regions for improving recognition accuracy. One method mixes DT-CWT, 2DICA and nearest neighbor classifier to classify traffic sign candidate and reject noise image. It can effectively extract features of candidate region, eliminate feature's redundancy and fast classify traffic sign. The other method is template matching based on intra pictograms of traffic sign. It employs color and RoIs analysis to extract intra pictograms and matches intra pictograms of test image with template database to recognize traffic sign. At the output stage, the result which fuses previous 2 different recognition results by some decision rules is output. Experimental results show that overall rate of proposed algorithm is more than 95%. These indicate that the proposed recognition method can classify traffic signs robustly, effectively, and nearly real-time in urban scenes.

References

1. Overett, G., Petersson, L., Andersson, L., et al.: Boosting a heterogeneous pool of fast hog features for pedestrian and sign detection. In: IEEE Intelligent Vehicles Symposium, Xi'an, China, pp. 584–590. IEEE, Piscataway, USA (2009)
2. Nunn, C., Kummert, A., Muller-Schneiders, S.: A two stage detection module for traffic signs. In: 2008 IEEE International Conference on Vehicular Electronics and Safety, Columbus, OH, USA, pp. 248–252. IEEE, Piscataway, USA (2008)
3. García-Garrido, M.Á., Sotelo, M.Á., Martín-Gorostiza, E.: Fast road sign detection using hough transform for assisted driving of road vehicles. In: Moreno Díaz, R., Pichler, F., Quesada Arencibia, A. (eds.) EUROCAST 2005. LNCS, vol. 3643, pp. 543–548. Springer, Heidelberg (2005). doi:10.1007/11556985_71
4. Belaroussi, R., Tarel, J.: Angle vertex and bisector geometric model for triangular road sign detection. In: 2009 Workshop on Applications of Computer Vision, Snowbird, UT, USA, pp. 1–7. IEEE, Piscataway, USA (2009)
5. de la Escalera, A., Armingol, J.M., Pastor, J.M., et al.: Visual sign information extraction and identification by deformable models for intelligent vehicles. IEEE Trans. Intell. Transp. Syst. 5(2), 57–68 (2004)
6. Hann, L.K., Phooi, S.K., Minn, A.L.: Intra color-shape classification for traffic sign recognition. In: 2010 International Conference of Computer Symposium, Tainan, Taiwan, pp. 642–647. IEEE, Piscataway, USA (2010)
7. Maldonado-Bascón, S., Lafuente-Arroyo, S., Gil-Jiménez, P., et al.: Road-sign detection and recognition based on support vector machines. IEEE Trans. Intell. Transp. Syst. 8(2), 264–278 (2007)
8. Akinlar, C., Topal, C.: EDCircles: a real-time circle detector with a false detection control. Pattern Recogn. 46(2013), 725–740 (2013)
9. Topal, C., Akinlar, C.: Edge drawing: a combined real-time edge and segment detector. J. Vis. Commun. Image Represent. 23(2012), 862–872 (2012)
10. Zi-Xing, C., Ming-Qin, G.: Traffic sign recognition algorithm based on shape signature and dual tree-complex wavelet transform. J. Central S. Univ. Technol. (English Edition) 20(4), 433–439 (2013)
11. Selesnick, W., Baraniuk, R.G., Kingsbury, N.C.: The dual-tree complex wavelet transform. IEEE Sig. Process. Mag. 22(6), 123–151 (2005)

Reversible Data Hiding Using Non-local Means Prediction

Yingying Fang and Bo Ou[✉]

College of Computer Science and Electronic Engineering, Hunan University,
Changsha 410082, China
{201308060210,oubo}@hnu.edu.cn

Abstract. In this paper, we propose a prediction-error expansion based reversible data hiding scheme by incorporating non-local means (NLM) prediction. The traditional local predictors reported in literatures rely on the local correlation and behave badly in predicting textural pixels. To remedy this, we propose to use NLM to achieve better prediction in texture regions and globally utilize the potential self-similarity contained in the image itself. More specifically, the textural pixels distinguished by its local complexity are predicted by NLM while the smooth pixels having high local correlation are predicted by a local predictor. The incorporation of NLM makes the proposed method possible to achieve accurate predictions in both smooth and texture regions. Optimal parameters in the method are obtained by minimizing the prediction-error entropy. Experimental results show that the proposed method can yield an improvement compared with some state-of-the-art methods.

Keywords: Reversible data hiding · Non-local means · Image similarity

1 Introduction

With the wide applications of digital multimedia and the Internet, digital data hiding was introduced as a technique for embedding extra information to covers such as image, audio and video for their notation, copyright protection, integrity authentication, etc. However, a drawback is that the insertion of information may bring out permanent degradation on original data even though they are usually imperceptible to the human visual system, which is intolerant for original data in some sensitive fields such as medical and judical imagery, etc. To meet such special requirement, the reversible data hiding to losslessly recover both the embedded and original data was proposed.

Basically, various reversible data hiding algorithms could be classified into four types: compression based, integer transform based, histogram shifting (HS) based and prediction-error expanding (PEE) based algorithms. Compression based algorithms [1] are mainly implemented by compressing the host data to save space for data embedding. Integer transform based algorithms [2–4] transform pixel pairs by reversible integer transforms and embed bits in the transform

© Springer International Publishing AG 2016
J. Carretero et al. (Eds.): ICA3PP 2016 Workshops, LNCS 10049, pp. 125–135, 2016.
DOI: 10.1007/978-3-319-49956-7_10

coefficients i.e. a well-known difference expanding (DE) proposed by Tian where features are the differences between two neighboring pixel. HS based algorithms [5,6] embed data into the pixels with the most occurrences in a special statistical quantity histogram (such as prediction-error histogram), and consequently splits the peak bin into two adjacent bins. Established on HS, PEE based algorithms [7–10] embed secret data according to such feature histogram, but it further incorporates difference expanding as its embedding modification. It divides the feature histogram into the inner and outer regions, and embeds data bits into inner-region pixels while shifting the outer-region ones. Regarded as a generalized version of DE and HS, larger embedding capacity can be achieved by this construction due to its good capability of capacity control and potential to well utilize the image correlation.

Up to now, PEE still attracts much attention of researchers to improve its performance by developing new prediction algorithms or histogram shifting manner in the two procedures of its mechanism: (1) to find an appropriate predictor, which shows an invariant relationship between the host and modified data, to generate the statistical quantity histogram and guarantee the reversibility, and (2) design an embedding strategy to optimize the histogram modification. With respect to prediction, the conventional PEE only focuses on exploiting local redundancies but neglects the utilization of non-local correlation of the whole image. This results in bad performances for highly textural images. From this point of view, PEE could be further improved.

In this paper, we propose an efficient reversible data hiding scheme in two following aspects:

- NLM prediction: The fact that natural images have much redundancy allows us to find many similar patches within the same image [11]. In fact, NLM can also be well incorporated into PEE to take advantage of such similarity of images. In NLM, a pixel p can be predicted by averaging the values of far away pixels whose neighborhoods resemble those of p. In this way, we can take advantage of the overall correlation of an image to obtain accurate predictions even for texture images.
- Adaptive prediction: The local and non-local predictors are combined to predict pixels according to the local complexity. Only the relative textural pixels with a certain amount of non-local similar patches are predicted by NLM. This action helps to maximize the benefits of NLM on textural pixels without causing worse predictions in smooth regions and reducing the computational complexity at the same time. The two kinds of predictors are switched adaptively without any extra flag bits.

The rest of this paper is organized as follows. The PEE technique is briefly introduced in Sect. 2. The details of the proposed algorithm are described in Sect. 3. The experimental results and performance comparison are discussed in Sect. 4. Finally, conclusions are made in Sect. 5.

2   Background

In this section, we will briefly review the mechanism of PEE based works in two phases: embedding and extraction.

In PEE, the secret data bits are concealed into pixels based on the prediction-error histogram. Such a histogram obeys a Laplace-Gaussian like distribution with the highest occurrence near zero value. It is well known that the more sharply distributed the prediction-error histogram, the better performance PEE gains. For a given pixel p, the prediction value $\hat{p}$ is calculated based on the neighboring pixels in conventional PEE predictors (such as MED [7], Mean [9] and GAP [10]):

$$\hat{p} = \Theta(p), \tag{1}$$

where the prediction function $\Theta(\cdot)$ returns an integer-valued prediction. The prediction-error is obtained as $e = p - \hat{p}$. For each pixel, if $e \in [T_l, T_r)$, it will be regarded as an inner one and embedded one bit through the prediction-error expansion $e^w = 2e + b$, where T_l, T_r are two parameters determined by the payload, b is a to-be-embedded data bit $0/1$ and e^w is the embedded prediction-error; else, if $e \in (-\infty, T_l) \cup [T_r, +\infty)$, it is taken as an outer one and shifted outwards T_l/T_r to create vacancy bins in the prediction-error histogram. Usually, we assume that $T_l < 0$ and $T_r \geq 0$. The larger the payload size, the bigger the value $|T_r - T_l|$. In summary, the embedded pixel p^w is generated as

$$p^w = \begin{cases} p + e + b, & e \in [T_l, T_r); \\ p + T_r, & e \in [T_r, +\infty); \\ p + T_l, & e \in (-\infty, T_l). \end{cases} \tag{2}$$

After PEE embedding, the prediction-error of inner and outer pixels are consequently changed to $e^w \in [2T_l, 2T_r)$ and $e^w \in (-\infty, 2T_l) \cup [2T_r, \infty)$, respectively. In terms of the definition of mean square error $MSE = \sum (p^w - p)^2$, the embedding distortion is determined by e, i.e. the smaller e, the less distortion for the same payload.

During data embedding, some pixel values may be outside of the range of the gray-scale image, e.g. $[0, 255]$, after modifications. To avoid such an overflow/underflow problem, a possible solution is to let these problematic pixels keep unchanged and mark them in the location map for the distinction at decoder. The location map should be transmitted as a part of side information to the decoder as well, and weakens the PEE performance to some extent as it consumes the embedding capacity. Fortunately, in practice the size of location map is affordable even without compression, because the maximum modifications on pixels in PEE are usually small for a huge payload size and the boundary pixels are few in natural images.

In the decoding phase, the side information is extracted in advance to help the decoder regain the prediction and distinguish the problematic pixels. Then the embedded prediction-error is obtained as $e^w = p^w - \hat{p}$. After generating the embedded prediction-error histogram, the inner and outer pixels can be classified with the help of T_l and T_r, and the original prediction-error e is recovered as

$$e = \begin{cases} \left\lfloor \frac{e^w}{2} \right\rfloor, & e^w \in [2T_l, 2T_r); \\ e^w - T_r, & e^w \in [2T_r, \infty); \\ e^w - T_l, & e^w \in (-\infty, 2T_l), \end{cases} \tag{3}$$

where $\lfloor \cdot \rfloor$ is the floor function. Accordingly, the pixel is restored in the inverse manner of embedding: $p = \hat{p} + e$. For the inner pixels whose $e^w \in [2T_l, 2T_r)$, the secret data bits are extracted by $b = e^w - 2 \left\lfloor \frac{e^w}{2} \right\rfloor$ until the payload size is met. Finally, both the original image and the secret data are recovered.

3   Proposed Algorithm

3.1   Non-local Means Prediction

In general, the prediction of a pixel is based on its neighboring pixels but neglects that some non-local patches can be applied to achieve better prediction. The benefit of NLM prediction is that it can provide extra correlation between pixels when the local correlation are somehow limited, and is therefore important for the prediction of textural pixels. Here, the double embedding pattern introduced by Sachnev et al. [9] is employed as shown in Fig. 1(a) and the diagram of NLM prediction is illustrated in Fig. 2.

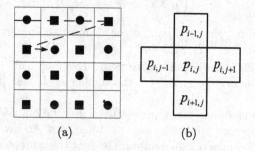

(a)   (b)

Fig. 1. (a) The double layer embedding, where the pixels are classified into two sets denoted by square and circle accordingly, (b) The basic patch unit in NLM.

A patch $P_{i,j}$, is regarded as a combination of the central pixel $p_{i,j}$ and its neighboring vector $V(p_{i,j}) = (p_{i-1,j}, p_{i+1,j}, p_{i,j-1}, p_{i,j+1})$ as shown in Fig. 1(b), which can be used to assess the similarity of two pixels. The NLM prediction $NL(p_{i,j})$ is given by the expression:

$$NL(p_{i,j}) = \frac{1}{\sum_k w_k} \sum_{\tilde{p}_k \in \tilde{P}_k} w_k \tilde{p}_k \tag{4}$$

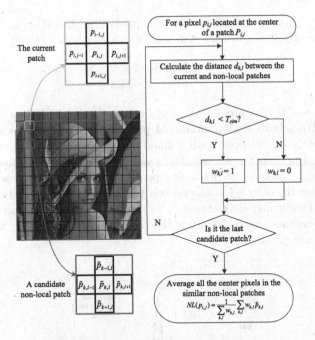

Fig. 2. The framework of NLM prediction.

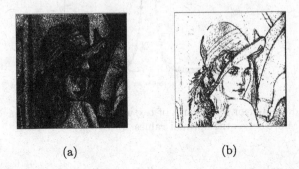

(a)   (b)

Fig. 3. The self-similarity of Lena for different T_{sim}, where the pixel having the similar non-local patches is marked white: (a) $T_{sim} = 0$, (b) $T_{sim} = 10$.

where the sign "$\sim$" represents a non-local element and w_k is the weighted value determined by the similarity between the current patch $P_{i,j}$ and the non-local one $\tilde{P}_k$. The similarity between $V(\tilde{p}_k)$ and $V(p_{i,j})$ is measured by the norm-2 distance as

$$d_k = \| V(\tilde{p}_k) - V(p_{i,j}) \|_2. \tag{5}$$

With the set of a similarity threshold T_{sim}, the patch with the distance below T_{sim} is judged to be similar to the current one while larger distance signifies that this dissimilar patch is not suitable for the prediction. Based on such partition, the associated weight w_k of each non-local patch can be adaptively assigned as

$$w_k = \begin{cases} 1, & d_k \leq T_{sim} \\ 0, & d_k > T_{sim}. \end{cases} \quad (6)$$

Referring to (4), the prediction of $p_{i,j}$ equals to the average value of those center-placed pixels in similar non-local patches. The pixel $\tilde{p}_k$ is assumed to be the similar non-local pixel with a small distance neigbor vetor to the to-be predicted pixel $p_{i,j}$. As the self-similarity is illustrated in the example Fig. 3, it shows that some basic structures are repeated dispersedly in the whole image and can be described by its homogeneous patches for prediction. Besides, as a result of the forwarding characteristic, an intuitive inference is that more non-local similar patches can be found at the beginning of data hiding than at the end as pixels are processed (Fig. 4).

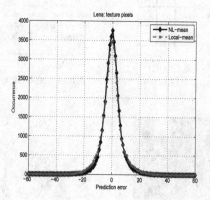

Fig. 4. The prediction-error histograms of textural pixels for Lena image, where T_{LV} and T_{sim} in NLM are set as the optimal values.

For smooth pixels, we use a local predictor for prediction, i.e., the local mean $M(p_{i,j})$,

$$M(p_{i,j}) = \frac{p_{i-1,j} + p_{i+1,j} + p_{i,j-1} + p_{i,j+1}}{4}. \quad (7)$$

3.2   Adaptive Prediction

To determine the class of predictor to a pixel, the local variance of a pixel $LV(p_{i,j})$ is computed to measure the local complexity, where $LV(p_{i,j}) = \sqrt{\frac{1}{4}\sum_{k=1}^{4}(v_k(p_{i,j}) - M(p_{i,j}))^2}$ and $v_k(p_{i,j})$ is the element in neighbor vector $V(p_{i,j})$. Note that $LV(p_{i,j})$ is constant both in the embedding and extraction phases. Then for a specific threshold T_{LV}, the pixels with $LV(p_{i,j}) \leq T_{LV}$ are referred to as smooth ones, while the others with $LV(p_{i,j}) > T_{LV}$ are referred to as textural ones. Now the pixel $p_{i,j}$ can be predicted as follows:

$$\hat{p}_{i,j} = \begin{cases} NL(p_{i,j}), & LV(p_{i,j}) > T_{LV} \text{ and } \sum w_k \geq 1 \\ M(p_{i,j}), & else, \end{cases} \tag{8}$$

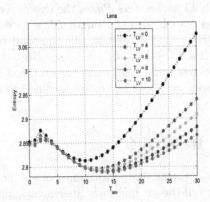

Fig. 5. The entropy of prediction-error histogram in the single layer embedding (only "square" pixels are used for embedding).

where $\sum w_k = 0$ indicates that no similar patch is available for NLM. The distribution of prediction-error histogram is measured by the entropy as

$$E(T_{sim}, T_{LV}) = -\sum_e p_r(e) \ln(p_r(e)), \tag{9}$$

where $p_r(\cdot)$ denotes the probability of an element, the prediction-error $e = p - round(\hat{p})$ and the function $round(\cdot)$ rounds the element into the nearest integer. So, the task of performance optimization is to estimate the best parameters $\{T_{sim}^*, T_{LV}^*\}$ which generate the smallest $E(T_{sim}, T_{LV})$ of prediction-error histogram from a given image:

$$\{T_{sim}^*, T_{LV}^*\} = \underset{T_{sim}, T_{LV} \geq 0}{\arg\min} \ E(T_{sim}, T_{LV}). \tag{10}$$

Here, an exhaustive search before embedding is adapted to find the solution of (10). Figure 5 gives an example that the entropy varies from T_{LV} and T_{sim} in a single layer embedding, where the minimum one is found by the full search. To ease the computation complexity in double layer embedding, the parameters of "circle" and "square" pixels (denoted by 1st layer and 2nd layer, respectively) are selected similarly. That is to say, the optimal parameters of 2nd layer can be empirically chosen in the nearby range of $T_{LV}^{1^{st}}, T_{sim}^{1^{st}}$ as $T_{LV}^{2^{nd}} \in [T_{LV}^{1^{st}} - \Delta T, T_{LV}^{1^{st}} + \Delta T], T_{sim}^{2^{nd}} \in [T_{sim}^{1^{st}} - \Delta T, T_{sim}^{1^{st}} + \Delta T]$, where ΔT is the window size. In fact, compared to the minimum entropy, the difference between the suboptimal and optimal entropy is negligible as shown in Fig. 5. Furthermore, a greedy-like algorithm could be applied to further reduce the complexity in both layers.

After finding the opitimal T^*_{sim} and T^*_{LV} by an exaustive search, we modify the derived optimal adaptive-prediction-error histogram to embed data bits according to PEE. To help the extraction work performed directly,the side information including threshold parameters $Para$, the size of secret data bits C and the compressed location map L with the length LL is necessary to be imbeded. Thus the payload size $PL = S + LL + C$, while the total size of the side information is $S = Para + \lceil \log_2 C \rceil + \lceil \log_2 LL \rceil + L$ bits. Note that S is concealed in the LSB of the first S pixels and these pixels are excluded from the embedding and extraction procedures, and both layers are assumed to be embedded with a half payload.

4   Experimental Results

In this section, we will evaluate the performance of the proposed method and compare it with the state-of-the-art methods. Specifically, four types of reversible data hiding algorithms including Hu *et al.*'s [8], Sachnev *et al.* [9], Luo *et al.*'s [6] and Wang *et al.* [3] are compared. Such algorithms are based on DE, PEE, HS

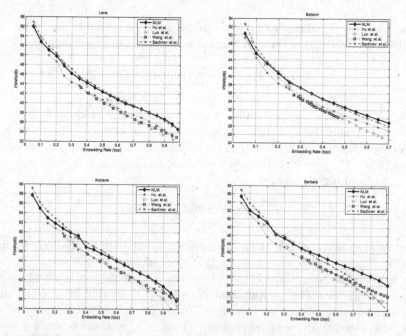

Fig. 6. Performance evaluation of the proposed method compared with other methods over standard test images.

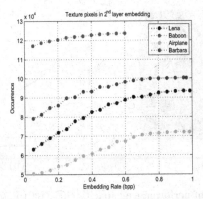

Fig. 7. The quantity of textural pixels in 2nd layer varying with the embedding rate.

and integer transform, respectively, and termed as Hu-DE, Sa-PEE, Luo-HS and Wang-IT, respectively. The tests are enforced on four 512×512 sized standard images including Lena, Baboon, Airplane and Barbara. Before going any further, the definitions of texture complexity and self-similarity are introduced to better illustrate our experimental results.

Definition 1. For a $H \times W$ sized image, the textural complexity of an image, denoted by TC, is calculated as the mean values of all local variances as

$$TC = \frac{1}{(H-2) \times (W-2)} \sum_{i=2}^{H-1} \sum_{j=2}^{W-1} LV(i,j), \tag{11}$$

where H, W are the height and width of the image, respectively. Obviously, TC decreases with the smoothness of the image.

Definition 2. The self-similarity of an image SS is defined to count the quantity of pixels which have non-local patches with identical neighborhood, i.e. $T_{sim} = 0$.

The capacity-distortion comparisons between the proposed method and the above five methods are depicted in Fig. 6. It can be seen that our method significantly outperforms Hu-DE, Sa-PEE, Luo-HS since the proposed adaptive-prediction-error histogram is more sharply distributed than theirs. For Sa-PEE, it employs the sorting technique to approximately arranges the magnitude of prediction-error in a descending order, which helps to reduce the distortion at low embedding rates. Compared with Sa-PEE, our method is slightly lower than Sa-PEE at low embedding rates, but make gains at the high embedding rate varying with the image type. To verify the superiority of NLM prediction, we can also utilize the sorting technique to further improve the performance of the proposed method as shown in Fig. 6. Besides, ours performs better for a huge payload because the 2nd layer goes textural when 1st layer is excessively embedded as shown in Fig. 7.

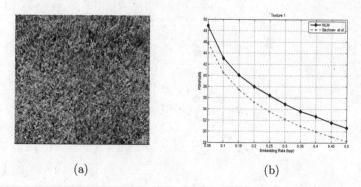

(a)   (b)

Fig. 8. The comparison of performance-capacity curve on the textural image. (a) Test image (b) Performance comparison

Furthermore, another experiment is designed to demonstrate the superiority of our proposed method on texture images. A textural image in USC-SIPI image database (http://sipi.usc.edu/database/) is tested (see Fig. 8(a)), and the corresponding capacity-distortion curve is given in Fig. 8(b). The test image is with strong texture or periodic structure, i.e., TC very high, meaning that they are weak in local correlation but still possess the redundancy overall. It is seen that the image is highly textural with tiny fragments while the others consist of bigger and regular fragments. By comparison, it shows that our method outperforms Sa-PEE especially for the images with tiny fragments, which also indicates that NLM prediction is more robust to local noise if the image consist of the repeated structures.

5   Conclusions

In this paper, we improve the conventional predictors in reversible data hiding schemes by using non-local means. Unlike the conventional predictors wholly dependent on the local correlation, the non-local pixels can be used of the prediction of the current one by globally utilizing the self-similarity in an image. Thus, our method achieve a deeper histogram exploiting the overall redundancy of the whole image. Compared with the state-of-the-art methods, the experimental results demonstrate that our method provides a good embedding performance especially for texture images.

Acknowledgement. This work is supported by the National Science Foundation of China (Nos. 61502160, 61472131, 61272546), Science and Technology Key Projects of Hunan Province (2015TP1004).

References

1. Celik, M.U., Sharma, G., Tekalp, A.M., Saber, E.: Lossless generalized-LSB data embedding. IEEE Trans. Image Process. **14**(2), 253–266 (2005)

2. Tian, J.: Reversible data embedding using a difference expansion. IEEE Trans. Circuits Syst. Video Technol. **13**(8), 890–896 (2003)
3. Wang, X., Li, X., Yang, B., Guo, Z.: Efficient generalized integer transform for reversible watermarking. IEEE Signal Process. Lett. **17**(6), 567–570 (2010)
4. Coltuc, D.: Low distortion transform for reversible watermarking. IEEE Trans. Image Process. **21**(1), 412–417 (2012)
5. Ni, Z., Shi, Y.Q., Ansari, N., Su, W.: Reversible data hiding. IEEE Trans. Circuits Syst. Video Technol. **16**(3), 354–362 (2006)
6. Luo, L., Chen, Z., Chen, M., Zeng, X., Xiong, Z.: Reversible image watermarking using interpolation technique. IEEE Trans. Inf. Forens. Security **5**(1), 187–193 (2010)
7. Thodi, D.M., Rodriguez, J.J.: Expansion embedding techniques for reversible watermarking. IEEE Trans. Image Process. **16**(3), 721–730 (2007)
8. Hu, Y., Lee, H.K., Li, J.: DE-based reversible data hiding with improved overflow location map. IEEE Trans. Circuits Syst. Video Technol. **19**(2), 250–260 (2009)
9. Sachnev, V., Kim, H.J., Nam, J., Suresh, S., Shi, Y.Q.: Reversible watermarking algorithm using sorting and prediction. IEEE Trans. Circuits Syst. Video Technol. **19**(7), 989–999 (2009)
10. Li, X., Yang, B., Zeng, T.: Efficient reversible watermarking based on adaptive prediction-error expansion and pixel selection. IEEE Trans. Image Process. **20**(12), 3524–3533 (2011)
11. Buades, A., Coll, B., Morel, J.-M.: A non-local algorithm for image denoising. In: IEEE Conference on Computer Vision and Pattern Recognition, vol. 2, pp. 60–65, June 2005

Secure Data Access in Hadoop Using Elliptic Curve Cryptography

Antonio F. Díaz[✉], Ilia Blokhin, Julio Ortega, Raúl H. Palacios,
Cristina Rodríguez-Quintana, and Juan Díaz-García

Department of Computer Architecture and Technology, University of Granada,
Granada and Andalusian Health Service (SAS), Granada, Spain
{afdiaz,jortega,raulhp,crodriguez}@ugr.es, djnib@correo.ugr.es,
juan.diaz.sspa@juntadeandalucia.es

Abstract. Big data analytics allows to obtain valuable information from different data sources. It is important to maintain control of those data because unauthorised copies could be used by other entities or companies interested in them. Hadoop is widely used for processing large volumes of information and therefore is ideal for developing big data applications. Its security model focuses on the control within a cluster by preventing unauthorised users, or encrypting data distributed among nodes. Sometimes, data theft is carried out by personnel who have access to the system so they can skip most of the security features. In this paper, we present an extension to the Hadoop security model that lets control the information from the source, avoiding that data can be used by unauthorised users and improving corporative e-governance. We use an eToken with elliptic curve cryptography that performs a robust operation of the system and prevents from being falsified, duplicated or manipulated.

Keywords: Hadoop · Big data · Security · Elliptic curve cryptography

1 Introduction

Processing large volumes of data requires specific tools that are optimised to manage them. Big Data paradigm opens up new possibilities and challenges to manipulate information in a efficient and safe way.

Traditional data analytics may not be able to handle such large quantities of data. Big data applications process data sets whose size is far beyond the capabilities of typical databases, storage, management and information processing.

In a basic configuration, data can be stored locally and accessible by only few users so that, it is a straightforward task how to restrict access. However, the big data scenario is more complex because there might be various data sources, multiple processing nodes and storage as well as a large number of users who

A.F. Díaz—This work has been partially supported by European Union FEDER and the Spanish Ministry of Economy and Competitiveness TIN2015-67020-P, FPA2015-65150-C3-3-P, and PROMEP/103.5/13/6475 UAEH-146.

© Springer International Publishing AG 2016
J. Carretero et al. (Eds.): ICA3PP 2016 Workshops, LNCS 10049, pp. 136–145, 2016.
DOI: 10.1007/978-3-319-49956-7_11

can access to the information, making it difficult to maintain data security at all stages. A current big data processing model is based on data providers that send the information to companies that process their data. If a valuable source believes that its data can not be copied, it should study what mechanisms have to be added to guarantee their safety.

Hadoop [2] is a versatile Java-based system used for processing big data. It solves the problem of storing data and distribute processing across multiple nodes allowing it to scale computing capacity. It can work with thousands of nodes and terabytes of data. Its distributed file system (HDFS) offers seamless transfer of data between nodes and the system can continue operating without interruption even if a node fails.

Hadoop consists of a distributed file system, a platform for analysis and data storage and a layer that manages parallel computing and administrative tools. Figure 1 shows the overall architecture of Hadoop, where the most significant elements are:

- HFDS: Fault tolerant distributed file system.
- YARN: It provides computing resources necessary for running applications.
- MapReduce: Data processing distribution mechanism among nodes.
- HBase: NoSQL database for data column.
- Pig: High level data-flow language that simplifies MapReduce programming.
- Hive: Data query application.
- Sqoop: It allows data transference between relational databases and Hadoop.

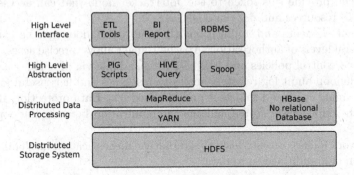

Fig. 1. Hadoop architecture.

This article describes a mechanism that complements and extends the current security model presented in Hadoop. The rest of the article is organised as follows: Sect. 2 provides an overview of the security features that implements Hadoop; Sect. 3 describes the main elements used in the model; In Sect. 4 the main features of the API developed are shown; Sect. 5 describes the proposed extended security model and finally in Sect. 6 the conclusions and future work are presented.

2   Hadoop Security

Security models in Hadoop have evolved due to the Internet exposure of computer resources and the users' requeriments [6]. In fact, some CVE vulnerabilities have been reported. Companies like Cloudera [4] or Hortonworks [10] have developed solutions where they solve the main security features and, books like Lakhe [16] describes practical way to afford those security enhancements. Some authors have revised Hadoop security model as Jam [13].

2.1   Main Elements

Hortonworks establishes a corporate security model based on five basic pillars: management, authentication, authorization, auditing and data protection.

To facilitate the administration is advisable to establish a centralised and coherent resource management model. Apache Ranger allows defining security policies that are applied to other components.

Hadoop can use its own authentication mechanism directly referring to the user information (Active Directory, LDAP, NFS, PAM, ...) or use a strong authentication mechanism based on Kerberos as shown in the Fig. 2.

In this case, encrypted delegate tokens services are used to validate access to Hadoop. The process is basically: the client requests a TGT (Ticket-Granting Ticket) and authenticates with the Kerberos KDC (Key Distribution Center) (1). The KDC validates the authenticity of the user (2) and returns the authentication token (3). The client uses the TGT to request a service key (4). Finally, the user can provide this token to the JobTracker node that can access to the Hadoop (5) resources and data in HDFS.

Different elements and applications that run on Hadoop can be controlled using several levels of authorisation. Apache Ranger allows precise access control to data and control policies and it is easily expandable via plugins.

The Hadoop audit log registers access to resources and it is useful for study of use, estimate costs and to detect unauthorised use. Data protection allows to encrypt the information stored and the communication between Hadoop applications.

This work focuses on establishing alternative authentication mechanisms and encryption and audit access to data.

2.2   Data Encryption

An important element to consider is the encryption of data because it may penalise the access speed and therefore it can affect the overall performance of data processing. Some studies have proposed the use of GPU to reduce the time penalty that may cause the encryption and decryption process. Al-Kiswany [11] defines a library primitives to accelerate hashing distributed storage systems. W.Sun [20] proposes an environment for combining the GPU in storage systems and implemented in the Linux kernel where the GPU-based AES encryption

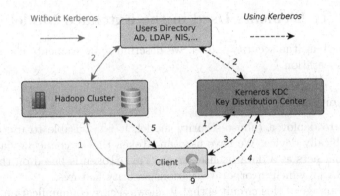

Fig. 2. Hadoop access.

getting a transfer rate of 4 Gbps, while the results with the CPU offered less than half of GPU performance.

Shredder [12] uses GPU to enhance computing and storage in Hadoop reducing Bottlenecks CPU. In general, works based on the GPU emphasise performance improvement but do not reveal energy efficiency or the real conditions in large cluster of computers where perhaps the number of nodes with GPU is usually smaller. Moreover, Intel has developed new enhancements such as Intel AES New Instructions (NI) [8] including encryption accelerators CPUs which significantly improves performance.

It has been proposed some alternative encryption schemes for Hadoop as HDFS-RSA & HDFS-Pairing [17] or Yang's proposal [22] that uses IDEA and RSA. Park [19] proposed an AES encryption based on the HDFS model. Other systems such as Kadre [15] that uses MapReduce combined with AES for encryption in parallel.

2.3 Additional Security Features

Rhino is an open source project that improves Hadoop platform with additional protection mechanisms and tries to eliminate potential security holes in the Hadoop stack. Among the variety of work undertaken within the framework of this project it is interesting to highlight a common abstraction layer that stablish a cryptographic API and the definition of a suitable environment for the resource distribution and key management.

Hadoop's perimeter security is based on the corporative firewall as the gateway Apache Knox. This mechanism offers a single point of authentication and access to services for multiple Hadoop clusters. Knox provides a central point of access to the Hadoop REST API and offers different levels of authorization, authentication, and SSO (Single Sign-On).

3   Security Elements Used in the Extended Model

Before describing the security model, we describe some elements necessary for such implementation.

3.1   eToken

If we want to deploy a robust security model, it is advisable to use a robust cryptographically device. We have used an eToken that is connects via USB to the node that acts as a data license server. This eToken is based on the Atmel ATECC508A [3] which incorporates various security features.

The advantage of this circuit is that it allows secure communication between its internal elements and verification software on the computer, preventing possible Man-In-the-Middle attacks that may capture data exchange between them. The circuit implements ECDSA and ECDSH algorithms (briefly described below). It includes asymmetric encryption algorithms based on elliptic curve cryptography (ECC), which is considerably more efficient than RSA. According to the recommendation of ECRYPT II and published by ENISA [1] a 256-bit ECC encryption requires 3248 bits in RSA. RSA algoriths would be slow because of the size of the keys, so the industry is shifting to ECC systems. In an Intel Xeon, the 256-bit ECDSA signature is approximately 9 times faster than a 2048-bit RSA signature.

3.2   ECDSA

Elliptic Curve Digital Signature Algorithm (ECDSA) [14] is a variant of the DSA algorithm based on Elliptic Curve. It was proposed by Scott Vanstone [21] in 1992 and was accepted as an ISO standard in 1998 (ISO 14888-3), ANSI standard (ANSI X9.62) in 1999, IEEE standard 1963-2000 in 2000 and FIPS standard (FIPS 186-2) in 2000. Examples of use are Bitcoins and a authentication mechanism implemented in TLS (Transport Layer Security). In particular, FIPS186-3 is used [5] in this circuit although there is an updated version of the standard FIPS186-4 2013.

Let's see how the algorithm is used to sign: Suppose Alice wants to sign a message with his private key (d_A) and Bob confirms Alice's signature Alice's public key (H_A). Thus, only Alice can sign and everyone can check it. The following steps are performed:

- A hash of the message is calculated and truncated to n bits (which is the order of the subgroup), value denoted as z.
- A random value is generated k.
- We apply the algorithm to the value with the private key d_A obtaining the firm (r, s).

We use (r, s) to verify the signature and the truncated hash of the message, z, which applied after the verification algorithm with the public key H_A can confirm the authenticity of the signature.

Although the algorithm is quite robust cryptographically, it must be used correctly because, if the recommendations are not followed, its application can be easily vulnerable. It is important that the number k has to be a good random number and change each time it is used. In fact, several vulnerabilities are documented, as an example: The PlayStation 3 video console games could run only signed by Sony with ECDSA and thus prevents other games on the market without his signature, but they used the same k. Although initially unknown, k could be calculated from two different games and from here you could obtain the private key. A similar problem was detected in various applications for Android Bitcoin wallets and OpenSSL where it was corrected in version 1.0.0e.

3.3   ECDH

The elliptic curve Diffie-Hellman algorithm (ECDH) is a safely key exchange protocol that can be used through an insecure channel. The circuit implements the NIST SP800-56A [9] standard, although there is an updated version (Rev 2) of the document.

If Alice and Bob want to share a secret key, first agree to an elliptic curve E over a finite body Z_p sufficiently secure and agree to a point $G \in E(Z_p)$ so that the subgroup generated by G is of a high order. They create their own private keys d_A and d_B and public $H_A = d_A G$ and $H_B = d_B G$. Then exchange their public keys H_A and H_B on the insecure channel. Finally, Alice estimates $S = d_A H_B$ and Bob $S = d_B H_A$. A man-in-the-middle attack could obtain the public keys of Alice H_A and Bob H_B but could not figure S.

$$S = d_A H_B = d_A(d_B G) = d_B(d_A G) = d_B H_A \tag{1}$$

The value of S can be used to create a symmetric safe key for the exchange of information between them. The keys can be static (always the same pair of public and private keys) or may change (new public and private keys are calculated every time the algorithm is used).

4   API eHTSecurity

It has been defined an API Token Security eHadoop (eHTSecurity) that stablish a robust encryption and authentication based on the chip mechanism and is available for Linux. The eHSecurity API consists of two separate modules: data server (eHTSecurity server) and data receiver (eHTSecurity client).

The API data server has three modules shown in the Fig. 3: Key management, eTokens Update and encryption.

Key management is responsible for creating and storing the symmetric encryption keys to encrypt data and asymmetric keys for authentication of customers. EToken allows updating the keys securely. When a eToken is validated, it is inserted the private key that will allow to authenticate and decrypt the symmetric key. The API data receiver verifies that the user or then node is authenticated and obtains the symmetric key to decrypt from the private key contained in the chip.

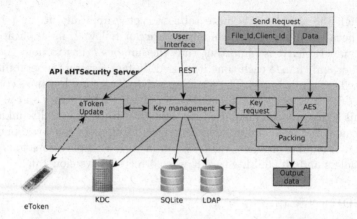

Fig. 3. API Server.

ECDSA is used by the module to check the chip and verify that the module code has not been tampered with. It is used to decrypt the key ECSH sent through the insecure channel(I2C+USB) so that the key is used to extract the data using the private key that is inside the chip. Figure 4 shows the communication process between the chip and the computer.

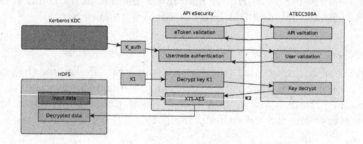

Fig. 4. Communication between API eSecurity and ATECC508A.

The API is integrated into the Hadoop security model on 2 levels: authentication and encryption. The advantage of using a token-based authentication is that it integrates the basic mechanisms of communication, which facilitates its implementation.

Although HDFS allows encryption, it is directed to local storage on data that is not accessible. In our case, the data is encrypted at the source and therefore the proper encryption HDFS is not necessary, although not it is not incompatible.

IEEE 1619-2007 standard is used [7] with the XTS (XEX-TCB-CTS) mode [18] for encrypting. The XTS provides greater protection for encryption block compared to other systems such as CBC and ECB. The XTS is also used in BitLocker, FileVault 2 TrueCrypt, FreeOTFE, dm-crypt among others as well as encryption of storage devices.

This system, as shown in Fig. 5, uses two keys, one for encryption AES block and another to encrypt the "Tweak Value" i. This encrypted value and is further modified with a polynomial function of Galois $GF(2^{128})$ and an XOR is performed with the plaintext and ciphertext of each block. The GF function provides greater randomness and ensures that identical data blocks not produce identical encrypted texts. This will avoid using IVs and chaining. Decryption of data is performed by reversing this process. Since each block is independent and there is a chain, if the data stored encrypted is damaged, only the data of that particular block will be unrecoverable. With chaining modes, these errors can spread to other blocks when decrypted. Another advantage of the XTS is that it can run in parallel, thus speeding up the processing of large volumes of data.

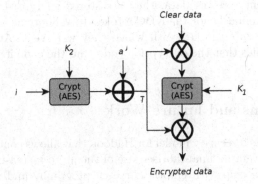

Fig. 5. Diagram of XTS-AES.

5   Extended Security Model

The proposed system establishes the following extensions from the current Hadoop's model:

- The data provider can send encrypted information and remotely control who has access to such data.
- The client authenticates the user (or user group) by Kerberos that verifies it with the eToken.
- The client incorporates a layer which is independent of decrypting encryption includes HDFS.
- Decryption incorporates a statistic that allows to audit the use of data.
- This service is validated by Kerberos tickets that is authenticated with eToken through the API.
- The eToken is managed in part by the data provider (which does not have to match the administrator running Hadoop cluster) and partly by the local administrator.

In this model, the data source encrypts data by controlling the cluster where processing is executed. This is useful when the source relies on a group of users, enabling corporate access, and avoiding that can be used outside of an authorised cluster. In this case, the eToken is located in any of the cluster nodes and that node acts as a license data server and the KDC validates authentication accessing that node.

This configuration consists of the following elements: Data provider (license server and data server) and the cluster processing (data receiver, licenser server and data processing nodes).

When the data server wants to send data to a client, it requests an encryption key to the license server. The encryption key is sent, but it is encrypted so that it can only be used by the client.

When the client receives data, they are stored encrypted on HDFS. If it comes to access them asks for the KDC a token to validate access, and the data license server decrypts the key with which they were sent. At this stage, the license server verifies that the decryption code, and the code itself has not been tampered with.

6 Conclusions and Future Work

This paper presents a security model for Hadoop that allows controlling userdata source control preventing unauthorised use of them. To increase their safety, an eToken based on a chip with elliptic curve cryptography and some additional resources have been protected against forgery or manipulation. The ESecurity API has been developed, and it performs the XTS-AES encryption, which provides access to the eToken and integrates with Hadoop components. As future work we are evaluating how to optimise the encryption layer to reduce the overhead and improve the interface configuration and management of eToken both local and remotely.

References

1. Algorithms, key size and parameters report - 2014. ENISA (2016)
2. Apache hadoop (2016)
3. ATECC508A Atmel CryptoAutentication Device. Atmel (2016)
4. Cloudera Apache Hadoop. Cloudera (2016)
5. FIPS PUB 186–3. Digital Signature Standard (DSS). FIPS (2016)
6. Hadoop in secure mode. Apache (2016)
7. IEEE P1619/D16 Standard for Cryptographic Protection of Data on Block-Oriented Storage Devices). IEEE (2016)
8. Intel Advanced Encryption Standard Instructions (AES-NI). Intel (2016)
9. NIST Spp. 800–56A Recommendation for Pair-Wise Key Establishment Schemes Using Discrete Logarithm Cryptography. NIST (2016)
10. What is Apache Hadoop? Hortonworks (2016)

11. Al-Kiswany, S., Gharaibeh, A., Santos-Neto, E., Yuan, G., Ripeanu, M.: Storegpu: exploiting graphics processing units to accelerate distributed storage systems. In: Parashar, M., Schwan, K., Weissman, J.B., Laforenza, D. (eds.), HPDC, pp. 165–174. ACM (2008)
12. Bhatotia, P., Rodrigues, R., Verma, A.: Shredder: Gpu-accelerated incremental storage and computation. In: Proceedings of the 10th USENIX Conference on File and Storage Technologies, FAST 2012, p. 14, Berkeley, CA, USA (2012). USENIX Association
13. Jam, M.R., Khanli, L.M., Javan, M.S., Akbari, M.K.: A survey on security of hadoop. In: 2014 4th International eConference on Computer and Knowledge Engineering (ICCKE), pp. 716–721, October 2014
14. Johnson, D., Menezes, A., Vanstone, S.: The elliptic curve digital signature algorithm (ecdsa) (2016)
15. Kadre, V., Chaturvedi, S.: Article: Aes - mr: A novel encryption scheme for securing data in hdfs environment using mapreduce. Int. J. Comput. Appl. 129(12), 12–19 (2015). Published by Foundation of Computer Science (FCS), NY, USA
16. Lakhe, B.: Practical Hadoop Security. Apress, Berkely (2014)
17. Lin, H.Y., Shen, Tzeng, W.G., Lin, B.S.P.: Toward data confidentiality via integrating hybrid encryption schemes and hadoop distributed file system. In: 2012 IEEE 26th International Conference on Advanced Information Networking and Applications (AINA), pp. 740–747, March 2012
18. Martin, L.: Xts: A mode of aes for encrypting hard disks. IEEE Secur. Priv. 8(3), 68–69 (2010)
19. Park, S., Lee, Y.: Secure hadoop with encrypted HDFS. In: Park, J.J.J.H., Arabnia, H.R., Kim, C., Shi, W., Gil, J.-M. (eds.) GPC 2013. LNCS, vol. 7861, pp. 134–141. Springer, Heidelberg (2013). doi:10.1007/978-3-642-38027-3_14
20. Sun, W., Ricci, R., Curry, M.L.: Gpustore: Harnessing gpu computing for storage systems in the os kernel. In: Proceedings of the 5th Annual International Systems and Storage Conference, SYSTOR 2012, pp. 9: 1–9: 12. ACM, New York, NY, USA (2012)
21. Vanstone, S.: Responses to NISTs proposal. Commun. ACM 35, 50–52 (1992). ACM
22. Yang, C., Lin, W., Liu, M.: A novel triple encryption scheme for hadoop-based cloud data security. In: 2013 Fourth International Conference on Emerging Intelligent Data and Web Technologies (EIDWT), pp. 437–442, Sept 2013

Statistical Analysis of CCM.M-K1 International Comparison Based on Monte Carlo Method

Chang-qing Cai[1], Xiao-ping Ren[1(✉)],
Guo-dong Hao[2], Jian Wang[1], and Tao Huang[1]

[1] National Institute of Metrology, Beijing 100029, People's Republic of China
{caichq, renxp, wjian, huangt}@nim.ac.cn
[2] Department of Intelligence Science and Engineering, Central South University,
Changsha 410083, People's Republic of China
haoguodong@csu.edu.cn

Abstract. The application of the Monte Carlo method is used in the processing of the measurement result of CCM.M-K1. This method can get over the limitations that apply in certain cases to the method described in GUM. Introduction and analysis of CCM.M-K1 measurement result was given out and commercial software named @RISK was used to purse numerical simulation and the result was compared with the final report of CCM.M-K1, which showed that differences between results of these two were negligible.

Keywords: Key comparison · Reference value · Degree of equivalence · Monte carlo method

1 Introduction

A key comparison is one of the set of comparisons selected by a Consultative Committee to test the principal techniques and methods in the field. For example, in mass filed, there have already several key comparisons holding in the past twenty years. In Table 1, it lists the details of CCM key comparisons.

The outputs of the statistical analysis of a CIPM key comparison are the key comparison reference value, the degrees of equivalence, and their associated uncertainties. So these three factors are very important during key comparison.

Besides, key comparisons carried out by regional metrology organizations are referred to as RMO key comparisons; this kind of key comparisons must be linked to the corresponding CIPM key comparisons by means of joint participants. Table 2 shows the status of APMP RMO comparisons.

The grants that have been received from the National Natural Science Funds of China (51405459), National Science and Technology Support Program (2011BAK15B06), Special-Funded Program on National Key Scientific Instruments and Equipment Development (2012YQ090208) are hereby acknowledged with much gratitude.

J. Carretero et al. (Eds.): ICA3PP 2016 Workshops, LNCS 10049, pp. 146–155, 2016.
DOI: 10.1007/978-3-319-49956-7_12

Table 1. CIPM key comparisons of mass standard

Key comparisons	Transfer artifacts	Date	Year of report	Number of labs
CCM.M.K1	2 × 1 kg	1995–1998	2004 [1]	15
CCM.M.K2	100 mg, 2 g, 20 g, 500 g, 10 kg	1998–1999	2003 [2]	14
CCM.M.K3	50 kg	2001–2002	2005 [3]	14
CCM.M.K3.1	2 × 50 kg	2009	2010 [4]	2
CCM.M.K4	2 × 1 kg	2011–2012	2014 [5]	16
CCM.M.K5	200 mg, 1 g, 50 g, 200 g, 2 kg	2000–2003	2011 [6]	19
CCM.M.K6	50 kg	2011–2013	2015 [7]	9
CCM.M.K7	500 mg, 5 g, 10 g, 100 g, 5 kg	2014–2015	/	10

Table 2. RMO key comparison of mass standard

APMP key comparisons	Transfer artifacts	Date	Year of report	Number of labs
APMP.M.M-K1	2 × 1 kg	1999–2001	2004	15
APMP.M.M-K1.1	1 kg	2008	2011	2
APMP.M.M-K2	100 mg, 2 g, 20 g, 500 g, 10 kg	2004–2007	2009	11
APMP.M.M-K2.1	100 mg, 2 g, 20 g, 500 g	2010	2011	2
APMP.M.M-K5	200 mg, 1 g, 50 g, 200 g, 2 kg	2015–2016	/	19
APMP.M.M-K6	100 mg, 2 g, 20 g, 500 g, 1 kg	2005–2006	2008	14

Cox gives guidelines for the statistical analysis of a CIPM key comparison [8]. This is based on the assumption that travelling standard having good short term stability and stability during transport. Besides, each NMI laboratory realizes its measurement independent of the others [9]. However, the key comparison may occur: some or all of the measurements are mutually dependent, or the travelling standard is not stable enough. We can know that many CIPM key comparisons are not simple; reference [8] does not apply to CIPM key comparisons at some situations. That's why researchers intend to develop further guidelines to cover these complications, and the Monte Carlo method (MCM) is used to overcome these limitations.

This paper uses a Monte Carlo method to re-analyze the measurement result of CCM.M-K1 comparison. Sections 2 and 3 are, respectively, an introduction and an analysis of CCM.M-K1 measurement result. In Sect. 4, we use Excel and Risk analysis software to re-calculate CCM.M-K1 result. In this section, we also give the key comparison reference value and its associated uncertainty based on the Monte Carlo method. A comparison between Monte Carlo and method in the final report appears in Sect. 5.

2 Status of CCM.M-K1 Comparisons

This comparison was carried out between 1995–02 and 1997–11. There were 14 laboratories taking parting inside this comparison except BIPM was pilot laboratory (PL).

Seven participating laboratories determined the mass of travelling standards VSL-1 and J2 (Group 1) while the remaining seven determined the mass of travelling standards VSL-2 and J3 (Group 2). BIPM determined the mass of each package at the beginning and the end of the comparisons and four times during the course of the comparisons. The measurement results are shown in Tables 3 and 4.

Table 3. Measurement result of group 1

Date	Lab	$m_{VSL1-1\ kg}$	$m_{J2-1\ kg}$	u_c/ug
Feb-95	BIPM	0.478	3.378	12
May-95	NMi,c	0.457	3.353	18
Jul-95	NPL	0.478	3.367	16
Sep-95	BIPM	0.471	3.365	12
Feb-96	VNIIM	0.529	3.396	24
May-96	BIPM	0.473	3.357	12
Aug-96	PTB	0.467	3.354	12
Dec-96	SMU	0.532	3.412	22
Feb-97	BIPM	0.474	3.383	12
Feb-97	BIPM	0.473	3.36	12
Mar-97	KRISS	0.468	3.357	14
Apr-97	BIPM	0.471	3.364	12
Jul-97	BNM	0.47	3.367	11
Sep-97	BIPM	0.468	3.359	12

Table 4. Measurement result of group 2

Date	Lab	$m_{VSL2-1\ kg}$	$m_{J3-1\ kg}$	u_c/ug
Feb-95	BIPM	0.042	3.564	12
Jul-95	NIST	0.01	3.54	19
Sep-95	NRC,c	0.012	3.54	16
Feb-96	NRLM,c	0.007	3.538	13
May-96	BIPM	0.024	3.554	12
Jul-96	CSIRO	0.025	3.557	14
Sep-96	BIPM	0.024	3.556	12
Oct-96	NIM	0.087	3.573	21
Feb-97	BIPM	0.083	3.586	12
Feb-97	BIPM	0.041	3.564	12
May-97	IMGC	0.034	3.561	13
Jun-97	BIPM	0.033	3.564	12
Sep-97	CENAM	0.031	3.556	13
Oct-97	BIPM	0.023	3.559	12

In this comparison, reference value was established based on the results of all participants. For the median has been proposed as a "robust" estimator for reference values [10]. So the reference value of this comparison is −3.0 µg (using all corrected results) and the std. deviation of reference value is 2.2 µg.

3 Analysis of Measurement Data and Processing Method in CCM.M-K1 Report

In the process of measurement result, examine the average mass and the average mass difference for each group is useful to check the unusual measurement result.

The first quantity depends sensitively on traceability to the international prototype (involving an important correction for air buoyancy) but averages over other influences. Figure 1(a) and (c) shows the average mass of two groups.

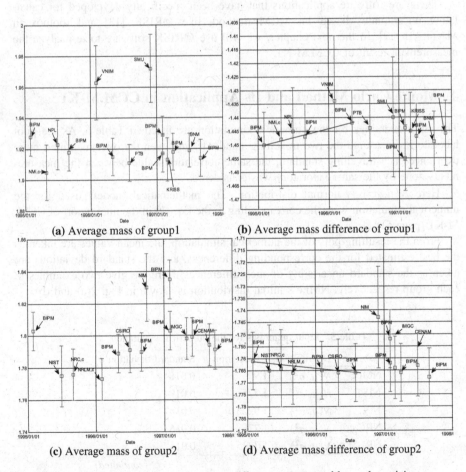

(a) Average mass of group1   (b) Average mass difference of group1

(c) Average mass of group2   (d) Average mass difference of group2

Fig. 1. The average value and average difference as reported by each participant

The second quantity more clearly indicates the relative stability of the travelling standards. Figure 1(b) and (d) shows the average mass difference of two groups.

From this data check, we can find VNIIM, SMU in group 1 and NIM in group 2 might have situation happening. This method is based on pilot laboratory's measuring result and it thus serves as a diagnostic tool. Now we can use chi-squared test to find the discrepant measurements [8].

A sound and well-established approach for evaluating the measurement uncertainty is set out in the "Guide to the expression of Uncertainty Measurement" (GUM). However, it is also clear that GUM approach encompasses a tedious and error-prone series of calculations [11].

In 1997, BIPM created the Joint Committee for Guides in Metrology (JCGM) with the mission of revising GUM in order to improve its ease of use and expand its range of application, since it displayed certain limitations. In the first of these supplements, an alternative procedure is described for the calculation of uncertainties: the Monte Carlo Method (MCM) [12].

There are software applications that have been specifically developed for calculating uncertainties based on MCM method, like @RISK [13] and toolbox in MATLAB [12]. In the next chapter, we will use @RISK software to re-analyze the measurement result of CCM.M-K1.

4   Monte Carlo Method and Its Application in CCM.M-K1

The input quantities for the numerical simulation are listed in Table 5. As the pilot laboratories measured the two travelling standards, and even the pilot measured more than once each travelling standard, the same correlation value between the measurements done by the same laboratory was considered.

Here $N(\mu, \sigma^2)$ is normal distribution. The mathematical models used for the numerical simulation were the corresponding to the Eq. (1) in the final report of CCM. M-K1 (page 5) [1].

From the resulting pdfs of the numerical simulation, the mean values are taken as the best estimated for the corresponding differences, and the standard deviations are taken as the standard uncertainty of such differences. Here we give two examples in each group respectively. NMi,c's initial distribution is shown in Fig. 2(a) and (b).

Table 5. Input quantities for the numerical simulation.

Lab.	Distribution	Expectation μ	Standard deviation σ
NMi,c	$N(\mu, \sigma^2)$	1.905	0.018
NIST	$N(\mu, \sigma^2)$	1.775	0.019
NPL	$N(\mu, \sigma^2)$	1.9225	0.016
NRC,c	$N(\mu, \sigma^2)$	1.776	0.016
NRLM,c	$N(\mu, \sigma^2)$	1.7725	0.013

(*continued*)

Table 5. (*continued*)

Lab.	Distribution	Expectation μ	Standard deviation σ
VNIIM	$N(\mu, \sigma^2)$	1.9625	0.024
CSIRO	$N(\mu, \sigma^2)$	1.791	0.014
PTB	$N(\mu, \sigma^2)$	1.9105	0.012
NIM	$N(\mu, \sigma^2)$	1.83	0.021
SMU	$N(\mu, \sigma^2)$	1.972	0.022
KRISS	$N(\mu, \sigma^2)$	1.9125	0.014
IMGC	$N(\mu, \sigma^2)$	1.7975	0.013
BNM	$N(\mu, \sigma^2)$	1.9185	0.011
CENAM	$N(\mu, \sigma^2)$	1.7935	0.013

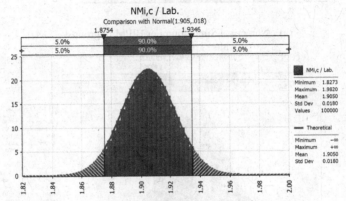

(a)   Numerical Simulation For NMi,c

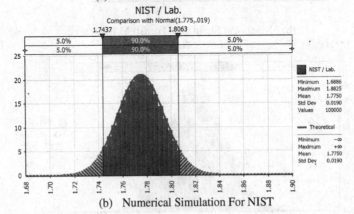

(b)   Numerical Simulation For NIST

Fig. 2. Histogram Resulting For NMi,c and NIST

To simulate the pdfs of pilot laboratory, each participant may have different measurement result of pilot laboratory. For example, before and after the NMi,c and NPL, the distribution of PL is $N(1.928, 0.012^2)$ and $N(1.918, 0.012^2)$. This is due to

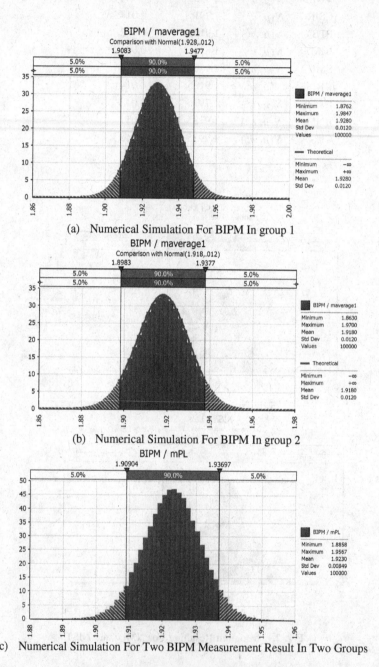

(a)   Numerical Simulation For BIPM In group 1

(b)   Numerical Simulation For BIPM In group 2

(c)   Numerical Simulation For Two BIPM Measurement Result In Two Groups

Fig. 3. Histogram resulting for pilot laboratory

PL had make two measurements before these participants. The Fig. 3 shows the two distributions of PL measurements and the average distribution of these two distributions $N(1.923, 0.0085^2)$.

After we got the distribution of average distributions of PL, we can use distribution of each participant to minus the average distribution of PL. for example, NMi,c's distribution minus PL, and the result is difference between participant and PL, which is $N(-0.018, 0.0202^2)$.

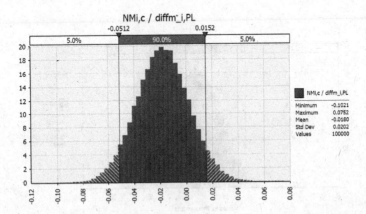

(a) Numerical Simulation For the Difference Between NMi,c and BIPM

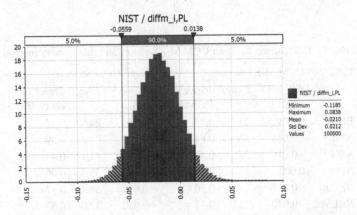

(b) Numerical Simulation For the Difference Between NIST and BIPM

Fig. 4. Histogram resulting for the difference between participant and PL

Table 6. Data of the median resulting of numerical simulation(/mg)

m_{RV}	-0.003
$u(m_{RV})$	0.007
$U(m_{RV})$, $k = 2$	0.014
$P[x_1, x_2]$	$[-15.5, 9.6]$

According to this method, we can give out all the distributions of mass differences. Results of some numerical simulation are shown in Fig. 4(a) and (b). The mean values of the pdfs, resulting from the numerical simulation, are taken as the best estimates of the output quantities and the standard deviations as the corresponding standard uncertainties.

The key comparison reference value and its dispersion are shown in Table 6. The histogram resulting from the numerical simulation is shown in Fig. 5.

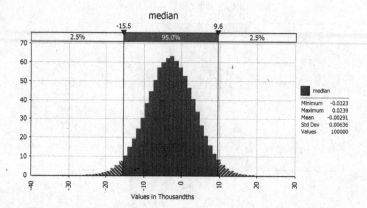

Fig. 5. Histogram resulting from simulation corresponding to KCRV and its uncertainty

Table 7. Comparison between CCM.M-K1 report and monte carlo method

Lab.	CCM.M-K1 Report			Monte Carlo Method		
	diff_mRV (mg)	$U(\mu g)$	degree of equivalence	diff_mRV (mg)	$U(\mu g)$	degree of equivalence
BIPM	0.003	24	0.13	0.003	24.8	0.13
NMi,c	−0.015	37	0.41	−0.015	39.3	0.39
NIST	−0.018	39	0.47	−0.018	41.1	0.44
NPL	0.002	32	0.07	0.002	35.3	0.06
NRC,c	−0.017	34	0.50	−0.017	36.4	0.47
NRLM,c	−0.020	28	0.72	−0.020	32.0	0.63
VNIIM	0.049	48	**1.03**	0.049	51.2	0.96
CSIRO	0.005	29	0.18	0.005	31.9	0.16
PTB	−0.001	26	0.04	−0.001	33.4	0.03
NIM	−0.001	46	0.03	−0.001	50.1	0.02
SMU	0.060	44	**1.37**	0.060	50.5	**1.19**
KRISS	−0.001	29	0.04	−0.001	31.8	0.04
IMGC	0.000	27	0.00	0.000	30.4	0.00
BNM	0.006	22	0.28	0.006	27.5	0.22
CENAM	0.002	27	0.08	0.002	30.7	0.07

Table 7 is a detail comparison of the degree of equivalence between results reported by CCM.M-K1 and the evaluation result from Monte Carlo Method. We can see that the result is almost the same and VNIIM is in the range of equivalence based on Monte Carlo method.

5 Conclusions

The paper summarizes the measurement results of CCM.M-K1, a key comparison of 1 kg weights. The measurement result was dealt based on the GUM. Recently, Monte Carlo method are adopted more often which was developed to overcome some of the limitations of the GUM, especially when an interval of confidence with a stipulated coverage probability is needed.

The numerical simulation in this paper was done in @Risk for Microsoft Excel 5.5 with 1×10^6 trials. The result of numerical simulation was compared with the result in CCM.M-K1 report. Differences between results of these two are negligible, and this result show that MCM leads to a better understanding of the measurement process.

References

1. Aupetit, C., Becerra, L.O., Bignell, N., et al.: Final Report on CIPM key comparison of 1 kg standards in stainless steel. Techn. Suppl. Metrologia **41**, 1–31 (2004)
2. Final Report on CIPM key comparison of multiples and submultiples of the kilogram (CCM.M-K2). Metrologia, 40(1A), 1–27 (2003)
3. Gosset, A., Madec, T.: Final report: CCM.M-K3 comparison / 50 kg mass. Metrologia **42**, 1–19 (2005)
4. Mann, G., Madec, T., Meury, P.A.: CCM.M-K3.1 comparison / 50 kg mass. Metrologia **47**, 1–10 (2010)
5. Becerra, L.O., Borys, M., et al.: Key comparison of 1 kg stainless steel mass standards CCM.M-K4. Metrologia **51**, 1–22 (2014)
6. Andel, I.V., Becerra, L.O., et al.: Report on CIPM key comparison of the second phase of multiples and submultiples of the kilogram (CCM.M-K5). Metrologia **48**(1), 40 (2011)
7. Abbott, P.J., Becerra, L.O., et al.: Final report Of CCM key comparison of mass standards CCM.M-K6, 50 kg. Metrologia **52**, 1–24 (2015)
8. Cox, M.G.: The evaluation of key comparison data. Metrologia **39**, 589–595 (2002)
9. Kacker, R.N., Datla, R.U., Parr, A.C.: Statistical analysis of CIPM key comparisons based on the ISO Guide. Metrologia **41**, 340–352 (2004)
10. Muller, J.W.: Possible advantages of a robust evaluation of comparisons. J. Res. Nat. Inst. Stan. Technol. **105**(4), 551–555 (2000)
11. Jurado, J.M., Alc´azar, A.: A software package comparison for uncertainty measurement estimation. Accred. Qual. Assur. **10**, 373–381 (2005)
12. Beascoa, M.S., Alegre, J.M., et al.: Implementation in MATLAB of the adaptive Monte Carlo method for the evaluation of measurement uncertainties. Accred. Qual. Assur. **14**, 95–106 (2009)
13. Sugiyama, Sam: Monte Carlo simulation/risk analysis on a spreadsheet: Review of three software packages. Foresight **9**, 36–42 (2008)

First International Workshop on Data Locality in Modern Computing Systems (DLMCS 2016)

Redundancy Elimination in the ExaStencils Code Generator

Stefan Kronawitter[1]([⊠]), Sebastian Kuckuk[2], and Christian Lengauer[1]

[1] University of Passau, 94030 Passau, Germany
{stefan.kronawitter,christian.lengauer}@uni-passau.de
[2] FAU Erlangen-Nürnberg, 91058 Erlangen, Germany
sebastian.kuckuk@fau.de

Abstract. Optimizing the performance of compute-bound codes requires, among other techniques, the elimination of redundant computations. The well-known concept of common subexpression elimination can achieve this in parts, and almost every production compiler conducts such an optimization. However, due to the conservative nature of these compilers, an external redundancy elimination can additionally increase the performance. For stencil codes using finite volume discretizations, an extension to eliminate redundancies between loop iterations is also very promising. We integrated both a classic common subexpression elimination and an extended version in the Exastencils code generator and present their impact on a real-world application.

Keywords: CSE · Common subexpression elimination · Vectorization

1 Introduction

Many scientific application fields, such as physics and chemistry simulations, require the solution of discretized partial differential equations (PDEs). This can be achieved efficiently by the usage of multigrid methods [8,16]. Since their composition and performance tuning can become quite complex and an application scientist is usually not interested in spending much time and effort on code optimization, a domain-specific language (DSL) is a good way to proceed. In project Exastencils[1] [12], we are developing a multi-layered DSL called ExaSlang [15] for geometric multigrid solvers and a corresponding code generator that is able to produce automatically optimized target code [11] for a given hardware description. The four layers of ExaSlang provide different levels of abstraction and are designed to address the needs of different user groups. Especially at the more concrete levels, the user can specify complex computations performed for the different multigrid components. Due to the regularity of stencil codes, there

S. Kronawitter—This work is supported by the German Research Foundation (DFG), as part of Priority Programme 1648 "Software for Exascale Computing" in project ExaStencils under contracts RU 422/15 and LE 912/15.

[1] http://www.exastencils.org.

© Springer International Publishing AG 2016
J. Carretero et al. (Eds.): ICA3PP 2016 Workshops, LNCS 10049, pp. 159–173, 2016.
DOI: 10.1007/978-3-319-49956-7_13

are various situations that may result in redundant computations. Therefore, the elimination of such redundancies both inside a single loop iteration and between loop iterations can be beneficial. The latter is especially useful in the context of finite volume discretizations.

We make the following contributions:

- a simple space-efficient extension of a common subexpression elimination (CSE) algorithm to eliminate redundancies between loop iterations,
- a detailed description of its implementation in the Exastencils code generator, along with useful preliminary steps and a subsequent vectorization,
- a demonstration of its usefulness for a real-world application.

The rest of the paper is organized as follows. Section 2.1 presents different approaches for a redundancy elimination and discusses their assets and drawbacks. Several preliminary steps to increase the yield of a redundancy elimination are described in Sect. 2.2. Two different CSE approaches implemented in the Exastencils code generator are introduced in Sects. 2.3 and 2.4 respectively. As the latter requires introducing additional code, which prevents vectorization in the first place, Sect. 2.5 describes how to overcome this limitation. An evaluation of the presented techniques using a fluid-flow simulation is given in Sect. 3. Section 4 introduces related work on redundancy elimination. Section 5 concludes.

2   Common Subexpression Elimination (CSE)

CSE [4] is frequently implemented in production compilers [2]. The basic idea is to remove repeated computations from expressions by reusing the result of the first computation. It is easy to see that this optimization can only be performed if none of the associated variables or memory regions are modified between the repeated evaluations of subexpressions. The drawback of this approach is that CSE potentially increases the register pressure since additional values must be preserved, which may lead to register spilling. But, in this case, the assumption is that, for larger expressions, the newly introduced memory access operations are faster than a recomputation of the expression.

2.1   Approaches to Common Subexpression Elimination

Text-Based CSE. There are different approaches for the detection of common subexpressions. The classic CSE searches for textual redundancies, introduces a new temporary variable, which holds the value of the common subexpression (CS), and replaces each occurrence by an access to the new variable. Figure 1a shows a simple code snippet, which contains the CS 2*i three times. Figure 1b shows an optimized version.

However, since redundant expressions are searched in the text, some optimization opportunities are missed. For example, there are two pairs of CSs in Fig. 2a. The first, 2*i, can be detected easily, but the other, 5+x respectively

```
                          cs = 2*i;
x = 2*i / j + 2*i;        x = cs / j + cs;
x = x * 2*i;              x = x * cs;
   (a) input code            (b) optimized code
```

Fig. 1. Example for a textual CSE.

5+y, varies in the last variable name and is therefore not detected, even though both variables have the same value. One can overcome this limitation by performing constant propagation and textual CSE repeatedly until a fixed point is reached. First, a CSE possibly introduces name aliases, which are resolved by a constant propagation. Second, since this may reveal new redundant expressions, a CSE must be reapplied. A dedicated detection of both pairs of subexpressions in Fig. 2a requires a semantic equivalence test, which is provided by, e.g., global value numbering (GVN).

```
x = 2 * i;            x = 2 * i;
y = 2 * i;            y = x;
a = 5 + x;            a = 5 + x;
b = 5 + y;            b = a;
  (a) input code        (b) optimized code
```

Fig. 2. Example for a semantic CSE based on GVN.

Global Value Numbering. GVN [3,5] is an analysis based on the static single-assignment form of a program. The first step is to assign a so-called value number to all variables such that two variables have the same value number iff their semantic equivalence can be proved. An optimal number mapping for the example in Fig. 2a would be $[i \rightarrow 1, x \rightarrow 2, y \rightarrow 2, a \rightarrow 3, b \rightarrow 3]$. According to this mapping, x and y, as well as a and b, are equal, which leads to the optimized code shown in Fig. 2b.

There are cases in which GVN is not able to identify a redundant computation that can be eliminated by a textual CSE. For example, the CS 2*i in Fig. 3a can be detected easily by a text-based CSE, while the value numbers of x and y must be different, since their values differ in sign if i is less than or equal to 0.

Loop-Carried Redundancies. Another opportunity for optimization arises from CSs between subsequent iterations of a surrounding loop as depicted in Fig. 4. The expression exp(0.5*i + 0.25) in iteration i-1 evaluates to the same value as the expression exp(0.5*i - 0.25) in the next iteration i:

$$exp(0.5*(i-1) + 0.25) == exp(0.5*i-0.5+0.25) == exp(0.5*i - 0.25)$$

Thus, the former can be reused. This incurs a higher detection effort, since some arithmetic conversions and simplifications are necessary due to the changing

```
x = 2 * i;              x = 2 * i;
if (i > 0)              if (i > 0)
  y = 2 * i;              y = x;
else                    else
  y = -(2 * i);           y = -x;
w = 5 + y;              w = 5 + y;
```

    (a) input code   (b) optimized code

Fig. 3. Example in which CSE is able to remove a redundancy not recognized by GVN.

value of the loop iterator. Also, the optimization shown in Fig. 4 requires that function `exp` is free of side-effects, so the analysis must be aware of this. One should further ensure that the CSs in different loop iterations do not overlap, i.e., do not share a part of the input code. For example, the redundant expression found above could be extended to `x = 4.2+exp(0.5*i + 0.25)` in iteration `i-1` and `y = 4.2+exp(0.5*i - 0.25)` in iteration `i`. But, since the summand `4.2` is now part of both expressions, the value for `A[i]` is `x + y - 4.2`. The additional subtraction of the shared summand `4.2` increases the complexity of the optimized code unnecessarily while reducing its benefit.

```
                                lcs = exp(0.5*0 - 0.25);
for (int i = 0; i < n; ++i) {   for (int i = 0; i < n; ++i) {
  A[i] = 4.2                       tcs  = exp(0.5*i + 0.25);
    + exp(0.5*i - 0.25)            A[i] = 4.2 + lcs + tcs;
    + exp(0.5*i + 0.25);           lcs  = tcs;
}                               }
```

    (a) input code   (b) optimized code

Fig. 4. Example of a loop-carried redundancy elimination.

The idea of such a loop-carried CSE is not restricted to a single encasing loop but, for multiple outer loops a separate value for each iteration of all inner loops must be remembered, which leads to a significant increase in memory consumption. Another drawback is that the reuse of data from the previous iteration effectively sequentializes a loop or, at least, requires a special treatment for a parallel execution.

2.2 Preliminary Transformations

The Exastencils code generator supports both types of redundancy elimination described in the previous subsection, namely a text-based and a loop-carried version. In order to facilitate the removal of as many and as large redundant computations as possible, a number of preliminary transformations is required.

Inlining. To start, two special inlining transformations, one global and one local, are executed. Besides leading to a better starting position, the former is necessary since multiple calls of arbitrary functions cannot be merged in general. Inlining the body of pure functions simplifies the redundancy detection. It is then only required to recognize and deal with pure calls to the standard C math library. All other function calls can be rejected, i.e., they are not allowed to be part of a CS.

The local inlining performed subsequently removes constant local variables, i.e., variables which are assigned exactly once, namely in their definition. This obviously introduces redundant computations, since every read of such a variable is replaced by the same expression. But it allows arithmetic optimizations and simplifications of the combined expressions, and the CSE applied later can potentially also detect larger redundant computations.

Arithmetic Simplifications. The arithmetic optimizations mentioned previously are the last step of the preprocessing. Since all transformations of the Exastencils code generator are performed on an abstract syntax tree (AST), the detection of redundant computations can be complex, as indicated by Fig. 5. In this example, the initializations of x and y are identical, but the corresponding ASTs are completely different. Even if the multiplication by 2 is factored out of the computation in the first line, the ASTs do not match because of the different order of the operands in the summation. For a binary addition, it is not sufficient to simply permute the children of each node, which exploits the commutativity law, but a more advanced restructuring analogously to the associativity law is required. To deal with this, the code generator uses a more general summation node with an arbitrary number of summands, of which a binary addition is a special case. A transformation to merge several nested additions into a single summation and to fix the permutation is straightforward. The same holds for multiplications, while subtraction and division must remain binary, since they are neither commutative nor associative. Note that one must take care when dealing with matrices and vectors, as the commutativity of the multiplication only holds for scalar values.

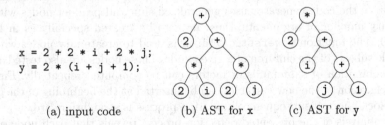

```
x = 2 + 2 * i + 2 * j;
y = 2 * (i + j + 1);
```

(a) input code   (b) AST for x   (c) AST for y

Fig. 5. Analysis example.

A normalization according to the distributivity law is a bit more complex. The heuristics implemented focuses mainly on affine computations, which is sufficient for the run-time-intense parts of the generated stencil codes. In a first step, the AST of the input expression is analyzed bottom up. The result is a key-value mapping which represents the given expression as a sum. Its keys are the summands and the associated values their constant coefficients. For each visited node, the mapping is generated either directly in case of an array or variable access, or for an operator by merging the mappings of their children accordingly. E.g., for an addition expression with the children mappings {i->3, j->1} and {i->1, k->4}, the result is {i->4, j->1, k->4}. This effectively normalizes the expression in the wrong direction: it maximizes the number of multiplications performed. But a reversal of this mapping factors out as many constants as possible. For the given example, the reversal is {4->i+k, 1->j} which results in the normalized expression 4*(i+k) + j.

2.3   Text-Based CSE

Although the loop-carried CSE described in the next subsection is performed first, it is based in both concepts and techniques on the traditional redundancy elimination, which justifies addressing the latter first. Section 2.1 introduced two different approaches to CSE, both with their own advantages and disadvantages. A value numbering would be the only transformation in the code generator that requires a static single-assignment form of the code. Therefore, an AST-based redundancy detection, analogously to a syntactical one, was implemented. In combination with the two inlining steps performed beforehand, most of the restrictions of this approach do not pose a hindrance. For example, both expressions for a and b from Fig. 2a read 5 + 2*i after x and y are inlined, which can now be optimized by any approach.

The detection begins with a search of variable accesses, array accesses, and constants in the input AST. Each instance found more than once is added to the initial set of redundant operations along with their ancestors. Note that the children of these nodes are ignored, i.e., array subscripts are not analyzed here, since there is a specialized optimization performing an address precalculation beforehand [11]. Starting with the initial list, larger CSs are detected inductively as presented in Algorithm 1: a larger CS can only be formed by a set of smaller CSs. Since the code generator uses generalized sum and product nodes with an arbitrary number of arguments, these have to be treated specially as in Lines 7 to 10. The function powerset_children is used to create new nodes with all possible subsets of the children of a given node. These nodes are also tested, since any combination of summands or factors can be computed repeatedly. Finally, the declaration of the new variables can be inserted at the beginning of the given code block and the subsequent elimination process is straightforward.

An analysis of the presented detection process reveals that each node of the input tree is added at most once to the list of potential CSs, namely as the parent of its child with largest depth. Therefore, in each step, the depth of the newly detected trees, which represent the new CSs, increases by exactly 1, so the depth of the input AST is an upper bound for the number of steps required.

```
       input  : set of initial common subexpressions CSs
       output : set of all common subexpressions
 1   newCSs = CSs
 2   while newCSs ≠ {} do
 3   │   newCSs' = newCSs
 4   │   newCSs = {}
 5   │   foreach expr ∈ locations(newCSs') do
 6   │   │   parent = parent(expr)
 7   │   │   if parent is sum or product then
 8   │   │   │   foreach parent' ∈ powerset_children(parent) do
 9   │   │   │   │   if children(parent') ⊆ CSs then
10   │   │   │   └     └  newCSs = newCSs ∪ {parent'}
11   │   │   else if children(parent) ⊆ CSs then
12   │   │   └     newCSs = newCSs ∪ {parent}
13   │   CSs = CSs ∪ newCSs
14   return CSs
```

Algorithm 1. Find larger CSs based on an input set of smaller ones.

After the first CS is removed, one could either update the set of the remaining ones carefully to choose how to continue, or simply restart the whole analysis. Due to its simplicity and low performance impact, the code generator currently restarts the CSE after each removed redundancy until either no new CS is found, or the largest one becomes too small to be profitable.

2.4   Loop-Carried CSE

The Exastencils code generator also supports loop-carried CSE, as described in Sect. 2.3, which is executed first. The basic idea is to detect and eliminate redundant expressions not only in a text sequence of statements, but also between statement instances of subsequent loop iterations, as described in Sect. 2.1.

Before the actual redundancy detection is started, each node of the AST gets its own unique integer identifier assigned as a preparation of a later overlap test. For the detection of redundancies between neighboring loop iterations, the body is duplicated and each occurrence of the loop iterator i is replaced by the expression i-str(i), while str denotes the stride of the given loop. The expressions in the modified body are then simplified using the transformation described in Sect. 2.2. As a result, the loop bodies of two subsequent iterations of the i-loop are available. These two versions of the loop body then form the input for the text-based CS detection described in the previous subsection. As explained in Sect. 2.1, only common subtrees that do not overlap in the unprocessed source are allowed to be eliminated. This is equivalent to the uniqueness test for the integral identifiers associated with each node among all common subtrees. From the remaining redundancies one must select an appropriate subset to be eliminated.

The selection of subexpressions to be eliminated in this approach is worth a closer look. Choosing the largest CS is not always sufficient. Figure 6a shows a loop in which one could reuse data from the previous loop iteration. The run time of this loop is clearly dominated by the calls of exp. While the original code contains four calls in each iteration, a text-based CSE can save two of them. But this code can also be optimized by a loop-carried CSE. On the one hand, Fig. 6b shows the resulting code if the largest possible redundancy, namely exp(0.5*i-0.25)+4.2 in iteration i-1 and exp(0.5*i+0.25)+4.2 in iteration i, is eliminated. However, it still contains two calls of exp, which can only be simplified by adding another variable to carry even more data between loop iterations. In this example, it would only require one additional scalar value but the problem can also arise in situations with a higher dimensionality, which could lead to a significantly higher memory usage. On the other hand, starting directly with the smaller redundancy exp(0.5*i-0.25) and exp(0.5*i+0.25) results in the code shown in Fig. 6c, which gets along with only a single exp call. Therefore, the code generator takes not only the size of a CS, but also the number of its occurrences into account. The heuristics used eliminates all redundancies larger than a fixed threshold, which leads to good results for all test cases mentioned before. A more advanced approach based on, e.g., the results of a roofline analysis or auto-tuning would be possible, too.

```
for (int i = 0; i < n; ++i) {
    A[i] = exp(0.5*i - 0.25) + exp(0.5*i + 0.25);
    B[i] = exp(0.5*i - 0.25) + 4.2;
    C[i] = exp(0.5*i + 0.25) + 4.2;
}
```

(a) input code

```
lcs = exp(0.5*0 - 0.25) + 4.2;
for (int i = 0; i < n; ++i) {
    tcs  = exp(0.5*i + 0.25);
    A[i] = exp(0.5*i - 0.25) + tcs;
    B[i] = lcs;
    C[i] = tcs + 4.2;
    lcs  = tcs + 4.2;
}
```

```
lcs = exp(0.5*0 - 0.25);
for (int i = 0; i < n; ++i) {
    tcs  = exp(0.5*i + 0.25);
    A[i] = lcs + tcs;
    B[i] = lcs + 4.2;
    C[i] = tcs + 4.2;
    lcs  = tcs;
}
```

(b) eliminating the largest CS   (c) eliminating a smaller CS

Fig. 6. Example in which eliminating a smaller CS results in a better performance.

The last part –the elimination itself– proceeds as follows. A new array to store the values computed in the previous loop iterations must be introduced. Its extent increases depending on how many loops are inside the one for which the loop-carried CSE is executed. E.g., for a three-fold loop nest with an iteration vector $(i, j, k) \in \{0, \ldots, 511\}^3$ and a redundancy between subsequent iterations of the i-loop, separate scalars for each of the inner 512*512 iterations are required. Its initialization is performed only in the first iteration of the i-loop using the redundant expression itself. This introduces a condition that is removed in a later optimization step by performing a partial unrolling. The CSs are replaced by an access to array element [j, k]. What remains is an update of the array with a new value from the current iteration. The expression for it can be generated from the CS by replacing each occurrence of i with i+str(i). This also introduces a new textual redundancy, which is eliminated by the successive text-based CSE.

The application of this approach is not limited to subsequent iterations; it can be easily extended to any step size. In our domain of stencil computations, however, this is usually not necessary.

2.5   Vectorization

One drawback of the presented loop-carried CSE is that it effectively sequentializes the corresponding loop, since data from the immediate predecessor is required.

On the one hand, employing multiple processor cores regardless of a previous redundancy elimination is easy if each thread executes one contiguous sequence of loop iterations. In this case, the initialization must be adapted to be executed not only in the first iteration of the loop but in the first one of each thread. Additionally, each thread must have its private buffer to carry information between different loop iterations.

On the other hand, vectorizing the innermost loop to load a single processor core to capacity is more complex, since it is equivalent to the concurrent computation of subsequent loop iterations. Excluding this loop from the loop-carried CSE is also not an option, as this is the most profitable one to optimize: it requires only a single scalar to carry data between iterations. However, the newly introduced data dependences do not prevent the vectorization in general, but require a more careful selection of the generated instructions for all three accesses to the new temporary variable. First, the initialization of the temporary need not be vectorized at all, as only the initial scalar has to be computed separately. Second, vectorizing a statement, which loads the value from the previous iteration, leads to two different situations, as shown in Fig. 7. For the first element of the vector, the required value is the one of the previous iteration stored in the temporary (thick arrow) while the values of all other elements are actually computed in the current iteration and used twice. This requires the corresponding elements of this iteration to be computed prior to the load operation and also to generate suitable data shuffling instructions. Third, the store of the newly computed value handed to the next iteration must be restricted to the last element of the computed vector. Alternatively, the whole vector could be preserved, which may reduce the number of shuffle instructions. But this also requires an additional load before the vectorized loop and a store after it to preserve data between different loops, such as a prolog or epilog loop if the number of iterations is not evenly divisible by the vector size.

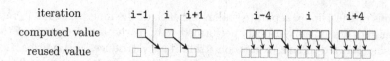

Fig. 7. Reusing a value from the previous iteration in the scalar and vectorized case. Arrows represent data copy operations. Thick ones are accross loop iterations.

3 Evaluation

Solving simple PDEs, such as Poisson's equation, is not suitable for the evaluation of the presented techniques since the resulting code is already quite simple. Consequently, subexpressions occur only rarely and if they do they are not very complex. Thus, we choose the application of simulating non-isothermal and non-Newtonian fluid flows instead. The targeted fluids have a high relevance in academia and industry alike. They are usually given by suspensions of particles or macromolecules and can be encountered as gels, pastes or foams. Relevant examples include organic fluids such as blood, food products such as fruit juice, and industrial fluids such as drilling fluids and mining pulps.

In recent decades, many approaches for such fluid flow simulations have been developed. Our implementation is based on the SIMPLE algorithm (Semi-Implicit Method for Pressure Linked Equations). A detailed derivation is beyond the scope of this paper but can be found in the literature [14,17]. The main idea of the SIMPLE algorithm is as follows: Instead of solving the entire non-linear system at once, linear systems of equations (LSEs) are set up for each of the velocity components. This step corresponds to freezing all other unknowns. Next, the single LSEs are solved. In our case, we use dedicated geometric multigrid solvers for this step. Since freezing components introduces some errors, a subsequent pressure correction has to be calculated and applied. In the classical SIMPLE algorithm, these steps are repeated until convergence is reached. For our problem, however, an extension towards incorporating temperature and thereby induced effects is required. Fortunately, this can be done similar to solving for the other components, i.e., by setting up another LSE and solving it. Due to the dependency of the five single LSEs on the current solution, a recomputation is required in every SIMPLE iteration. In total, an algorithm as detailed in Algorithm 2 emerges. The function 'update quantities' includes the modeling of temperature-induced behavior and the chosen model for non-Newtonian behavior.

Concerning discretization, we rely on a finite volume approach on non-uniform staggered grids, as depicted in Fig. 8. The specifics can be found elsewhere [17,18]. Generally, finite volume discretizations, especially on staggered grids, require frequent interpolation and integration of values and expressions with respect to control volume interfaces. Usually, at least parts of these computations on interfaces are independent of the direction of the evaluation. Consider, e.g., the evaluation of a physical quantity located at the cell centers on the East (right) interface. This evaluation will yield the same value when performed for

```
foreach time step do
   while not converged do
      update quantities
      set up LSEs for u, v and w, and solve
      set up LSE for pressure correction and solve
      apply pressure correction
      set up LSE for temperature and solve
```

Algorithm 2. SIMPLE algorithm.

the West (left) interface from the point on the next cell. Consequently, a loop-carried CSE has the potential to benefit most codes based on these types of discretizations.

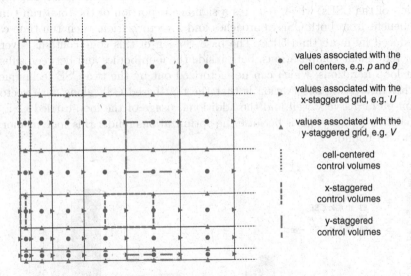

Fig. 8. 2D illustration of the lower left part of a non-equidistant, staggered grid. Velocity components are associated with the centers of edges (resp. faces in 3D). Staggered control volumes get halved at the boundary.

All experiments were executed on Intel Xeon E5-2690 v2 processors. They consist of ten Ivy Bridge EP cores, each running at 3.2 GHz. The complete simulation with 10,000 time steps was implemented in our DSL ExaSlang 4 and compiled to C++ code for the given architecture by the Exastencils code generator. Some basic optimizations, such as address precalculation are always applied, while the effect of the presented optimizations are evaluated in detail. The C++ code was compiled with gcc 5.2 using aggressive optimizations (-O3) and enabling AVX instruction generation (-mavx). For a single simulation, four execution times were extracted: the time to update physical properties such as viscosity (update quantities), the time to set up the LSEs for all variables (compile LSEs) and to solve them (solve LSEs), as well as the total time which consists of the previous mentioned and other factors such as convergence checks. Each of these times is the average over all 10,000 time steps for a single simulation. Additionally, every simulation was executed five times for a grid size of 64^3, and their median is shown in Fig. 9. On the one hand, it can be seen that neither the update of the quantities, nor the solving of the LSEs do benefit from the CSE techniques. This is an expected result, since the corresponding codes do not contain any redundant computation between different loop iterations. And the ones found by the text-based CSE are too small to influence the run time. Vectorization also does not affect the performance of solving the LSEs, since they are clearly memory-bandwidth-bound. However, it does increase the performance of the quantity update, which can be explained by a frequent usage of the square-root function, whose vectorized version is considerably faster than the one in the math library shipped with gcc 5.2. On the other hand, the compilation of the LSEs, which requires a significant portion of the total run time, does benefit from both CSE approaches and a vectorization: their run time can be reduced by more than 50 %. The base version of this code contains several larger redundant computations, both inside the loop bodies and between subsequent loop iterations, which can be factorized out by the two CSE techniques. Another interesting observation is that the text-based CSE along with vectorization performs very well and the additional usage of the loop-carried CSE is only slightly better. This is because the optimizations render this code memory-bandwidth-bound.

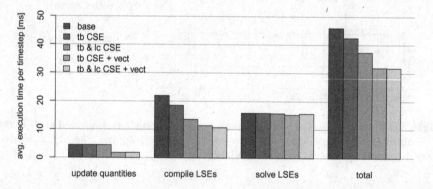

Fig. 9. Average execution times per time step for the presented text-based (tb) and loop-carried (lc) CSE optimizations applied. Total run time is divided into the update of physical properties such as viscosity, compiling the LSE, i.e., updating the stencil coefficients, solving them, and other factors not shown such as convergence checks.

4   Related Work

CSE and GVN are well-known and also well-understood compiler optimization techniques incorporated in almost all production compilers [2,5,13]. These implementations are suitable for removing redundancies introduced by the compiler itself, e.g., when it creates address-computation instructions from abstract array accesses. However, CSs at source-code level are not always identified as such, since the target compiler must make worst-case assumptions for aliasing and other language features. More powerful CSE techniques were presented by Debray [6] and Saabas et al. [1], and elsewhere. Additionally, there exist several specialized CSE approaches, which focus on problems in different application domains, such as digital signal processing [10,17].

Neither of these take redundancies between loop iterations into account. Hammes et al. present a temporal CSE for a special type of loops from the language SA-C [9]. For these loops, the programmer can explicitly specify a so-called window for the data structure to traverse. This window defines how many neighboring elements are accessed per loop iteration. It is also used to identify redundancies between subsequent loop iterations, which simplifies the detection process but also limits the applicability. A more powerful approach was presented by Faber et al. [7]. It is based on the polyhedral model and can therefore detect redundancies between any loop iterations. On the downside, this approach only detects CSs for which the non-array parts are structurally equivalent, i.e., the example of Fig. 4a cannot be optimized. Additionally, even if a single scalar would be sufficient to carry information from one loop iteration to the next, every instance of this value gets its own memory location. In contrast to the presented loop-carried CSE from Sect. 2.4, this unnecessarily increases memory consumption.

5   Conclusion

We presented redundancy-elimination optimizations implemented in the Exastencils code generator. These contain a traditional text-based version of a CSE, along with a small set of preliminary transformations to increase both the size and the number of CSs found. The latter consists of an inlining step to allow removing redundancies across function boundaries, and arithmetic simplifications to prevent the commutativity and associativity law of addition and multiplication to interfere with the CS detection.

Based on the simplification transformation we also formulated a simple extension of the text-based CSE to be also applicable across loop boundaries. This allows reusing already evaluated subexpressions from the previous iteration of any surrounding loop. However, it comes at a cost: for outer loops not only a single scalar must be preserved, but for each inner loop iteration an additional value has to be stored. Vectorizing the optimized code also requires special treatment, since the reuse of values from a previous loop iteration introduces an additional data dependency.

Finally, we demonstrated the usefulness of the presented techniques with a real-world application, namely a non-isothermal and non-Newtonian fluid-flow simulation. The performance of the affected code parts was doubled and the optimizations were able to render them memory-bandwidth-bound. A text-based version can be profitable, or at least not harmful, for any stencil computation, while a loop-carried approach is especially useful for finite volume discretizations.

References

1. Aceto, L., Ingolfsdottir, A., Saabas, A., Uustalu, T.: Program and proof optimizations with type systems. J. Logic Algebraic Prog. **77**(1–2), 131–154 (2008)
2. Aho, A.V., Lam, M.S., Sethi, R., Ullman, J.D.: Compilers - Principles, Techniques and Tools, 2nd edn. Addison-Wesley, Boston (2007)
3. Click, C.: Global code motion/global value numbering. In: Proceedings of ACM SIGPLAN 1995 Conference on Programming Language Design and Implementation (PLDI), pp. 246–257. ACM, June 1995
4. Cocke, J.: Global common subexpression elimination. In: Proceedings of Symposium on Compiler Optimization, pp. 20–24. ACM, Jul 1970
5. Cocke, J., Schwartz, J.T.: Programming Languages and Their Compilers: Preliminary Notes, 2nd edn. Courant Institute of Mathematical Sciences, New York University (1970)
6. Debray, S.K.: Compiler optimizations for low-level redundancy elimination: An application of meta-level prolog primitives. In: Pettorossi, A. (ed.) META 1992. LNCS, vol. 649, pp. 120–134. Springer, Heidelberg (1992). doi:10.1007/3-540-56282-6_8
7. Faber, P., Griebl, M., Lengauer, C.: Loop-carried code placement. In: Sakellariou, R., Gurd, J., Freeman, L., Keane, J. (eds.) Euro-Par 2001. LNCS, vol. 2150, pp. 230–235. Springer, Heidelberg (2001). doi:10.1007/3-540-44681-8_34
8. Hackbusch, W.: Multi-Grid Methods and Applications. Springer-Verlag, Heidelberg (1985)
9. Hammes, J., Böhm, A.P.W., Ross, C., Chawathe, M., Draper, B.A., Rinker, B., Najjar, W.A.: Loop fusion and temporal common subexpression elimination in window-based loops. In: Proceedings of 8th IPDPS Reconfigurable Architectures Workshop (RAW), 8 p. IEEE Computer Society, April 2001
10. Kamal, H., Lee, J., Koo, B.: An improved non-CSD 2-bit recursive common subexpression elimination method to implement FIR filter. ETRI J. **33**(5), 695–703 (2011)
11. Kronawitter, S., Lengauer, C.: Optimizations applied by the ExaStencils code generator. Technical Report MIP-1502, Faculty of Informatics and Mathematics, University of Passau, 10 p., January 2015
12. Lengauer, C., et al.: ExaStencils: advanced stencil-code engineering. In: Lopes, L., et al. (eds.) Euro-Par 2014. LNCS, vol. 8806, pp. 553–564. Springer, Heidelberg (2014). doi:10.1007/978-3-319-14313-2_47
13. Muchnick, S.S.: Advanced Compiler Design and Implementation. Morgan Kaufmann Publishers Inc., San Francisco (1997)
14. Patankar, S.V., Spalding, D.B.: A calculation procedure for heat, mass and momentum transfer in three-dimensional parabolic flows. Int. J. Heat Mass Transfer **15**(10), 1787–1806 (1972)
15. Schmitt, C., Kuckuk, S., Hannig, F., Köstler, H., Teich, J.: ExaSlang: A domain-specific language for highly scalable multigrid solvers. In: Proceedings of 4th International Workshop on Domain-Specific Languages and High-Level Frameworks for High Performance Computing (WOLFHPC), pp. 42–51. ACM (2014)

16. Trottenberg, U., Osterlee, C.W., Schüller, A.: Multigrid. Academic Press, New York (2000)
17. Vasco, D.A., Moraga, N.O., Haase, G.: Parallel finite volume method simulation of three-dimensional fluid flow and convective heat transfer for viscoplastic non-Newtonian fluids. Numer. Heat Transf. Part A: Appl. **66**(2), 990–1019 (2014)
18. Versteeg, H.K., Malalasekera, W.: An Introduction to Computational Fluid Dynamics: The Finite Volume Method, 2nd edn. Pearson Education Limited, Upper Saddle River (2007)

A Dataflow IR for Memory Efficient RIPL Compilation to FPGAs

Robert Stewart[1]([✉]), Greg Michaelson[1], Deepayan Bhowmik[2],
Paulo Garcia[2], and Andy Wallace[2]

[1] School of Mathematical and Computer Sciences,
Heriot-Watt University, Edinburgh, UK
R.Stewart@hw.ac.uk
[2] School of Engineering and Physical Sciences,
Heriot-Watt University, Edinburgh, UK

Abstract. Field programmable gate arrays (FPGAs) are fundamentally different to fixed processors architectures because their memory hierarchies can be tailored to the needs of an algorithm. FPGA compilers for high level languages are not hindered by fixed memory hierarchies. The constraint when compiling to FPGAs is the availability of resources.

In this paper we describe how the dataflow intermediary of our declarative FPGA image processing DSL called RIPL (Rathlin Image Processing Language) enables us to constrain memory. We use five benchmarks to demonstrate that memory use with RIPL is comparable to the Vivado HLS OpenCV library without the need for language pragmas to guide hardware synthesis. The benchmarks also show that RIPL is more expressive than the Darkroom FPGA image processing language.

Keywords: Domain specific languages · FPGAs · Data locality

1 Introduction

1.1 Memory Costs of High Level FPGA Languages

General Purpose Languages. Programming with C++ for FPGAs often relies heavily on the programmer's use of language pragmas to control how data structures should be implemented in hardware. For example when using Xilinx Vivado HLS [13], if a 3×3 window for applying a 2D filter is needed, the programmer must use an array partition pragma to partition the 3×3 pixel window array into individual scalar elements, to avoid its implementation using BRAM.

Image Processing Languages and Libraries. Domain specific languages (DSLs) offer potential for clearer syntax, stronger semantic checks, type-system-based guarantees and compiler optimisation for improved code execution. Compared to compiling C/C++ with HLS tools, DSLs can capture domain knowledge to abstract hardware templates that encapsulate common data access patterns that can more easily be analysed, *e.g.* for FIFO depth and bitwidth requirements.

© Springer International Publishing AG 2016
J. Carretero et al. (Eds.): ICA3PP 2016 Workshops, LNCS 10049, pp. 174–188, 2016.
DOI: 10.1007/978-3-319-49956-7_14

A DSL may be an existing collection of language primitives ported to FPGAs, *e.g.* the Vivado HLS support [10] for a subset of the OpenCV [2] library. OpenCV C++ library code is not synthesisable directly, instead OpenCV function calls in existing software code must be replaced with corresponding function calls from the HLS library. In this restricted setting, it is not possible to use dynamic memory allocation *e.g.* in the construction of image whose dimensions are decided at runtime. For good performance using this library, the programmer must use explicit pragmas to guide hardware generation.

Alternatively, DSLs may be embedded within the programming model of an existing language, *e.g.* the Darkroom [5] FPGA image processing DSL is embedded within Terra [4]. Darkroom is compiled to line-buffered pipelines, with all intermediate values in local line-buffer storage. Images at each stage of computation are specified as pure functions from 2D coordinates to the values at those coordinates.

Our RIPL DSL for FPGAs is implemented as a standalone language, *i.e.* it has its own syntax and its stream processing based programming model is not hindered by a programming model of any general purpose host language. The memory performance and expressivity of HLS OpenCV, Darkroom and RIPL is compared in Sect. 5.

1.2 Data Locality

Fixed memory architectures comprise very fast cache access, off chip DDR memory access, or slow disk storage. Each application must fit into a fixed memory architecture representing a single large hierarchical memory space. A common approach is to build data locality aware compilers [11], *e.g.* locality aware scheduling of OpenMP tasks on multicore CPUs [9] and mapping nested access patterns on GPUs [8]. Minimising cache misses involves profiling cache traces, moreover trading function inlining with executable size, and managing memory pressure. Minimising memory requirements is a particular problem for close to sensor real-time image processing on FPGAs, where hard choices must be made in trading off memory and processing.

1.3 FPGA Memory

An important FPGA language implementation choice is whether on chip or off chip memory should be used to store data structures. Utilising off chip memory is sometimes unavoidable depending on the data transforms an algorithm requires, *e.g.* transposing or rotating an image, both of which require an image frame buffer. However, frequently using off chip memory from different parts of FPGA circuits does not scale, because only one memory read from an on chip circuit can be performed in each clock cycle. This can sequentialise execution and hence hurt throughput performance. Moreover, off chip memory access can take multiple clock cycles compared to latency-free LUT RAM or one cycle to access BRAM. On chip memory provides contention free local buffer access for different parts of the application specific circuit, because it is distributed across the FPGA's fabric.

Compilers of high level real-time languages should therefore prioritise wholly on chip memory implementations. However, the scarcity of BRAM introduces its own set of constraints for programming language designers to consider.

Memory layout on FPGA chips is fundamentally different to fixed processor architectures. Instead of compiling a program to map efficiently to fixed memory hierarchies, synthesis of high level languages builds a custom memory architecture on chip tailored for the needs of an algorithm. The constraint when compiling high level languages to FPGAs is the available resources, *e.g.* on chip memory ranges from 4 Mb to 68 Mb. The challenge for HLS compilers is therefore to minimise memory use from algorithms expressed with high level software languages. Synthesis tools can choose to implement memory using registers, lookup tables (LUTs), or block RAM (BRAM). Unlike cache contention issues on multicore CPUs, there is no contention to access BRAM memory because it is distributed across the fabric of an FPGA.

2   FPGA Memory Constraints

2.1   Image Buffer Capacity

The main FPGA resource for implementing memory is BRAM blocks. For example, the Z-7020 chip on the Zedboard has 140 36 Kb BRAM blocks amounting to 4.4 Mb. The XC7K480T chip on the Kintex-7 board has 1,910 18 Kb blocks and 995 36 Kb blocks amounting to 34 Mb. The XC7VX1140T chip on the Virtex-7 board has 3,760 18 Kb blocks and 1,880 36 Kb blocks amounting to 68 Mb. A single channel image pixel is 8 bits, or 1 byte. A 320×240 image with a single colour channel is $76,800$ bytes, a 512×512 image is $262,144$ bytes, a 1024×768 image is $786,432$ bytes, and a 1920×1080 image is $2,073,600$ bytes.

Storing entire image frame buffers on FPGAs does not scale. The cost of buffering entire image frames on chip is shown in Fig. 1. The Zedboard can store up to seven 320×240 frame buffers and just two 512×512 frame buffers. The Kintex-7 can store up to five 1024×768 buffers and two 1920×1080 buffers, and the Virtex-7 is able to store four 1920×1080 buffers. Localised pixel, row and region buffers should instead be generated by high level language compilers.

2.2   Eliminating Intermediate Buffers with Compiler Optimisation

When compiling high level programs to FPGAs, it is important to eliminate intermediate data structures because on chip BRAM is a scarce resource. A motivating example is shown in Fig. 2. This C++ code applies a Sobel edge detection filter with a nested *for* loop, and then brightens the result with another nested *for* loop. It uses the OpenCV *Mat* class for two intermediate images, *image2* and *image3*. The *xGradient()* and *yGradient()* functions are omitted for brevity. Whilst these intermediate image structures could be offloaded to off chip DDR memory, this would result in a latency of multiple clock cycles for every memory access, compared to a single cycle for on chip access. There is a need for

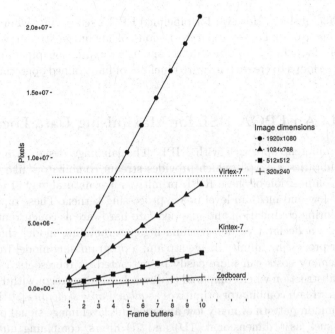

Fig. 1. Storing multiple frame buffers with on chip FPGA Memory

```
Mat image2;
/* Sobel filter */
for(int y = 1; y < image1.rows - 1; y++) {
  for(int x = 1; x < image1.cols - 1; x++) {
      gx = xGradient(image1, x, y);
      gy = yGradient(image1, x, y);
      sum = abs(gx) + abs(gy);
      image2.at<uchar>(y,x) = sum;
  }
}

Mat image3;
/* brighten image2 */
for(int y = 1; y < image2.rows - 1; y++) {
  for(int x = 1; x < image2.cols - 1; x++) {
      newPixel = image2.at<uchar>(y, x) + 50;
      image3.at<uchar>(y,x) = newPixel > 255 ? 255 : newPixel;
  }
}
```

Fig. 2. Intermediate images using OpenCV's *Mat* class

FPGA language compilers to avoid wasteful memory resources on intermediate images *image2* and *image3*.

One data locality approach in data parallel language compilers is to start from an imperative language with loops, and fuse the successive loops over the input *image1* into an expression tree in a single loop, to improve cache locality and on chip register locality *e.g.* [6,12]. For CPU or GPU scheduling, this expression tree can be duplicated to apply the same fused computation on image chunks in a data parallel fashion. However for pipelined FPGA scheduling, where different computations are applied to separate regions of an image stream, a compiler would apply loop fusion optimisations, and then expression pipelining in the body of those loops to create hardware pipelines of fine grained operator dataflow graphs.

3   RIPL: An FPGA DSL for Maximising Data Locality

We take a different approach with RIPL. The language design is inspired by streaming libraries *e.g.* [7], which provides stream combinators like *map*, *fold* and *sum*. Composition of these RIPL primitives is a natural way of expressing pipelines of low and medium level image processing kernels. These pipelines are preserved during compilation and mapped into hardware as concurrent circuits.

RIPL has a declarative non-terminating programming model that is constrained for processing infinite image stream, a programming model from which minimal memory costs can more easily be extracted. It represents a high programming abstraction when compared to direct hardware design with HDLs. We term RIPLs stream combinator primitives as *algorithmic skeletons* [3]. They capture the common pattern of many low and medium level image signal processing operations such as 1 dimensional (1D) and 2D filters, combining images, and global operations such as finding the maximum pixel value. Intermediate images in RIPL programs are transformed to streams that are shared through parallel hardware pipelines, rather than copying whole images for each pipeline phase to process. The RIPL implementation is available online[1].

3.1   RIPL Skeletons

RIPL skeletons abstract common data access patterns, to which the user supplies functions and values. They have been designed such that dataflow analysis can be performed on their composition, and to extract the minimal memory requirements of their use. The RIPL program in Fig. 3 broadly corresponds to the OpenCV C++ in Fig. 2, though RIPLs *convolve* and *filter2D* skeletons also mirrors edge pixels over image boundaries to apply the kernel function to edge pixels. When compiled to hardware, the image stream *image1* is incrementally processed, first by hardware logic that computes Sobel edge detection and then by logic that brightens each pixel in the stream.

Skeleton API. The RIPL skeletons are shown in Fig. 4, using a standard notation for function type signatures, *e.g. map* is a skeleton that takes two arguments: an $M \times N$ image, and function from a vector of A pixels to a vector of B pixels. It returns an $M \times N$ image. Each skeleton is repeatedly applied over an image stream. Types in Fig. 4 are annotated with pixel major order, vector lengths and image dimensions. For example, $[P]_A$ is a vector of pixels of length A, so an argument in a function of the form $\lambda[a, b]$ has an implicit type $[P]_2$.

---

[1] https://github.com/robstewart57/ripl.

```
image1 = imread 512 512;
/* Sobel filter */
image2 = filter2D image1 (3,3)
    (\p1 p2 p3 p4 p5 p6 p7 p8 p9 ->
        abs ((p1 + (2*p2) + p3) - (p7 + (2*p8) + p9))
      + abs ((p3 + (2*p6) + p9) - (p1 + (2*p4) + p7)));

/* brighten image2 */
image3 = map image2 (\[pixel] -> [min 255 (pixel + 50)]);
```

Fig. 3. RIPL equivalent of the OpenCV C++ in Fig. 2

$$imread_{M,N} : (M : Int) \rightarrow (N : Int) \rightarrow I^R_{(M,N)}$$

$$map_{M,N,A,B} : I^R_{(M,N)} \rightarrow ([P]_A \rightarrow [P]_B) \rightarrow I^R_{(M*(B/A),N)}$$

$$map_{M,N,A,B} : I^C_{(M,N)} \rightarrow ([P]_A \rightarrow [P]_B) \rightarrow I^C_{(M,N*(B/A))}$$

$$imap_{M,N,A} : I_{(M,N)} \rightarrow ([P]_A \rightarrow P) \rightarrow I_{(M,N)}$$

$$convolve_{M,N,A,B} : I_{(M,N)} \rightarrow (A, B) : (Int, Int) \rightarrow [K]_{(A*B)} \rightarrow I_{(M,N)}$$

$$filter2D_{M,N,A,B} : I_{(M,N)} \rightarrow (A, B) : (Int, Int) \rightarrow ([P]_{(A*B)} \rightarrow P) \rightarrow I_{(M,N)}$$

$$zipWith_{M,N,A} : I_{(M,N)} \rightarrow I_{(M,N)} \rightarrow ([P]_A \rightarrow [P]_A \rightarrow [P]_A) \rightarrow I_{(M,N)}$$

$$zipWithScalar_{M,N,A} : I_{(M,N)} \rightarrow P \rightarrow (P \rightarrow P \rightarrow P) \rightarrow I_{(M,N)}$$

$$zipWithVector_{M,N,A,B} : I_{(M,N)} \rightarrow [P]_A \rightarrow ([P]_A \rightarrow P \rightarrow P) \rightarrow I_{(M,N)}$$

$$unzip_{M,N,A} : I^R_{(M,N)} \rightarrow ([P]_A \rightarrow P) \rightarrow ([P]_A \rightarrow P) \rightarrow (I^R_{(M/2,N)}, I^R_{(M/2,N)})$$

$$unzip_{M,N,A} : I^C_{(M,N)} \rightarrow ([P]_A \rightarrow P) \rightarrow ([P]_A \rightarrow P) \rightarrow (I^C_{(M,N/2)}, I^C_{(M,N/2)})$$

$$scan_{M,N} : I_{(M,N)} \rightarrow Int \rightarrow (P \rightarrow Int \rightarrow Int) \rightarrow I_{(M*N)}$$

$$foldScalar_{M,N} : I_{(M,N)} \rightarrow Int \rightarrow (P \rightarrow Int \rightarrow Int) \rightarrow Int$$

$$foldVector_{M,N,A} : I_{(M,N)} \rightarrow Int \rightarrow (A : Int) \rightarrow (P \rightarrow [Int]_A \rightarrow [Int]_A) \rightarrow [Int]_A$$

$$transpose_{M,N} : I^R_{(M,N)} \rightarrow I^C_{(M,N)}$$

$$transpose_{M,N} : I^C_{(M,N)} \rightarrow I^R_{(M,N)}$$

Fig. 4. RIPL skeletons

An image $I^R_{(M,N)}$ is M pixels wide and N pixels high, and whose pixels are in row (R) major order. RIPLs *map* and *unzip* skeletons are implicitly directional, sliding linearly either row wise or column wise over a one dimensional vector of pixels. This meta information about stream order, image dimensions and vector lengths is not specified by the programmer; it is inferred by the RIPL compiler.

Skeletons with Non-overlapping Sliding Windows. The *map* skeleton slides over an image and applies the user defined function with a non-overlapping 1D vector on each execution. The *zipWith* skeleton is similar, though it slides a vector window of the same length over two images in lock step. The *map* and *zipWith* skeletons are stateless and do not carry state between executions. Their memory costs are therefore solely determined by the length of the sliding vector that they consume. The *zipWithScalar* skeletons combines every pixel and a scalar value with a user defined function, and similarly *zipWithVector* allows the programmer to use a random access vector to modify an image.

As an example of non-overlapping sliding windows, the following RIPL assignment combines two images using *zipWith* with a mean average combinator. The memory cost is 2 8 bit integers, one each for pixels *p1* and *p2* from images *image1* and *image2* respectively.

```
image3 = zipWith image1 image2 (\[p1] [p2] -> [(p1+p2)/2]);
```

Skeletons with Overlapping Sliding Windows. The *imap* skeleton is useful for applying 1D filters to an image. It is an *indexed* map that slides over contiguously positioned pixels in a non-discrete fashion. The *imap* syntax differs from *map*, because *imap* applies a function from a pixel *position [.]* to a new value for that position, using the current pixel value and its neighbouring pixels using *+/-*, e.g. *[.-1]* points to the pixel to the left of *[.]* in an I^R image. The difference in how *map* and *imap* traverses an image is depicted in Fig. 5, which is labelled with repeated execution counts show the difference in their data processing rates of an image row. Figure 6 shows the expression of a 1D blur filter in RIPL, along with its memory cost. The hardware implementation of this *imap* consumes pixels into a 3 element circular buffer, updating the mid point index for *[.]*, before executing the user defined blur function.

(a) traversing images with *map*   (b) traversing images with *imap*

Fig. 5. Comparison of *map* with *indexed map*

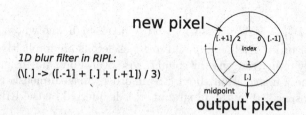

1D blur filter in RIPL:

(\[.] -> ([.-1] + [.] + [.+1]) / 3)

Fig. 6. Memory requirements of 1D blur with *imap* satisfied with a circular buffer

RIPLs *unzip* skeleton is for splitting apart an image into two images, and shares the pixel position syntax with *imap*. The hardware memory generated from *unzip* is similar to *imap*, the difference being its scheduling – the hardware for *unzip* creates two image streams, which are produced by alternating the execution of the two user defined functions.

Skeletons for 2D Filters. Many 2D filters can be implemented by combining the results of two 1D filters, one in the horizontal direction and one in the vertical direction. This implementation approach is possible in RIPL by applying a 1D horizontal filter with *imap*, transposing the result with *transpose*, then applying a vertical 1D filter with *imap*. However, this is a very memory costly composition, because *transpose* generates a frame buffer. For better stream data locality, RIPL has two 2D filters *convolve* and *filter2D*. The *convolve* skeletons modifies each pixel by applying a convolution of its neighbours using a small user defined $M\ PLH\ N$ kernel. The following example applies 3×3 kernel to sharpen an image.

```
image2 = convolve image1 (3,3) {0,-1,0,-1,5,-1,0,-1,0};
```

The *filter2D* skeleton provides more expressivity than *convolve*. When using *filter2D* with a 3×3 window, the programmer is provided 9 pixel values that can be used in their own function body, as shown earlier in Fig. 3 which computes the approximate magnitude $|G| = |Gx| + |Gy|$ for Sobel edge detection.

The memory requirements for *convolve* and *filter2D* is shown in Fig. 7. This has the capacity to store two rows and a further three pixels. Stream based processing begins once one row and two pixels are streamed into the corresponding buffer, which is when the top left pixel can be processed.

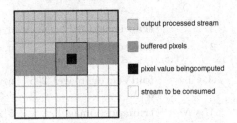

Fig. 7. Memory cost for *convolve* and *filter2D*

Stateful Skeletons. Stateful programming is achieved with RIPL using two skeletons, *foldScalar* and *foldVector*. They apply user defined reduction operations on images or image regions. Reducing an image to a scalar value is done using *foldScalar*, *e.g.* finding the maximum pixel value. The *scan* skeleton is similar to *foldScalar*, but returns a stream of intermediate successive reduced values. Reducing an image to a vector is done using *foldVector*, *e.g.* computing a colour histogram with each bin initialised to 0. Maximum pixel and histogram calculations are expressed as:

```
maxValue  = foldScalar image1 0 (\p currMax -> max p currMax);
histogram = foldVector image1 0 255 (\p hist -> hist[p]++);
```

4   RIPL Memory Costs

4.1   Memory Costs for Computation

RIPL programs are compiled to a dataflow intermediary of small computational actors and FIFOs. The memory costs for each RIPL skeleton in bytes is shown

Table 1. Memory costs for RIPL skeletons

Skeleton	buffer size	Example		
		RIPL code	$M \times N$	buffer size
$map_{M,N,A,B}$	A	**map** image1 $(\lambda[a,b,c] \rightarrow ...)$	n/a	3
$imap_{M,N,A}$	$A+1$	**imap** image1 $(\lambda[.] \rightarrow ([.-1]+[.]+[.+1])/3)$	n/a	4
$zipWith_{M,N,A}$	$A*2$	**zipWith** image1 $(\lambda[a,b]\ [c,d] \rightarrow ...)$	n/a	4
$zipWithScalar_{M,N,A}$	$A+1$	**zipWithScalar** image1 $(\lambda[a,b]\ x \rightarrow ...)$	n/a	3
$zipWithVector_{M,N,A,B}$	$A+B+1$	**zipWithVector** image1 $(\lambda[a,b]\ vect \rightarrow ...)$	n/a	$3+B$
$unzip_{M,N,A}$	$A+1$	**unzip** image1 $(\lambda[a,b] \rightarrow ...)\ (\lambda[c,d] \rightarrow ...)$	n/a	3
$convolve_{M,N,A,B}$	$M*2+3$	**convolve** image1 (3,3) kernel	512×512	1027
$filter2D_{M,N,A,B}$	$M*2+3$	**filter2D** image1 (3,3) $(\lambda... \rightarrow ...)$	512×512	1027
$scan_{M,N}$	2	**scan** image1 0 $(\lambda.. \rightarrow ..)$	n/a	2
$foldScalar_{M,N}$	2	**foldScalar** image1 0 $(\lambda.. \rightarrow ..)$	n/a	2
$foldVector_{M,N,A}$	$A+1$	**foldVector** image1 255 0 $(\lambda.. \rightarrow ..)$	n/a	256
$transpose_{M,N}$	$M*N$	**transpose** image1	512×512	262144

in Table 1. The *map*, *imap*, *zipWith* and *unzip* skeletons are implemented with either overlapping or non-overlapping sliding vectors, and hence their memory requirements are not determined by an image's dimensions. These costs are calculated from their offsets in stream access, analogous to array access offset analysis in *for* loops in imperative languages. The *map* and *zipWith* memory costs are solely determined by the vector length of the λ argument in the user defined function. The memory cost of *zipWithScalar* and *zipWithVector* is the stored scalar or vector, and the next incoming pixel value. The memory costs for *imap* are determined by the biggest X in $[.+X]$ occurrences in the output expression, minus the biggest Y in $[.-Y]$ occurrences.

The memory cost for the *foldScalar* and *scan* skeletons is the folded scalar and the next pixel from the image stream. The *foldVector* skeleton's memory requirements are determined by the programmer's choice of output vector length which is folded through each execution, and the next pixel from the image stream. The *convolve* and *filter2D* skeleton's memory requirements are determined by the processed image's width. The most costly skeleton is *transpose*, because it requires an entire image to be stored in a buffer before being outputted with a transpose index.

4.2 Memory Costs for Communication

An addition memory cost is the depth of dataflow wires to ensure deadlock free RIPL execution. Dataflow wires are derived by data dependencies in RIPL programs, *i.e.* if the output of one skeleton is used as an input to another, then a FIFO point-to-point connection is created in hardware to support that data sharing. When the output of one RIPL skeleton is used in just one place in a program, only one output FIFO will be connected from the hardware implementing that skeleton, shown in Fig. 8a. In these cases, the required FIFO depth is determined by the vector length of the λ argument in the receiving skeleton. For example, if a *map* takes $\lambda[a, b, c]$ then the required depth is 3. The overall memory cost for FIFOs in Fig. 8a is 2 8 bit integers.

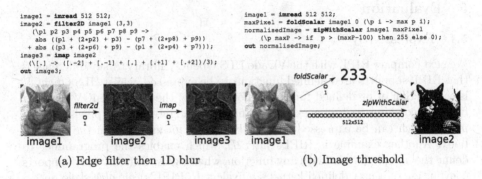

(a) Edge filter then 1D blur   (b) Image threshold

Fig. 8. Memory costs for dataflow FIFOs

If the output image of one skeleton is used in multiple places, then depth requirements can increase, shown in Fig. 8b. This RIPL program finds the biggest pixel value of 233 with *foldScalar*, which is used to threshold the original image using *zipWithScalar* with a threshold of 233 − 100. The generated hardware duplicates image *image1* over two FIFOs, one to the dataflow actor for computing the maximum value, and the other to threshold the image. Pixel tokens are transmitted to both FIFOs in lock step. Therefore in order for $maxP$ to be computed, the actor executing *foldScalar* needs to receive all tokens, so the FIFO to the threshold actor needs capacity to buffer the entire 512×512 image for the $maxP$ value to be computed. The overall memory cost for FIFOs in Fig. 8b is $(2 + 512 \times 512)$ 8 bit integers.

4.3 FPGA Memory Implementation

Once RIPL programs are compiled to dataflow graphs, actor computation code and dataflow wires are compiled to HDL using an open source dataflow compiler [1], which makes choices about how to implement memory. For scalar integer values it uses FPGA slice registers used as memory. For small arrays that the RIPL compiler generates to support *convolve*, *filter2D* and *foldVector*, the dataflow compiler may also use slice registers depending on the overall memory requirements of the complete hardware design. The benefit of implementing these memories with slice registers is that the larger BRAM blocks are available for other parts of an algorithm, and because BRAM access is one clock cycle whilst LUTs RAM can be accessed without any latency. BRAM is used to support larger arrays generated by the RIPL compiler to support *convolve* and *filter2D* on big images, and for *transpose* which needs an entire image buffer.

FIFOs are compiled to HDL as generic memories, leaving the FPGA synthesis tools to choose how to implement them. Rendevous single token FIFOs will be implemented using registers or LUTs. Small FIFOs, *e.g.* to buffer a single row, are likely to be implemented with LUTs, whilst large FIFO depths, *e.g.* to support duplicating image streams in Fig. 8b, will likely be implemented using BRAM.

5   Evaluation

5.1   Expressivitiy

We next compare RIPL with the Vivado HLS OpenCV library. A key difference is that RIPL supports used defined functions to be expressed, whilst HLS OpenCV is a collection of predefined functions. For example, the HLS OpenCV *hls::Max* function combines two images by retaining the brighter of the pixels at each point, which can be expressed using RIPL's *zipWith* and *max* in the function body. Another example is RIPLs *filter2D*, which enables the programmer to define the mid pixel point with any function, whereas *hls::Filter2D* only supports convolution of a user defined kernel, equivalent to RIPL's *convolve* skeleton.

Another difference between RIPL and HLS OpenCV is image sharing. When an image is used in two places in a RIPL program, the image stream is automatically duplicated and shared to both consuming skeletons. With the HLS OpenCV model, an equivalent program would deadlock because the first function that uses the image will consume its pixels, emptying the FIFO. The *hls::Duplicate* function must be used explicitly to avoid this.

OpenCV programming requires explicit dimension and bitwidth information for each image declaration. The $hls::Mat <>$ template class is used to initialise an image, *e.g.* $hls::Mat < 512, 512, HLS\_8UC1 >$ defines a 512×512 single channel image, using 8 unsigned bits per pixel. In contrast, the RIPL compiler infers the dimension of every image, by following dimension transformations performed by skeletons through the implicit dataflow paths starting from *imread*, the only place where dimensions are explicit. The compiler also infers pixel bitwidths automatically, by calculating maximum upper bounds on bitwidth requirements as image data flows through arithmetic operators. Another difference is the inference of FIFO depths. The default FIFO depth in both RIPL and HLS OpenCV is 1. However, when an image is used in multiple places the RIPL compiler increases the FIFOs automatically to frame buffers (Sect. 4.2).

```
hls::Mat<512,512, HLS_8UC1> img_0(rows,cols);
hls::Mat<512,512, HLS_8UC1> img_1(rows,cols);
hls::Mat<512,512, HLS_8UC1> img_2(rows,cols);
hls::Mat<512,512, HLS_8UC1> img_3(rows,cols);

// explicit depth for img_2 to prevent deadlock
#pragma HLS stream depth=262144 variable=img_2.data_stream

// convert AXI4 stream data to hls::mat format
hls::AXIvideo2Mat(INPUT_STREAM1, img_0);

// duplicate the img_0 stream
hls::Duplicate(img_0,img_1,img_2);

// find the maximum pixel of img_1 duplicate
int maxP, minP;
hls::Point p1,p2;
hls::MinMaxLoc(img_1,&minP,&maxP,p1,p2);

// threshold the img_2 duplicate using the max pixel - 50
int threshold = maxP - 50;
hls::Threshold(img_2,img_3,threshold,255,HLS_THRESH_TOZERO);
```

Fig. 9. Thresholding with HLS OpenCV using a maximum pixel value

The HLS compiler does not make this inference, leaving the programmer to use FPGA co-simulation to identify deadlocks. The user then programmatically uses $#pragma\ HLS\ stream\ depth = <N>$ to specify the FIFO depth to avoid deadlock. Figure 9 shows a HLS OpenCV example that demonstrates the need for explicit image duplication and explicit FIFO depths. The RIPL compiler infers both of these properties automatically.

The final difference is how image processing pipelines are constructed. Pipelined parallelism in RIPL is automatic. When two skeletons are composed in sequence over an input image, they will execute in parallel over different regions of the image stream. In HLS OpenCV, the programmer must specify *#pragma HLS dataflow* above the function calls intended to be pipelined over the image stream.

One similarity between HLS OpenCV and RIPL is the implementation of image data structures. An OpenCV image is a *hls::Mat*. The Vivado HLS FPGA implementation of *hls::Mat* images uses *hls::stream* internally, so OpenCV images on FPGAs are FIFOs, which is also true for RIPL. Hence random image access is not possible in either case.

Darkroom can be used to express benchmarks 1 and 2 (✓), but not 3, 4 or 5 (✗). Global reductions are not supported, because Darkroom's line buffers cannot be used to store values beyond a traversing a single line. Such a buffer is required to compute the maximum pixel value (3) and the histogram (4). RIPL is the only language of the three compared that supports image transposition, which again requires a frame buffer that uses 64 BRAMs.

5.2 Space Performance

We use five benchmarks to compare the space performance of RIPL and OpenCV compiled to FPGAs using Vivado HLS. The benchmarks are (1) brighten each pixel in an image by 50, (2) 2D Sobel edge detection, (3) find the maximum pixel $maxPixel$ value then threshold the image with $(maxPixel - 50)$, (4) compute a sum histogram for an image then normalise the image using the histogram, and (5) transpose an image. All programs are compiled for the Xilinx Zedboard XC7Z020 for 512×512 single channel images. The memory use performance of Darkroom cannot be compared because the line buffer to Verilog compiler backend is not publicly available.

Table 2. Memory implementation and expressivity results

Benchmark	RIPL		HLS OpenCV		Darkroom
	BRAM	LUTs	BRAM	LUTs	
1	Image brighten	0 (0 %)	118 (0 %)	0	450 (0 %)	✓
2	Sobel 2D edge detection	1 (0 %)	12273 (23 %)	3 (1 %)	713 (1 %)	✓
3	Threshold with max pixel	64 (45 %)	280 (0 %)	64 (45 %)	9172 (1 %)	✗
4	Histogram normalisation	64 (45 %)	799 (1 %)	3 (1 %)	2918 (5 %)	✗
5	Image transposition	64 (45 %)	321 (0 %)	✗		✗

The synthesis results in Table 2 are for RIPL and HLS OpenCV. RIPL and OpenCV occupy very similar memory resources for image brightening (1) and image thresholding (3). For Sobel edge detection (2), RIPL uses 2 BRAMs less than OpenCV by instead using more LUTs. Thresholding and histogram normalisation (4) in RIPL require a FIFO depth equal to the number of pixels in the image in RIPL's hardware backend. To support 8 bit pixels, the synthesis tools use BRAMs in 32Kb mode, so storing a 512×512 image requires 64 BRAM blocks for these two benchmarks. The same is true for HLS OpenCV for thresholding, but not histogram normalisation. This is because of an optimisation built into $hls::EqualizeHist()$, which normalises frame $N + 1$ using the histogram computed for the previous frame N. This results in more efficient BRAM use compared to RIPL. We plan this optimisation for RIPL.

6 Conclusion

Memory resources on FPGAs can be tailored to the needs of an algorithm, so FPGA compilers are not hindered by fixed memory hierarchies such as those on CPUs and GPUs. They are however constrained by the limited amount of on chip BRAM and LUT memory resources. This paper describes the memory efficiency aspects of RIPL, our image processing DSL for FPGAs. RIPL is more concise than Vivado HLS OpenCV, because it automatically infers upper bounds on bitwidths and the required FIFO depths for image streams, and image streams are automatically duplicated when necessary. Despite these abstractions, RIPL memory use is competitive on three of the four benchmarks expressible with the Vivado HLS OpenCV. RIPL is more expressive than the Darkroom image processing DSL, because Darkroom compiles to line buffers so does not support global image reductions. Future work will explore temporal video processing capabilities in RIPL, where new opportunities for dataflow analysis for data locality may arise. We also wish to explore the applicability of RIPL for FPGA acceleration of other stream based domains beyond image processing.

Acknowledgements. We acknowledge the support of the Engineering and Physical Research Council, grant reference EP/K009931/1 (Programmable embedded platforms for remote and compute intensive image processing applications).

References

1. Bezati, E.: High-level synthesis of dataflow programs for heterogeneous platforms. Ph.D. thesis, STI, EPFL, Switzerland (2015)
2. Bradski, G.R., Kaehler, A.: Learning OpenCV - Computer Vision with the OpenCV library: Software that Sees. O'Reilly, Beijing (2008)
3. Cole, M.: Algorithmic Skeletons: Structured Management of Parallel Computation. MIT Press, Cambridge (1991)
4. DeVito, Z., Hegarty, J., Aiken, A., Hanrahan, P., Vitek, J.: Terra: a multi-stage language for high-performance computing. In: ACM SIGPLAN Conference on Programming Language Design and Implementation, Seattle, WA, USA, June 16–19, 2013, pp. 105–116. ACM (2013)
5. Hegarty, J., Brunhaver, J., DeVito, Z., Ragan-Kelley, J., Cohen, N., Bell, S., Vasilyev, A., Horowitz, M., Hanrahan, P.: Darkroom: compiling high-level image processing code into hardware pipelines. ACM Trans. Graph. **33**(4), 1–11 (2014)
6. Kennedy, K., McKinley, K.S.: Maximizing loop parallelism and improving data locality via loop fusion and distribution. In: Banerjee, U., Gelernter, D., Nicolau, A., Padua, D. (eds.) LCPC 1993. LNCS, vol. 768, pp. 301–320. Springer, Heidelberg (1994). doi:10.1007/3-540-57659-2_18
7. Kiselyov, O.: Iteratee IO: Safe, Practical, Declarative Input Processing. In: 11th International Symposium on Functional and Logic Programming. LNCS, vol. 7294, pp. 166–181 (2012)
8. Lee, H., Brown, K.J., Sujeeth, A.K., Rompf, T., Olukotun, K.: locality-aware mapping of nested parallel patterns on GPUs. In: 47th Annual IEEE/ACM International Symposium on Microarchitecture, MICRO 2014, Cambridge, UK, December 13–17, 2014, pp. 63–74. IEEE (2014)
9. Muddukrishna, A., Jonsson, P.A., Brorsson, M.: Locality-aware task scheduling and data distribution for openmp programs on NUMA systems and manycore processors. Sci. Program. **2015**, 981759: 1–981759: 16 (2015)
10. Stephen Neuendorffer, T.L., Wang, D.: Accelerating OpenCV Applications with Zynq-7000 All Programmable SoC using Vivado HLS Video Libraries. Technical report, Xilinx, June 2015
11. Tate, A., et al.: Programming abstractions for data locality. In: Workshop on Programming Abstractions for Data Locality, Swiss National Supercomputing Center, Lugano, Switzerland, April 2014

12. Wieser, V., Grelck, C., Haslinger, P., Guo, J., Korzeniowski, F., Bernecky, R., Moser, B., Scholz, S.: Combining high productivity and high performance in image processing using Single Assignment C on multi-core CPUs and many-core GPUs. J. Electron. Imaging **21**(2), 21116 (2012)
13. Xilinx: Implementing Memory Structures for Video Processing in the Vivado HLS Tool. Technical report, Xilinx, September 2012

Ultrascale Computing for Early Researchers (UCER 2016)

Exploring a Distributed Iterative Reconstructor Based on Split Bregman Using PETSc

Estefania Serrano[1]($\boxtimes$), Tom Vander Aa[2], Roel Wuyts[2], Javier Garcia Blas[1], Jesus Carretero[1], and Monica Abella[1,3]

[1] University Carlos III, Madrid, Spain
{esserran,fjblas,jcarrete}@inf.uc3m.es
[2] ExaScience Life Lab at imec, Leuven, Belgium
{Tom.VanderAa,Roel.Wuyts}@imec.be
[3] Instituto de Investigacion Sanitaria Gregorio Marañon (IiSGM), Madrid, Spain
mabella@hggm.es

Abstract. The proliferation in the last years of many iterative algorithms for Computed Tomography is a result of the need of finding new ways for obtaining high quality images using low dose acquisition methods. These iterative algorithms are, in many cases, computationally much more expensive than traditional analytic ones. Based on the resolution of large linear systems, they normally make use of backprojection and projections operands in an iterative way reducing the performance of the algorithms compared to traditional ones. They are also algorithms that rely on a large quantity of memory because they need of working with large coefficient matrices. As the resolution of the available detectors increase, the size of these matrices starts to be unmanageable in standard workstations. In this work we propose a distributed solution of an iterative reconstruction algorithm with the help of the PETSc library. We show in our preliminary results the good scalability of the solution in one node (close to the ideal one) and the possibilities offered with a larger number of nodes. However, when increasing the number of nodes the performance degrades due to the poor scalability of some fundamental pieces of the algorithm as well as the increase of the time spend in both MPI communication and reduction.

Keywords: Computed tomography · CT · PETSc · MPI · Iterative reconstruction

1 Introduction

Medical imaging is a multidisplinary field that includes physicians, mathematicians or computer scientists with the objective of obtaining better images for

E. Serrano—This work has been partially supported under the COST Action IC1305 "Network for Sustainable Ultrascale Computing Platforms" (NESUS), the grant TIN2013-41350-P, *Scalable Data Management Techniques for High-End Computing Systems* from the Spanish Ministry of Economy and Competitiveness, FPU14/03875 from the Spanish Ministry of Education, NECRA RTC-2014-3028-1, TEC2013-47270-R and RTC-2014-3028-1 project.

© Springer International Publishing AG 2016
J. Carretero et al. (Eds.): ICA3PP 2016 Workshops, LNCS 10049, pp. 191–200, 2016.
DOI: 10.1007/978-3-319-49956-7_15

diagnosis and the study of diseases in human beings. One of the important techniques nowadays is CT (Computed Tomography). CT uses X-Ray images and a computational processing pipeline to obtain the inner images of the body thanks to the different rate of absorption of the rays depending on the materials. This computational pipeline normally consists on the application of different algorithms, which, over time, have been developed to increase the quality of the final images in different unfavorable situations.

The proliferation in the last years of many iterative algorithms for CT is a result of the need of finding new ways for obtaining high quality images using low dose acquisitions. These iterative algorithms are, in many cases, computationally much more expensive than traditional analytic methods. The general approximation of iterative reconstruction algorithms is the continuous improvement of the final resulting image, taking into account the characteristics of the input radiographies. They are also algorithms that rely on a large amount of memory because they work with large and dense coefficient matrices. As the resolution of the available detectors increase, the size of these matrices becomes unmanageable in standard workstations.

In this work, we present an iterative reconstruction algorithm adapted to a distributed environment using the PETSc library. With this approach, it is possible to overcome the memory limits of single node executions and increase the computational resources. This solution could be applied to other type of iterative algorithms or even to standard analytical methods in the reconstruction of large volumes. For the construction and implementation of the iterative algorithm we have started from a parallel CT simulator containing basic operations [10].

This work is divided in the following sections. In Sect. 2 we present a brief summary of different approaches that have been taken to accelerate iterative reconstruction algorithms. The iterative algorithm implemented is explained in detail in Sect. 3 and we provide a graphical description of the flow of the application. Then, in Sect. 4 we explain the approach taken in this work to distribute the computations through the use of PETSc and MPI. We evaluate our implementation in terms of performance in Sect. 5. Finally, major conclusions of our work are presented in Sect. 6.

2   Related Work

There have already been works discussing different optimizations of iterative algorithms for CT. The works proposed in [4,6,8] are focused on the optimization of the projection and backprojection methods included in the iterative reconstruction. The approach is similar to the one taken by us, since the kernel operators are normally the tasks that are more time consuming thus requiring a larger optimization effort. Works in [4,6] follow the parallelization approach, dividing the planes to process them separately in a CUDA compatible device and comparing with a CPU implementation. Another approach is the one taken by Rit et al. in [8], in which the authors present novel techniques for truncating and reducing the number of operations of the kernel, obtaining a faster algorithm.

Distribution of the computation has also been a studied topic. Palenstijn et al. [7] present a similar approach to the work shown here. They implement a version of SIRT algorithm from the ASTRA Toolbox in a distributed way using MPI and GPUs for the backprojection and projection methods. MPI over the Cloud have been used by Rosen [9] for the implementation of a penalized weighted least-squareswith ordered subsets (PWLS-OS) reconstruction algorithm. Finally, changing of paradigm from MPI to MapReduce, we have the work of Meng et al. [5], which parallelizes with MapReduce large 4D reconstruction studies for FDK (Feldkamp, Davis and Kress) non iterative reconstruction algorithms, obtaining a speedup of 10 over the one node version when using Hadoop relying on 200 nodes. All these distributed versions perform considerably better than their one node versions and prove the feasibility of reconstructing large problems. However, the scalability of some of these approaches is not near ideal.

3   Iterative Reconstruction Algorithm

Iterative reconstruction algorithms rely on the iterative refinement of the final image until a point of convergence or a minimal noise rate are reached. There exist multiple types of iterative algorithms and innumerable variations. One of the main characteristics of an iterative algorithm is the progressive refinement of the image to be reconstructed. This is carried out through the application of specific operators: backprojection and projection.

The backprojection operator consists on the transformation of the projection images (or radiographies) to a 3D volume that contains the information of the inside of the scanned object. The projection operator is just the opposite: from a 3D volume it is able to recover the radiographies. In other words, it projects the volume onto different planes. Simplifying, both of them are based on the computation of ray trajectories that traverse the voxels in the volume to reach the detector. Then, it computes the integral of the values in the voxels or pixels reached. Therefore, the computational complexity of these algorithms is, respectively: $O(dim\_u * dim\_v *dim\_z)$ and $O(dim\_ps * dim\_pz *dim\_v)$ being dim_u, dim_v and dim_z the number of voxels in the final volume in each of the axis, and dim_ps and dim_pz the number of pixels of the detector.

In our case, we work on a new iterative algorithm based on the split Bregman method [3] that includes a Krylov subspace solver [2]. The main purpose of the Krylov solver is to resolve the equation system:

$$Ax = b, \tag{1}$$

where A is the system matrix and x and b are vectors representing volume data.

The system matrix A is a large matrix representing the relationship between the value of the voxels in the volume and the pixel value in the detector. In medium and large studies the size of this matrix increases, as well as the cost to compute it. Thus, it is easier to employ backprojection and projection algorithms than their system matrix representation. For this reason we execute an independent function to compute Ax, which results in a much smaller vector than the system matrix A and requires the usage of a matrix-free compatible solver. We also provide the vector b, being an approximation of the final volume. The specific Krylov space solver employed in this work was BiCGSTAB (Bi Conjugate Gradient Stabilized method) [11] in its matrix-free form without any preconditioners.

Although this algorithm contains a variety of vector operations, the execution time is conditioned by the two previously explained analytical operators.

4   Distributed Implementation

The basis of the distributed implementation is the possibility of, not only increasing the computation power due to the increase in the number of processors or accelerators available, but also to increase the memory which allows the reconstruction of bigger volumes and the use of higher number of projections.

4.1   PETSc and MPI

For the implementation of the algorithm in a distributed environment we employed the library PETSc (Portable, Extensible Toolkit for Scientific Computation) [1], which relies on MPI (Message Passing Interface) for the communication between different nodes. This library contains several methods for matrix and vector computation, as well as optimized and distributed versions of the most popular solvers including BiCGSTAB. It also allows integration with several external mathematical libraries and even can take advantage of specialized hardware like GPUs.

The implementation of the distributed routines is based on the use of parallel structures included in PETSc, the distributed memory distributed arrays (DMDAs), which describe the parallel structure of an object (a vector or matrix) including the partitioning, ordering, interpolations, and ghost or stencil regions. Developing the distributed functions taking into account this structure leads to a partitioning-independent implementation, which provides a more flexible execution of the application in diverse environments.

Its compatibility with MPI allows the programming of hybrid algorithms that combine native MPI functions with PETSc structures and methods.

4.2   Distribution Strategy

The distribution and parallelization strategy were constructed around the division of the output data (the volume) in different chunks. This division is done in the z axis (as seen in Fig. 1) to encourage data locality and to avoid unnecessary communication. Since most of the operations are voxel independent (sum of vectors, vector scaling, vector subtraction) and others are independent in the different u-v planes, the partitioning of the vector through the z axis was the most reasonable option. However, there exist a dependency in the z plane regarding the algorithm: the execution of the backprojection and projection step over a partition of the volume generates incomplete information. The backprojection is an operator in which the generation of each of the voxels is totally independent, and the same happens for projection on the different pixels. However, if we want to obtain a complete and correct volume, the projections must also be complete. As shown in Fig. 1, the application of the projection operator over independent chunks of the volume generates incomplete projections in the z axis leading to the computation of incorrect voxel values in the subsequent backprojection step. To overcome this problem it is necessary to obtain the complete and correct projections in all distributed processes, thus creating a synchronization point. At this synchronization point, the interpolation zones of each projection in each process must be reduced to obtain the final correct value.

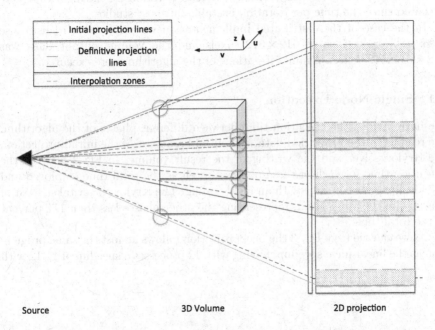

Fig. 1. Interpolation zones that must be reduced inside the volume and projection. Each partition of the volume is held by a different node.

This division strategy provides good results for the backprojector operator, but it does not scale for the case of the projector. This is due to the fact that projector's complexity, $O(dim\_ps * dim\_pz * dim\_v)$ does not depend of the partitioned variable, the dimension of the volume in z. To provide scalability, we had to decrease the size of the computed projections for each partitioned volume computing the maximum and minimum projections lines. These projection lines (red dot lines in Fig. 1) represent the limits of the contribution of the partial volume to the projection.

5 Experimental Study

We have executed a preliminary evaluation of the implementation on a single node and in a distributed environment composed of 12 nodes. The purpose was to evaluate the scalability of the application for a different number of MPI processes. The evaluation was done on nodes with an Intel(R) Xeon(R) CPU X5660 @ 2.80 GHz with 12 physical cores and 96 GB of memory. The version of MPI used was MPICH 2 with the Hydra manager. The application was compiled with GCC 4.9 and the execution was configured to have the processes bound to the physical cores of the node. The PETSc version employed was 3.7.

The application was tested with real data: 360 projections of 128×128 pixels of a crocodile scapula for the single node execution. The output data consisted on a volume of 128×128x128 voxels. Only two iterations of the algorithm were executed since the time per iteration is stable for most studies.

In the case of the distributed implementation we employed a realistic use case: 180 projections of 512×512 pixels and the volume output data was 512×512x512 voxels. Again 2 iterations of the algorithm were executed.

5.1 Single Node Execution

We have divided the execution time between different phases of the algorithm: the reading of the projection data, the initial broadcast of the initial projection, the Krylov solver and the writing of the result volume. In Fig. 2 we plot the execution time for each of these phases as well as the total time employed and the ideal progression time with an ideal scaling. The Krylov solver takes most of the time of the application, representing the other phases less than 1 % percent of the total time.

As we can see from Fig. 3 the backprojection follows almost the same progression as the linear ideal speedup, having with 12 processes a speedup of 11.12 with

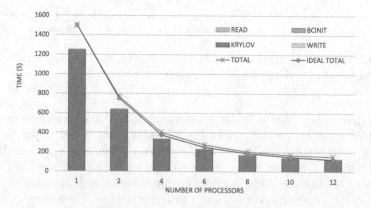

Fig. 2. Execution time of the application for different number of processors and stages.

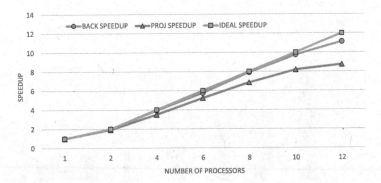

Fig. 3. Speedup for the backprojection and projection phases for different number of processors vs ideal speedup.

respect of the execution with just one MPI process. The scalability of the projection kernel is worse than that of the backprojection kernel. This is an expected behaviour since, as explained before, the projection does not scale directly with the partition variable, but with the projection of the divided volume over the detector. This means that the scalability of the projection will be worst than that of the backprojection and that also depends of variables such as the distance between source, object and detector and pixel and voxels sizes. In these first experiments the influence of the reduction of the projections is not high because of the low number of processes. However, in further evaluation in larger scales, this reduction could represent a problem to be tackled.

5.2   Distributed Execution

For the distributed execution we chose a larger data set with less projection simulating a realistic use case. We show the total execution time compared with the ideal one for different number of processors in Fig. 4. The MPI processes are always distributed equally between nodes.

As in the evaluation with the single node, the Krylov solver represents a large percentage of the execution time of the application although, a larger gap with the total time is observed. This gap includes minor functions such as matrix substractions and vector multiplications as well as the projection reduction. Studying the execution time for all the projection reductions performed during the execution (both included and not included inside the Krylov solver) we can see in Fig. 5 that the combination of results to obtain the final projection planes (the reduction) now represents a higher percentage of the total time, being, with 144 processors almost 50 % of the total.

This naturally influences the maximum speedup that can be obtained taking into account parallelization as we show in Fig. 6. The backprojection operator scales neraly ideally, however the inadequate scaling of the projection operator due to the previously explained reasons, as well as the problem introduced with the projection reduction cost reduce significantly the total speedup of the application that reaches a maximum of 40 when using 144 processors.

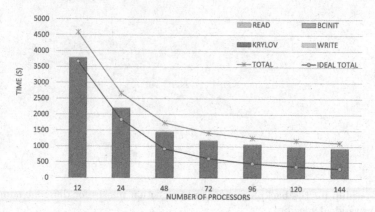

Fig. 4. Execution time of the application for different number of processors and stages.

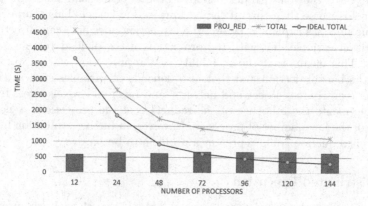

Fig. 5. Execution time of the application for different number of processors and stages including time spent in projection reduction.

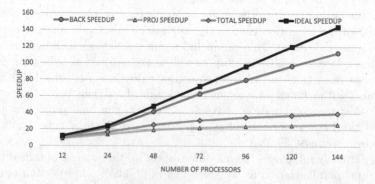

Fig. 6. Speedup for the backprojection and projection phases for different number of processors vs ideal speedup.

6   Conclusions

In this paper, we have presented the implementation and evaluation of an iterative reconstruction method for CT in a distributed environment. For the distribution of the application we have chosen PETSc, a mathematical library on top of MPI that already implemented some of the algorithms needed for our method. We have partitioned the main output dataset to provide scalability as well. In the first preliminary evaluation, we observed that our implementation scales in the main computational parts (backprojector and projector operators) and it is possible to execute in parallel with little differences in the final result. However, when distributing over several nodes, the specific characteristics of the projection operation along with the increasing cost of the projection reduction impacts negatively on the overall performance providing poor speedups.

Further scalability evaluations with larger volumes will be done in the future with both GPU and CPU alternatives for the main operators. Additionally, we plan to optimize the reduction of the projections with a division of the reduction in different groups, taking into account their contribution to the projection lines. Finally, further studies for the improvement of the scalability of the projection operator will be done, taking into account other possible partitioning variables that can give a more balanced solution for this operator.

References

1. Balay, S., Abhyankar, S., Adams, M.F., Brown, J., Brune, P., Buschelman, K., Dalcin, L., Eijkhout, V., Gropp, W.D., Kaushik, D., Knepley, M.G., McInnes, L.C., Rupp, K., Smith, B.F., Zampini, S., Zhang, H., Zhang, H.: PETSc Web page (2016). http://www.mcs.anl.gov/petsc
2. de Molina, C., Abascal, J., Desco, M., Abella, M.: Study of the possibilities of surface-constrained compressed sensing (SCCS) method for limited-view tomography in CBCT systems. In: Proceedings of the 4th International Meeting on Image Formation in X-Ray CT, pp. 491–494 (2016)
3. Goldstein, T., Osher, S.: The split bregman method for l1-regularized problems. SIAM J. Imaging Sci. **2**(2), 323–343 (2009)
4. Jian-Lin, C., Lei, L., Lin-Yuan, W., Ai-Long, C., Xiao-Qi, X., Han-Ming, Z., Jian-Xin, L., Bin, Y.: Fast parallel algorithm for three-dimensional distance-driven model in iterative computed tomography reconstruction. Chin. Phys. B **24**(2), 28703 (2015)
5. Meng, B., Pratx, G., Xing, L.: Ultrafast and scalable cone-beam CT reconstruction using MapReduce in a cloud computing environment. Med. Phys. **38**(12), 6603–6609 (2011). http://scitation.aip.org/content/aapm/journal/medphys/38/12/10.1118/1.3660200
6. Nguyen, V.G., Jeong, J., Lee, S.J.: Gpu-accelerated iterative 3d ct reconstruction using exact ray-tracing method for both projection and backprojection. In: 2013 IEEE Nuclear Science Symposium and Medical Imaging Conference (NSS/MIC), pp. 1–4. IEEE (2013)
7. Palenstijn, W.J., Bdorf, J., Batenburg, K.J., King, M., Glick, S., Mueller, K.: NWO: A distributed SIRT implementation for the ASTRA Toolbox. None, June (2015). https://repository.cwi.nl/noauth/search/fullrecord.php?publnr=23719

8. Rit, S., van Herk, M., Sonke, J.J.: Fast distance-driven projection and truncation management for iterative cone-beam ct reconstruction
9. Rosen, J.M., Wu, J., Wenisch, T.F., Fessler, J.A.: Iterative helical CT reconstruction in the cloud for ten dollars in five minutes. In: Proceedings International MTG on Fully 3D Image Recon. in Rad. and Nuc. Med. pp. 241–244 (2013). http://web.eecs.umich.edu/~fessler/papers/lists/files/proc/13/web/rosen-13-ihc.pdf
10. Serrano, E., Blas, J.G., Molina, C., Garcia, I., Carretero, J., Desco, M., Abella, M.: Design and evaluation of a parallel and multi-platform cone-beam X-ray simulation framework. In: Proceedings of 4th International MTG on Image Formation in X-ray CT, pp. 423–426 (2016)
11. Van der Vorst, H.A.: Bi-cgstab: a fast and smoothly converging variant of bi-cg for the solution of nonsymmetric linear systems. SIAM J. Sci. Stat. Comput. **13**(2), 631–644 (1992)

Implementation of the Beamformer Algorithm for the NVIDIA Jetson

Fran J. Alventosa[1], Pedro Alonso[1(✉)], Gema Piñero[2], and Antonio M. Vidal[1]

[1] Department of Information Systems and Computation (DSIC),
Universitat Politècnica de València, Valencia, Spain
{fraalrue,palonso,avidal}@dsic.upv.es
[2] Instituto de Telecomunicaciones y Aplicaciones Multimedia (iTEAM),
Universitat Politècnica de València, Valencia, Spain
gpinyero@iteam.upv.es

Abstract. Nowadays, the aim of the technology industry is intensively shifting to improve the ratio Gflop/watt of computation. Many processors implement the low power design of ARM architecture like, e.g. the NVIDIA TK1, a chip which also includes a GPU embedded in the same die to improve performance at a low energy consumption. This type of devices are very suitable target machines to be used on applications that require mobility like, e.g. those that manage and reproduce real acoustics environments. One of the most used algorithms in these reproduction environments is the Beamformer Algorithm. We have implemented the variant called Beamformer QR-LCMV, based on the QR decomposition, which is a very computationally demanding operation. We have explored different options differing basically in the high performance computing library used. Also we have built our own version with the aim of approaching the real-time processing goal when working on this type of low power devices.

Keywords: Audio processing · Beamformer · GPU-CPU Processing · Heterogeneous QR Factorization

1 Introduction

In High Performance Computing (HPC), the challenge is not only to improve the performance of applications that have a very high computational cost but also to improve another type of applications, those that require a low computational power but are characterized however by the immediacy of the result, i.e. applications with real-time constraints. The Beamformer Algorithm, object of study in this work, is a typical algorithm used in digital signal processing contexts whose purpose is to separate different sound sources simultaneously broadcast on the

This work has been supported by projects TEC2015-67387-C4-1-R of the Spanish Ministerio de Economía y Competitividad and PROMETEOII/2014/003 of the Generalitat Valenciana.

© Springer International Publishing AG 2016
J. Carretero et al. (Eds.): ICA3PP 2016 Workshops, LNCS 10049, pp. 201–211, 2016.
DOI: 10.1007/978-3-319-49956-7_16

same channel so that they are, therefore, mixed [3]. A typical example is of several people speaking at the same time in the same room. The main objective of a "Beamformer" application is to separate those different sources and try to extract the original independent signals in real-time.

Another challenge we address nowadays is to use mobile low-power devices to perform this task. Both mobility and a long battery life are requirements to the applicability of these devices. However, a real-time response of the application and the use of low-power devices can be incompatible. The problem is exacerbated by the fact that, in order to achieve an accurate solution, the amount of numerical operations increases exponentially with the problem size.

However, on the positive side of the scales, currently we count on low-power processors based on ARM architecture that incorporate an embedded GPU in the same die. They are the NVIDIA TK1 and the NVIDIA TX1 processors. These processors can be found in tablets (NVIDIA Shield) under the Android operating system or under the Linux operating system (Jetson Development Kit). Being in the same chip, both the CPU and the GPU share the same physical address space in main memory allowing thus to access shared data very fast. Hence, using the CPU in combination with the GPU can help to reach the real-time threshold if we can develop an optimized version of our algorithm for this processor. Furthermore, the ratio gflops per watt is large for these devices thanks to the GPU, allowing thus to save energy.

In this work we start the way to a real-time Beamforming Algorithm on low-power devices which feature an embedded GPU. In particular, we have implemented codes corresponding to the Beaformer QR-LCMV (Linearly Constrained Minimum Variance) Algorithm presented in [4]. In the implementation we have employed different high performance computing libraries that contain linear algebra solvers, i.e. implementations of BLAS and LAPACK. We used OPENBLAS [8] and PLASMA [2], which are optimized and parallel libraries that work with the cores of the CPU. To work with the GPU we used CUBLAS [5], the NVIDIA optimized implementation of BLAS for its GPUs. And, finally, we also used MAGMA [9], which is a library containing hybrid routines that let to use both the CPU and the GPU when possible. As we will see in the results, none of these libraries are completely satisfactory to exploit the capabilities of a Jetson processor. This is why we added to the set of possibilities our own implementation of the Beaformer QR-LCMV Algorithm, taking advantage of the peculiarities of the hardware employed, in this case the NVIDIA Jetson TK1.

The paper is structured as follows. The following section explains the mathematical model which is in the base of the Beamformer QR-LCMV Algorithm, which is a summary of the proposal presented in [4]. Next, in Sect. 3 we show how the algorithm has been implemented. Section 4 shows the experimental results obtained running the algorithm with different HPC libraries. The paper ends with some conclusions.

2   Mathematical Background of the Beamformer Algorithm

Figure 1 shows graphically the problem that solves the application that we address in this paper. Concretely, this problem model presents two speakers that emit one different signal each and an array of three microphones, each one located at a different point of a room, that capture the sound signal coming from the sound sources. In these systems, it is required that the number of listeners is larger than the number of sources.

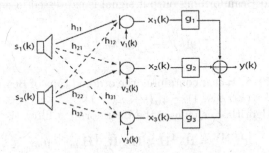

Fig. 1. Beamformer model

Formally, the Beamformer model is described as follows. Each S_m, for $m \in 1, 2$, represents a speaker of the model. Through V_n, for $n \in 1, 2, 3$, we represent the microphones located at different points of the room. Variable h_{mn} represents the existing channel between the m-th speaker and the n-th microphone. The array g_z, for $z \in 1, 2, 3$, is the filter to be applied to microphone z in order to get the sought-after signal k. Finally, array $y(k)$ represents the output signal as the result of applying filter g to the signals captured by the microphones.

Let $s_m(k)$, $m = 1, \ldots, M$, be signals emitted by M loudspeakers, the goal is to develop N filters g_n, $n = 1, \ldots, N$, being N the number of microphones in the system, that allow to rebuild the original source signals once cleaned from noise and room reverberation. To this end, we use channel responses of the room, represented as h_{nm}, for the values n and m stated before.

The output of the n-th microphone is given by:

$$x_n(k) = \sum_{m=1}^{M} \sum_{j=1}^{L_h} h_{nm}(j) s_m(k - j) + v_n(k),$$

where L_h is the length of longest room impulse response of all the acoustic channels h_{nm}, and $v_n(k)$ is the noise signal. (For the sake of clarity, we will not consider the noise term hereafter.) Also for clarity and computation efficiency, we rewrite the form of the output signal of each microphone as

$$x_n(k) = \sum_{m=1}^{M} \mathbf{h}_{nm}^T \mathbf{s}_m(k),$$

where $\mathbf{s}_m(k)$ is the column vector defined as

$$\mathbf{s}_m(k) = \left[\, s_m(k)\, s_m(k-1) \cdots s_m(k - L_h + 1)\,\right]^T,$$

and $\mathbf{h}_{nm}$ is the $\mathbb{R}^{L_h \times 1}$ acoustic channel vector from loudspeaker m to microphone n.

Considering now the problem of recovering source signals $s_m(k)$ from the recorded observations $x_n(k)$, Beamforming filters g_n have to be designed so that the output signal $y(k)$ is a good estimate of $s_m(k)$, that is, $y(k) = \hat{s}_m(k - \tau)$ with minimum error. Given a maximum length of L_g taps for each of the N filters g_n, the broadband Beamforming output signal is expressed in a similar form as

$$y(k) = \sum_{n=1}^{N} \mathbf{g}_n^T \mathbf{x}_n(k),$$

where $\mathbf{g}_n$ is the $\mathbb{R}^{L_g \times 1}$ vector containing the ordered taps of Beamforming filters g_n, and $\mathbf{x}_n(k) = [x_n(k) x(k-1) \cdots x_n(k - L_g + 1)]^T$.

The LCMV Algorithm calculates the Beamforming filters as:

$$\mathbf{g}^{\mathrm{LCMV}} = \hat{\mathbf{R}}_x^{-1} \mathbf{H}_{:m}[\mathbf{H}_{:m}^T \hat{\mathbf{R}}_x^{-1} \mathbf{H}_{:m}]^{-1} \mathbf{u}_m, \qquad (1)$$

where the solution array $\mathbf{g}^{\mathrm{LCMV}}$ is formed by the concatenation of filters $\mathbf{g}_n$, i.e. $\mathbf{g}^{\mathrm{LCMV}} = [\mathbf{g}_1^T, \ldots, \mathbf{g}_N^T]^T$, and matrix $\mathbf{H}_{:m}^{(NL_g) \times (L_g + L_h - 1)}$ is a partition of the channel impulse matrix that only includes the impulse responses from the m-th source to the N microphones used in *Sylvester* matrix form. Matrix $\hat{\mathbf{R}}_x$ is the correlation matrix of the recorded signals, and $\mathbf{u}_m$ is a vector set to zeros except for one entry which is set to one at the proper position in order to compensate the room impulse response delay.

The implementation of the LCMV Algorithm proposed seeks for efficiency and accuracy, and for this reason is mainly based on the QR decomposition. Firstly, we form the following matrix $\mathbf{X} \in \mathbb{R}^{NL_g \times K}$,

$$\mathbf{X} = \frac{1}{\sqrt{K}} \begin{pmatrix} \mathbf{x}_1(k) & \mathbf{x}_1(k+1) & \ldots & \mathbf{x}_1(k+K-1) \\ \mathbf{x}_2(k) & \mathbf{x}_2(k+1) & \ldots & \mathbf{x}_2(k+K-1) \\ \vdots & \vdots & & \vdots \\ \mathbf{x}_N(k) & \mathbf{x}_N(k+1) & \ldots & \mathbf{x}_N(k+K-1) \end{pmatrix},$$

where $K \,(> NL_g)$ is the number of samples used. The algorithm computes the $\mathbf{QR}$ decomposition of $\mathbf{X}^T$, i.e. $\mathbf{X}^T = \mathbf{QR}$, where $\mathbf{Q}$ is orthogonal and $\mathbf{R}$ is upper triangular. Thus, in order to use LAPACK routines we build directly matrix X^T in column major order representation. Using matrix $\mathbf{X}$, matrix $\hat{\mathbf{R}}_x$ (1) can be computed as

$$\hat{\mathbf{R}}_x = \mathbf{X}\mathbf{X}^T = \mathbf{R}^T \mathbf{Q}^T \mathbf{Q} \mathbf{R} = \mathbf{R}^T \mathbf{R}.$$

Now, we define for convenience matrix $\mathbf{W} = \hat{\mathbf{R}}_x^{-1} \mathbf{H}_{:m}$ so that the LCMV Beamformer filter $\mathbf{g}^{\mathrm{LCMV}}$ (1) can be expressed as

$$\mathbf{g}^{\mathrm{LCMV}} = \mathbf{W}[\mathbf{H}_{:m}^T \mathbf{W}]^{-1} \mathbf{u}_m. \qquad (2)$$

Algorithm 1. The QR-LCMV Beamformer Algorithm

Require: Xmicro, N, LG, tam
Ensure: Y
1: Construction of matrix X.   (Algorithm 2)
2: Computation of the QR decomposition of matrix X.
3: Computation of the Beamformer filter (G).   (Algorithm 3)
4: Apply filter Beamformer (vector G) to get the output (vector Y).

We also define a matrix named $\mathbf{Z}$ which is the solution of the linear system

$$\mathbf{R}^T \mathbf{Z} = \mathbf{H}_{:m},$$

so that using the $\mathbf{QR}$ decomposition of matrix $\mathbf{X}$ we have

$$\mathbf{W} = \hat{\mathbf{R}}_x^{-1} \mathbf{H}_{:m} = (\mathbf{R}^T \mathbf{R})^{-1} \mathbf{H}_{:m} = \mathbf{R}^{-1} \mathbf{R}^{-T} \mathbf{H}_{:m} = \mathbf{R}^{-1} \mathbf{Z},$$

where clearly matrix $\mathbf{W}$ is the solution of the linear system $\mathbf{RW} = \mathbf{Z}$.

The path to obtain the Beamforming filters proceeds by solving the linear system

$$\mathbf{A}\mathbf{b}_m = \mathbf{u}_m, \tag{3}$$

where $\mathbf{A} = \mathbf{H}_{:m}^T \mathbf{W} = \mathbf{H}_{:m}^T \mathbf{R}^{-1} \mathbf{Z} = \mathbf{Z}^T \mathbf{Z}$. Also here, the solution of the linear system (3) is obtained through a $\mathbf{QR}$ factorization, in this case, of matrix $\mathbf{Z}$. Let $\mathbf{Z} = \mathbf{Q}'\mathbf{R}'$ be the $\mathbf{QR}$ decomposition of matrix $\mathbf{Z}$, then vector $\mathbf{b}_m$ can be computed by solving the following two triangular linear systems:

$$\mathbf{R}'^T \mathbf{y} = \mathbf{u}_m,$$
$$\mathbf{R}' \mathbf{b}_m = \mathbf{y}.$$

Finally, it is easy to see that the Beamformer filter presented in (1) can be computed through these last objects, i.e. $\mathbf{R}$, $\mathbf{Z}$, and $\mathbf{b}_m$, this way:

$$\mathbf{g}^{\text{LCMV}} = \mathbf{R}^{-1} \mathbf{Z} \mathbf{b}_m,$$

which involves a matrix vector product and a triangular linear system solution.

3   Implementation of the QR-LCMV Algorithm

We call QR-LCMV Algorithm to the LMCV Algorithm derived in the previous section whose computation is based on the QR decomposition. This algorithm can be easily described at the highest level of abstraction through four sequential steps that are summarized in Algorithm 1.

Matrix X, of size $rows \times cols$, has a rectangular structure characterized by a number of rows which is much greater than the number of columns ($rows \gg cols$), being $rows$ and $columns$ functions of the filter length LG and the number of microphones N. This matrix is built as shown in Algorithm 2. For the

Algorithm 2. Construction of matrix X

Require: Xmicro, N, LG, tam
Ensure: X

```
 1: pXmicro = Xmicro+LG-1;
 2: pmatrixX = X;
 3: for(i=0; i<N; i++) {
 4:   pXmicroaux = pXmicro;
 5:   for(r=0; r<LG; r++) {
 6:     for(j=0; j<k; j++) {
 7:       *pmatrixX = *(pXmicroaux+j);
 8:       *pmatrixX++;
 9:     }
10:     pXmicroaux--;
11:   }
12:   pXmicro += tam;
13: }
```

Algorithm 3. Computation of the Beamformer filter G

Require: rows, cols, lda, l, R, H
Ensure: G

```
 1: // Z = R*H
 2: memcpy(Z,H,n*l);
 3: strsm_(L,U,T,N,&cols,&l,&alpha,R,&lda,Z,&cols);
 4: // A = Z*Z';
 5: memcpy(A,Z,cols*l);
 6: calculateQR(cols,l,cols,A);
 7: // B[] = zeros; B[lg]=1
 8: spotrs_(U,&l,&right,A,&cols,B,&l,&info);
 9: sgemv_(N,&cols,&l,&alpha,Z,&cols,B,&right,&zero,G,&right);
10: strsv_(U,N,N,&cols,R,&rows,G,&right);
```

---

construction of X, we use an entry data matrix (Xmicro) which contains a set of values corresponding to the impulse response of the room and represents thus the physical features of the transmission channel. The integer tam is associated with some dimension of matrix Xmicro.

The second step of Algorithm 1 is solved by calling a LAPACK routine of the most suitable package. The libraries used exploit the ARM cores both in sequential and in parallel. Furthermore, some libraries allow to use the GPU alone or together the CPU cores. However, we did not find any implementation of the QR decomposition able to use the four ARM cores together the GPU. Hence, we performed a reimplementation of the LAPACK routine larfb, used by the driver routine geqrf, so that the GPU can be used in the QR decomposition (using CUBLAS library) at the same time the CPU cores can be used in parallel to perform another parts of the QR decomposition. This strategy is very similar to that implemented by MAGMA for multicore with a GPU attached. However, we decided to perform our own implementation since the results obtained with the MAGMA routine in the Jetson were very disappointing.

The third step of Algorithm 1 is devoted to the computation of filter G and its description is depicted in Algorithm 3. The last step involves simply operations needed to compute the final solution.

4   Analysis of the Results

In this work, we have employed the hardware platform NVIDIA Jetson TK1 [6]. The NVIDIA Jetson is a development kit running Linux that includes the processor Tegra K1 of NVIDIA, a processor which is also included in a wide variety of mobile devices like the Tablet NVIDIA Shield. The K1 chip features a quad-core ARM Cortex-A15 [1] processor and a Kepler [7] GPU with 192 cores. The NVIDIA Jetson includes 2 GB of main memory shared by the ARM processors and the GPU. It has, in addition, a great variety of connection interfaces: USB 3.0, mini-PCIE, GygaEthernet, SATA 3, HDMI..., that make of this device a very useful tool for a wide set of applications.

In the experimental tests the system used is made of 3 microphones and 2 loudspeakers. We worked with two filter lengths: 319 and 1499, which are upper and lower thresholds of usual filter lengths for this type of system.

The two first tests were performed to compare different versions of libraries BLAS and LAPACK optimized for the NVIDIA Jetson TK1. Optimized versions of these libraries can be found, e.g. in ATLAS and OPENBLAS. Tables 1 and 2 show the execution time using these two libraries, respectively, when running on one core. It can be easily observed that the optimization performed by OPENBLAS is slightly better than that of ATLAS for this hardware.

Table 1. Results of the Beamformer algorithm using ATLAS with 1 core.

	LG = 319		LG = 1499	
	TIME	%	TIME	%
MatrixX	0.022 s	1%	0.44 s	0%
QR of MatrixX	2.327 s	85%	224.03 s	86%
G Filter	0.373 s	14%	35.57 s	14%
Total time	2.722 s	100%	260.04 s	100%

The tables show three parts of the algorithm that correspond with those described in Algorithm 1, taking into account that the last two steps are merged in only one execution time (**G Filter**). We clearly observe, by analyzing the profile of the algorithm, that the most time consuming operation of the algorithm is the QR factorization of matrix X. The cost of this operation is all above 80 % of the total cost. This disparity in the cost of each part of the algorithm dictates

Table 2. Results of the Beamformer algorithm using OPENBLAS with 1 core.

	LG=319		LG=1499	
	TIME	%	TIME	%
MatrixX	0.015s	1 %	0.28s	0 %
QR of MatrixX	2.049s	85 %	191.19s	86 %
G Filter	0.348s	14 %	30.91s	14 %
Total time	2.413s	100 %	222.37s	100 %

that the optimization effort should be addressed to the QR decomposition of matrix X.

As a natural step forward we tested the behaviour of this algorithm when using more than one core. In this case there are 4 cores available to operate with. Libraries OPENBLAS and PLASMA both provide with a parallel implementation of the LAPACK routine that allows to obtain the QR factorization of a general matrix in parallel. Table 3 shows the execution time, also partitioned in the parts of the algorithm, when using 4 cores and OPENBLAS. The results with 4 cores using PLASMA are shown in Table 4. As in the case of using libraries ATLAS and OPENBLAS with a single core, also here OPENBLAS is better than PLASMA when using the four 4 cores of the TK1.

Table 3. Results of the Beamformer algorithm using OPENBLAS with 4 cores.

	LG=319		LG=1499	
	TIME	%	TIME	%
MatrixX	0.015s	2 %	0.28s	0 %
QR of MatrixX	0.639s	84 %	55.19s	86 %
G Filter	0.108s	14 %	8.91s	14 %
Total time	0.763s	100 %	64.37s	100 %

Table 4. Results of the Beamformer algorithm using PLASMA with 4 cores.

	LG=319		LG=1499	
	TIME	%	TIME	%
MatrixX	0.013s	1 %	0.32s	0 %
QR of MatrixX	0.709s	74 %	56.48s	75 %
G Filter	0.236s	25 %	18.20s	24 %
Total time	0.958s	100 %	75.00s	100 %

Table 5. Results of the Beamformer algorithm using OPENBLAS with 4 cores and MAGMA.

	LG=319		LG=1499	
	TIME	%	TIME	%
MatrixX	0.013s	1%	0.40s	1%
QR of MatrixX	1.117s	87%	36.65s	83%
G Filter	0.158s	12%	6.99s	16%
Total time	1.289s	100%	44.03s	100%

Table 6. Results of the Beamformer algorithm using OPENBLAS with 4 cores and CUBLAS.

	LG=319		LG=1499	
	TIME	%	TIME	%
MatrixX	0.015s	1%	0.30s	1%
QR of MatrixX	1.056s	83%	31.45s	81%
G Filter	0.206s	16%	6.93s	18%
Total time	1.277s	100%	38.68s	100%

Next, we used the embedded GPU of the processor TK1. We firstly used the only package (to the best of our knowledge) that allows to use a general purpose processor together a GPU, i.e. MAGMA (Table 5). We checked that the MAGMA implementation is still not properly optimized, and that a specialized work must be done to tune the hybrid implementation for processors like the NVIDIA TK1. Following the idea inspired by MAGMA, we made our own implementation of a hybrid algorithm that uses the four CPU cores plus the GPU device, using OPENBLAS for the CPU and CUBLAS for the GPU. Table 6 shows that our implementation outperforms MAGMA.

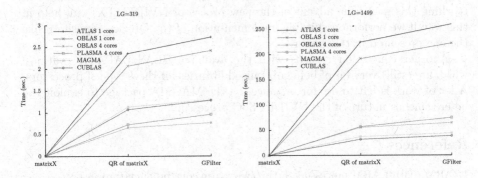

Fig. 2. Profile of the Beamformer algorithm with regard to the library employed.

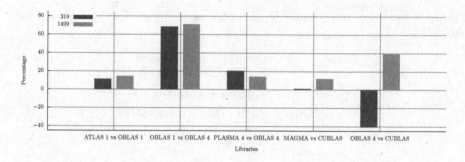

Fig. 3. Peer comparison of libraries (percentage of improvement).

Figure 2 summarizes the results with each different library and/or setting for the two filter lengths, i.e. LG = 319 and LG = 1499, to compare them all.

In addition, Fig. 3 depicts the percentage of improvement by pairs of libraries for both filter lengths. For instance, the first tick shows that OPENBLAS with 1 core performs better than ATLAS with 1 core for both filter lengths. On the other side of the figure, the negative value shows that it is worse using CUBLAS (the GPU) than using the four cores with OPENBLAS for a small filter length (LG=319) but, on the contrary, for a large filter length it is better to use the GPU instead of the 4 ARM cores. In general, we observe that the GPU plays a more significant role as the problem size increases.

5 Conclusions

The very large computational cost of the QR decomposition in which is based the QG-LCMV Beamformer Algorithm makes this method not suitable for real-time processing of digital sound reproduction systems when we try to use mobile devices based on ARM technology. However, the combination of a processor like the NVIDIA TK1, which contains a GPU accelerator embedded, with a proper implementation of the QR decomposition opens the door to the possibility of reaching this goal. The advent of the new processor NVIDIA TX1 can help in this way if we perform a suitable implementation of the QR decomposition like the one presented in this paper.

Another conclusion regards with the available BLAS/LAPACK routines, which are (still) very far of being optimized libraries for these type of processors. A lot of work is left to do, for instance, on the MAGMA package to exploit the heterogeneous nature of the NVIDIA SoC processors.

References

1. ARM. (2016) ARM processors. http://www.arm.com/products/processors/
2. Dongarra, J., et al.: "PLASMA users' guide", Electrical Engineering, Computer Science Department, Univesity of Tennessee, Knoxville, Tennessee 37996, Technical report (2015). http://icl.cs.utk.edu/plasma

3. Benesty, Y.H.J., Chen, J., Dmochowski, J.: On microphone-array beamforming from a mimo acoustic signal processing perspective. IEEE Trans. Audio Speech Lenguage Process. **15**, 1053–1065 (2007)
4. Lorente, J., Piñero, G., Vidal, A., Belloch, J., González, A.: Parallel implementations of beamforming design and filtering for microphone array applications. In: Proceedings of the 19th European Signal Processing Conference (EUSIPCO), Barcelona, Spain, pp. 501–505 (2011)
5. NVIDIA: NVIDIA CUDA Basic Linear Algebra Subroutines. https://developer.nvidia.com/cublas
6. NVIDIA. (2015) NVIDIA Jetson TK1. http://www.nvidia.es/object/jetson-tk1-embedded-dev-kit-es.html
7. NVIDIA. (2016) NVIDIA Kepler. http://www.nvidia.es/object/nvidia-kepler-es.html
8. OpenBLAS: An optimized BLAS library. http://www.openblas.net/
9. Tomov, S., Dongarra, J., Baboulin, M.: Towards dense linear algebra for hybrid GPU accelerated manycore systems. Parallel Comput. **36**(5–6), 232–240 (2010). http://icl.cs.utk.edu/magma

MARL-Ped+Hitmap: Towards Improving Agent-Based Simulations with Distributed Arrays

Eduardo Rodriguez-Gutiez[1](✉), Francisco Martinez-Gil[2](✉),
Juan Manuel Orduña[2](✉), and Arturo Gonzalez-Escribano[1](✉)

[1] Departamento de Informática, Universidad de Valladolid,
Campus Miguel Delibes s/n, 47011 Valladolid, Spain
{eduardo,arturo}@infor.uva.es
[2] Departamento de Informática, Universidad de Valencia,
Avenida Universidad s/n, Burjassot, 46100 Valencia, Spain
{francisco.martinez-gil,juan.orduna}@uv.es

Abstract. Multi-agent systems allow the modelling of complex, heterogeneous, and distributed systems in a realistic way. MARL-Ped is a multi-agent system tool, based on the MPI standard, for the simulation of different scenarios of pedestrians who autonomously learn the best behavior by Reinforcement Learning. MARL-Ped uses one MPI process for each agent by design, with a fixed fine-grain granularity. This requirement limits the performance of the simulations for a restricted number of processors that is lesser than the number of agents. On the other hand, Hitmap is a library to ease the programming of parallel applications based on distributed arrays. It includes abstractions for the automatic partition and mapping of arrays at runtime with arbitrary granularity, as well as functionalities to build flexible communication patterns that transparently adapt to the data partitions.

In this work, we present the methodology and techniques of granularity selection in Hitmap, applied to the simulations of agent systems. As a first approximation, we use the MARL-Ped multi-agent pedestrian simulation software as a case of study for intra-node cases. Hitmap allows to transparently map agents to processes, reducing oversubscription and intra-node communication overheads. The evaluation results show significant advantages when using Hitmap, increasing the flexibility, performance, and agent-number scalability for a fixed number of processing elements, allowing a better exploitation of isolated nodes.

Keywords: Agents · Crowd simulation · Message-passing · Programming tools · Distributed arrays

---

A. Gonzalez-Escribano—This work has been funded by Spanish MINECO and the EU ERDF program under grants HomProg-HetSys TIN2014-58876-P, TIN2015-66972-C5-5-R, CAPAP-H5 network TIN2014-53522-REDT, and COST Program Action IC1305: Network for Sustainable Ultrascale Computing (NESUS).

J. Carretero et al. (Eds.): ICA3PP 2016 Workshops, LNCS 10049, pp. 212–225, 2016.
DOI: 10.1007/978-3-319-49956-7_17

1   Introduction

Multi-agent systems allow the modelling of complex, heterogeneous, and distributed systems, in a realistic way. They assign an agent to each entity involved in the real-world environment [17,18]. This software paradigm is particularly appropriated for the study of pedestrian dynamics, where autonomous interactions among individuals generate global system behaviors. MARL-Ped [13] is a multi-agent distributed tool where each agent (pedestrian) learns its own behavior by Reinforcement Learning (RL) [15], allowing the simulation of pedestrian groups (ranging from a few ones to crowds) in different scenarios (queue forwarding, congestion scenarios, evacuation of enclosed ares, etc.). The great computational workload added by the learning process of each agent, together with the required number of agents in medium and large scale scenarios require the use of High Performance Computing platforms. Indeed, the number of agents tested in learning environments is usually limited by the available computing resources. MARL-Ped is based on the MPI message-passing standard which provides portability across distributed- and shared-memory environments. It uses one MPI process for each agent by design, with a fixed fine-grain granularity. This requirement limits the performance of the simulations for a restricted number of processors that is lesser than the number of agents. On the other hand, Hitmap [7] is a library designed to ease the task of programming parallel applications by using distributed arrays. It includes abstractions for the automatic partitioning and mapping of arrays with arbitrary granularity, as well as the automatic construction of flexible communication patterns adapted to the partition.

In this work, we present the methodology and techniques of granularity selection in Hitmap applied to the simulations of agent systems, using MARL-Ped as a case of study. Hitmap allows to transparently map agents to processes. We show the benefits of using this mechanism for improving the performance of agent-based applications executed in a restricted number of processing elements that is lesser than the number of agents. It eliminates oversubscription effects, and reduces intra-node communication overheads by grouping communications. The application of the Hitmap methodology does not increase the development effort. The comparative performance evaluation shows that the version using Hitmap uses more efficiently the computing resources, becoming more scalable in terms of the number of simulated agents.

The rest of the paper is organized as follows: Sect. 2 shows some related work. Section 3 introduces MARL-Ped and Hitmap tools. Next, Sect. 4 describes how Hitmap has been included in the MARL-Ped original application. Then, Sect. 5 presents an experimental evaluation of the modified application. Finally, Sect. 6 discusses some conclusion remarks and future work to be done.

2   Related Work

Pedestrian-dynamics models were improved and extended in the 80 s with the advent of low cost computers. Many different models have been used: the social forces model [9], models based on cellular automata [2], or continuum models based on gas kinetics equations [10]. However, the most extended ones are agent-based models [14], due to the ease of extracting global behavior as the sum of individual behaviors. In the last years, some efforts have been made to add machine learning technique to agent-based pedestrian models [12], in such a way that the agents learn their individual behavior by themselves, releasing the programmer of this task. Since the behavior learning is a complex task, it has become the main challenge for the pedestrian models. On the other hand, the microscopic simulation of pedestrian in crowded scenarios requires parallel processing. In this sense, specific architectures have been proposed for these simulations [1], and parallel architectures, where interconnected servers share the computational workload, have been developed [16]. Even architectures based on many-core processors have been used for simulating a marathon of one million runners [19].

Hitmap offers an intermediate abstraction layer, halfway between the manual programming of distributed data structures on message-passing models, and PGAS languages (Partitioned Global Address Space), like Chapel [3] or UPC [11]. Hitmap also provides mechanisms for the construction of reusable communication patterns at runtime that adapt to the data partition, creating a low number of aggregated communications. This leads, for example, to a performance efficiency comparable to UPC, with a reduced programming complexity and development effort [7]. Hitmap is used as a runtime system for the Trasgo parallel programming framework [8], that offers an approach similar to PGAS languages. Hitmap extends and generalizes the hierarchy creation and data partition functionalities of other libraries or distributed arrays models, such as HTAs [5] o Parray [4]. It allows to use transparent partition policies, either regular or irregular, defined as interchangeable modules with a common interface. This hides to the programmer the decisions about granularity and synchronization across hierarchical levels. Hitmap has also been extended to support data structures such as sparse matrices, or graphs, using the same methodology and interface [6].

3   MARL-Ped and Hitmap

3.1   MARL-Ped

MARL-Ped is a multi-agent system tool for pedestrian simulation which uses reinforcement learning (RL) [15] in each agent to learn the individual behavior of a single pedestrian. The purpose of the RL algorithm is to compute a control function which will be used by the agent to select at a given moment the action to do, based on the sensorized local state. MARL-Ped includes two types of agents: (a) Pedestrian (Learning) agents, which execute the RL algorithms and store the control function learned; and (b) an Environment agent, which executes the physical system simulation of the scenario, and sensorizes the state of each agent. The scenario is a 3D virtual world where the physical model engine named Open Dynamic Engine (ODE) simulates the collisions and forces moving the

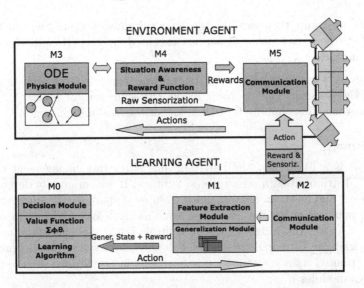

Fig. 1. MARL-Ped scheme showing the types of agents and their relationships.

pedestrians. Figure 1 shows a graphic scheme of the system, including both types of agents, and the communications exchange. These communications take place exclusively between the Environment agent and the rest of agents.

MARL-Ped has two working modes: learning mode and simulation mode. Both modes include the same communications between learning agents and the environment. The only difference is that RL algorithms are active in the learning mode to incrementally compute the control function, that will be used in the simulation mode. Both modes are synchronous, and composed of the classical cycle of observation-action-reward:

1. The Environment agent queries the ODE about the dynamic situation of each agent, consisting of position, speed, distance to the closest n pedestrians, and the distance to the closest n objects. In learning mode, the Environment agent also assigns a reward for each pedestrian agent depending on different facts: if it has reached the target, if it has collisioned with other agents or objects, etc.

2. The Environment agent sends the state and reward information to the Learning agents.

3. Each Learning agent uses the received information to build the local state and the immediate reward value. In the learning mode, the data built will be used by the RL algorithm to update the control function. In the simulation mode, the control function is not updated.

4. The agent queries the current control function to obtain the new action to be executed. The action indicates a change in direction and/or speed of the pedestrian.

5. The agents send their actions to the Environment agent, which in turn translate them into physical actions executed by the ODE in the virtual environment.

This cycle is repeated a given number of times which is a configuration parameter of the system. In the learning mode with some tens of agents, this parameter can range from hundreds of thousands to several million times.

3.2   Hitmap

Hitmap [7] is a library for the partition, mapping, and management of hierarchically distributed data structures at runtime. It was originally designed for dense arrays, and has been also extended to support sparse data structures, such as sparse matrices or graphs, using the same methodology and interface [6]. It is based on an SPMD (Single Program Multiple Data) model and the message-passing paradigm. Hitmap defines several abstractions to write parallel programs using distributed data structures. The functions in the library are grouped in three main modules.

Tiling functions. They allow the definition and management of hierarchically tiled data structures. These functionalities can be used independently of the rest of the library to improve locality on sequential code. They define classes to represent domains of indexes in a compact form. A class named *HitTile* represents the association between the elements of the indexes-domain space and the actual data, allowing the accesses to data with the same efficiency as manually developed codes without the tile abstraction. A process can declare and allocate a subspace of the original domain, in order to create a distributed data structure.

Mapping functions. They include interchangeable modules that implement policies to automatically part and map domains in terms of the processes of a virtual topology. The virtual topologies are also generated by another class of policy modules at runtime. Neighbor relations across processes are established by these policies. The partitions are represented by objects named *HitLayouts* that can be queried to obtain the indexes subdomain mapped to the local, a neighbor, or any other remote virtual process.

Communication functions. They are an abstraction of the message-passing model for tiles or tiles parts across virtual processes. They allow the creation of *HitCom* objects that store the information needed to marshall/unmarshall and exchange selected tile data across processes. Several interfaces for different types of point-to-point and collective communications are available. More complex patterns composed of multiple communication operations involving one or more tiles (several *HitCom* objects), are implemented as *HitPattern* objects. The constructor functions have always *HitLayout* parameters that are queried internally to automatically determine who communicates and what. Thus, these objects are transparently adapted on construction to the target platform details and the actual data distribution selected. The communication objects have a method that can be called at any time, and as many times as needed, to execute the communications. Internally, these objects exploit efficient MPI techniques such as derived data types, asynchronous communications, etc.

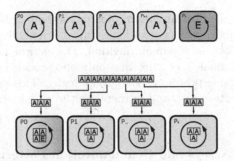

Fig. 2. Global structure of the simulation and task distribution across processors in the original MARL-Ped design (top) and after applying Hitmap (bottom).

4 Applying Hitmap Techniques and Methodology

In this section we describe how the Hitmap methodology and techniques can be applied to agent-based simulation applications to adapt the granularity of tasks to the available processing resources. We show this process using MARL-Ped as a case of study.

4.1 Structural Changes

The structure of the MARL-Ped application has been redesigned. The Hitmap version applies the concept of distributed arrays to group learning agents in processes, instead of using a single MPI process for each one, and a different process for the environment agent. Figure 2 (top) shows the conceptual distribution of the computation in the original MARL-Ped version. Each process executes the code of a single agent (*RLAgent* class). The last process performs the environment simulation (*RLEnvironment* class). The objects of these classes have several methods that implement the corresponding operations of the simulation loop that is repeatedly executed.

One of the first design decisions for the Hitmap version is to distribute agents across the available processes without reserving a special process for the environment. The environment code will be executed by one of the processes that will also have learning agents assigned, as the main computation for the learning agents and environment never overlap in time. Hitmap provides the tools needed for the balanced distribution of agents between the available processes as depicted in Fig. 2 (bottom). Each process should be able to execute, for each iteration of the simulation loop, the code of several learning agents.

In addition, the process in which the environment agent is mapped should execute its code. Thus, the simulation loop code cannot be placed inside the environment or learning agent classes. The application must be redesigned to execute the simulation loop in the main function. The simulation loop must iterate across the number of agents mapped to the process. To achieve this, the codes of the simulation loop are removed from the methods of the learning and environment classes. The private and protected methods called inside the loops are redeclared as public. The control logic that do the calls is relocated inside the new simulation loop at the main function. The environment control logic is wrapped with conditionals to ensure that only one process executes it. Hitmap automatically labels one process as the group leader. This process can identify itself by using a function call, and is therefore the one selected to execute the environment logic.

4.2   Distributed Arrays and Communication Patterns

The MPI-based communications in original MARL-Ped code have been replaced by distributed-array management functions provided by Hitmap. All data structures involved in communications are substituted by *HitTile* structures.

During the initialization stage of the program, the distributed arrays and objects of type *HitCom* and *HitPattern* are created to contain the specifications of the communications that will be invoked from the new simulation loop. Control signals are represented by a single integer-type variable at each process, independently of the number of assigned agents. On the other hand, two distributed arrays are declared for each data flow between the environment and the learning agents. These arrays have a global index domain equal to the number of learning agents. For one of the arrays, we use a distribution policy that maps its elements evenly across the processes. For the other one, we use a policy that maps all of the domain elements to the process running the environment. Given these two arrays with the same domain but different distribution policies, Hitmap allows the creation of a *HitPattern* object with a single function call. This object implements a communication pattern capable of redistributing the data from one array to the correspondent local or remote elements of the other array. This technique allows the construction of communication objects that will transparently move the data between the two copies of each array; the one actually distributed and the other one having the entire index domain at the environment process. The communication pattern adapts (at construction time) to the results of the partition policies, regardless of the number of agents and processes. This mechanism solves, in a unique way, the construction of the communication flows.

5   Experimental Study

This section describes an experimental study to show the advantages of using Hitmap on agent-based simulation programs. The study is focused on two areas. The first one is the code complexity and development effort. The second one is the performance when the number of agents grows above the number of available processing elements.

Table 1. Measurements of complexity and development effort.

	MARL-Ped	MARL-Ped+Hitmap
KDSI (code lines)	1970	1888
McCabe's C.C	209	171
Halstead	19.38×10^6	18.26×10^6

5.1 Development Effort

The first part of this experimental study shows that programming with Hitmap introduces granularity flexibility, even with a slightly lower development effort and code complexity than the original agent-per-process approach. We have measured several metrics both in the original MARL-Ped source code and in the modified Hitmap version: (a) The KDSI metric of the COCOMO methodology, based in the total number of source code lines; (b) McCabe's cyclomatic complexity; and (c) Halstead development effort metric. We have applied these metrics on the main function of the programs and the three classes modified when redesigning the original application. We have considered both the code of the modified functions and the header files, excluding comments and removing conditional compilation parts related to versions, alternatives or details of the MPI libraries used, etc. The modified code represents 16 % of the total application code, that has approximately 12 200 lines of code.

The results in Table 1 show that the version directly designed and programmed using Hitmap presents slightly lower complexity and effort than the original MPI version. Programming a direct MPI version with the agent distribution and load balancing capacity of the Hitmap version would clearly increase the programming effort, since the programmer would have to include code dealing with decisions about distributed array partition and management, that are transparently implemented in Hitmap.

5.2 Experimental Methodology for Performance Studies

The second part of the experimental study includes performance measurements of both the original MARL-Ped program and the Hitmap-based version. This work is focused on the MARL-Ped learning process, which is the most computationally demanding mode, and does not imply input/output operations during the main computation and communication loop. The code has been instrumented in order to measure the execution time for each distributed process. We have measured the time elapsed from the start of the initialization of parallelism-related structures (MPI or Hitmap) to the end of the execution of the learning process, before writing the results in files. Since each execution of the whole program gives one time measurement for each process, we consider as the global result the time of the slowest process, the one that has required the longer time to be completed. In addition, each experiment has been repeated several times in

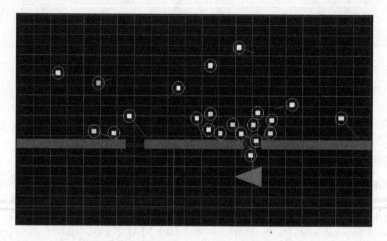

Fig. 3. Snapshot of the simulated scenario.

order to test the variability of the results. Both codes have been executed in multicore platforms, where communication costs are lower and potential overheads have a higher impact on the overall performance. These potential overheads can be associated to changes in execution structure, handling of internal Hitmap data structures, or computations and choices about the particular communications, among others. We have selected two machines, one with 8 cores (named *Miami*), and the other with 12 cores (named *Chimera*). Both machines had the *hyperthreading* option enabled. Table 2 summarizes the characteristics of these platforms as well as the development tools used in the study.

Since the execution time required for a full learning process execution is extremely long (RL is based on a long iterative process), the program has been limited to only 100 training iterations in all cases, in order to analyze a search space that is broad enough in terms of execution parameters. This threshold has been experimentally set to produce both a large computational load, and a significant number of communication and synchronization steps. The test scenario selected for the experiments has been validated in previous works [13]. This scenario reproduces a classic navigation problem in pedestrian dynamics called "shortest path vs. quickest path". In this scenario, a group of pedestrians must move from the room where they are initially located to a target place located outside of the room. This room has two exits, one of them being closer to the target than the other one. Agents must learn that if all of them head for the nearest exit, then a bottleneck is formed, making the overall evacuation time longer. A better solution implies that approximately half of the agents use the nearest exit, while the other half leaves the room through the most distant one, leading to a quicker evacuation. The configuration chosen places 28 agents in a 30-meter by 30-meter square room with two possible exits. Each exit has a width of one meter in order to prevent passage of more than one pedestrian at the same time. The goal of the agents is to reach the meeting point placed outside the room. Figure 3 illustrates the considered scenario, showing a snapshot of the simulation.

5.3   Performance Effect of the Agents Grouping

One of the objectives of this work is to obtain a better scalability when the number of agents grows, for a restricted number of processing elements in single cluster nodes. It is achieved using the Hitmap strategy of grouping several agents to the same process. This first performance study experimentally tests the difference in performance when the number of agents increases above the number of available processing elements in a given machine. Both programs (the original MARL-Ped version and the Hitmap-based version) have been run in learning mode with the number of MPI processes set to the number of cores available on each machine, and we have progressively increased the number of agents above that number.

Figure 4 shows the execution times required by *Miami* and *Chimera* machines (using 8 and 12 MPI processes respectively) for simulations of 100 learning iterations with different numbers of learning agents. In the original MARL-Ped tool (whose plots are labeled as MARL-Ped in the figure), the number of MPI processes is the number of agents plus one. In the MARL-Ped+Hitmap tool (whose plots are labeled as Hitmap in the figure), the number of processes has been fixed to be the number of actual cores of the machine. The structure of these simulation applications, that make use of collective communications with clear global synchronization points around the execution of the simulation engine, does not present a *parallel slackness* property. This property appears in certain applications when several processes assigned to the same element alternate communication and computation phases without overlapping.

Table 2. Characteristics of the machines used in the experimental study.

		Miami	Chimera
Processor		2x Intel X5550	2x Intel E5-2620 v2
Clock speed		2.66 GHz	2.10 GHz
Cores		8	12
Main memory		32 GB DDR3-1333	8 GB DDR4-1866
Cache	L1	128 K	32 K
	L2	1024 K	256 K
	L3	8192 K	15360 K
Operative system		CentOS 7.2.1511 x64	CentOS 7.0.1406 x64
C++ Compiler		GCC 4.8.5 20150623	GCC 4.8.2 20140120
Compilation flags		-O3	-O3
MPI implementation		MPICH 3.0.4	MPICH 3.1.3

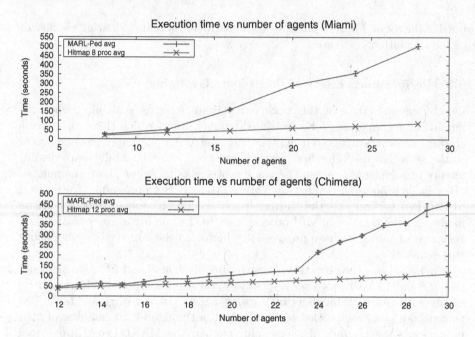

Fig. 4. Execution time vs. number of agents for 100 iterations of learning. The plots show with error bars the standard deviation of six different executions.

Figure 4 shows a very similar behavior in both platforms: the required execution time is slightly longer for MARL-Ped than for the Hitmap version while the number of agents does not reach double the number of existing cores in the machine. From this value up, the execution time required by MARL-Ped is significantly higher, linearly increasing with a high slope. These plots show how the additional costs of *oversubscription* (executing simultaneously more processes than processing elements available) has a negative impact on the application performance. Thus, in the Chimera machine, with 12 cores and hyperthreading enabled, the effect is much more remarkable starting at 24 agents, where MARL-Ped uses 25 MPI processes, increasing the oversubscription ratio to more than two. When there is oversubscription, the way in which task schedulers swap processes becomes relevant. Thus, we can observe slightly higher differences between maximum and minimum execution times in both *Miami* and *Chimera* machines for the original MARL-Ped program. On the contrary, the Hitmap plots remain almost flat regardless of the number of agents, showing much shorter execution times than the original MARL-Ped. This behavior is due to the fact that Hitmap can limit the number of processes, executing sequentially on each process the code of several agents in a more efficient way.

5.4   Impact of the Amount of Processes

This section studies the impact of modifying the number of processes, and therefore the agents distribution per process, when MARL-Ped+Hitmap is used.

Figure 5 shows the results obtained for a fixed number of 28 agents in the two machines. For MARL-Ped+Hitmap, we include plots for several consecutive experiments to show the variability of the results. The execution results of MARL-Ped+Hitmap are better than those of the original MARL-Ped in all cases, because of the oversubscription effects discussed in the previous section. It can be seen that the results for the Hitmap version when executed with a single process are slightly improved when the number of processes grows up to the number of cores in the machine, since the parallelism level increases. However, when the number of processes exceeds the number of real cores (without taking hyperthreading into account), the performance decreases and results become more unstable, due to stochastic negative effects of oversubscription. The process scheduling policy of the operative system also contributes to make the results more unpredictable. Due to the execution order of the processes during the context switching, in some cases execution times are as short (good) as before the start of the oversubscription, while in other cases the results are worse, but with a clear upper limit. Once the number of processes exceeds the number or available threads, taking hyperthreading into account, the results considerably worsen.

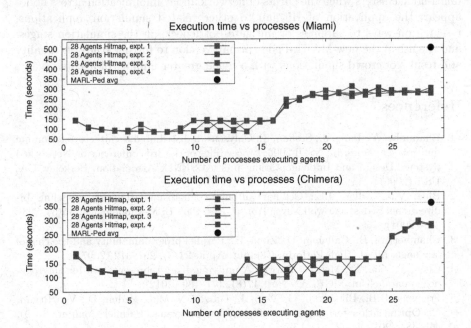

Fig. 5. Execution time vs. number of processes for 100 iterations of training, with a fixed number of 28 agents.

These results indicate that the number of processes to select in MARL-Ped+Hitmap in training mode is predictable, and can be adapted to the features of the target machines when the application is launched. The execution times are shorter and more stable when the number of processes is equal to the number of real processing elements, without taking into account the hyperthreading option.

6   Conclusions

This article presents the application of the techniques and tools of the Hitmap library to control the granularity of agent to processes map in agent-based simulation applications. As a first approximation, we use the MARL-Ped multi-agent pedestrian simulation software as a case of study for intra-node cases. The performance evaluation results show that MARL-Ped+Hitmap allows simulations with a number of agents greater than the number of processing elements available in a machine, while keeping execution times stable and predictable. These results show that the use of distributed arrays and automatic data partitions improves the performance agent-based simulation tools, due to the ability of Hitmap of transparently map a high number of agents to a constricted number of processes.

Future work includes the study of the scalability of Hitmap techniques in multi-node clusters when the effects of network and communication across nodes appear; the application of Hitmap to other related simulation applications; research on ways to suppress or mitigate bottlenecks in the simulation stages; and the use of the new MARL-Ped+Hitmap version to further study the quality and results of crowd simulations with a much greater number of agents.

References

1. Bharambe, A., Pang, J., Seshan, S.: Colyseus: a distributed architecture for online multiplayer games. In: NSDI 2006: Proceedings of the 3rd conference on Networked Systems Design and Implementation, p. 12. USENIX Association, Berkeley, CA, USA (2006)
2. Blue, V.J., Adler, J.L.: Cellular automata microsimulation for modeling bi-directional pedestrian walkways. Transp. Res. Part B: Methodological **35**(3), 293–312 (2001)
3. Chamberlain, B., Callahan, D., Zima, H.: Parallel programmability and the chapel language. Int. J. High Perform. Comput. Appl. **21**(3), 291–312 (2007)
4. Chen, Y., Cui, X., Mei, H.: Parray: A unifying array representation for heterogeneous parallelism. SIGPLAN Not. **47**(8), 171–180 (2012)
5. Fraguela, B.B., Bikshandi, G., Guo, J., GarzaráN, M.J., Padua, D., Von Praun, C.: Optimization techniques for efficient hta programs. Parallel Comput. **38**(9), 465–484 (2012)
6. Fresno, J., Gonzalez-Escribano, A., Llanos, D.: Blending extensibility and performance in dense and sparse parallel data management. IEEE Trans. Parallel Distrib. Syst. **25**(10), 2509–2519 (2014)

7. Gonzalez-Escribano, A., Torres, Y., Fresno, J., Llanos, D.: An extensible system for multilevel automatic data partition and mapping. IEEE Trans. Parallel Distrib. Syst. **25**(5), 1145–1154 (2014)
8. Gonzalez-Escribano, A., Llanos, D.R.: Trasgo: a nested-parallel programming system. J. Supercomput. **58**(2), 226–234 (2011)
9. Helbing, D., Molnár, P.: Social force model for pedestrian dynamics. Phys. Rev. E **51**, 4282–4286 (1995)
10. Hughes, R.L.: The flow of human crowds. Annu. Rev. Fluid Mech. **35**, 169–182 (2003)
11. Mallón, D.A., Gómez, A., Mouriño, J.C., Taboada, G.L., Teijeiro, C., Touriño, J., Fraguela, B.B., Doallo, R., Wibecan, B.: Upc performance evaluation on a multicore system. In: Proceedings of the Third Conference on Partitioned Global Address Space Programing Models, pp. 9: 1–9: 7. PGAS 2009, NY, USA. ACM, New York (2009)
12. Martinez-Gil, F., Lozano, M., Fernández, F.: Multi-agent reinforcement learning for simulating pedestrian navigation. In: Vrancx, P., Knudson, M., Grześ, M. (eds.) ALA 2011. LNCS (LNAI), vol. 7113, pp. 54–69. Springer, Heidelberg (2012). doi:10. 1007/978-3-642-28499-1_4
13. Martinez-Gil, F., Lozano, M., Fernández, F.: MARL-ped: A multi-agent reinforcement learning based framework to simulate pedestrian groups. Simul. Model. Pract. Theor. **47**, 259–275 (2014)
14. Reynolds, C.: Steering behaviors for autonomous characters. In: Game Developers Conference, pp. 763–782. Miller Freeman Game Group, San Francisco, California (1999)
15. Sutton, R.S., Barto, A.G.: Reinforcement Learning: An Introduction. MIT Press, Cambridge (1998)
16. Vigueras, G., Orduña, J.M., Lozano, M.: A read-copy update based parallel server for distributed crowd simulations. J. Supercomput. **64**(1), 156–166 (2013)
17. Wooldridge, M.: Multi-Agent Systems. Intelligent Agents. MIT Press, Cambridge (2013)
18. Wooldridge, M., Jennings, N.: Intelligent agents: theory and practice. Knowl. Eng. Rev. **10**, 115–152 (1995)
19. Yilmaz, E., Isler, V., Cetin, Y.Y.: The virtual marathon: Parallel computing supports crowd simulations. IEEE Comput. Graph. Appl. **29**(4), 26–33 (2009)

Efficiency of GPUs for Relational Database Engine Processing

Samuel Cremer$^{(\boxtimes)}$, Michel Bagein$^{(\boxtimes)}$, Saïd Mahmoudi$^{(\boxtimes)}$,
and Pierre Manneback$^{(\boxtimes)}$

Computer Science Department, University of Mons,
Rue de Houdain, 9, 7000 Mons, Belgium
`samuel.cremer@heh.be`,
`{michel.bagein,said.mahmoudi,pierre.manneback}@umons.ac.be`

Abstract. Relational database management systems (RDBMS) are still widely required by numerous business applications. Boosting performances without compromising functionalities represents a big challenge. To achieve this goal, we propose to boost an existing RDBMS by making it able to use hardware architectures with high memory bandwidth like GPUs. In this paper we present a solution named CuDB. We compare the performances and energy efficiency of our approach with different GPU ranges. We focus on technical specificities of GPUs which are most relevant for designing high energy efficient solutions for database processing.

Keywords: In-Memory DB · RDBMS · GPU · SoC

1 Introduction

In recent years, it has became common to use GPUs as co-processing units for scientific simulations in HPC environment or for computer vision applications, either for faster processing or for energy saving. Consumption of data still grows in order to deal higher needs on data storage and processing (social network, IoT, distributed applications, data externalization, etc.). To contain energy growing needs, numerous researches [1] show that GPUs are more efficient than CPUs for high and intensive computing but only for a limited number of specific applications. Our vision of energy saving is more based on improving efficiency of usual components. Data RDMS SQL engine is one of the most spread and used component, targeting operating systems, personal applications, CRM, ERP up to largely distributed applications (DropBox, Skype) and either for small devices (Smartphone) up to datacenters. Using RDBMS components in applications is largely driven by the high flexibility of SQL language for data definition and manipulation. The counterpart of this flexibility is the computing complexity (parsing, query plan generation and execution, data retrieval) in term of CPU cycles per data manipulation. Starting from this situation, we focused in boosting such engines, in order to improve this last ratio. One of the usual ideas that might be proposed for such a purpose is to parallelize such engine on all CPU

© Springer International Publishing AG 2016
J. Carretero et al. (Eds.): ICA3PP 2016 Workshops, LNCS 10049, pp. 226–233, 2016.
DOI: 10.1007/978-3-319-49956-7_18

available cores in order to speedup performances with a limited power overhead. This approach is limited by the number of cores sharing a common memory space on one computing node. To overcome this limit, one way is to exploit more efficient processing accelerators.

The main GPU efficiency advantage is given by its hardware architecture: many synchronized arithmetic and logic units (ALU) are driven by only one instruction decoder enabling large vectorized data process. In contrast, CPU cores are fully asynchronous, enabling multiple concurrent processes running together, but each ALU requires its own decoder. ALUs, which are the real data processing worker, can be more populated in GPU die (more than 2000 cores) than in CPU die. Again, thanks to its architecture, GPU brings a second advantage over CPU: the memory bandwidth. On GPU cards, memory chips implantation is dedicated to processor data bus which can be much wider than the usual 64 bit buses of DIMM RAM memories. In term of speed, high end GPU memory bandwidths (480 GB/s for 384-bit GDDR5X memory of a Titan X) are currently more than ten time faster than RAM memories (25,6 GB/s for a PC4-25600 DDR4).

Most of database treatments are extraction queries. A same extraction query is generally applied on multiple data rows which is a valid workflow for a SIMT (Single Instruction Stream Multiple Threads) architecture like a GPU. That is why GPUs can deliver high performance and fast responsiveness when they are used for database treatments while improving energy efficiency. The first objective of this paper is to show that a database engine which uses GPUs can outperform a conventional CPU implementation. Our second objective is to investigate which type of GPU architecture and which technical specificities are most relevant to build an efficient solution for database treatments.

2   Positioning and Related Works

Previous research thematic focused on improving processing speed of database engines with GPUs can be subdivided in 3 categories: (1) proposals for conceptions of RDBMS engines, (2) NoSQL engines, and (3) studies of abilities of GPUs to process some specific functionality of RDBMS engines. First category of previous researches contains GPUQP [2], where the authors describe the potentiality to execute each relational operator of generated query plan, either on CPU or GPU. The authors focused on the processing of single join-queries and contributed to provide a foundation for many other researches. An important contribution is Sphyraena [3], where the authors proposed to accelerate the SQLite open source database engine with GPUs. This work has inspired us in going some steps further. Firstly, with new designs of faster storage and join engines for increasing responsiveness and secondly with a multithreaded CPU co-processing engine to maintain highest speed accelerations on tiny datasets. In the second category we can find - for example Mega-KV [4], a Key-Value store running on GPUs. With Mega-KV, data are hosted in CPU side RAM-memory while GPU memory only hosts a hash table of keys. Incoming queries are regrouped and launched concurrently on GPU. Global performances are interesting with high number of incoming queries but an isolated query is not running faster as with a classical CPU implementation. Unlike Mega-KV, our solution is based on a RDBMS: in order to improve processing time, each query exploits the available parallel cores of GPU. This approach offers better response times for each query. In last category, proposals like GPUTx [5] focused on transaction mechanisms of GPU RDBMs. It can execute only pre-compiled procedures and is not able to process single queries. In 2013, Pietron et al. published a paper presenting the implementation of *"SELECT WHERE"* and *"SELECT JOIN"* queries with non-indexed data on a GPU-database [6]. Join operations were implemented as Cartesian products of tables which procure a quadratic time complexity for a simple join operation. With CuDB, those kinds of queries are dynamically resolved, thanks to temporary indexation mechanisms, on linearithmic time complexity which provide faster executions.

3   Boosting a RDBMS with GPUs

According to DB-Engines ranking [7], RDBMs are still more popular and are not yet being overthrown by NoSQL engines. Hosting relational databases of multiple clouds with hybrids nodes (CPU + GPU) can deliver better performances while improving energy efficiency of datacenters. Our solution, named CuDB, is an In-Memory RDBMS where data is mainly processed by GPU, based on the SQLite open source RDBMS. In order to achieve an easy migration of existing applications, CuDB preserves same API and query compiler of SQLite. As those two mechanisms are intrinsically sequential processes, they cannot benefit from parallel architecture of GPUs and they are still processed by the CPU. The two last modules, data processing and storage engines which required most of processing resources, are implemented on GPU side. Most part of processing is computed in parallel by the GPU cores and the entire database is hosted in GPU memory in order to benefit from its higher memory bandwidth. Because the entire database resides into the GPU global memory, and unlike many other GPU applications, each query processing has to transfer a very limited amount of data from CPU to GPU. The amount of data to transfer is essentially limited to size of the query plan, which represents around one kilobyte per query. A query plan generated by query compiler is sent to GPU and executed by all GPU threads. Every GPU thread process the query plan on its own data subset. This scheme is able to deal with the SIMT specificities of GPU architectures while taking advantages either of massively parallel cores than large GPU memory buses.

To maximize performances, memory accesses of GPU-threads have to be coalesced [8]. Given that each CUDA thread works on its own record and on the same column, a column-oriented data structure is able to provide coalesced memory access in order to mask high latency times of GPU global memory. Coalesced memory accesses can be obtained when data-structure uses fixed-size columns, but this is a constraint for variable-length strings and blob values. Those types of data are managed as pointers. Pointers are stored into the column-oriented storage zone and refer to associated values stored in a row-oriented storage zone.

Column-oriented and row-oriented tables are located side by side in order to minimize memory foot-print and increasing data locality (cache optimization). Fixed-length strings are entirely stored into the column-oriented storage zone, like numerical values. However, in the context of non-extensible GPU memory size, the main drawback of this storage method is the data compactness induced by fixed size columns. CuDB storage engine supports also storage tables organized in row-oriented to maximize data compactness, this it implies a 20% to 300% performance drop depends on query type and data types.

To be more efficient than CPU, GPU processing needs a minimal amount of data to process. With queries on tiny tables, CPU processes faster than GPU. In order to maintain the maximal performances for all situations, a switch and a threshold are implemented to redirect query execution of tiny tables from GPU to CPU side. Equivalent processing and storage engines are implemented at CPU side. Theses CPU engines are designed on the same parallel principles of the GPU counterpart engines, with POSIX multithreading. This way, queries that involve small datasets are processed by CPU, with as drawback that we have to maintain duplicated tiny tables (less than 1000 records) at CPU memory side. In upcoming work, the threshold (1000 records per table) will be dynamically managed.

4   Experimental Results

For the equity of the performance comparison, with SQLite we used an in-memory stored database. Given that the query parser remains identical for CuDB and SQLite we did not take into account its execution time. For all versions, we only measured the elapsed time of the query-plan executions. Results generated by GPU are asynchronously exported to central RAM (Pinned Memory). When all GPU jobs are finished, CPU can access entire results and measure of execution time is evaluated at this instant. In order to smooth variations generated by the overall system load, all results reports average of hundred executions of same queries. As time variations of same queries were less than 5%, they are not reported to preserve the readability of this paper. We consider that average measures are sufficiently relevant to be presented as valid results. We test multiple forms of *SELECT* queries, with single table scans and multiple table joins. We used an experimental database setup wherein tables contain one *char(80)* column and multiple integer columns. Rows selected by our queries are, in most cases, randomly spread inside tables.

For the veracity of our evaluations we choose to test a panel of several GPUs. Given that there is currently no entry level GPU for newer Maxwell generation, we chose to make our benchmark with the Kepler family. All of them are issued from a same Kepler generation and are manufactured in 28 nm. GPU1 represent a high end GPU with numerous cores and a higher memory bandwidth. GPU2 is a little GPU but with best ratio of core/bandwidth and core/L2 cache. GPU3 is a cheap entry level GPU with slower GDDR3 memory. We also think that it should be relevant to test performances with a SoC version: the Tegra K1. This

Table 1. Hardware specifications

	CPU	GPU1	GPU2	GPU3	SoC
Name	Core i7 2600 K	GTX770	GT740	GT720	Tegra K1
Cores	4 + HT	1536	384	192	4(CPU) + 192(GPU)
Frequency	3.4 GHz	~1 GHz	~1 GHz	~0.8 GHz	~0.8 GHz
L2 Cache	8 MB	512 kB	256 kB	128 kB	128 kB
Mem. Bandwidth	21 GB/s	220 GB/s	80 GB/s	15 GB/s	15 GB/s
TDP	95 W	230 W	64 W	19 W	11 W

kind of low-power platform can be considerate like the next generation of mobiles devices where efficiency improvement can increase battery autonomy. We used a "Jetson TK1" development kit which embeds 192 GPU Kepler cores, quad 32bits ARM Cortex-A15 CPU cores and one battery-saver core on the same die. Only one unified memory space is used by GPU and CPU cores. Main hardware specifications we used for performances tests are listed in Table 1.

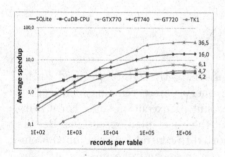

Fig. 1. Average speedups   **Fig. 2.** Energy efficiency improvements

Figure 1 shows the average speedups obtained with our different test platforms with SQLite on the Core i7 2600 K as reference. The multithreaded CPU version is always faster than SQLite and provide a maximal speedup of 4,1. The discrete GPUs need quite a thousand of records to become more efficient and reach a peak speedup of 37 for the fastest GPU, 6 for the slowest and 4,7 for Tegra K1.

During our tests, we also measured the power consumption of the whole system with an external power meter. From those values we have subtracted the idle power consumption with the purpose of showing only the consumptions involved by database processing's. Figure 2 shows the gains in energy efficiency with our different platforms. It seems that, when volume of data is sufficient, using a GPU-RDBMS is always more energy efficient than CPU In-Memory implementations. Also cheap entry levels GPUs performs very well. This observation should however be tempered by the fact that our reference processor is an outdated second generation Core i7 CPU (32 nm) with a TDP of 95W. Current

14 nm sixth generation of Core i7, like 6920HQ available in laptops has a TDP of only 45 W while delivering similar performances. Anyway, with an energy efficiency starting at 1700% for GPU1 and rising up to 5800% with the Tegra platform, GPUs are still far ahead.

4.1   PCI-Express Bus: The Bottleneck

PCI-Express bus is a bottleneck when a query returns numerous records. Figure 3 shows the results with a trivial *"SELECT * FROM T WHERE 1"* query. That kind of query works just like a memory dump where GPU cores just read values and send it directly back to the CPU through PCI-Express bus.

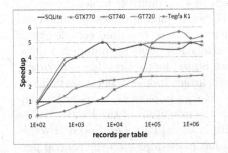
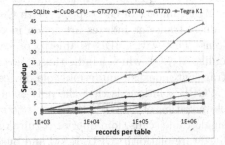

Fig. 3. Speedup with *SELECT* all   **Fig. 4.** Speedup with *SELECT WHERE*

The performances of GPU1 and GPU2, plugged on a PCI Express 16x interfaces, are similar (5x and 4,7x) despite GPU1 is theoretically 4 times faster. GPU3 is about 2 times slower (2,75x) because it is plugged on 8x PCI-Express interface. The SoC platform becomes here the fastest solution when enough data are involved with a speedup of 5,4x. With a Tegra K1, there is no PCI Express bottleneck. Data are directly copied through the main memory bus but it is still a disappointment that on those kinds of SoC architecture, data still needs to be copied between CPU and GPU space memory; we expected a real shared memory space, which could avoid all data transfers/duplications between CPU and GPU. We had tested the "unified memory" mechanisms provided by CUDA 6 which allow using a single memory pointer for CPU and GPU code. It seems it is only a developer's easiness: data are still duplicated/transferred in background by the driver what results in noticeable performance loss and even with the Tegra K1. CuDB current implementation preserves separated CPU and GPU memory pointers in order to maximize performances. With conventional usages of RDBMs, queries generally return only a small proportion of the processed data. Figure 4 shows average speedups obtained with different *"SELECT WHERE"* queries. For those tests, the amount of returned records vary from 10 rows up to 2000 rows for queries on the largest datasets. If we compare results of Figs. 3 and 4, we can see that PCI-Express bus has much less influence. GPU3 suffer from its 8x bus when it has to send more than a thousand of records back to RAM memory.

4.2   Comparison Between Versions of a Same GPU

As shown on Table 1, GPU specificities of Tegra K1 SoC are similar to a GeForce GT720. The main differences are: (1) one is embedded into a SoC and the other is a graphic card, and (2) one shares its memory with the CPU cores while the other has to transfer data through a slow PCI Express 8x bus. To compare both implementations of a same GPU we "underclocked" our Core i7 CPU to 1.6 GHz and the DDR3-1333 Memory to 800 MHz to be closer to the performances of ARM cores of Tegra K1. HyperThreading and Intel Turboboost were also disabled. We notice that with this configuration, our desktop CPU is still 11% faster than the Tegra K1 CPU cores. For full table scans and with this high performance degradation of our Core i7 CPU, we notice no relevant performance drop of the GT720. With join queries which involve multiple tables, we notice a higher impact of CPU speed. With CuDB, before joining tables on unindexed values, transient indexes are made in order to reduce the time complexity of joins. This way, CuDB is able to process really fast joins on unindexed data, unlike MySQL which handle those joins with nested loops. Creating and sorting transient indexes require multiple device synchronizations. A big constraint for GPGPU solutions is that the only reliable way to implement barriers for synchronization of all GPU threads, is to stop the execution of the kernel. Unlike single table scans, join queries require multiple kernel launches. Speed of whole hardware platform (CPU, RAM and buses) has more impact on the general performances of join queries. Compared to GT720 with "underclocked" CPU, Tegra K1 is multiple times slower while processing join queries on tiny datasets. This performance gap decreases up to 40% for processing queries on biggest tables. Slower processing speed of Tegra K1 for join queries is due to the shared memory bus and slower CPU cores.

If we are focused on pure energy consumption, Tegra K1 is potentially the most efficient solution but it needs enough data (500 k) before it becomes really interesting. The fact that K1 become efficient when it has to treat large datasets is contradictory with the fact that its memory, shared with CPU cores, is quiet limited (2 GB), and remains not extensible. Another drawback of the SoC platform is that performances are not consistent. During our tests we had a variance of 107% while discrete GPUs offered a great stability with a variance of only 5%. This instability in performances is again explained by the fact that the memory is shared with CPU cores. Moreover, ARM CPU cores of Tegra K1 are relatively slow. With the SoC platform, our GPU kernels need 1.2 ms to start while 0.14 ms are sufficient with the desktop hardware. This explains why Tegra K1 is always slower than other GPU solutions when it has to process small datasets.

4.3   Summary

In view of our different results, entry level GPUs are cheap and energy efficient but, with their slower memory bus, they are only 50% faster than a quadcore CPU. This performance gain is not enough to justify managing constraints involved by GPGPU solutions. A SoC platform, like a Jetson TK1, procures a high energy efficiency but it suffers from same drawbacks than entry level GPUs, adding the fact that CPU cores and memories are even more limited. We did not test our solution with Tegra X1 SoC which is theoretically around 50% faster but it preserves similar memory limitations. If we take a closer look at results of GPU1 and GPU2, for a boosted GPU-RDBMS we deduce the follow rule: memory bandwidth and amount of L2 cache per core are more significant than number of cores. GPU1 is not 4 times faster than GPU2 though it has 4 times more cores. GPU2 is nearly 3 times faster than GPU3 while having similar power efficiency, even though it has only 2 times more cores. For database processings, the most efficient solution should be mid-range GPU (less than 1000 cores) with the same amount of cache and same memory bandwidth than high end GPUs.

5   Conclusion and Future Works

In this paper, we presented CuDB, a solution able to boost performances of an open source RDBMs by using GPU architectures. We showed that GPUs are able to speed up most of extraction queries while reducing the global energy consumption. The biggest challenges we still have to resolve is to deal with memory limitations of GPUs and adding a full transaction support. In this paper, we also showed that for building an energy efficient solution, all ranges of GPUs has to be taken into account and not only the faster ones. CuDB includes also a multithreaded CPU processing engine which already procures substantial speedups for query on tiny tables. To complete our study, it should be interesting to test our multithreaded CPU engine on Many-Core platforms like Xeon Phi's. Relevance of memory bandwidth has been pointed and, regarding specificities of next generation of GPUs and Xeon Phi's (no prominent increase of number of cores but massive memory improvements), it seems that industry agrees with our observations.

References

1. Huang, S., Xiao, S., Feng, W.: On the energy efficiency of graphics processing units for scientific computing. In: IPDPS 2009, Sichuan (2009)
2. Fang, R., He, B., Lu, M., Yang, K., Govindaraju, N.K., Luo, Q., Sander, P.V.: GPUQP: query co-processing using graphics processor. In: SIGMOD/PODS 2007, Beijing, pp. 1061–1063 (2007)
3. Bakkum, P., Skadron, K.: Accelerating SQL database operations on a GPU with CUDA. In: 3rd Workshop on GPGPU, Pittsburgh, pp. 94–103 (2010)
4. Zhang, K., Wang, K., Yuan, Y., Lei, G., Lee, R., Zhang, X.: Mega-KV: a case for GPUs to maximize throughput of in-memory key-value stores. VLDB Endowment, col. 8(11), 1226–1237 (2015)
5. He, B., Xu, Yu, J.: High-throughput transaction executions on graphics processors. VLDB Endowment 4(5), 314–325 (2011)
6. Pietron, M., Russek, P., Wiatr, K.: Accelerating select where and select join queries on a GPU. Comput. Sci. (AGH) 14(2), 243–252 (2013)
7. DB-Engines Ranking. http://db-engines.com/en/ranking
8. van den Braak, G., Mersman, B., Corporaal, H.: Compiletime GPU memory access optimizations. In: ICSAMOS 2010, Samos, pp. 200–207 (2010)

Geocon: A Middleware for Location-Aware Ubiquitous Applications

Loris Belcastro[1]([⊠]), Giulio Di Lieto[1], Marco Lackovic[2],
Fabrizio Marozzo[1], and Paolo Trunfio[1]

[1] DIMES, University of Calabria, Rende, Italy
{lbelcastro,fmarozzo,trunfio}@dimes.unical.it
[2] Helmes AS, Tallinn, Estonia
marco.lackovic@helmes.ee

Abstract. A core functionality of any location-aware ubiquitous system is storing, indexing, and retrieving information about entities that are commonly involved in these scenarios, such as users, places, events and other resources. The goal of this work is to design and provide the prototype of a service-oriented middleware, called Geocon, which can be used by mobile application developers to implement such functionality. In order to represent information about users, places, events and resources of mobile location-aware applications, Geocon defines a basic metadata model that can be extended to match most application requirements. The middleware includes a *geocon-service* for storing, searching and selecting metadata about users, resources, events and places of interest, and a *geocon-client* library that allows mobile applications to interact with the service through the invocation of local methods. The paper describes the metadata model and the components of the Geocon middleware. A prototype of Geocon is available at https://github.com/SCAlabUnical/Geocon.

1 Introduction

With the widespread diffusion of mobile technologies and location-based services, it is possible to provide ubiquitous access to context-aware information (e.g., interesting attractions or events in a given place being visited). A core functionality of any location-aware ubiquitous system is storing, indexing, and retrieving information about entities that are commonly involved in these scenarios, such as (mobile) users, places, events and other resources (e.g., photos, media, comments). The goal of this work is to design and provide the prototype of a service-oriented middleware, called Geocon, which can be used by mobile application developers to implement such functionality. Geocon can be used to discover location-aware content, to share context-related information, and to facilitate interaction among users of mobile apps. Examples of services that can

This work has been partially supported by Project PON04a2_D DICET-INMOTO-ORCHESTRA funded by MIUR.

J. Carretero et al. (Eds.): ICA3PP 2016 Workshops, LNCS 10049, pp. 234–243, 2016.
DOI: 10.1007/978-3-319-49956-7_19

be implemented in a mobile app using Geocon are: (*i*) discovery of cultural places to be visited during a trip; (*ii*) publication of user reviews about hotels and restaurants; (*iii*) sharing of real-time information about events, traffic, and so on.

A key benefit for developers using Geocon is the possibility to focus on the front-end functionality provided by their mobile application, without the need of implementing by scratch back-end components for data storing, indexing and searching, since they are provided by the middleware. In order to represent information about users, places, events and resources of mobile location-aware applications, Geocon defines a basic metadata model that can be extended to match most application requirements. The widely-used *JavaScript Object Notation* (JSON) format is employed to represent such metadata. The architecture of the middleware includes a *geocon-service* that exposes methods for storing, searching and selecting metadata about users, resources, events and places of interest, and a *geocon-client* library that allows mobile applications to interact with the service through the invocation of local methods. The interaction between service and client is based on the REST model.

Given the huge number of users, places, events and resources that may be involved in location-aware ubiquitous applications, scalability plays a fundamental role [8]. Geocon was designed to ensure scalability through the use of a NoSQL indexing and search engine, Elasticsearch, that can scale horizontally on a very large number of nodes as the system load increases. Elasticsearch is used in combination with an external NoSQL database, MongoDB, which is more focused on constraints, correctness and robustness. Data stored in MongoDB can be asynchronously pushed to Elasticsearch, making it possible to persist in Elasticsearch a subset of the data stored in the external database.

The remainder of the paper is organized as follows. Section 2 discusses related work. Section 3 describes the metadata model. Section 4 describes the middleware architecture and components. Finally, Sect. 5 concludes the paper.

2   Related Work

The European research project CRUMPET [5] (*Creation of User-Friendly Mobile Services Personalised for Tourism*) was developed in the early 2000s, before the mass diffusion of smartphones, for addressing issues related to the mobility of tourists. Taking into account different user's travel purposes (e.g. business, leisure, entertainment, education), CRUMPET aims to provide information services meeting the different tourists' needs. It exploits information about users' personal interests and their geographical position to filter the content available to them. One of the primary goals of CRUMPET was to implement and improve FIPA[1](*Foundation for Intelligent Physical Agents*) specifications for mobile applications. The project used the explicit/implicit feedback concepts and the GML (*Geography Markup Language*) standard for storing geographic data.

---

[1] http://www.fipa.org.

Yu and Chang [10] extended the CRUMPET project ideas by seeking new intelligent solutions for overcoming the limitations of handheld devices in terms of reduced screen size for displaying information and limited bandwidth for transmitting data over a mobile network. Schmidt-Belz and Poslad [7] presented another study connected to the CRUMPET project, which aims to assess the quality of CRUMPET usability from the end user's point of view. The study takes into account four European locations (i.e., Heidelberg, Helsinki, London and Aveiro) and makes use of the standard questionnaire SUMI[2] (*Software Usability Measurement Inventory - ISO/IEC 9126*) to evaluate quality of software usability. This questionnaire was replaced in 2011 by SQuaRE[3](*Systems and software quality Requirements and evaluation - ISO/IEC 25010*).

Some works have been devoted to the development of context aware-mobile applications that use context to provide information and/or services relevant to the user, in which the relevance depends on the user's intentions [1]. An example is COMPASS [9] (*Context-aware Mobile Personal Assistant*), which provides services and information based on user's interests and position. For selecting relevant services, COMPASS uses two types of criteria: (*i*) *strict criteria*, which are used for discarding irrelevant results; and (*ii*) *soft criteria*, for sorting results and assigning a relevance score to each service/information. The application is based on the WASP platform [4] that provides general support services, such as context manager and indexing services. WASP can be integrated with other services and can be easily applied to other domains, such as taxi reservation or dwelling search.

3   Metadata Model

We defined a metadata model for representing information about users, places, events and resources of mobile location-aware applications. The model identifies a number of categories for indexing items in the domain of interest, which are generic enough to satisfy most of the application contexts. In particular, the metadata model is divided into four categories:

- *User:* defines basic information about a user (e.g., name, surname, e-mail).
- *Place:* describes a place of interest (e.g., square, restaurant, airport), including its geographical coordinates.
- *Event:* describes an event (e.g., concert, exhibition, conference), with information about time and location.
- *Resource:* defines a resource (e.g., photo, video, web site, web service) associated to a given place and/or event, including its Uniform Resource Identifier (URI).

Tables 1, 2, 3 and 4 present the basic metadata fields for each of the four categories listed above. Metadata are meant to be extensible, i.e., it is possible

---

[2] http://sumi.ucc.ie/.

[3] http://www.iso.org/iso/catalogue_detail.htm?csnumber=35733.

Table 1. Basic User metadata.

Name	Type	Description
id	String	Unique user identifier
name	String	Given name
surname	String	Family name
email	String	E-mail
token	String	Authentication token

Table 2. Basic Place metadata.

Name	Type	Description
id	String	Unique place identifier
name	String	Name of the place
description	String	Textual description of the place
latitude	Real	Latitude of the place
longitude	Real	Longitude of the place
address	String	Full address of the place
user_id	String	Id of the user who created the place

to include additional fields based on the specific application. For example, the user schema may be extended to include birth date, city, linked social network accounts, and so on.

Table 3. Basic Event metadata.

Name	Type	Description
id	String	Unique event identifier
name	String	Name of the event
description	String	Textual description of the event
start_date	String	Date and time when the event begins
end_date	String	Date and time when the event ends
place_id	String	Id of the place where the event is held
user_id	String	Id of the user who created the event

To represent metadata, the *JavaScript Object Notation* (JSON) is used. JSON is a widely-used text format for the serialization of structured data that is derived from the object literals of JavaScript [2]. Figure 1 shows an example of JSON metadata describing a User. Beyond the basic metadata (id, name, etc.), it includes some additional fields (city, linked accounts and food preferences).

Table 4. Basic Resource metadata.

Name	Type	Description
id	String	Unique resource identifier
name	String	Name of the resource
description	String	Textual description of the resource
URI	String	Link to the resource
place_id	String	Id of the place to which the resource is associated
event_id	String	Id of the event to which the resource is associated
user_id	String	Id of the user who created the resource

```
{
"id": "jdoe",
"name": "John",
"surname": "Doe",
"email": "john.doe@example.com",
"token": "19800308",
"city": "New York, NY, USA",
"linked-accounts": [
{"name":"facebook", "token":"424911363"},
{"name":"google", "key":"23467223454"}
],
"food-preferences": ["sushi", "pizza"],
"date-created": "2016-03-27T08:05:43.511Z"
}
```

Fig. 1. Example of User metadata in JSON.

```
{
  "id": "534",
  "name": "Kabuki",
  "description": "Japanese Restaurant",
  "latidude": "38.897683",
  "longitude": "-77.006081",
  "address": "Union Station 50, Washington, DC, USA",
  "user_id": "jdoe",
  "tags": ["Japanese", "sushi"]
}
```

Fig. 2. Example of Place metadata in JSON.

Figure 2 shows an example of Place metadata, regarding the "Kabuki" restaurant in Washington, DC, USA, which is tagged as a Japanese and sushi specialties restaurant using an additional "tags" field.

4 Middleware

Figure 3 describes the architecture of the middleware, which includes two main components:

– *geocon-service*, which contains a central registry for indexing users, resources, events and places of interest; it exposes methods for storing, searching and selecting metadata about these entities.
– *geocon-client* is a client-side library that allows mobile applications to interact with *geocon-service* through the invocation of local methods.

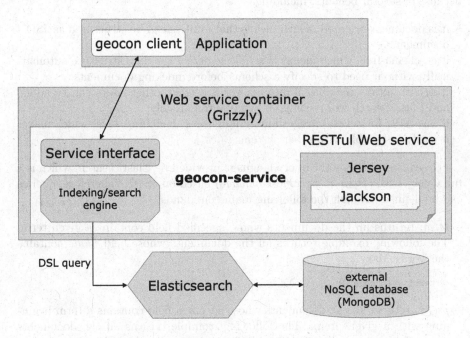

Fig. 3. Architecture of the middleware.

The interaction between service and client is based on the REST model [6]. To this end, a complete support to *CRUD* (Create, Read, Update, and Delete) operations on the metadata has been defined through Java APIs.

4.1 Geocon-Service

The geocon-service has been implemented as a RESTful Web service and exposed via the Web service container Grizzly [4], which was deployed on the Microsoft

---

[4] https://grizzly.java.net.

Azure platform that ensures scalability, reliability, and access to external data analytics [3].

The framework used in our implementation to develop RESTful Web services is *Jersey*[5], an open source framework that implements JAX-RS (Java API for RESTful Web Services) using annotations to map a Java class to a Web resource, and natively supports JSON representations through the integrated library *Jackson*[6].

The core component of *geocon-service* is the indexing and search engine, which has been implemented using Elasticsearch[7]. Elasticsearch is an open-source, distributed, scalable, and highly available search server based on Apache Lucene[8], and provides a RESTful web interface. Elasticsearch has been chosen because of several benefits, including:

- it is document-oriented, which means that entities can be structured as JSON documents;
- it is schema-free, which means it is able to detect the data structure automatically without need to specify a schema before indexing documents;
- it is horizontally scalable: if more power is needed, other nodes can be added and Elasticsearch will reconfigure itself automatically;
- it has APIs for several programming languages, including Java, which makes it easily integrable with other systems.

Geocon-service uses the query language provided by Elasticsearch, which is a full Query DSL (*Domain Specific Language*) based on JSON. Therefore, queries can be defined through the following main commands:

- *term*: returns all the documents whose specified field contains a given term. The following example returns all the documents whose field *name* contains the word "Mary":

```
{"term" : { "name" : "Mary" }}
```

- *prefix*: returns all the documents whose specified field contains a term beginning with a given prefix. The following example returns all the documents whose field *surname* begins with "Ro":

```
{"prefix" : { "surname" : "Ro" }}
```

- *bool*: returns all the documents containing a boolean combination of queries. It is built using one or more boolean clauses (i.e., *must, must_not, should,* and the parameter *minimum_should_match* that is the minimum number of clauses to be met). The following example returns all the users whose *name* is "Mary", that are not between 10 and 20 years old, and that like eating sushi or pizza:

---

[5] Jersey: http://jersey.java.net/.

[6] Jackson: http://jackson.codehaus.org/.

[7] https://www.elastic.co/.

[8] https://lucene.apache.org/.

```
{"bool" : {
    "must" : { "term" : { "name" : "Mary" } },
    "must_not" : {
      "range" : {"age" : { "from" : 10, "to" : 20 }}
    },
    "should" : [
      { "term" : { "food-preferences" : "sushi" } },
      { "term" : { "food-preferences" : "pizza" } }
    ],
    "minimum_should_match" : 1
  }}
```

Due to some limitations of Elasticsearch (e.g., absence of transaction support, possible loss of write operation during cluster reforming/splitting), we use it in combination with an external NoSQL database, MongoDB[9], which is more focused on constraints, correctness and robustness. Compared to relational databases, MongoDB provides several benefits in terms of simplicity, flexibility, and scalability. Data stored in MongoDB can be asynchronously pushed to Elasticsearch. In such way, it is possible to persist in Elasticsearch a subset of the data stored in the external database, possibly using a different data format.

4.2   Geocon-Client

Geocon-client is the library used by mobile applications to interact with *geocon-service*. The library aims to facilitate communication with the *geocon-service* methods, hiding some low-level details (e.g., authentication, REST invocation, etc.) and providing users with a complete set of functions for executing CRUD operations. These functions are implemented using a set of objects and methods provided by the client library to the application layer.

Geocon-client consists of five classes: four classes are used to represent the metadata categories (*User*, *Place*, *Event* and *Resource*), while a fifth class (*SearchEngine*) is used to expose the methods for storing and searching data on *geocon-service*. For each class representing a metadata category, the *SearchEngine* class provides a set of CRUD methods: *register*, *get*, *update*, and *delete*. As an example, Table 5 shows the CRUD methods provided to register, get, update and delete Resource elements in the service.

Table 5. CRUD methods for Resource elements.

Method	Description
register (Resource r)	Registers a resource to the service
get (Resource r)	Returns the metadata of a resource
update (Resource r)	Updates the metadata of a resource
delete (Resource r)	Deletes a resource

---

[9] https://www.mongodb.com.

5   Conclusions

Geocon is a service-oriented middleware designed to help mobile developers to implement location-aware ubiquitous applications. In particular, Geocon provides a service and a client library for storing, indexing, and retrieving information about entities that are commonly involved in these scenarios, such as (mobile) users, places, events and other resources (e.g., photos, media, comments). A key benefit for developers using Geocon is the possibility to focus on the front-end functionality provided by their mobile application, without the need of implementing by scratch back-end components for data management, which are provided by the middleware.

Geocon defines a basic metadata model to represent information about users, places, events and resources of mobile location-aware applications, which can be easily extended to match most application requirements. In order to ensure a high level of decoupling and efficient communication between client and service, the REST model has been adopted. Moreover, given the huge number of users, places, events and resources that may be involved in location-aware ubiquitous applications, Geocon uses the Elasticsearch engine that can scale horizontally on a very large number of nodes. A prototype implementation of Geocon is available at https://github.com/SCAlabUnical/Geocon.

References

1. Abowd, G.D., Dey, A.K., Brown, P.J., Davies, N., Smith, M., Steggles, P.: Towards a better understanding of context and context-awareness. In: Gellersen, H.-W. (ed.) HUC 1999. LNCS, vol. 1707, pp. 304–307. Springer, Heidelberg (1999). doi:10.1007/3-540-48157-5_29
2. ECMA. Ecma-262: ECMAscript Language Specification, 5th edn. ECMA (European Association for Standardizing Information and Communication Systems) (2009)
3. Marozzo, F., Talia, D., Trunfio, P.: A cloud framework for big data analytics workflows on azure. Adv. Parallel Comput. **23**, 182–191 (2013)
4. Martin, S., Leduc, G.: An active platform as middleware for services and communities discovery. In: Sunderam, V.S., Albada, G.D., Sloot, P.M.A., Dongarra, J. (eds.) ICCS 2005. LNCS, vol. 3516, pp. 237–245. Springer, Heidelberg (2005). doi:10.1007/11428862_33
5. Poslad, S., Laamanen, H., Malaka, R., Nick, A., Buckle, P., Zipl, A.: CRUMPET: creation of user-friendly mobile services personalised for tourism. In: Second International Conference on 3G Mobile Communication Technologies, (Conf. Publ. No. 477), pp. 28–32 (2001)
6. Richardson, L., Ruby, S.: RESTful web services. O'Reilly Media Inc. (2008)
7. Schmidt-Belz, B., Poslad, S.: User validation of a mobile tourism service. In: Proceedings of the Workshop on HCI in Mobile Guides, pp. 57–62. University of Udine (2003)
8. Talia, D., Trunfio, P., Marozzo, F.: Data Analysis in the Cloud. Elsevier, USA (2015)

9. Setten, M., Pokraev, S., Koolwaaij, J.: Context-aware recommendations in the mobile tourist application COMPASS. In: Bra, P.M.E., Nejdl, W. (eds.) AH 2004. LNCS, vol. 3137, pp. 235–244. Springer, Heidelberg (2004). doi:10.1007/978-3-540-27780-4_27

10. Yu, C.-C., Chang, H.: Personalized location-based recommendation services for tour planning in mobile tourism applications. In: Noia, T., Buccafurri, F. (eds.) EC-Web 2009. LNCS, vol. 5692, pp. 38–49. Springer, Heidelberg (2009). doi:10.1007/978-3-642-03964-5_5

I/O-Focused Cost Model for the Exploitation of Public Cloud Resources in Data-Intensive Workflows

Francisco Rodrigo Duro[✉], Javier Garcia Blas, and Jesus Carretero

Computer Science and Engineering Department, University Carlos III, Leganes, Spain
{frodrigo,fjblas,jcarrete}@inf.uc3m.es

Abstract. Ultrascale computing systems will blur the line between HPC and cloud platforms, transparently offering to the end-user every possible available computing resource, independently of their characteristics, location, and philosophy. However, this horizon is still far from complete. In this work, we propose a model for calculating the costs related with the deployment of data-intensive applications in IaaS cloud platforms. The model will be especially focused on I/O-related costs in data-intensive applications and on the evaluation of alternative I/O solutions. This paper also evaluates the differences in costs of a typical cloud storage service in contrast with our proposed in-memory I/O accelerator, Hercules, showing great flexibility potential in the price/performance trade-off. In Hercules cases, the execution time reductions are up to 25% in the best case, while costs are similar to Amazon S3.

Keywords: Cloud · Amazon · Data-intensive · Cost model · Workflows

1 Introduction

The popularization of the cloud computing paradigm brought a new scenario to the scientific computing field. Based on the virtually limitless resources offered in a pay-per-use approach, research centers have the possibility to use cloud resources instead of the traditional HPC infrastructures. It could be even possible to combine the benefits offered by both approaches, owning an HPC cluster or supercomputer for testing and development, while deploying experiments in this HPC infrastructure augmented with as much cloud computing resources as needed or as possible given the budget of the project. This combination will lead the path to Ultrascale systems [2], large-scale complex systems that join parallel and distributed computing systems, reaching two to three orders of magnitude larger than todays systems. The research line for achieving Ultrascale systems should focus on the simplification of this scenario with mixed infrastructures, by

F. Rodrigo Duro—This work was supported by the project TIN2013-41350-P "Scalable Data Management Techniques for High-End Computing Systems" from the *Ministerio de Economía y Competitividad*, Spain.

J. Carretero et al. (Eds.): ICA3PP 2016 Workshops, LNCS 10049, pp. 244–257, 2016.
DOI: 10.1007/978-3-319-49956-7_20

transparently taking advantage of every possible computing resources available, independently of their characteristics, location, or philosophy.

However, the current technology is far from this ideal scenario. Interfaces in both HPC and cloud platforms differ and difficult its use in a combined way. The philosophy differences in cloud and HPC infrastructures, especially in the I/O subsystems, are still an unsolved inconvenience for generic applications. For tackling with this limitation, in previous works we proposed Hercules [5,9], an in-memory generic I/O architecture for data-intensive applications, as an alternative to current infrastructure-specific I/O solutions.

This lack of generic approaches does not only affect to the computing infrastructures, but also to the scientific applications. Since the introduction of the MapReduce paradigm, we have seen a change in the trends of scientific application paradigm, from the classical CPU-intensive applications (large-scale simulations, complex mathematical problems, etc.) to data-intensive applications. However, most of the technological breakthroughs emerged from the Big Data field are not fully applied to data-intensive scientific applications executed on HPC infrastructures. In the recent years, the use of workflow engines for the design, implementation, and execution of data-intensive applications in different infrastructures, is seen as the best generic approach for scientific computing.

Future Ultrascale systems will be in charge, not only of transparently offering every available resource to the users, but they will also be responsible of scheduling each computing job to the platform with the best fit for the characteristics of the application. In order to better understand when the pay-per-use cloud resources are the best option for a specific workload, it is indispensable to fully understand the incurred costs of executing an application in the cloud. In this work, we propose a model for calculating potential costs derived from the deployment of a data-intensive application over an IaaS cloud platform. This model takes especially into account the costs related with I/O operations, including the impact of deploying our proposed in-memory I/O accelerator, Hercules, as an alternative to the default cloud storage service. We have also applied this model to a study case that involves the execution of a data-intensive application, demonstrating that our solution better suits the pay-per-use philosophy for I/O operations over temporary data, flexibly adapting the performance and costs to the user requirements.

The remainder of the paper is organized as follows. Section 2 overviews previous works related to data-intensive applications in clouds. Section 3 introduces Hercules. Section 4 proposes a model for calculating the costs of deployment of an application in an IaaS cloud platform. Section 5 applies our model to the execution of a data-intensive application, comparing Amazon S3 and Hercules. Finally, Sect. 6 presents the conclusions of this work.

2   Related Work

Workflow engines, such as DMCF [8], Pegasus [1], and OmpSs [4] are software systems for designing and executing data analysis workflows. Most workflow engines rely on the default shared storage. This implies that the I/O performance of tasks is limited by the performance of the default storage and can be greatly affected by contention. Thus, currently, the costs of working with large datasets mainly depends on infrastructures, where storage and computation resources are not completely decoupled as in the case of HDFS.

As a result, data locality-aware techniques and in-memory storage are becoming more and more important, avoiding these problems. Recent solutions like Tachyon [7] have shown the importance of data locality and in-memory storage for improving performance in data-intensive applications. Chiu et al. [3] evaluated the effects of reducing the data transfers through the use of a cooperative cache. In this work, we demonstrate that our in-memory cache solution also reduces applications production costs compared with the Amazon S3 storage system.

Yuan et al. [10] presented a novel intermediate data storage strategy for reducing the cost of the scientific cloud workflows. This strategy is based on the automatic store of the most appropriate intermediate datasets. In [11], the same authors proposed a dataset storage cost model for managing the intermediate data in a scientific cloud-aware workflow systems. Our approach differs from this one by considering both application and hardware characteristics.

3   Hercules Background

Hercules is a generic I/O architecture based on in-memory key-value stores. Hercules can be deployed as an I/O subsystem alternative to existing storage solutions such as parallel shared file system in HPC systems and cloud storage services in cloud platforms. It is especially designed for the acceleration of I/O operations over temporary data in data-intensive applications.

The main characteristics offered by Hercules are: easy deployment, flexibility, portability, scalability, and performance. Based on its easy deployment, Hercules can be flexibly configured with as many I/O nodes as necessary, depending on the requirements of the application or even depending on the requirements of each execution of the same application. A larger number of I/O nodes deployed is translated to the (several) network interfaces available, implying a greater aggregated throughput available for the applications.

Additionally, based on the generic characteristics of the architecture, Hercules can be deployed in a wide range of different infrastructures, including HPC systems [5] and cloud platforms [9], showing potential performance improvements while providing portability for existing and legacy applications. Hercules is also capable of being deployed for sharing resources with the compute nodes, enabling the possibility of exposing data locality in order to be exploited by locality-aware schedulers. However, this feature is out of the scope of this work.

4   Costs Model for In-Memory Storage on Clouds

In this section, we present a model with the objective of calculating the costs associated with the execution of a data-intensive workflow application in a public cloud platform. We have based this model on the Amazon AWS platform, but given the similarity in billing concepts of the different existing IaaS providers, this model should be applicable to other cloud providers (i.e., Microsoft Azure). Application modeling is focused on workflow applications, represented as a Directed Acyclic Graph (DAG).

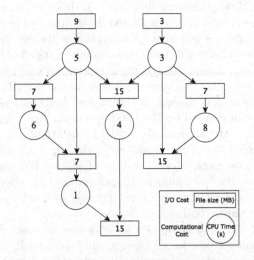

Fig. 1. Workflow model for the cost analysis.

Figure 1 shows how graph nodes (circles) represent the computational cost of each task (CPU time in seconds) while boxes represent data communication between tasks. Each box corresponds with one file, representing the file size measured in MB. Links associating tasks and files represent I/O dependencies, being write operations the links with task-to-file direction and read operations the file-to-task links. Any number of workflow instances can be executed depending on the number of existing input files.

$$C_{TOTAL} = C_{CSS} + C_{CCI} \tag{1}$$

The *total execution cost* of an application (C_{TOTAL}) is denoted as the sum of the costs of the cloud storage services (C_{CSS}) and the costs of compute instances (C_{CCI}). Both costs depend on the characteristics of the application, the characteristics of the infrastructure, and the execution time, i.e. the time needed for executing an application is lower using two computing instances than using one, but the cost of deploying two virtual machines (VMs) is greater than deploying one during the same amount of time.

4.1   Cloud Storage Service Costs

The cloud storage service costs (C_{CSS}) refers to the costs related with the I/O operations (amount of data stored, number of read/write operations, etc.) and can be calculated as:

$$C_{CSS} = \sum_{i \in F} FSize_i \cdot S_{cost} \cdot t_{ex} + \sum_{j \in E} Ein_j \cdot PUT_{cost} + \sum_{j \in E} Eout_j \cdot GET_{cost} \quad (2)$$

where F and E are respectively the sets of involved files and the in/out edges of the application. Every existing link has two different associated input and output costs. These costs will be considered depending on the nature of the I/O operation: write operations will have $IN = 1, OUT = 0$ costs (represented also as Ein), while read operations will have these values changed ($IN = 0, OUT = 1$, represented as $Eout$). Each of these costs represents one I/O operation over a specific file. $FSize$ is the *file size* of one file object in MB and S_{cost} is the store cost of files. Amazon charges the storage as USD/GB per month, so the total storage cost will depend on the total execution time (t_{ex}), introduced in Eq. 6. We only take into account the cost of execution, but any data stored before/after the execution of the workflow in the cloud storage service will be billed. Based on these parameters, the cost of storing files can be calculated. Ein and $Eout$ represent the number of input and output operations over each file, while GET_{cost} and PUT_{cost} represent the cost of every operation (a billing concept existing in most cloud storage services).

The C_{CSS} cost can be decomposed in more specific costs depending on the nature of the I/O operations. In our case, it will be especially useful to measure the cost of operations performed over input and output files ($C_{CSS_{in}}, C_{CSS_{out}}$) independently from the rest of I/O operations ($C_{CSS_{tmp}}$), as shown in Eq. 3.

$$C_{CSS} = C_{CSS_{in}} + C_{CSS_{tmp}} + C_{CSS_{out}} \quad (3)$$

where $C_{CSS_{in}}$, $C_{CSS_{out}}$, and $C_{CSS_{tmp}}$ take into account only storage costs and I/O operation costs related with input, output, and temporary files, respectively.

4.2 Computing Resources Costs

For the second part of the Eq. 1, the objective is to calculate the costs related with the use of computing resources. These costs include the VM instances used for executing the application and depend on the total execution time:

$$C_{CCI} = t_{ex} \cdot \sum_{i \in V} VM_{cost_i} \quad (4)$$

where V is the set of VM instances deployed during the execution of the application. In order to better represent the costs associated with the deployment of the Hercules I/O accelerator, the former equation can be decomposed differentiating the VM instances executing the application and the VM instances deployed for the Hercules I/O back-end servers:

$$C_{CCI} = t_{ex} \cdot \left(\sum_{i \in C} VM_{cost_i} + \sum_{j \in H} VM_{cost_j} \right) \quad (5)$$

where C and H are the sets of VM instances deployed during the execution of the application, for computation and Hercules purposes, respectively. t_{ex} is the *total execution time* of the application (in seconds) and VM_{cost} is the price of deploying each VM during one second (in USD/s). This cost calculation introduces the first simplification of our proposed model. In the Amazon EC2 platform, VM instances are billed for full hours, independently of being used 1 s or 59 min. In our model, we consider paying only for the useful time in seconds. This simplification can be explained by the use of the infrastructure for executing multiple batch applications. In this simplified scenario, configuration, initialization, and full hour costs can be discarded. When multiple applications are executed by the same infrastructure, these costs are diluted between all the executions. Other cloud platforms, like Microsoft Azure[1], allow per minute billing. This advanced billing model can even better fit our model.

The total execution time depends on two different factors: time spent in computation (t_{CPU}) and time spent during I/O operations ($t_{I/O}$):

$$t_{ex} = t_{CPU} + t_{I/O} \tag{6}$$

Both CPU and I/O times are affected by the characteristics of the infrastructure used during the execution of the application. t_{CPU} will be reduced depending on the number of compute instances used during the execution of the application:

$$t_{CPU} = \frac{\sum_{i \in T} t_i}{n(C)} \tag{7}$$

T is the task set of the application, while C is the set of VM instances deployed during the execution of the application for computation purposes. t_i represents the execution time of each task of the workflow and $n(C)$ is the number of VM machines deployed. The second simplification of our model consists on considering all the tasks as perfectly scalable and as executable by any instance (without taking into account dependencies), fully utilizing all the available resources, resulting in a perfect distribution of the load where the total execution time is divided by the number of VM instances. Our model suppose homogeneous VM instances where the CPU load has been previously profiled in order to measure the CPU time required by each task on this specific VM instance.

Finally, the I/O time ($t_{I/O}$) is calculated taking into account both the I/O characteristics of the application and the infrastructure used. The performance achieved for read and write operations using the Amazon S3 service greatly vary, leading to the distinction in the following equation:

$$t_{I/O} = \frac{\sum_{i \in W} FSize_i}{n(C) \cdot BW_{write}} + \frac{\sum_{j \in R} FSize_j}{n(C) \cdot BW_{read}} \tag{8}$$

---

[1] http://azure.microsoft.com/en-us/pricing/.

where W and R represent the sets of write operations and read operations in the application, while $FSize$ represents the size of these operations in MB. $n(C)$ represents the number of VM instances deployed and affects the total available bandwidth of I/O operations (BW is the bandwidth perceived by each node for I/O operations in MB/s). The way of considering the total available bandwidth introduces the third simplification of our model, which is the perfect scalability of the I/O operations, without taking into account network congestion and I/O contention. If one VM instance requires 10 s to write 10 files containing 100 MB of data each (1 GB total), two virtual instances will ideally perform the same operations in 5 s. Again, the simplification excludes any kind of data dependencies, dividing the total I/O work between the available compute VM instances, in a perfectly balanced scenario.

Given the fact that Hercules only affects I/O operations performed over temporary data, it is necessary to decompose the previous I/O time in three different factors:

$$t_{I/O} = t_{I/O_{input}} + t_{I/O_{tmp}} + t_{I/O_{output}} \tag{9}$$

The time needed for reading the input files of the application from Amazon S3 ($t_{I/O_{input}}$) and the time needed to write the results to persistent storage ($t_{I/O_{output}}$), is the same in the S3-only cases and the cases where Hercules is present. It can be modeled as:

$$t_{I/O_{input}} = \frac{\sum_{i \in IN} FSize_i}{n(C) \cdot BW_{read}} \tag{10}$$

$$t_{I/O_{output}} = \frac{\sum_{i \in OUT} FSize_i}{n(C) \cdot BW_{write}} \tag{11}$$

where IN is the set of read operations performed over input files and OUT is the set of write operations performed over result files during the execution of the application. The time needed for executing the I/O operations over temporary files ($t_{I/O_{tmp}}$) is modeled differently for S3 ($t_{I/O_{tmp}}(S3)$) and Hercules ($t_{I/O_{tmp}}(HER)$), as detailed in the two following equations:

$$t_{I/O_{tmp}}(S3) = \frac{\sum_{i \in TW} FSize_i}{n(C) \cdot BW_{write_{s3}}} + \frac{\sum_{j \in TR} FSize_j}{n(C) \cdot BW_{read_{s3}}} \tag{12}$$

$$t_{I/O_{tmp}}(HER) = \frac{\sum_{i \in TW} FSize_i}{MIN_{VM} \cdot BW_{write_{HER}}} + \frac{\sum_{j \in TR} FSize_j}{MIN_{VM} \cdot BW_{read_{HER}}} \tag{13}$$

$$MIN_{VM} = min(n(C), n(H)) \tag{14}$$

where W and R represent the sets of write operations and read operations performed over temporary files during the execution of the application and $n(H)$ represents the number of VM instances deployed for the Hercules infrastructure. The total available bandwidth over files stored in Hercules depends, not only on the number of compute VM instances, but also on the number of Hercules I/O nodes available. We have selected the minimum of both values, denoted as MIN_{VM}, because it will be the limiting factor in the maximum available bandwidth. As example, in the case of a low number of compute nodes using a large Hercules infrastructure, the limiting factor will be the bandwidth available at client side: two compute instances will perform I/O operations in half the time required by one computing VM. However, this assumption is only true when the I/O nodes outnumber the computing infrastructure. In case of a lesser number of I/O nodes, the limiting factor will be the available bandwidth exposed by the Hercules infrastructure, i.e. four compute instances accessing concurrently to only one Hercules node, will share the maximum possible bandwidth offered by this node. This model is consistent with the results shown in the experimental evaluation of our solution. The rest of variables remain as described for Eq. 8.

As a summary, there are three main differences presented by the use of Amazon S3-only solutions in contrast with a hybrid solution using Amazon S3 for I/O files and Hercules for any I/O operation performed over temporary files. First, Hercules requires the deployment of a greater number of VM instances (or VMs with more RAM when deployed sharing resources with the compute nodes), incurring in a greater computation costs (pay-per-use of VM instances). Second, Hercules deployment can result in time reductions due to the acceleration of I/O operations, obtaining a reduction of the total execution time of the application, potentially lowering the costs related to the computing infrastructure (VM instances). Third, through the use of Hercules instead of Amazon S3 for I/O operations performed over temporary files, the cost of using the storage service can be lowered, which is especially important in the targeted data-intensive applications.

The next section presents the evaluation of a use case application, consistent with the data intensive target, in order to analyze this balance in different scenarios.

5 Costs Analysis of a Data-Intensive Application

In order to show the usefulness of our proposed model, we are going to define a data-intensive application with realistic characteristics. This costs analysis will show the budget impact of I/O-related operations in the execution of a data intensive application in a public cloud platform, as well as presenting the execution costs of the application performing every I/O operation over Amazon S3 in comparison with performing I/O operations over temporary data stored in Hercules.

5.1 Application Description

As a study case, we have used an I/O intensive workflow application where both computation and I/O times are balanced. Figure 2 depicts the workflow phases, where an image file is read by the *filter task*, creating three new image files. The filtering task can be any kind of lightweight image-processing computation, such as applying three different filters and decomposing the image in RGB colors. These new image files are afterwards read by the *combine task*, combining the images or selecting one of the images (this combination/selection can be based on any criteria: quality, randomness, patterns, etc.) writing a final image file as a result of the workflow. Every image in the workflow has roughly the same size and any number of images can be used as input files.

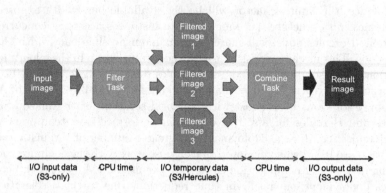

Fig. 2. Image processing data-intensive workflow used as study case for analyzing the costs derived of the deployment of Hercules over a cloud infrastructure. (Color figure online)

When Hercules is deployed and temporary files are stored in Hercules I/O nodes. In our study case, the images created by the *filter task* and read by the *combine task* (depicted in orange) are temporary files. Input and resulting files are stored in the Amazon S3 storage service in every evaluated case for durability reasons. The selected Hercules deployment consists of sharing resources with compute nodes, while deploying VM instances with a greater amount of RAM for the in-memory storage of data. Based on that logic, in the Amazon S3-only case we have deployed *m4.xlarge* VM instances (4 cores, 16 GB RAM, 0.264 USD/hour) and *r3.xlarge* memory optimized VM instances for the Hercules case, which are equivalent VM instances with more RAM (4 cores, 31.5 GB RAM, 0.371 USD/hour). In the table, the cost of VM instances for the Hercules infrastructure appears as *+0.107 USD/hour*, showing the price difference of the additional main memory required. Additionally, *r3.xlarge* come with 80 GB SSD space, which can be utilized for data.

Tables 1, 2, and 3 present the specific configuration of every configurable variable of our model, describing the characteristics of the application in Table 1, the characteristics of the architecture in Table 2, and the billing concepts and prices applied based on Amazon AWS costs in Table 3. Every variable representing costs is presented as provided by the cloud operator (Amazon) and normalized to our model when necessary. Amazon S3 and Hercules bandwidths are based on previous works [6].

Table 1. Input parameters for the costs analysis of the study case: Characteristics of the application.

Parameter	Value
Total input files	8,192
Size of input files	128 MB
Total size of input files	1 TB (8,192 * 128 MB)
Generated temporary files	24,576 (3 * 8,192)
File size of temporary files	128 MB
Total size of temporary files	3 TB (128 MB * 24,576)
Generated result files	8,192
File size of result files	128 MB
Total file size of result files	1 TB (128 MB * 8,192)
No. GET operations	32,768 (4 * 8,192)
No. PUT operations	32,768 (4 * 8,192)
Filter task CPU time	20 s
Combine task CPU time	10 s

Table 2. Input parameters for the costs analysis of the study case: Characteristics of the infrastructure running the application.

Parameter	Value
No. compute VM instances (C)	32
No. Hercules I/O nodes (H)	**4 to 32**
$BW_{read_{S3}}$	90 MB/s[a]
$BW_{write_{S3}}$	20 MB/s[a]
$BW_{read_{HER}}$	90 MB/s[a]
$BW_{write_{HER}}$	90 MB/s[a]

[a]Based on our previous work [6].

We have selected 30 s of computation time for balancing the I/O-to-computation ratio. Based on an image file size of 128 MB, reading the image from Amazon S3 at around 90 MB/s implies ~1.4 s while writing the same image at around 20 MB/s is translated in ~6.4 s. The workflow consists of a total of five image files, with one read and one write operation per file (with the exception of input and output files which are only read or written, not both), up to a total of 4 read operations and 4 write operations, resulting in ~31.2 s. CPU time can be distributed as 20 s for the *filter task* and 10 s for the *combine task*. Figure 3 shows the details of this data intensive application following the workflow model presented in Fig. 1. As can be seen in Table 1, in this configuration the application processes 8,192 images, leading to 8,192 executions of the workflow that can be carried out in parallel in different computing resources with a proper scheduler.

Table 3. Input parameters for the costs analysis of the study case: billing concepts and prices in the Amazon AWS platform.

Parameter	Value
Storage cost	0.0300 USD per GB[a]
Normalized storage cost	1.13e−11 USD per MB per sec
Total CPU time	245,760 s (30 * 8,192 s)
Compute VM instances cost	0.239 USD/hour per node[b]
Normalized comp. VM instances cost	0.000066 USD/sec per node
Hercules I/O nodes cost	+0.107 USD/hour per node[b]
Normalized Hercules I/O nodes cost	0.000029 USD/sec per node
GET operations cost	0.004 USD per 10,000 op.[a]
Normalized GET operations cost	0.0000004 USD
PUT operations cost	0.005 USD per 1,000 op.[a]
Normalized PUT operations cost	0.000005 USD

[a]Based on Amazon S3 prices https://aws.amazon.com/s3/pricing/.
[b]Based on Amazon AWS prices for Amazon EC2 m4.xlarge and r3.xlarge instances https://aws.amazon.com/ec2/pricing/.

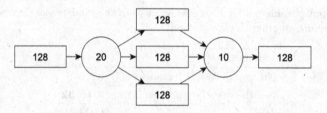

Fig. 3. Model of the image processing data-intensive workflow used as study case, including tasks, CPU cost (CPU time), I/O operations, and I/O cost (file size).

5.2 Costs Analysis

Figure 4 plots the breakdown of the total execution time of the experiment over different I/O infrastructures. *S3* case represents executions where every I/O operation is performed over the Amazon S3 storage service, while every other case rely on different Hercules deployments for temporary data accesses (using 4, 8, 16 and 32 I/O nodes deployed sharing resources with the compute nodes). The black line represents the total cost of the execution of this workflow, based on the previously presented costs model. Figure 4 clearly shows how the flexibility of Hercules can be used for finding a trade-off between cost and execution time. Using 4 I/O nodes, Hercules presents a poor execution time compared with the *S3* case. However, as the number of I/O nodes increases, the total execution time is reduced. This behavior is produced by the increased performance of I/O operations performed over temporary data, using Hercules as I/O accelerator. Every other phase of the workflow execution time remains constant for every

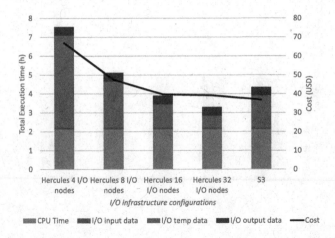

Fig. 4. Breakdown of the total execution time comparing the use of the cloud storage service (S3) for every I/O operation with the deployment of different Hercules configurations for temporary data. The black line represents the total execution cost (secondary Y axis). Computing infrastructure is 32 VM instances for every case.

experiment (including the S3 case): reading the input files, writing the results, and computation time.

The trend shown by the costs line seems counter-intuitive for two main reasons. First, total execution costs are similar in some Hercules and S3-only cases, which seems incorrect given the additional resources needed for the Hercules I/O infrastructure. Second, Hercules costs are reduced at the same pace as more Hercules I/O nodes are deployed, which again seems unrealistic given the fact that costlier VMs are necessary. Figure 5 presents a breakdown of the execution costs, detailing the cost related with three different billing concepts: S3-related costs (storage and PUT/GET operations), the costs of the VM instances deployed as computing resources. and the cost of VM instances running as Hercules backends. The combination of Figs. 4 and 5 shows how the usage of Hercules for temporary data both reduces the total execution time and reduces the amount of data stored over Amazon S3. On the one hand, the reduction of the total execution time affects the amount of time where VM instances are deployed, reducing the costs related with computation and I/O instances. On the other hand, the reduction of data stored over S3 minimizes the costs related with the use of the S3 API, both in persistent data storage and PUT/GET operations costs.

It is also interesting to highlight how the performance scales as the price is reduced in Hercules. The flexibility in the deployment of the Hercules infrastructure offers to the users the ability of trading-off execution time and cost efficiency, depending on their necessities. The specific characteristics of the application or the cloud provider used may vary these results, but we consider the study case presented as a fair example of data-intensive application (balanced CPU and

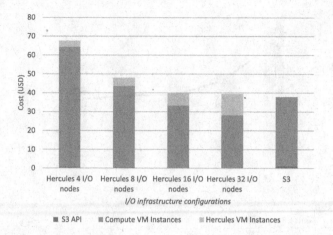

Fig. 5. Breakdown of the total execution cost comparing the use of Amazon S3 for every I/O operation with the deployment of different Hercules configurations for temporary data. Computing infrastructure is 32 VM instances for every case.

I/O time, large amount of temporary data produced) and cloud provider (being Amazon AWS one of the most used IaaS cloud providers).

Our cost analysis shows how data-intensive applications can be benefited by the deployment of Hercules, resulting in reductions in total execution time with a comparable cost. Depending on the execution time reductions achieved by applying Hercules for temporary I/O operations, it could be possible to even obtain cost reductions in applications with a great amount of temporary data in comparison with Amazon S3. Total execution time is reduced due to the increased I/O performance offered by our proposed I/O accelerator. In the costs reduction side, on the one hand, the additional costs related with the deployment of additional or costlier VM instances for the Hercules I/O infrastructure can be compensated with a reduction in total execution time (less total execution time is translated in less time using the deployed VM instances). On the other hand, the costs of storing and accessing temporary data in a persistence-oriented service like Amazon S3 can be avoided by using Hercules I/O nodes.

6   Conclusions

This work has presented a model for calculating potential costs derived from the deployment of data-intensive applications over IaaS cloud platforms. This model takes especially into account the costs related with I/O operations, including the impact of deploying our proposed in-memory I/O accelerator (Hercules) as an alternative to default cloud storage services. Additionally, we have applied the proposed model to a data-intensive image processing application, comparing the costs of execution performing every I/O operation over the default cloud storage service in contrast with deploying Hercules for temporary data.

We can conclude that the performance of data-intensive applications with a large amount of temporary data can be improved while maintaining the execution costs. The main benefit offered by our solution for future Ultrascale systems is the flexibility in configuration, targeting different objectives depending on the requirements of the application and the available budget. The user choose to save money or save time in comparison with the default cloud storage service, even beating both price and performance in balanced configurations.

In the future we should focus on the extension of the costs model for taking into account data locality issues, which should expose even better performance and costs in Hercules cases. Additionally, the model can be applied to other IaaS public cloud providers like Microsoft Azure.

References

1. Deelman, E.: Pegasus, a workflow management system for science automation. Future Gen. Comp. Syst. **46**, 17–35 (2015)
2. Carretero, J., et al.: Memorandum of understanding. In: Network for Sustainable Ultrascale Computing (NESUS), p. 30 (2014). http://www.nesus.eu
3. Chiu, D., Agrawal, G.: Evaluating caching and storage options on the Amazon Web Services Cloud. In: 11th IEEE/ACM International Conference on Grid Computing, pp. 17–24 (2010)
4. Duran, A., Ayguade, E., Badia, R.M., Labarta, J., Martinell, L., Martorell, X.: OmpSs: a proposal for programming heterogeneous multi-core architectures. Parallel Process. Lett. **21**(02), 173–193 (2011)
5. Duro, F.R., Blas, J.G., Isaila, F., Wozniak, J.M., Carretero, J., Ross, R.: Flexible data-aware scheduling for workflows over an in-memory object store. In: CCGRID 2016, pp. 321–324, May 2016
6. Duro, F.R., Garcia-Blas, J., Isaila, F., Carretero, J.: Experimental evaluation of a flexible I/O architecture for accelerating workflow engines in cloud environments. In: DISCS 2015, pp. 6:1–6:8 (2015)
7. Li, H., Ghodsi, A., Zaharia, M., Shenker, S., Stoica, I.: Tachyon: Reliable, memory speed storage for cluster computing frameworks. In: Proceedings of the ACM Symposium on Cloud Computing, pp. 1–15. ACM (2014)
8. Marozzo, F., Talia, D., Trunfio, P.: JS4Cloud: script-based workflow programming for scalable data analysis on cloud platforms. Concurrency Comput. Pract. Experience **27**(17), 5214–5237 (2015)
9. Rodrigo Duro, F., Marozzo, F., Garcia Blas, J., Talia, D., Trunfio, P.: Exploiting in-memory storage for improving workflow executions in cloud platforms. J. Supercomputing **72**(11), 4069–4088 (2016)
10. Yuan, D., Yang, Y., Liu, X., Chen, J.: A cost-effective strategy for intermediate data storage in scientific cloud workflow systems. In: IPDPS 2010, pp. 1–12 (2010)
11. Yuan, D., Yang, Y., Liu, X., Chen, J.: On-demand minimum cost benchmarking for intermediate dataset storage in scientific cloud workflow systems. J. Parallel Distrib. Comput. **71**(2), 316–332 (2011)

SCDT-2016: Supercomputing Co-Design Technology Workshop

Cellular ANTomata as Engines for Highly Parallel Pattern Processing

Arnold L. Rosenberg(⊠)

Computer and Information Science, Northeastern University,
Boston, MA 02115, USA
rsnbrg@ccs.neu.edu

Abstract. One important approach to high-performance computing has a (relatively) simple physical computer architecture *emulate* virtual algorithmic architectures (VAAs) that are highly optimized for important application domains. We expose the *Cellular ANTomaton* (CANT) computing model—*cellular automata* enhanced with mobile FSMs (*Ants*)—as a highly efficient VAA for a variety of pattern-processing problems that are inspired by biocomputing applications. We illustrate the CANT model via a *scalable* design for an $n \times n$ CANT that solves the following bio-inspired problem in *linear time*.

The Pattern-Assembly Problem.

Inputs: a length-n *master pattern* Π and r *test patterns* $\pi_0, \ldots, \pi_{r-1}$, of respective lengths $m_0 \geq \cdots \geq m_{r-1}$.

The problem: Find every sequence $\langle \pi_{j_0}, \ldots, \pi_{j_{s-1}} \rangle$ of π_k's, possibly with repetitions, that "assemble" (i.e., concatenate) to produce Π; i.e., $\pi_{j_0} \cdots \pi_{j_{s-1}} = \Pi$.

Timing: $m_1 + \cdots + m_r + O(n)$ steps, with a quite-small big-O constant.

Keywords: HPC via emulation · Cellular ANTomata · Pattern assembly

1 Introduction

1.1 (PA + VAA) = (Path Toward HPC)

Ever since the development, in the 1970s, of technologies that enable massively parallel computers, the value of "indirection" in the development of algorithms for such computers has been recognized. Rather than cope explicitly, for each successive desired application, with the complex *physical architectures* (*PAs*) of such computers, one could fruitfully design domain-optimized *virtual algorithmic architectures* (*VAAs*) that the PAs would *emulate* efficiently. This approach employed a genre of *co-design:* the structure of each VAA carefully accommodated both the fixed features of the PA and the data- and communication-flow needed by algorithms that performed the computations that achieved the target

This research was supported in part by US NSF Grant CSR-1217981.

© Springer International Publishing AG 2016
J. Carretero et al. (Eds.): ICA3PP 2016 Workshops, LNCS 10049, pp. 261–277, 2016.
DOI: 10.1007/978-3-319-49956-7_21

application. This computational paradigm, as enunciated in [19] and elsewhere, has led to a varied and valuable literature that explored the problem of designing VAAs for myriad important applications; see, e.g., [1,14,18,22,25]. One exciting recurring observation in this decades-spanning literature is that many VAAs can lead to high-performing algorithms for broad, diverse genres of applications.

In order for emulation-based co-design to be an effective avenue for achieving high performance computing, one must have access to a repertoire of VAAs that (a) can be optimized for important specific application domains and (b) can be efficiently emulated on relatively simple PAs. The current paper adds yet more evidence that the *Cellular ANTomaton* (CANT) computing model of [21] is such a VAA. We support this claim here by designing CANTs that *scalably* provide high performance (algorithmic) solutions for a variety of pattern-processing problems of the sort encountered in the increasingly important applications that arise in biologically inspired computing.

1.2   The Computing Model

(a) Meshes. The $n \times n$ *mesh* $\mathcal{M}_n$ is an array of *cells* indexed by nonnegative integers: each cell has a distinct index $\langle i, j \rangle$, with $0 \leq i, j < n$. $\mathcal{M}_n$'s *row-k* cells are: $\langle k, 0 \rangle, \ldots, \langle k, n-1 \rangle$; its *column-k* cells are: $\langle 0, k \rangle, \ldots, \langle n-1, k \rangle$. We posit *King's-move* adjacencies: cells $\langle i, j \rangle$ and $\langle i', j' \rangle$ are adjacent iff $\max(|i - i'|, |j - j'|) = 1$.

(b) Cellular automata. An $n \times n$ *cellular automaton* (CA) is obtained by placing a copy of a single *finite-state machine* (*FSM*) $\mathcal{F}$ within each cell of $\mathcal{M}_n$; $\mathcal{F}^{\langle i, j \rangle}$ denotes the copy of $\mathcal{F}$ within cell $\langle i, j \rangle$. FSMs in adjacent cells exchange one message per step.

(c) Cellular ANTomata. An $n \times n$ *Cellular ANTomaton* (CANT) is obtained by deploying a (possibly heterogeneous) team of *mobile finite-state machines* (called *Ants*) atop an $n \times n$ CA, at most one Ant per cell. Each Ant exchanges messages at each step with the FSM in its current cell and with each Ant on an adjacent cell.

CANTs provide a powerful computing model that finds application in several application domains. Our earlier work studied CANTs working on problems inspired by *robotics* [21]; The present paper illustrates CANTs solving pattern-processing problems that are inspired by *bioinformatic* applications.

We merely mention two inviting, as-yet unexplored, areas in which CANTs may make signficant contributions: (i) as discrete versions of *feedback-intense continuous biological systems*—such as, e.g., the immune system in the liver [8]; (ii) as engines for *big data*-inspired applications: the Ants bring processing power to where it is needed, while the underlying CA moves data in a more-or-less regular fashion.

Elaboration and Clarification. (1) *The nature of FSMs.* Regrettably, FSMs are saddled historically with the name "machines," hence are usually thought of as hardware constructs. In fact, FSMs can fruitfully serve as an easily implemented *programming model*; cf. [20,24]. Thus viewed, CANTs become *virtual*, *algorithmic* constructs. (2) *The nature of Ants*. Ants can be either physical or virtual. Even in purely algorithmic studies, *virtual Ants* can simplify algorithmics. (3) *Timing within* CANTs. We design CANTs that operate *semi-synchronously*: neighboring FSMs/Ants never get out of synch by as much as an entire state transition. By careful programming, CANTs can behave as though they were fully synchronous; cf. [7,26]. (4) *Enforcing (algorithmic) scalability*. We achieve *scalable* CANT-designs by having $n \times n$ CANTs operate with n as an *unknown*; algorithms can exploit only "finite-state" properties of n (such as parity).

To conserve space, we describe CANTs via text and/or small examples. One easily formalizes our anthropomorphically described CANT-designs and analyses.

1.3   Algorithmic Tools that Enhance the Power of CANTs as VAAs

(a) Virtual tracks. It is convenient to view $\mathcal{M}_n$'s rows and columns as having *tracks*, which allow symbols in FSMs' memories to "pass by" or "cross over" one another. By endowing all rows and columns with tracks, we can view $\mathcal{M}_n$ as having multiple *layers* (of course, only a fixed finite number). We use *structured symbols* to implement virtual tracks; e.g.: (*i*) $\langle \sigma_1, \sigma_2 \rangle$ can represent two vertical tracks $\boxed{\sigma_1 \, , \, \sigma_2}$ or two horizontal tracks $\boxed{\begin{array}{c} \sigma_1 \\ - \\ \sigma_2 \end{array}}$; (*ii*) $\langle \sigma_1, \sigma_2 \rangle \langle \sigma_3, \sigma_4 \rangle \langle \sigma_5, \sigma_6 \rangle$ can represent a pile of three cells, each with two vertical tracks $\boxed{\begin{array}{c} \sigma_1 \, , \, \sigma_2 \\ \sigma_3 \, , \, \sigma_4 \\ \sigma_5 \, , \, \sigma_6 \end{array}}$, or two adjacent cells, each with two horizontal tracks $\boxed{\begin{array}{c|c|c} \sigma_1 & \sigma_3 & \sigma_5 \\ - & - & - \\ \sigma_2 & \sigma_4 & \sigma_6 \end{array}}$. We simplify exposition by discussing tracks as though they were physical, not virtual.

(b) Synchrony and synchronization. CAs and CANTs operate *semi*-synchronously— i.e., do not require full synchrony; they monitor every action that affects more than one FSM. This is formalized by orchestrating state transitions into sequences of sub-transitions; cf. [20,21]. CANTs precede every global action by a *barrier synchronization* implemented, say, via the *firing squad protocol (FSP)* [17]. The *FSP* begins with all *targeted* FSMs—i.e., those that are to be synchronized—in a "dormant" state. An *initiator* FSM orchestrates a program of message-exchanges among the FSMs, which guarantees that all targeted FSMs enter a designated *active* state at the same time-step. It is shown in [11] that: *$2n-1$ synchronous steps suffice for the FSP to simultaneously activate all FSMs, both in a linear array of n FSMs and in an $n \times n$ CA or CANT.*

(c) Using mesh walls for navigation [21]. Let FSM $\mathcal{F}$ initiate walks within $\mathcal{M}_n$ whose slopes are $\pm 45°$, beginning and ending at (possibly distinct) edge-cells of $\mathcal{M}_n$. These walks can be used to *replicate* or *complement* distances along $\mathcal{M}_n$'s edges, *scalably, without any explicit computation*. Focus, for illustration, on a walk that begins at a top-edge cell $\langle 0, j \rangle$. If $j < n - 1$, then $\mathcal{F}$ can take a *southeasterly* step, which leads it to cell $\langle 1, j + 1 \rangle$; if $j = n - 1$, then $\mathcal{M}_n$'s right edge), then $\mathcal{F}$ would "fall off" $\mathcal{M}_n$. Similarly, if $j > 0$, then $\mathcal{F}$ can take a *southwesterly* step, which leads it to cell $\langle 1, j-1 \rangle$; if $j = 0$, then on $\mathcal{M}_n$'s left edge), then $\mathcal{F}$ would "fall off" $\mathcal{M}_n$. Therefore—cf. Fig. 1—if we focus on any integer $r \leq n/2$:

- if $\mathcal{F}$ begins at cell $A = \langle 0, r \rangle$, then its *southwesterly* walk ends at cell $B = \langle r, 0 \rangle$; and its *southeasterly* walk ends at cell $C = \langle n-r-1, n-1 \rangle$.
- if $\mathcal{F}$ begins at cell $D = \langle 0, n-r-1 \rangle$, then its *southwesterly* walk ends at cell $E = \langle n-r-1, 0 \rangle$; and its *southeasterly* walk ends at cell $F = \langle r, n-1 \rangle$.

Clerical adjustments accommodate source- and destination-cells along any edges.

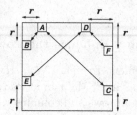

Fig. 1. Trajectories that lead an FSM to the *mirrors* of the cell it begins on. The point is that when the slopes of all indicated trajectories are (multiples of) 45°, then the indicated distance equalities hold (as elaborated in the text).

This algorithmic strategem provides two benefits. (*i*) It allows one to avoid certain (possibly) costly multi-precision calculations involving n when n is huge. (*ii*) It enables simple $O(n)$-step CA-computations that (cf. Fig. 2) answer questions such as: Is the word along row 0 of $\mathcal{M}_n$ a palindrome (does it read the same forwards and backwards)? Is the word along row 0 the reversal of the word along row $n-1$?

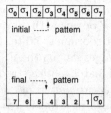

Fig. 2. $\mathcal{M}_8$ with a word along row 0 and the reversal of that word along row 7.

(d) **Programmability.** The *algorithmic* benefits of VAAs have received much attention over the decades, but there has been less focus on the advantages of VAAs regarding *algorithm specification*, or, *programmability*. VAAs that are based on FSMs, such as CAs and CANTs, have received some welcome attention, via general-purpose specification systems such as CARPET [24] and via broadly applicable special-purpose systems as studied in [2]. As exposed in [18], these systems encompass the important data-flow ideas underlying *systolic arrays* [15].

1.4 Our Highlighted Case Study: Pattern Assembly by CANTs

The best way to illustrate the use of CANTs as a VAA is to design a CANT that incorporates several sophisticated algorithmic ideas to solve a significant problem. To that end, we now develop a CANT that provides a *linear-time, scalable* solution to a pattern-processing problem that is inspired by bioinformatic applications.

The (parameter-n) Pattern-Assembly Problem (PAP).

Inputs: (a) a length-n *master pattern* Π; (b) a sequence $\langle \pi_1, \ldots, \pi_r \rangle$ of *test patterns*, of respective lengths $m_1 \geq \cdots \geq m_r$ (each $m_i \leq n$).

Problem: Discover every *multi-sequence* $\langle \pi_{j_1}, \ldots, \pi_{j_s} \rangle$ of test patterns that "assembles" to produce pattern Π. In detail, allowing each π_{j_k} to appear multiple times (perhaps 0), we must have

$$\Pi = \pi_{i_1} \pi_{i_2} \cdots \pi_{i_k}. \tag{1}$$

We design an $n \times n$ CANT $\mathcal{C}$ that scalably solves the parameter-n PAP in *linear time*, specifically, within $m_1 + \cdots + m_r + O(n)$ steps, with a quite-small big-O constant. (Note that the big-O constant-factor uncertainty involves only n, not the m_i.)

1.5 Related Work

The PAP is a quite natural problem, so it is not surprising that variants have been studied in other contexts. Specifically, the version of the PAP in which the test patterns are fixed *a priori* (rather than being dynamically specified inputs that can vary in length and "content") has been called the *word break* problem, and $O(n^2)$-step dynamic programming solutions to this problem have been announced. See, e.g., [28–30].

Focusing on the model rather than the algorithmic problem: CAs have been known for decades to combine mathematical simplicity with levels of computational efficiency that make them feasible platforms for many real computational tasks; cf. [10, 21, 24, 27]. Indeed, CAs are remarkably efficient for a broad range of tasks that require tight coordination of many simple agents [5, 6, 9, 13, 16]. A variant of CAs underlies the *DFMS* model of [3], which implements a specialized *laboratory-on-a-chip*. Several recent CA-based robotics-motivated studies appear in [23]. The preceding models deviate from CANTs in fundamental ways: they support algorithms that are: fully synchronous (there is a single clock); centrally controlled (there is a central planner); not scalable (the central planner knows and exploits the size of the system). Some models are centrally programmable, using systems such as CARPET [24]; their global name spaces preclude scalability. CAs have also been used for a rather general suite of parallel-computing applications in [24] and related works. More closely related to our study are the (*one-dimensional*) CAs used in [13] for (bio-inspired) pattern matching. Also relevant, in a formal sense, are studies of formal languages in a two-dimensional setting, e.g., [4]. Our prior work on CANTs, which appears in [21] has developed efficient algorithms for three *robotics-inspired* problems involving path-planning and exploration:

1. Parking: Route $\leq n$ Ants to maximally compact configurations in their closest corners of $\mathcal{M}_n$. *Time*: $O(n^2)$ steps.
2. Food-finding: Pair $\min(r, s)$ out of r Ants with $\min(r, s)$ out of s "food items." *Time*: take $O(\min(nr, n\sqrt{s}))$ steps.
3. Maze-threading: Route an Ant from a maze entrance to a designated maze exit. *Time*: $O(\text{shortest path})$ steps.

Space limitations force us to ignore three bodies of literature that are only marginally relevant to our study: CAs as parallel computers, e.g., [9, 24]; ant-inspired models of "swarm intelligence," e.g., [12]; myriad (applied) automata-theoretic studies of the (in)ability of FSMs to explore graphs with goals such as finding "entrance"-to-"exit" paths or exhaustively visiting all nodes or all edges of input graphs.

2   A CANT-Design for the Pattern Assembly Problem (PAP)

Instance $\mathcal{P} = \langle \Pi, P \rangle$ of the PAP is specified by the following inputs from the "outside world": a length-n *master pattern* $\Pi = \sigma_0 \cdots \sigma_{n-1}$ and a *sequence* $P = \langle \pi_1, \ldots, \pi_r \rangle$ of distinct *test patterns*, of respective lengths: $m_1 \geq \cdots \geq m_r$, where each $m_i \leq n$. The goal is to determine whether there is a *multi-sequence* $\widehat{P} = \langle \pi_{i_1}, \ldots, \pi_{i_k} \rangle$ of test patterns—i.e., a sequence with possible repetitions—whose concatenation, *in the indicated order*, equals Π, in the sense of Eq. 1. We call $\widehat{P}$ a *solution* to instance $\mathcal{P}$. We design a CANT $\mathcal{C}$ that *scalably* solves instance $\mathcal{P}$; our design is based on the following reformulation of the PAP.

Focus on any solution to instance $\mathcal{P} = \langle \Pi, P \rangle$ of the PAP. As exposed by Eq. 1, each copy of a test pattern $\pi_{i_j} \in \widehat{P}$ is characterized by two position-indices within Π:

π_{i_j}'s *begin-index* b_{i_j} (resp., *end-index* e_{i_j}) is the position within the specification of Π in Eq. 1 where π_{i_j}'s first symbol (resp., π_{i_j}'s last symbol) occurs.

These indices jointly identify π_{i_j} as the length-$(m_{i_j} = e_{i_j} - b_{i_j} + 1)$ subpattern of Π:

$$\pi_{i_j} = \sigma_{b_{i_j}} \sigma_{b_{i_j}+1} \cdots \sigma_{e_{i_j}-1} \sigma_{e_{i_j}}.$$

Call $\langle b_{i_j}, e_{i_j} \rangle$ the *instance-span of* π_{i_j} *under Eq. 1. The challenge* of the PAP under this reformulation is that $\mathcal{C}$ must determine whether there is a sequence $\widetilde{P} = \langle \langle b_{i_1}, e_{i_1} \rangle, \ldots, \langle b_{i_k}, e_{i_k} \rangle \rangle$ of instance-spans from P such that:

$$\text{(a) } b_{i_1} = 0; \quad \text{(b) } b_{i_{j+1}} = e_{i_j} + 1 \ \text{ for } \ 0 \le j < n - 1; \quad \text{(c) } e_{i_k} = n - 1. \qquad (2)$$

We exploit this equational view to design our CANT $\mathcal{C}$ that solves instance $\mathcal{P}$.

2.1   Discovering Instance-Spans

Our PAP-solving CANT $\mathcal{C}$ invokes three algorithmic tools: *broadcast-replication* (Sect. 2.1A); *zip-matching* (Sect. 2.1B); *pipelining* (Sect. 2.1C). Figure 3 illustrates the first two of these. Focus on a single length-m test pattern $\pi = \tau_0 \cdots \tau_{m-1}$ that begins, left-justified, on row $n - 1$, having been input from the "outside world" one step earlier. Because (as we see imminently) $\mathcal{C}$ will create $n - m$ copies of π, we enhance legibility by embellishing π and its symbols with a *copy-index*, as $\pi^{(0)} = \tau_0^{(0)} \cdots \tau_{m-1}^{(0)}$.

A. Broadcast-replication

> **Step A1**: *(Broadcast):* In $m - 1$ successive steps, $\mathcal{C}$ staggers the symbols of $\pi^{(0)}$ as they climb to row 0: $\tau_0^{(0)}$ stays on row $n - 1$; $\tau_1^{(0)}$ moves up to row $n - 2, \ldots, \tau_{m-1}^{(0)}$ moves up to row $n - m$. $\mathcal{F}^{\langle n-1, m-1 \rangle}$, which contains $\tau_{m-1}^{(0)}$, recognizes its rightmost status by the emptiness of cell $\langle n - 1, m \rangle$. It initiates $\tau_{m-1}^{(0)}$'s ascent immediately after receiving input $\tau_{m-1}^{(0)}$. Each other $\mathcal{F}^{\langle n-1, i \rangle}$ that contains a symbol of $\pi^{(0)}$ initiates its symbol's ascent when it senses that its eastward neighbor's symbol has moved (i.e., vacated its cell). $\pi^{(0)}$ moves northward for $n - m$ steps, until $\tau_{m-1}^{(0)}$ encounters σ_{m-1} along row 0.
>
> **Step A2a**: *(Replication):* As an essential adjunct to the broadcast operation, $\mathcal{C}$ initiates the replication of $\pi^{(0)}$. Say that $\mathcal{F}^{\langle i, j \rangle}$ holds a symbol τ of $\pi^{(0)}$. If $\mathcal{F}^{\langle i, j \rangle}$'s easterly neighbor, $\mathcal{F}^{\langle i, j+1 \rangle}$, does *not* hold a symbol of π, then, *in addition to* sending τ to its northerly neighbor, $\mathcal{F}^{\langle i-1, j \rangle}$, $\mathcal{F}^{\langle i, j \rangle}$ sends τ to its northeasterly neighbor, $\mathcal{F}^{\langle i-1, j+1 \rangle}$.
>
> **Step A2b**. After broadcast-plus-replication, $n - m$ copies $\{\pi^{(i)}\}$ of π climb toward row 0. All copies of all $\pi^{(i)}$s' last symbols $\tau_{m-1}^{(i)}$ arrive at row 0 simultaneously. As each $\tau_{m-1}^{(i)}$ reaches cell $\langle 0, n - m + i \rangle$ (its target on row 0), $\mathcal{C}$ activates a *virtual Ant* at that cell. That Ant will "shepherd" $\pi^{(i)}$ through the zip-matching process.

B. Zipped pattern matching

The *zipped pattern-matching* strategy is illustrated using test pattern $\pi^{(0)} = \tau_0^{(0)} \tau_1^{(0)} \tau_2^{(0)}$ in Fig. 3. (The operator "$\cdot$" denotes LOGICAL AND.)

> **Step B1a**. The Ants activated in Step A2b initiate the *concurrent* zip-matching of all copies of test pattern π. Although the actual match-tests occur along

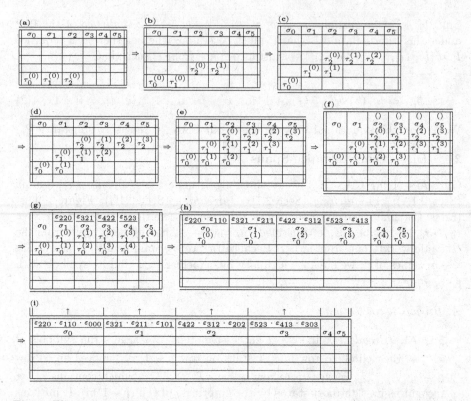

Fig. 3. Illustrating zipped pattern-matching on a length-($n = 6$) master pattern Π (along row 0) and a length-($m = 3$) test pattern π (along row $n - 1 = 5$). Symbols of copies of π have superscripts (0)–(3) to aid legibility. Steps (a)–(f): the copies are broadcast-replicated to prepare for zip-matching. Steps (g)–(i): the copies are zip-matched, and match-results are accumulated, by LOGICAL ANDing the truth-values of match-variables $\varepsilon_{ijk} \equiv [\sigma_i = \tau_j^{(k)}]$ ($k = 0$ in the figure). Vertical arrows ($\uparrow$) [Step (i)] indicate Ants' transmitting results to the "outside world."

row 0, symbols of copies of π that are below row 0 continue to climb as the match-tests proceed. The tests proceed as follows. First, all copies of τ_{m-1} are compared with their adjacent symbols from master pattern Π, and each result is recorded as the truth-value of a match-variable $\varepsilon_{ijk} \equiv [\sigma_i = \tau_j^{(k)}]$ (in our example, $k = 0$). Next, all copies of τ_{m-2} are compared with their adjacent symbols from Π, . . . ; finally, all copies of τ_0 are compared with their adjacent symbols from Π. Note how each sequence of matches is reminiscent of the closing of a zipper (whence the algorithm's name). As successive matches are performed, each Ant AND-accumulates the results of its tests in a register— depicted initially by empty parentheses in Fig. 3 and thence by underscored logical expressions that AND the truth-values of match-variables. Thus, an Ant concurrently:

- walks westward along Π (which serves as the "top" half of the "zipper")
- accesses successive lower-index symbols of π (the "bottom" half of the "zipper").

$\mathcal{C}$ enables this access by continuing to move the symbols of π northward.

A harmless feature here is that extraneous copies of symbols of π arrive at row 0, to the east of all of the Ants—because, for simplicity, we did not provide a termination mechanism for the replication process. $\mathcal{C}$ has row-0 FSMs to the east of all Ants erase all encountered extraneous symbols. This is possible because Ants are activated and travel westward *as a block*.

Step B1b. After m westward steps, symbols of copies of π stop arriving, which tells the Ants that the zip-match is complete. At that point, each Ant's ε-register contains the YES/NO "decision" whether the copy of π that it shepherded is a subword of Π. The Ant announces its decision to the "outside world." In detail: the Ant that finishes the zip-match process on cell $\langle 0, j \rangle$ has completed zip-matching copy $\pi^{(j)}$ of π; and it announces whether a copy of π begins at position j of Π.
Timing. Each symbol of each copy of a length-m pattern π follows a trajectory comprising $n - 1$ northward moves, followed by m westward moves. Because of concurrency, $\mathcal{C}$'s decisions about copies of π are available (simultaneously) within $n + m$ steps.

C. Processing multiple test patterns

One can pipeline the zip-matching process in order to discover instance-spans of multiple test patterns relative to a fixed master pattern Π. To this end one needs simply feed the desired sequence of test patterns, $\pi_1, \ldots, \pi_r$, one after the next, into row $n - 1$, left-justified, *in nondecreasing order of length*. In detail:

One feeds test patterns $\pi_0, \ldots, \pi_{r-1}$, of respective lengths $m_0 \geq \cdots \geq m_{r-1}$ (each $m_i \leq n$), left justified into row $n - 1$ of $\mathcal{C}$, in such a way that each π_{i+1} arrives m_i steps after π_i.

The following observations enable a pipelined algorithm that discovers instance-spans for multiple test patterns. When processing a length-m test pattern π, $\mathcal{C}$ eventually vacates portions of $\mathcal{M}_n$, which can then be used to zip-match another test pattern. In particular: (*i*) $\mathcal{C}$ vacates row $n-1$ after m steps. It vacates rows with successively lower indices at each subsequent step. Vacated rows are available for processing new test patterns. (*ii*) Activated Ants travel westward as a block in row 0. Cells eastward of that block are available for zip-matching new test patterns.

The pipelined algorithm and its timing analysis proceed as follows.

Step C1. Test pattern π_0 is processed as in Sects. 2A, 2B within $n + m_0$ steps.

Step C2. Test patterns $\pi_1, \ldots, \pi_{r-1}$. Focus on the end of the processing of π_i, where $i \geq 0$. As each symbol of π_i vacates row $n - 1$, the symbol's FSM announces that its cell is available for inputting π_{i+1}. Because $m_i \geq m_{i+1}$ all symbols of π_{i+1} can be input to row $n - 1$. $\mathcal{C}$ inserts π_{i+1} "backwards," from last symbol to first, to facilitate zip-matching. Symbols enter the broadcast-replication process immediately.

Timing: π_{i+1} climbs into position at row 0 in n steps; it takes m_{i+1} more steps for π_{i+1} to get zip-matched. However, n of these $n + m_{i+1}$ steps overlap n of the steps for processing π_i. Thus, the *net* additional time for π_{i+1} is m_{i+1} steps.

Summation: $\mathcal{C}$ discovers instance-spans for the sequence of test patterns π_0, $\ldots, \pi_{r-1}$ within $n + m_0 + \cdots + m_{r-1}$ steps.

Note the absence of constant factors!

2.2   Computing with Instance-Spans

A. *Representing instance-spans compactly and efficiently*
  Equation 2 allows us to focus only on instance-spans of test patterns, rather than on the patterns that form the instances. This simplifies the design of $\mathcal{C}$ because an instance-span ι can be represented using only three symbols. As in the example $\iota = [\diagdown\diagdown \cdots \diagdown\diagdown]$, the compound symbol "$[\diagdown$" denotes ι's leftmost symbol; the compound symbol "$\diagdown]$" denotes ι's rightmost symbol; all of ι's intermediate symbols are instances of "$\diagdown$". Having $\mathcal{C}$ represent each instance-span by means of a southeasterly diagonal sequence, as suggested in Fig. 4, facilitates processing distinct instance-spans in parallel, using an

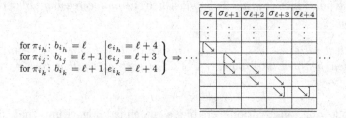

$$\left.\begin{array}{l}\text{for } \pi_{i_h}: b_{i_h} = \ell \quad \left| e_{i_h} = \ell + 4 \right. \\ \text{for } \pi_{i_j}: b_{i_j} = \ell + 1 \left| e_{i_j} = \ell + 3 \right. \\ \text{for } \pi_{i_k}: b_{i_k} = \ell + 1 \left| e_{i_k} = \ell + 4 \right.\end{array}\right\} \Rightarrow \cdots$$

Fig. 4. The "calculus" of result-coalescing. Three positive matches (perforce, from different patterns): π_{i_h} and π_{i_k} share end-index $\ell + 4$; π_{i_j} and π_{i_k} share begin-index $\ell + 1$.

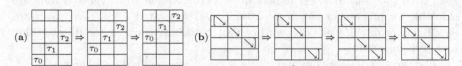

Fig. 5. (a) A northward-bound pattern of symbols. (b) A southward-bound instance-span.

algorithmically convenient *compact* representation. For pattern-instances π_{i_j} and π_{i_h}: (i) If π_{i_j} and π_{i_h} share a begin-index (i.e., $b_{i_j} = b_{i_h}$), then one pattern is a prefix of the other, so the span of the shorter one "nests in the shadow" of the longer; see π_{i_j} and π_{i_k} in Fig. 4. (ii) If π_{i_j} and π_{i_h} share an end-index (i.e., $e_{i_j} = e_{i_h}$), then the spans of both patterns share the shadow-symbols of the shorter one; see π_{i_h} and π_{i_k} in Fig. 4.

B. *When instance-spans move*

When patterns of symbols (e.g., copies of test patterns) move within $\mathcal{M}_n$, the understanding is that each symbol of each pattern moves at each step until it reaches its destination, as in Fig. 5(a). In contrast, when instance-spans move, the understanding is that they do so *at half-speed*, as in Fig. 5(b). The delays built into this worm-like pattern allow time for an (instance-span) symbol to inform its northwesterly neighbor to stop moving southward. $\mathcal{C}$ thereby orchestrates the movements of instance-spans so that they end up in a southeasterly staggered formation, with the southeast-most symbol at row $n - 2$, as suggested by Fig. 4.

A final detail: An FSM knows that it is on row $n - 2$, i.e., has the "name" $\mathcal{F}^{\langle n-2, j \rangle}$, because its southerly neighbor, $\mathcal{F}^{\langle n-1, j \rangle}$, recognizes that *it* has no southerly neighbor.

C. *Computing instance-spans via augmented zipped pattern-matching*

Our PAP-solving CANT $\mathcal{C}$ produces and processes (representations of) instance-spans efficiently by using an augmented version of zipped pattern-matching; Fig. 6 shows a small example: four copies of a length-3 test pattern $\pi = \tau_0 \tau_1 \tau_2$ being zip-matched against a length-6 master pattern $\Pi = \sigma_0 \sigma_1 \sigma_2 \sigma_3 \sigma_4 \sigma_5$. The figure begins from Step (f) of Fig. 3; therefore, we describe here only the processing of instance-spans.

The virtual Ants in Fig. 6 generate the sequences of instance-spans exposed by Eq. 2. Note that the formulation of the PAP embodied in Eq. (2) employs only instance-spans that arise from *positive* copies of a test pattern π, i.e., copies that the zipped pattern-matcher identifies as subpatterns of master pattern Π. But, $\mathcal{C}$ cannot know whether the copy of π that is processed by Ant A—call it $\pi^{(A)}$—is positive until A completes zip-matching $\pi^{(A)}$. Rather than wait for such knowledge—at the cost of time and/or bookkeeping complication—$\mathcal{C}$ has Ants proceed *optimistically*, but with an efficient mechanism for later eliminating false-positives. Specifically, as Ant A begins to zip-match $\pi^{(A)}$, it anticipates that $\pi^{(A)}$ *is* a positive copy of π, so A generates "$\diagdown$", the rightmost symbol of a positive instance-span, and A dispatches this symbol southward. Continuing thus, as A zip-matches the intermediate symbols of $\pi^{(A)}$, it generates and dispatches instances of "$\diagdown$", the intermediate symbol of a positive instance-span. Only when A finally zip-matches the *initial* symbol of $\pi^{(A)}$—which is when it knows whether $\pi^{(A)}$ is, indeed, positive—does it modify its optimistic behavior. At this point, A consults its AND-accumulating ε_{ijk}-value register to determine whether $\pi^{(A)}$ is positive. If $\pi^{(A)}$ *is* positive, then A generates "$\diagdown$", the leftmost

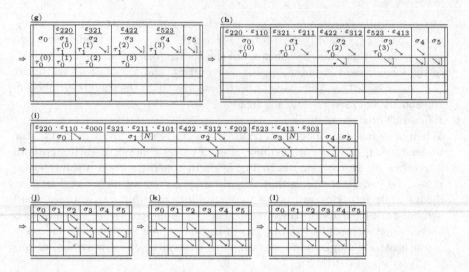

Fig. 6. The *augmented* zipped pattern-matcher for a single test pattern π. $\mathcal{C}$ broadcast-replicates π to achieve Step (g), where $n - m$ copies have reached row 0. Virtual Ants zip-match copies against Π, producing the ANDed values of match-variables ε_{ijk}. Outcomes are memoized via an instance-span (abbreviated "i-s") for each copy. The i-s of a copy that occurs in Π (a "YES", as, e.g., copies (0) and (2)) travels southward until its end-index reaches row $n - 2$; the i-s of a copy with a "NO" (as, e.g., copies (1) and (3)) is erased.

symbol of a positive instance-span, and it dispatches this symbol southward. If $\pi^{(A)}$ is *not* positive, then A generates a *negation symbol* "$[N]$", which announces $\pi^{(A)}$'s *nonpositive* status, and it dispatches this symbol southward.

Each pattern that represents a *positive* instance-span travels southward in the southeasterly staggered fashion depicted in Fig. 6, until its rightmost symbol ("$\searrow]$") encounters row $n - 2$. Because instance-spans travel at half-speed, $\mathcal{C}$ can have each positive instance-span halt with its last symbol on row $n - 2$ and its earlier symbols on successively northward cells. As *nonpositive* instance-spans travel southward, they are followed by the negation symbol $[N]$. In contrast to all other symbols from instance-spans, $[N]$ travels *southeasterly* at full speed— and it *erases* every occurrence of "$\searrow$" or "$\searrow]$" that it encounters. $[N]$ continues this erasing until it reaches row $n - 2$, at which point it self-erases.

When the virtual Ant in cell $\langle 0, 0 \rangle$ finishes its last zip-match, it has $\mathcal{F}^{\langle 0,0 \rangle}$ initiate an FSP-synch throughout $\mathcal{M}_n$. The $2n - 1$ time-steps of this action allow $\mathcal{C}$ to complete two phase-completing actions. (1) $\mathcal{C}$ uses this time to "clean up," by ensuring that: (i) the (last symbols of the) *positive* instance-spans have reached row $n - 2$; (ii) the *nonpositive* instance-spans have been erased. (2) $\mathcal{C}$ also triggers the final phase of solving the PAP, which process is initiated by $\mathcal{F}^{\langle n-1,n-1 \rangle}$.

2.3 Completing the PAP-Solving Process

Once positive instance-spans are in place, $\mathcal{F}^{\langle n-1,n-1\rangle}$ initiates the final phase of the PAP-solving process via an FSP-synch. This is essentially a *breadth-first* construction of a DAG $\mathcal{G}_{\mathcal{P}}$ that we associate with instance $\mathcal{P}$ of the PAP. $\mathcal{G}_{\mathcal{P}}$'s vertices comprise all prefixes of master pattern Π that are concatenations of multi-sequences of test patterns, including the null prefix, [NULL]. For each vertex x and each test pattern $\pi \in P$, there is an arc $(x \rightarrow x\pi)$ from x to $x\pi$ *if and only if* pattern $x\pi$ is a prefix of Π. Any path from vertex [NULL] to vertex Π describes a solution to instance $\mathcal{P}$ of the PAP.

$\mathcal{C}$ attempts to construct DAG $\mathcal{G}_{\mathcal{P}}$ "backwards," from sink to source. $\mathcal{C}$ assumes optimistically that pattern Π *is* a vertex of $\mathcal{G}_{\mathcal{P}}$, so it begins its construction with a DAG $\mathcal{G}$ that contains Π as its sole vertex. $\mathcal{C}$ then tries to augment $\mathcal{G}$ by means of a breadth-first search along the *reversed* arcs of $\mathcal{G}_{\mathcal{P}}$, with the hope of discovering a path from source [NULL] to sink Π. $\mathcal{C}$ proceeds inductively from the initial $\mathcal{G}$. For each newly discovered vertex/pattern x, $\mathcal{C}$ generates every prefix y of x for which there exists a test pattern π such that $x = y\pi$. Call such a prefix y *viable*. $\mathcal{C}$ adds all viable prefixes to the vertex-set of the evolving $\mathcal{G}$. This inductive process ends in one of two ways.

1. $\mathcal{C}$ eventually adds to DAG $\mathcal{G}$'s vertex-set a vertex x that is a test pattern. $\mathcal{G}$ thereby becomes a sub-DAG of $\mathcal{G}_{\mathcal{P}}$ whose vertex-set contains both [NULL] and Π—which means that $\mathcal{G}$ encodes a solution to instance $\mathcal{P}$ of the PAP. By continuing to add vertices to $\mathcal{G}$, $\mathcal{C}$ arrives at a maximal version of $\mathcal{G}$ that contains all paths from source [NULL] to sink Π, hence, all solutions to instance $\mathcal{P}$ of the PAP.

2. $\mathcal{C}$ eventually reaches a point at which no vertex x of $\mathcal{G}$ has a viable prefix, so the final version of $\mathcal{G}$ *does not contain vertex/pattern* [NULL]. It follows that DAG $\mathcal{G}_{\mathcal{P}}$ does not contain vertex/pattern Π, so there is no solution to instance $\mathcal{P}$ of the PAP.

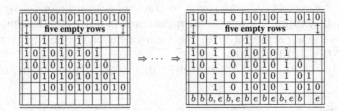

Fig. 7. Illustrating the final phase of solving the PAP, with master pattern $\Pi = 101010101010$ and test patterns from the set $\{010, 101, 1010, 10101\}$. Symbols b and e denote, respectively, the beginnings and ends of discovered instance-spans.

2.4   A Small Example

Figure 7 illustrates our solution process when the master pattern is $\Pi = 101010101010$, and the test patterns form the set $\{010, 101, 1010, 10101\}$. Figure 7(left) depicts the initial configuration after all positive instances have reached their target positions within $\mathcal{M}_n$. Figure 7(right) depicts the final configuration, after all (beginnings and ends of) arcs of $\mathcal{G}_\mathcal{P}$ have been discovered; symbols "b" and "e" along row $n - 1$ denote, respectively, the beginnings and ends of discovered arcs. To enhance legibility: (i) We portray actual (sample) patterns, rather than "shadows"; (ii) we mark the initial symbol of each positive instance with a "hat"; the remainder of each instance extends thence diagonally down to row $n - 2$. In detail, when activated by the FSP-synch, $\mathcal{F}^{\langle n-1,n-1 \rangle}$ initiates the construction of $\mathcal{G}_\mathcal{P}$ as follows. First, it adds the *end-of-instance-span* symbol "e" to cell $\langle n - 1, n - 1 \rangle$. From that step on, inductively:

1. Whenever symbol "e" is added to a cell $\langle n - 1, k \rangle$, $\mathcal{C}$ searches upward along the diagonal path that ends in that cell, looking for *beginning-of-instance-span* symbols "b". In Fig. 7(right), the traversed northwesterly path from cell $\langle n - 1, n - 1 \rangle$ encounters the string $010\hat{0}\hat{1}$. (*Remember that this is being done from right to left.*) Whenever a "hatted" symbol is encountered, $\mathcal{C}$ sends the symbol "b" vertically downward to row $n - 1$.

2. Whenever a cell $\langle n - 1, i \rangle$ along row $n - 1$ receives a *beginning-of-instance-span* symbol "b", $\mathcal{F}^{\langle n-1,i \rangle}$ tells its lefthand neighbor $\mathcal{F}^{\langle n-1,i-1 \rangle}$ (*if it exists*) to insert an *end-of-instance-span* symbol "e" into its cell. The rationale is that *if* we are identifying a solution to Eq. 1, then some pattern from P (at cell $\langle n - 1, i - 1 \rangle$) must end immediately before a new pattern from P begins (at cell $\langle n - 1, i \rangle$). $\mathcal{C}$ does *not* add the symbol e to any cell $\langle n - 1, i \rangle$ whose northward neighbor $\langle n - 2, i \rangle$ does not contain a symbol: such a cell cannot contain the end of a prefix of Π. (Note the leftmost two cells along row $n - 1$ in Fig. 7(right).)

Once the described process has completed, one can read the "answer" for the subject instance of PAP; moreover, by tracing backward along diagonals, one determines all solutions to the problem instance. In our example, the answer is "YES": there is a parsing of Π of the form in Eq. 1. We find four witnessing parsings of $\Pi = 101010101010$:
$\langle 101, 010, 101, 010 \rangle$; $\langle 1010, 10101, 010 \rangle$; $\langle 1010, 1010, 1010 \rangle$; $\langle 10101, 010, 1010 \rangle$

2.5   Timing

(1) As in Sect. 2.1, we can use zipped pattern-matching to discover the instance-spans associated with instance $\mathcal{P}$, within $n + m_1 + \cdots + m_r$ steps. (2) The algorithm of Sect. 2.3 positions all positive instance-patterns in northwest-to-southeast diagonal paths that end in row $n - 2$. Most of this is achieved within the "time-shadow" of zipped pattern matching, so the net time-cost for achieving this configuration is $O(n)$ steps, with a quite-small big-O constant, including the

time for all instance-patterns to reach their final homes. (3) Constructing DAG $\mathcal{G}_\mathcal{P}$ involves an n-step east-to-west traversal of row $n-1$ that is accompanied by marches up the diagonal instance-patterns. $\mathcal{C}$ marches along row $n-1$ at *half pace*, to ensure that it reaches a cell $\langle n-1, k \rangle$ at the same time-step when a symbol "b" (if there is any) destined for that cell arrives. In detail, when instance-pair "b_{i_j}"-"e_{i_j}" instance-pair is processed: all trajectories followed by $\mathcal{C}$—the north-westward trajectory along the diagonal, the southward trajectory that delivers symbol "b", and the westward trajectory to the home for that symbol along row $n-1$—have identical lengths, $e_{i_j} - b_{i_j}$. When $\mathcal{C}$ marches westward at half pace, all three trajectories complete in precisely $2(e_{i_j} - b_{i_j})$ time-steps. Thus, $2n$ steps suffice for traversing row $n-1$ westward and processing all "b_{i_j}"-"e_{i_j}" instance-pairs.

Thus, $\mathcal{C}$ solves instance $\mathcal{P}$ of the PAP within $m_1 + \cdots + m_r + O(n)$ steps, with a quite-small big-O constant.

3   Conclusion

CANts were invented in [21] to augment the known benefits of CAs as a parallel computing model. The focus in [21] was on robotics-inspired path-planning and exploration problems. The current study introduces the use of CANts in the realm of bioinformatic algorithms, specifically with focus on the significant Pattern-Assembly Problem (which also entails pattern-matching). In companion work in progress, we achieve efficient matching of test patterns within master patterns when the test patterns are allowed to *wrap around* the master pattern. The power of CANts that is witnessed by our perspicuous *scalable, linear-time* CANt-designs, combines with the amply-demonstrated ease of implementing CANts on simple PAs (cf., [1,2,7,9,14,15,19,22,24,25] to argue for adding CANts to the arsenal of valuable VAAs that enable high-performance computing.

References

1. Annexstein, F., Baumslag, M., Rosenberg, A.L.: Group action graphs and parallel architectures. SIAM J. Comput. **19**, 544–569 (1990)
2. Avis, D., Bremmer, D., Deza, A. (eds.): Polyhedral Computation. In: CRM Proceedings and Lecture Notes, vol. 48. American Mathematical Society (2009)
3. Böhringer, K.F.: Modeling and controlling parallel tasks in droplet-based microfluidic systems. IEEE Trans. Comput. Aided Des. Integr. Circ. Syst. **25**, 329–339 (2006)
4. Borchert, B., Reinhardt, K.: Deterministically and sudoku-deterministically recognizable picture languages. In: 2nd International Conference on Language and Automata Theory and Applications (2007)
5. Chen, L., Xu, X., Chen, Y., He, P.: A novel ant clustering algorithm based on cellular automata. In: IEEE/WIC/ACM International Conference, Intelligent Agent Technology (2004)

6. Chowdhury, D., Guttal, V., Nishinari, K., Schadschneider, A.: A cellular-automata model of flow in ant trails: non-monotonic variation of speed with density. J. Phys. A: Math. Gen. **35**, L573–L577 (2002)
7. Fisher, A.L., Kung, H.T.: Synchronizing large VLSI processor arrays. IEEE Trans. Comput. **C-34**, 734–740 (1985)
8. Folcik, V.A., An, G.C., Orosz, C.G.: The basic immune simulator: an agent-based model to study the interactions between innate and adaptive immunity. Theor. Biol. Med. Model. **4**, 39 (2007)
9. Folino, G., Mendicino, G., Senatore, A., Spezzano, G., Straface, S.: A model based on cellular automata for the parallel simulation of 3D unsaturated flow. Parallel Comput. **32**, 357–376 (2006)
10. Goles, E., Martinez, S. (eds.): Cellular Automata and Complex Systems. Kluwer, Amsterdam (1999)
11. Gruska, J., Torre, S., Parente, M.: Optimal time and communication solutions of firing squad synchronization problems on square arrays, toruses and rings. In: Calude, C.S., Calude, E., Dinneen, M.J. (eds.) DLT 2004. LNCS, vol. 3340, pp. 200–211. Springer, Heidelberg (2004). doi:10.1007/978-3-540-30550-7_17
12. Hu, X., Zhang, J., Li, Y.: Orthogonal methods based ant colony search for solving continuous optimization problems. J. Comput. Sci. Technol. **23**, 2–18 (2008)
13. Laurio, K., Linaker, F., Narayanan, A.: Regular biosequence pattern matching with cellular automata. Inf. Sci. **146**(1–4), 89–101 (2002)
14. Leighton, F.T.: Introduction to Parallel Algoithms and Architectures. Morgan Kaufmann Publ., San Mateo (1992)
15. Leiserson, C.E.: Systolic and semisystolic design. In: IEEE International Conference on Computer Design, pp. 627–630 (1983)
16. Marchese, F.: Cellular automata in robot path planning. In: EUROBOT 1996, pp. 116–125 (1996)
17. Moore, E.F.: The firing squad synchronization problem. In: Moore, E.F. (ed.) Sequential Machines, Selected Papers, pp. 213–214. Addison-Wesley (1962)
18. Quinton, P.: Automatic synthesis of systolic arrays from uniform recurrence equations. In: 11th IEEE International Symposium on Computer Architecture, pp. 208–214 (1984)
19. Rosenberg, A.L.: Better parallel architectures via emulations. In: Meyer, F., Monien, B., Rosenberg, A.L. (eds.) Nixdorf 1992. LNCS, vol. 678, pp. 30–36. Springer, Heidelberg (1993). doi:10.1007/3-540-56731-3_4
20. Rosenberg, A.L.: The Pillars of Computation Theory: State, Encoding, Nondeterminism. Universitext. Springer, New York (2009)
21. Rosenberg, A.L.: Cellular ANTomata. Adv. Complex Syst. **15**(6) (2012). doi:10.1142/S0219525912500701
22. Rosenberg, A.L., Scarano, V., Sitaraman, R.K.: The reconfigurable ring of processors: efficient algorithms via hypercube simulation. Parallel Proc. Lett. **5**, 37–48 (1995). (Special Issue on Dynamically Reconfigurable Architectures)
23. Sirakoulis, G., Adamatzky, A. (eds.): Robots and Lattice Automata. Emergence, Complexity and Computation, vol. 13. Springer, Switzerland (2014)
24. Spezzano, G., Talia, D.: The CARPET programming environment for solving scientific problems on parallel computers. Parallel Distr. Comput. Prac. **1**, 49–61 (1998)
25. Ullman, J.D.: Computational Aspects of VLSI. Computer Science Press, Rockville (1984)
26. Williams, T.: Clock skew and other myths. In: IEEE International Symposium on Asynchronous Circuits and Systems (2003)

27. Wolfram, S. (ed.): Theory and Application of Cellular Automata. Addison-Wesley, Reading (1986)

28. (2011).   http://thenoisychannel.com/2011/08/08/retiring-a-great-interview-problem

29. (2016). http://www.geeksforgeeks.org/dynamic-programming-set-32-word-break-problem

30. (2016). http://ideone.com/53LMkr

Educational and Research Systems for Evaluating the Efficiency of Parallel Computations

Victor Gergel[(✉)], Evgeny Kozinov, Alexey Linev, and Anton Shtanyk

Lobachevsky State University of Nizhni Novgorod, Nizhni Novgorod, Russia
gergel@unn.ru,
{evgeny.kozinov,alexey.linev,anton.shtanyuk}@itmm.unn.ru

Abstract. In this paper we consider the educational and research systems that can be used to estimate the efficiency of parallel computing. ParaLab allows parallel computation methods to be studies. With the ParaLib library, we can compare the parallel programming languages and technologies. The Globalizer Lab system is capable of estimating the efficiency of algorithms for solving computationally intensive global optimization problems. These systems can build models of various high-performance systems, formulate the problems to be solved, perform computational experiments in the simulation mode and analyze the results. The crucial matter is that the described systems support a visual representation of the parallel computation process. If combined, these systems can be useful for developing high-performance parallel programs which take the specific features of modern supercomputing systems into account.

Keywords: High-performance system · Parallel computations · Parallel algorithm · Numerical experiment · Simulation · Parallel speedup · Parallel efficiency

1 Introduction

The computational power of modern supercomputer systems is rapidly increasing. In 2008, performance exceeded the petaflops level (10^{15} operations per second). Currently, the performance of Sunway TaihuLight (China), the most powerful supercomputer system, already exceeds 100 Pflops. This system consists of 10.5 million computational elements (a more than 100-fold performance increase over the last 8 years). Due to their enormous computational power, supercomputer systems can solve many problems of modern society (Grand Challenge Problems).

These huge supercomputer capabilities should be used efficiently. It should be noted that despite the fact that standard Linpack test results are 70–90% for the maximum

This research was supported by the Russian Science Foundation, project No 16-11-10150 "Novel efficient methods and software tools for time-consuming decision making problems using supercomputers of superior performance."

J. Carretero et al. (Eds.): ICA3PP 2016 Workshops, LNCS 10049, pp. 278–290, 2016.
DOI: 10.1007/978-3-319-49956-7_22

supercomputer performance, for a large number of scientific and engineering problems the performance of supercomputer computations is significantly lower (as low as 10%).

The efficiency of high-performance computing system applications is currently one of the main challenges of supercomputer technologies. Methods and software programs need to use efficient algorithms, provide efficient parallelization and employ the specific features of supercomputer systems to the maximum extent. All these problems should be analyzed, which usually requires performing a large number of computational experiments.

Estimating parallel program efficiency requires a corresponding integrated environment that is utilized to execute computational experiments. Thus, it is necessary to have access to several supercomputer systems with differing architectures and computer equipment. Executing computational experiments can be relatively time-consuming and, thus, may require large resources. It should also be noted that analyzing the results of computational experiments is very complicated due to the large volume of data and the various visual methods required to represent these data.

The high cost and complexity of supercomputer computational experiments can be significantly reduced by developing and broadly applying educational and research software systems, which provide the tools to model various high-performance systems, to formulate the problems to be solved, to execute the computational experiments in simulation mode and to analyze the results.

The application of educational and research software systems to evaluate parallel algorithms is actively being researched (see, for example, [1–4]). One of the first methods for visually representing parallel systems is described in [5]. Estimating the efficiency of tools for animating and visualizing the program execution process is studied in [6–8]. Some of the available educational and research software systems are considered in [9, 10]. One widely used approach is to use Matlab for visualizing algorithms and programs [11].

In this article we discuss some educational and research software systems that were developed at the University of Nizhni Novgorod and are actively used to educate specialists in the field of supercomputer technologies [4].

The rest of the paper is organized as follows. In Sect. 2, we consider ParaLab (Parallel Laboratory) [12–14], which is an integrated environment for studying and researching the solutions of parallel algorithms that are used in a majority of "classical" computational problems (matrix computations, sorting, graph processing, optimization, etc.). The wide range of tools available for visualizing the execution process for experiments and for analyzing their results provides the ability to evaluate the efficiency of various parallel algorithms on various computational systems, evaluate the scalability of these algorithms and determine the speedup that can be achieved by parallel computations. Computational experiments are executed on personal computers with a single CPU running the Windows OS in parallel computations simulation mode.

In Sect. 3, we consider a library of parallel algorithms ParaLib (Parallel Library) [15, 16], which is intended for studying and developing modern parallel technologies and programming languages, and provides examples of parallel algorithm implementations for a large number of mathematical computation problems. Using examples of computational problems and their parallel solution methods, we can compare the computational complexity of parallel algorithms and the efficiency of parallel programs. The experiments can be executed either on a personal computer or on a computational system with distributed memory. Software to implement parallel methods are developed using various parallel programming languages and technologies, including the OpenMP parallel programming technology for systems with shared memory [17], the MPI parallel programming technology for systems with distributed memory [18], the Chapel parallel programming language [19] and the Co-Array Fortran parallel programming language [20].

In Sect. 4, we consider the Globalizer Lab system (Global Optimization Laboratory) [21], which is an integrated software environment for computational experiments for analyzing global search methods. Multiextremal optimization problems are commonly encountered in practical applications. They are computationally intensive and can be solved only by using high-performance computing systems. Globalizer supports the formulation of optimization problem, allows the selection of a global search algorithm, executes computational experiments and analyzes global search results.

At the end of the paper, we provide a conclusion and discuss possible areas of future research.

2   The ParaLab System for Evaluating Parallel Methods

The ParaLab system (*Parallel Laboratory*) [12–14] is an integrated software environment that enables both real parallel computations on a multiprocessor computing system and the simulation of such experiments on a personal computer with the ability to visualize the parallel processing of complex computational problems.

ParaLab provides the following.

1. **Simulation of parallel computing systems.** During the simulation process, the user can *determine the topology* of the parallel computing system that will be used to implementation the experiments, *set the number of CPUs* for the selected topology (Fig. 1), *determine the CPU performance* and select *the communication properties* and *method*.

   The ParaLab system provides support for the following main computing system topologies: line, ring, star, grid, hypercube and complete graph.

   ParaLab can perform computational experiment simulations on multiprocessor (SMP) and multi-CPU (multicore) architectures. At the highest level, a computer system is represented as a set of computers (computing nodes). Each computer consists of one or more processors, and each processor contains one or more cores.

2. **Determining the computational experiment parameters.** To set the parameters, a user can *formulate the computational problem* for which the ParaLab system implements parallel algorithms. For a selected problem, the user can determine the *problem parameters*. For the solution of the formulated problem can be selected the *parallel method*.

The ParaLab system supports computational experiments for multiplying matrices by a vector, matrix multiplication, solving linear equation systems, sorting, processing graphs, solving PDE and multiextremal optimizations.

3. **Visualization parameters.** The ParaLab system allows users *to set the visualization parameters* and select the required demonstration mode, the visualization mode for exchanging data between processors, and the level of detail for visualizing executed parallel computations (see Fig. 2).

4. **Computational experiments.** ParaLab can *perform experiments* with parallel solutions for selected problems. The system also can determine several *problems for experiments* with different types of multiprocessor systems, problems and parallel computation methods. The execution of these experiments can be performed simultaneously (in time-shared mode); the simultaneous execution of experiments for several problems provides a convenient demonstration for solving one original problem with different methods, using different topologies and with varying parameters. For a *series of experiments* that requires a long time to perform computations, the system provides an automatic execution mode where the results are stored in an *experiment register*, so it is possible to analyze the resulting data later.

5. **Accumulation and analysis of computational experiment results.** ParaLab supports the *accumulation and analysis of experimental results*; the results that were stored in the experiment register can be utilized to build plots that describe how parallel computation parameters (*computation time, acceleration, efficiency*) depend on the problem parameters and the properties of the computational system (see Fig. 3).

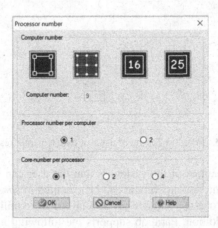

Fig. 1. Dialog window for selecting the number of processors and computational cores

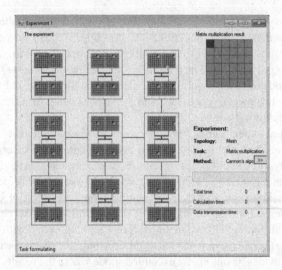

Fig. 2. ParaLab window for executing computational experiments

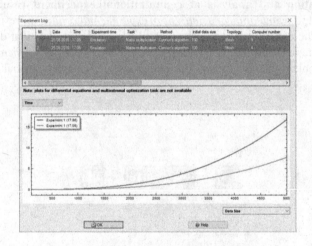

Fig. 3. Window for the register of experimental results

One of the main features of the system is that the user can select the method for executing an experiment. An experiment can be executed *in simulation mode*, i.e. it is executed on a single processor without any special software utilities such as message-passing libraries. In addition, ParaLab supports the following methods for executing *real computational experiments*:

- *on a single computer* with a message-passing library MPI (multithreaded execution); this library has a public version that can be downloaded from the internet and installed on computers running the MS Windows operation system,
- *on a real multiprocessor computational system*,
- *in remote access mode* for the computational clusters.

If we perform an experiment on a multiprocessor computing system or in remote access mode, then ParaLab allows the type of computational nodes to be selected.

To determine the dependencies of performance characteristics from problem and computing system parameters for experiments executed in simulation mode, the system utilizes theoretical estimations based on the available parallel computation models [22–24]. For experiments on multiprocessor computing systems, the dependencies are constructed based on the results of prior computational experiments. Any previously performed experiments can be restored and performed again. In addition, the system provides an experiment register in which the problem statement, computing system parameters and the computational results are stored.

The ParaLab system can be freely used and downloaded from the Supercomputer Technologies Centre of University of Nizhni Novgorod website [14].

3   ParaLib Parallel Computational Methods Library

The ParaLib (*Parallel Library*) library [15, 16] is designed for the study and comparative examination of various parallel algorithmic languages and parallel software development technologies. For executing parallel experiments, the library provides a control system. Its dialog window is shown in Fig. 4.

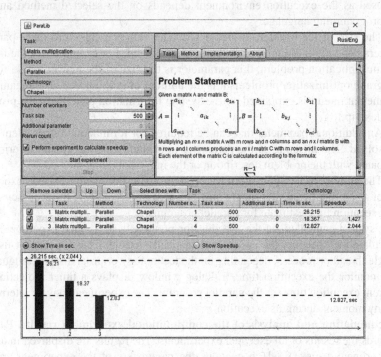

Fig. 4. Dialog window of the ParaLib control system

The ParaLib control system provides the following.

1. **Selection of problem and solution method.** For executing parallel experiments, the ParaLib system allows the user to select the problem to be solved, its solution method and the technology and programming language to be used to implement the method.

   ParaLib contains methods for solving of a number of "classical" mathematical computation problems, which are used to study the basics of parallel programming. For solving the problems ParaLib provides both serial and parallel methods. Method implementations are provided for all problems based on OpenMP and MPI [17, 18]. For the problem of matrix multiplication ParaLib provides implementation methods based on the Co-Array Fortran and Chapel parallel programming languages [19, 20].

2. **Context information.** ParaLib provides the required information on selected algorithms and implementation methods. The system information panel displays the problem statement, a description of the selected method and examples of the algorithm implementations. In addition, it displays the general information on the ParaLib library and the problems and methods currently implemented in the library.

3. **Execution of computational experiments.** In the ParaLib system, the user can determine the specific conditions for executing a computational experiment with the help of the following parameter set:

   - The number of execution threads. The computational threads or processes are used as the execution environment depends on the selected method and the programming language.
   - The size of the problem to be solved. The values assigned to these parameters depend on the type of problem to be solved. For example, for the matrix multiplication problem, this parameter is the size of the matrix, while for the graph optimization problems it is the number of graph nodes. The meaning of the parameter is explained on the system information panel with the problem description.
   - An additional parameter that can be required for formulating the problem to be solved. The meaning of the parameter is explained on the system information panel with the problem description or the implementation method.
   - The number of iterations for the computational experiment. Repeated execution of a computational experiment may be necessary to increase the accuracy of the execution time estimate for parallel programs.

   The system can calculate the speedup for previously performed experiments. To calculate the speedup, the system automatically executes the experiment using a single thread or process, depending on the technology or programming language.

   To monitor the execution time, a dialog window displays a timer indicating the current execution time for the parallel program. The experiment may be interrupted at any moment during its execution.

4. **Accumulation and analysis of the computational experiment results.** ParaLib records the results of all executed experiments. The results are displayed in a table (experiment register), which contains the parameters of the experiment and the parallel program execution time.

If the volume of results becomes too large, the user can delete or hide the results of selected experiments. As a default, the execution time and the speedup of computational efficiency are displayed for all experiments.

For the data analysis, the experimental results can be shown in the table in a desirable order. For analytic convenience, the user can select experimental results as needed based on the problem to be solved, method and technology.

5. **Visual comparison of experimental execution time.** To provide a visual representation of the results, ParaLib displays a chart with the results of the computational experiments, where the horizontal axis represents the serial number of the experiment and the vertical axis represents the execution time or the speedup. The chart also displays the maximum and minimum execution time, as well as the ratio between the maximum and minimum values. The corresponding values for the execution time or the speedup are displayed next to each column on the chart.

To implement all of the described functions, the parallel algorithm architecture library and control system is organized as a system of functionally-oriented software layers, or levels (see Fig. 5).

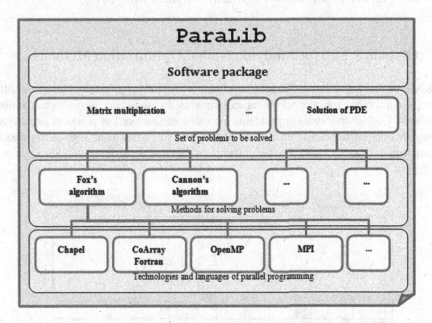

Fig. 5. Architecture of the ParaLib library

The upper level consists of the control system. The system sets the conditions for computational experiments, runs the executable modules for different initial conditions, accumulates data from the executed experiments and estimates the feasibility of a chosen technology or parallel programming language for solving a particular problem.

The next level is the subsystem containing the computational problems for which the library provides implemented solutions. This subsystem also contains information and descriptions of all problems stored in the library.

The next level is the subsystem which, for each problem from the prior level provides available solution methods and their implementations based on different parallel programming languages and technologies. In addition, this subsystem also contains descriptions for parallel algorithm implementations.

At the lowest level is a subsystem containing the implementations of algorithms by applying different methods, technologies and programming languages. Each implementation in this subsystem consists of several files (each with source code and an executable module). In the ParaLib framework, executable modules accept four parameters – the size of the problem, the number of iterations of the algorithm, the number of threads or processes and an optional parameter, which depends on the specific problem. As the result of running the executable module, the systems tracks the run-time and records it in a separate line of the experiment register.

The ParaLib library can be freely used and downloaded from the Supercomputer Technologies Centre of University of Nizhny Novgorod website [16].

4   GlobalizerLab for Studying Global Optimization Methods

The Globalizer Lab (*Global Optimization Laboratory*) [21] system is an integrated software environment for computational experiments for analyzing global optimization methods. Global optimization problems are often encountered in practical situations. They are computationally intensive and can only be solved by using high-performance computing systems [25–29]. The general view of the Globalizer dialog window is shown in Fig. 6.

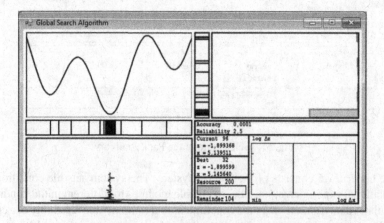

Fig. 6. Dialog window of the Globalizer Lab system

The Globalizer systems provides the following.

1. **Formulation of optimization problems**. The system supports several different problem formulation methods. The objective function can be selected from a standard set of test problems that are commonly used in global optimization. Minimization functions can also be selected using the symbolic formula or can be generated by a random generator. The function determined by any of these methods can be modified in the graphical editor included in the system. All of the above methods for setting the functions are easy to use and provide methods for formulating complex one-dimensional multiextremal optimization problems with the required characteristics (presence of a "plateau," "wide" and "narrow" minimums, "oscillations", etc.).

2. **Selection of the global optimization algorithm** from the optimization methods built-in in the system. Globalizer contains 10 multiextremal optimization methods that are well known in the theory and practice of global optimization. The system also supports extending the set of available methods using integrated tools, without applying algorithmic programming languages.

3. **Determine the visual indicators** for observing the global search process. Based on these indicators, the system can demonstrate a graph of the minimizing function or it's piecewise linear approximation, utilizing the function values from each iteration, as well as determine the distribution, density and sequence of iteration points and the corresponding function values. Monitoring the visual indicators during the global search process helps to develop the necessary skills for practically applying and further developing multiextremal optimization methods.

4. **Execution of computational experiments**. Experiments can be executed in serial or parallel modes (see Fig. 7). The latter method allows us to visually compare the dynamics for various optimization methods executed in time-shared mode. The system also provides executing serial experiments that are performed in automatic mode with storing optimization results for further data analysis. In addition, experiments can be performed in the manual search mode when the iterations points are determined by the user (this mode can be used to test different hypotheses that could be utilized as global search patterns).

5. **Accumulation and analysis of the results of previous experiments**. The Globalizer system estimates the efficiency (operational characteristics) of the methods and provides an experiment register to record optimization results. The accumulated data can be presented in different visual forms (tables, plots, diagrams) that are very convenient for analysis. Computational results can be stored in the Globalizer system archive, printed or copied to the Windows clipboard as text, graphics or tables and imported into a text editor, Word, Excel or other Windows OS programs for further processing (including their reproduction for papers, reports, etc.).

The Globalizer Lab system can be used freely and downloaded from the Supercomputer Technologies Centre of University of Nizhni Novgorod website [21].

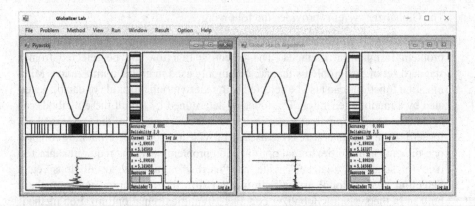

Fig. 7. Example of the simultaneous execution of several experiments

5   Conclusion

In this paper we consider educational and research systems that can be used to estimate efficiency of parallel computations. ParaLab enables the evaluation of parallel computation methods. With the ParaLib library, we can compare parallel programming languages and technologies. The Globalizer Lab system is capable of estimating the efficiency of algorithms for solving computationally intensive global optimization problems. These systems provides to model various high-performance systems, formulate problems, perform computational experiments in simulation mode and analyze the results. The *crucial matter* is that the described systems visually represent the parallel computation process. In general, these systems can be useful for developing high-performance parallel programs which take the specific features of modern supercomputing systems into account.

An important area for further research is the scalability of these systems in order to add new parallel programming problems, methods and technologies. It is also necessary to be able to execute experiments for simulated systems with a large number of processors and computational cores.

References

1. A Survey on Training and Education Needs for Petascale Computing. http://www.prace-ri.eu/IMG/pdf/D3-3-1_document_final.pdf
2. Rague, B.: Teaching parallel thinking to the next generation of programmers. J. Educ. Inform. Cybern. **1**(1), 43–48 (2009)
3. Voevodin, V., Gergel, V., Popova, N.: Challenges of a systematic approach to parallel computing and supercomputing education. In: Hunold, S., et al. (eds.) Euro-Par 2015. LNCS, vol. 9523, pp. 90–101. Springer, Heidelberg (2015). doi:10.1007/978-3-319-27308-2_8

4. Gergel, V., Liniov, A., Meyerov, I., Sysoyev, A.: NSF/IEEE-TCPP curriculum implementation at the State University of Nizhni Novgorod. In: IPDPSW 2014 Proceedings of the 2014 IEEE International Parallel & Distributed Processing Symposium Workshops, pp. 1079–1084. IEEE Computer Society, Washington, DC, USA (2014)

5. Kraemer, E., Stasko, J.T.: The visualization of parallel systems: an overview. J. Parallel Distrib. Comput. **18**, 105–117 (1993)

6. Hundhausen, C.D., Dougla, S.A., Stasko, J.T.: A meta-study of algorithm visualization effectiveness. J. Vis. Lang. Comput. **13**(3), 259–290 (2002)

7. Urquiza-Fuentes, J., Velázquez-Iturbide, J.Á.: Towards the effective use of educational program animations: the roles of student's engagement and topic complexity. Comput. Educ. **67**, 178–192 (2013)

8. Lazaridis, V., Samaras, N., Sifaleras, A.: An empirical study on factors influencing the effectiveness of algorithm visualization. Comput. Appl. Eng. Educ. **21**, 410–420 (2013)

9. Ben-Ari, M., Bednarik, R., Ben-Bassat, L.R., Ebel, G., Moreno, A., Myller, N., Sutinen, E.: A decade of research and development on program animation: the Jeliot experience. J. Vis. Lang. Comput. **22**(5), 375–384 (2011)

10. Sorva, J., Karavirta, V., Malmi, L.: A review of generic program visualization systems for introductory programming education. ACM Trans. Comput. Educ. (TOCE) **13**(4), 15 (2013)

11. Teaching with Data, Simulations and Models. Topical Resources. http://serc.carleton.edu/NAGTWorkshops/data_models/toolsheets/MATLAB.html

12. Gergel, V., Labutina, A.: The ParaLab system for investigating the parallel algorithms. In: Hsu, C.-H., Malyshkin, V. (eds.) MTPP 2010. LNCS, vol. 6083, pp. 95–104. Springer, Heidelberg (2010). doi:10.1007/978-3-642-14822-4_11

13. Kozinov, E., Shtanyuk, A.: Learning parallel computations with ParaLab. In: CEUR Workshop Proceedings, vol. 1513, pp. 11–20 (2015)

14. The ParaLab system website (2016). http://hpc-education.unn.ru/en/trainings/teachware/paralab. Accessed

15. Kozinov, E., Gergel, V., Line, A., Shtanyuk, A.: Educational and research systems for studying of parallel methods. In: CEUR Workshop Proceedings, vol. 1482, pp. 779–786 (2015). (in Russian)

16. The ParaLib Library website (2016). http://hpc-education.unn.ru/en/trainings/teachware/paralib. Accessed

17. Chandra, R., Dagum, L., Kohr, D., Maydan, D., McDonald, J., Melon, R.: Parallel Programming in OpenMP. Morgan Kaufmann Publishers, San-Francisco (2000)

18. Group, W., Lusk, E., Skjellum, A.: Using MPI. Portable Parallel Programming with the Message-Passing Interface. MIT Press, Cambridge (1994)

19. Reid, J.: JKR Associates, UK Coarrays in the next Fortran Standard, 21 April 2010. ftp://ftp.nag.co.uk/sc22wg5/n1801-n1850/n1824.pdf

20. The Chapel Parallel Programming Language. http://chapel.cray.com/

21. The Globalizer Lab system website (2016). http://hpc-education.unn.ru/en/trainings/teachware/globlab. Accessed

22. Kumar, V., Grama, A., Gupta, A., Karypis, G.: Introduction to Parallel Computing. The Benjamin/Cummings Publishing Company, Inc., San Francisco (1994)

23. Quinn, M.J.: Parallel Programming C with MPI and OpenMP. Mccraw-Hill, New York (2004)

24. Gergel, V.P.: Theory and Practice of Parallel Computations. Binom, Moscow (2007). (in Russian)

25. Strongin, R.G., Sergeyev, Ya.D: Global Optimization with Non-convex Constraints Sequential and Parallel Algorithms. Kluwer Academic Publishers, Dordrecht (2000)

26. Gergel, V.P.: A method of using derivatives in the minimization of multiextremum functions. Comput. Math. Math. Phys. **36**(6), 729–742 (1996)
27. Gergel, V., Grishagin, V., Israfilov, R.: Local tuning in nested scheme of global optimization. Procedia Comput. Sci. **51**, 865–874 (2015)
28. Barkalov, K., Gergel, V.: Parallel global optimization on GPU. J. Global Optim. **66**, 1–18 (2015). doi:10.1007/s10898-016-0411-y
29. Lebedev, I., Gergel, V.: Heterogeneous parallel computations for solving global optimization problems. Procedia Comput. Sci. **66**, 53–62 (2015)

Generalized Approach to Scalability Analysis of Parallel Applications

Alexander Antonov$^{(\boxtimes)}$ and Alexey Teplov

Moscow State University, Moscow, Russia
asa@parallel.ru, alex-teplov@yandex.ru

Abstract. This article describes an approach to scalability analysis of parallel applications, which is a major part of the algorithm description used in AlgoWiki, the Open Encyclopedia of Parallel Algorithmic Features. The proposed approach is based on the suggested definition of generalized scalability of a parallel application. This study uses joined and structured data on an application's execution and supercomputing co-design technologies. Parallel application properties are studied by analyzing data collected from all available sources of its dynamic characteristics and information about the hardware and software platforms corresponding with the features of an algorithm and its implementation. This allows reasonable conclusion to be drawn regarding potential reasons of changes in the execution quality for any parallel applications and to compare the scalability of various programs.

Keywords: Scalability · Dynamic characteristics · Efficiency · Parallel computing · Supercomputing co-design

Introduction

Scalability is one of the most important properties of parallel algorithms and programs. Its analysis is given special attention in the AlgoWiki Open Encyclopedia of Parallel Algorithmic Features project [1]. It is important for the encyclopedia that this property can be used in a comparative analysis of various parallel algorithms [2] and can be complemented by other studies on the same topic. However, the existence of various definitions of scalability and approaches to its analysis prevents researchers from comparing the results of studies conducted in different terms.

Many different definitions of scalability can be found in academic publications. These mainly point to the changes in dynamic characteristics (namely, speed-up and performance) for one and the same application under different startup conditions.

The results were obtained in Moscow State University with the financial support of the Russian Science Foundation, agreement N 14-11-00190, and the Russian Foundation for Basic Research, grant N 16-07-01003 (Sect. 4), and grant N 16-07-00972 (Sect. 5).

© Springer International Publishing AG 2016
J. Carretero et al. (Eds.): ICA3PP 2016 Workshops, LNCS 10049, pp. 291–304, 2016.
DOI: 10.1007/978-3-319-49956-7_23

The scalability of a parallel application is often shown as a chart illustrating the dependency of the program's speed-up or performance on the number of processors or processing cores used. However, researchers usually point out that this correlation also depends on other factors and provide the specific values of those factors for which it was obtained. For example, the influence of problem size produced terms like strong and weak scalability [3], and wide scalability [4].

The definition used in [5] is abstract, as it defines scalability simply as an *ability*, i.e. a property of the application itself, not relating it to the dependency of performance characteristics on changes in the environment. In [6], the author links the notion of scalability strictly to the dependence between the speed-up of a parallel application and the number of processors, without defining what this speed-up should be compared with. In [7], the idea of scalability is related to changes in performance, which should be proportional to the hardware resources available. Other authors [8] call an algorithm scalable only if the number of processors changes, singling out efficiency as the most interesting feature. There are many other definitions of this term.

An analysis of the advantages and disadvantages of existing definitions helps to identify their common features. Most authors agree that algorithm performance is substantially affected by the hardware and software platform, and therefore either conclude that this is a fixed correlation, or point to the need to use co-design technologies to find an optimal solution. The wide range of definitions [9–13] shows that different authors approach this term from different angles. On the one hand, this illustrates the complexity and importance of scalability while, on the other hand, it indicates the need to deeply analyze this property for parallel applications. The fact that a single term has such a great number of definitions is also a sign that it requires a more concise, yet more generalized and universal definition if we want it to describe the properties of a parallel application.

1   Introducing the Term of Generalized Scalability

The term "scalability" only recently entered academic literature. To some level, this explains the existence of numerous definitions of this term. In most cases the term is defined as a dependency between some property of the program and certain startup conditions.

The main drawback of most of these definitions is that the authors only describe the dependency between one specific program property and one (rarely two) startup parameter. Moreover, even looking at just one integral indicator from the entire range of characteristics available does not show the entire picture of the changes in the executed program's characteristics, and doesn't explain, even indirectly, the reasons for such changes.

What unites all of the different definitions of this term is that almost everyone relates it to the dependency of various characteristics of the program (speed-up, performance, efficiency, etc.) on the number of processors involved in its execution.

Dynamic characteristics [14] are those indicators of a parallel application that describe the process of its execution. These can include execution time, speed-up, performance, efficiency, etc. They can be averaged over some period of time or measured instantly. Dynamic characteristics can be divided into two groups [15], depending on how they are obtained.

The first group includes *measurable dynamic characteristics*. These are, for example: the program execution time, the number of cache misses, the number of bytes sent over the communication network during its execution, the number of memory read/write operations during its execution, etc.

The second group includes *calculated dynamic characteristics*, which are derived from measurable dynamic characteristics. These include: speed-up, performance, network data transfer rate, the number of cache misses per second, instant and average efficiency, etc.

By *startup parameter* [14], we mean any parallel application parameter that has an impact on its execution process. Startup parameters for a parallel application do not include those parameters that do not affect its execution (such as the number of comments in the program code, the names of variables in the program, etc.).

Startup parameters can be divided into the following types:

1. *hardware parameters* — those related to the system's hardware (CPU, RAM, computing node, interconnect);
2. *system parameters* — those related to the operating system, compilers, libraries, system applications and their settings;
3. *software parameters* — those that affect the program logic or its computational complexity, as well as various parameters considered by the application developer (data amount, data format, data output parameters, logical forking, various algorithm parameters, etc.).

To understand the properties of a parallel application and the reasons for discovered scalability features, it is important to consider all available startup parameters and dynamic characteristics. We should view scalability as a more general property of a parallel application, which includes both the dependency of dynamic characteristics on various startup parameters, and the connections between changes in the values of various dynamic characteristics.

Therefore it is advisable to define *scalability* [14] as *a property of a parallel application that describes the dependency of changes in the full range of dynamic characteristics for that program on the full range of its startup parameters*.

With this definition, the term "scalability" allows the execution of a parallel application to be described and to get an idea of how computing resource usage changes upon changes in various program startup parameters. This allows the user to draw conclusions about the factors affecting an application's efficiency, to identify the consistency of the algorithm, its implementation and the computing system, and to find potential ways to improve execution efficiency by making changes to the application and to the hardware and software platform.

To determine the correlation between a program's execution quality and some of its startup parameters, any dynamic characteristic can be used. Any startup parameter can be used as an argument. This approach effectively treats scalability as a multi-dimensional dependency reflecting the changes in the entire combination of dynamic characteristics, while reviewing the entire diversity of factors affecting program execution. Most other definitions of the term "scalability" are in fact particular cases of the proposed definition.

Figure 1 shows a three-dimensional representation of scalability of a parallel application that performs dense matrix multiplication, which is understood as the dependency of performance on the number of processors and the matrix size. Cross-sections of the charts are shown for a fixed problem size (A) and a fixed number of processes (C), which correspond to strong scalability and wide scalability.

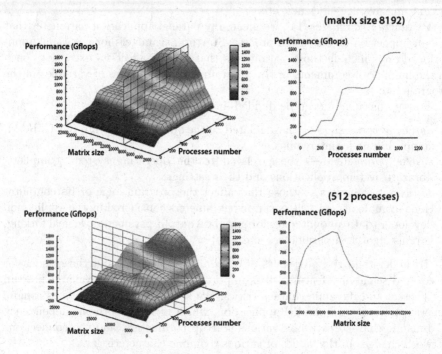

Fig. 1. Cross-section of the data representation for generalized scalability of dense matrix multiplication given a fixed problem size (A) and a fixed number of processes (C) demonstrates strong scalability (B) and wide scalability (D), respectively.

If we intersect the generalized scalability data with a plane located at an angle to the axes of reference, we will get a weak scalability chart. One can point to a connection between the proposed definition and the definition of the isoefficiency function [12] if implementation efficiency is used as the dynamic characteristic of the same program instead of performance. By crossing the obtained surface with a constant efficiency value, we will get a cross-section describing the dependency of the problem size on the number of processors. With this change of parameter values, program execution efficiency will remain constant.

Correspondingly, most of the known definitions of scalability can be derived from the proposed definition by using various combination of startup parameters and dynamic characteristics of the application being analyzed.

Thus, we can say that using the proposed approach to defining scalability does not conflict with existing definitions of this term, but rather expands and generalizes them relative to the currently used parameters of program execution quality and startup parameters.

As a result, existing studies of scalability can be supplemented by different startup parameters and different dynamic characteristics of the same algorithm or its implementation. This approach allows to create an extensible library with information on the scalability properties of an algorithm and its implementations. New studies will only enhance the overall picture.

2   Key Principles of Scalability Studies

The proposed principles for studying scalability [16,17] imply merging all available data on the execution of a parallel application and analyzing the impact of each individual factor and its combination with its related dynamic characteristics. In this case, data on the program's scalability can be presented as a vector function of several variables. The arguments to this function will be the variable program startup parameter values. The function's values can be presented as a vector, where the value of each element is the value of a dynamic characteristic obtained while executing the parallel application.

The key focus when analyzing the data will be on the dependencies arising between various dynamic characteristics. As the nature of the data used for analysis differs, and the amount of data increases greatly, the analysis itself becomes a more complex task too. However, finding the connections between changes in various dynamic characteristics enable conclusions to be made regarding what causes these mutual impacts. When studying scalability under the proposed approach, researchers can combine the results of various studies of the same parallel application with different startup parameters and supplement the existing information on the program's scalability.

The analysis of the data collected in this case is intended to identify the dependencies between integral dynamic characteristics [18] and dynamic characteristics obtained from system monitoring.

The proposed analytical approach helps to consider the impact of various factors, to find reasons for changes in algorithm characteristics, and to draw conclusion about how execution efficiency can be improved, using co-design technologies if necessary.

Another important part of the proposed principles for scalability studies using dynamic characteristics is a more in-depth analysis of each individual dynamic characteristic. This allows the impact of each individual factor to be evaluated regarding the entire program's scalability.

3   Analysis of Factors that Reduce Scalability Using System Monitoring Data

The reasons that impact a program's scalability can include factors related to the program's execution algorithm, its implementation features, and the properties of the programming technologies used. Importantly, the factors that affect a program's scalability also include the characteristics of the hardware and software environment in which the parallel application is executed.

However, when analyzing the program's scalability, it is less important to observe the impact of each individual factor separately, than determining how this impact is affected by changes in the program startup parameters.

The factors that have the maximum impact on the scalability of parallel applications can be divided into several groups for convenience.

The first group includes factors related to using communication networks as one of the most important components of a supercomputer. The second group includes factors related to elements of a supercomputer's computing node usage. Finally, the third group includes factors related to the characteristics of the algorithm used or the parallel application studied.

The analysis of the system monitoring data is based on usage of a certain set of sensors that report the status of the hardware and software environment. Depending on the purpose of the study, information is collected from the relevant subset of sensors. As a result, we obtain a historical record of the computing system's states at various moments during the application execution. It should be noted that system monitoring data can only be used to develop hypotheses about the factors affecting a system's dynamic characteristics. Carefully collected and properly calculated statistics, with subsequent analysis of the results obtained, help to identify the reasons for certain patterns in the computing system's behavior with higher accuracy.

By analyzing a computing system's monitoring data, we can determine a very wide range of factors affecting scalability.

For example, an analysis of networking activity helps isolate the causes of problems like high latency or low bandwith of the communication network. In the example below, network bandwith will determine how much time is used to send each message. The more processes that send messages, the more load will be experienced by the switches connecting the computing nodes.

Let's look at launching the same application — a specially designed test, with startup parameters corresponding to sending messages of different length (1; 1,000,000; 100,000,000).

The Infiniband data transmission chart (Fig. 2A) shows low network usage intensity, with a rate of about 100 MB/sec when the message length equals 1. As the message length is increased to 1,000,000 (Fig. 2B), network usage intensity increases to 900 MB/sec. The difference between the minimum and maximum data transfer rate values increases as well. Average data send and receive rates fluctuate from the maximum to the minimum value and then back. This behavior can indicate that individual nodes have reached their maximum capacity, which results in transmission delays for many messages of great length.

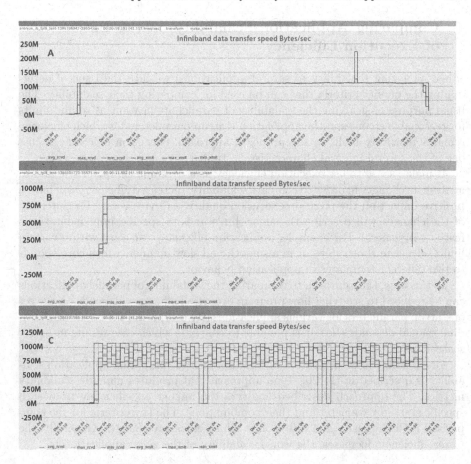

Fig. 2. Data transfer rate over an Infiniband network (A — length 1; B — length 1,000,000; C — length 100,000,000).

In the third experiment with the same test, the message length is increased to 100,000,000 (Fig. 2C). The maximum data transfer rate increases up to 1,100 MB/sec, which is higher than the value in the previous experiment (900 MB/sec). However, the minimum data send and receive rate decreases to 650 MB/sec. This is much lower than in the previous experiment (850 MB/sec), which wasn't too far from the maximum value. The transmission pattern remains the same, but the gap between maximum and minimum transmission rates is much larger. The minimum data transmission rate falls lower than in the experiment with shorter messages. Deviations in the average transfer rate also increase substantially and acquire a stepped structure. This confirms our assumption about a bandwith threshold being reached on the communication network.

Other examples of the various factors that affect application scalability based on the system monitoring data are provided in [19].

4   Comparing Application Scalability on the Basis of Execution Efficiency

When analyzing scalability of several applications, we face the issue of determining the quality criteria that can be used for comparing their scalability. The usual purpose of studying the scalability of parallel applications is to find limits for reasonable changes in the application startup parameters for which efficiency remains relatively high. In the proposed approach, execution efficiency is just one of the several integral characteristics studied.

It makes sense to use execution efficiency as a dynamic characteristic and to analyze its changes in order to compare scalability. Increased efficiency will have a positive impact on the program execution quality, and vice versa. The intensity of the changes will describe the algorithm's and its specific implementation's features in general. For example, application efficiency can vary within certain limits, either in sharp steps or in a smooth and slow manner, which corresponds to two different templates in application behavior.

In this case, the approach to comparing the scalability of parallel applications can be reduced to studying how program execution efficiency depends on the set of startup parameters for various applications. By comparing the resulting multidimensional dependencies, it is possible to conclude which case results in better scalability.

One possible implementation of this approach to comparing application scalability is described in [14, 20] — an approach that produces numeric scalability metrics. The approach described analyzes the impact on efficiency from each specific startup parameter and their combinations. The key criteria for the comparison is the intensity and direction in which efficiency changes. Generally, the faster efficiency decreases, the worse scalability of the given application is.

5   An Example of Scalability Analysis According to the Proposed Approach

As an example of the practical application of the universal principles of scalability analysis described above, we can present a study of a Linpack benchmark implementation (HPL).

As part of this research, we used Job Digest reports [21] to obtain system monitoring data. The report data was analyzed for dependencies between various charts produced from system sensors.

When studying the HPL benchmark, two variable startup parameters were used: the number of processes and the matrix size. The number of processors varied in the [8; 128] limits with increments of 8 processes, while the matrix size changed in the [1000; 100,000] range, with increments of 1000. A constant calculation block size of 224 was used.

The study was conducted using the Lomonosov MSU supercomputer [22], on computing nodes with four quad-core Intel Xeon 5570 CPUs, 8 GB RAM each. 8 processes were launched per computing node, one for each CPU core.

Increasing the number of processes in steps of 8 provided a uniform distribution of processes over computing nodes, fully loading all CPU cores at each node.

The results are depicted in Fig. 3 as a surface, for which the X and Y coordinates correspond to the number of processes and the matrix size respectively, with Z indicating the test execution efficiency.

When considering the resulting dependency, it is important to point out the rather high efficiency of the test on the given computing system. For most combinations of the startup parameters, efficiency was close to 80%. However, with a large matrix size and a small number of processes, the efficiency dropped sharply to 0%. This corresponds to the matrix size no longer fitting in the available random-access memory.

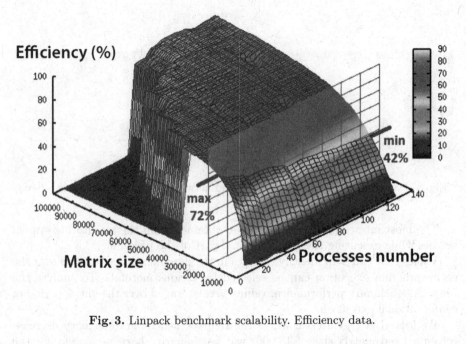

Fig. 3. Linpack benchmark scalability. Efficiency data.

The efficiency also drops smoothly as the number of processes grows given a fixed matrix size. The figure shows a cross-section of the resulting surface with a fixed matrix size of 15,000. The cross-section shows how execution efficiency dropped as the number of processes increased. Efficiency dropped from about 72% to about 42% as the number of processors increased from 4 to 128. A 30% efficiency drop for a matrix of this size is quite substantial. To understand its causes, it is useful to look at system monitoring data for each launch of the program.

Looking at the behavior of other dynamic characteristics, it is obvious that they were not constant during the program execution, and changed over time following a complex pattern. Figure 4 shows an example of Infiniband data transfer

rate (in Megabytes and packets per second) for one run of the Linpack benchmark using a matrix size of 50,000. The biggest challenge when looking at these
series of values is to single out those that will be characteristic for the given
application and will show that the intensity of communication network usage
changes with the startup parameters (the number of processes in this example).

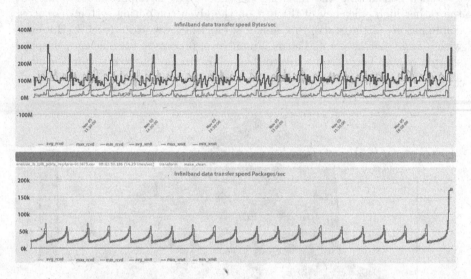

Fig. 4. Data transfer rate over an Infiniband network in MB/sec and packets/sec.

The most interesting values are those obtained from the monitoring system
sensors while executing the *computational* part of the program.

Values that can help identify changes in the dynamic characteristics over the
entire program execution can be selected by various methods. To analyze the
Linpack benchmark performance, values were averaged over the entire period of
computational execution.

We looked at the interval where the Linpack benchmark efficiency decrease
(given a fixed matrix size of 15,000) was particularly sharp — namely for the
number of processes varying from 16 to 48. The benchmark efficiency drops 14%
over this period, which is quite a significant indicator. This allows changes in
the behavior of the hardware's dynamic characteristics to be noted while substantially reducing the amount of data analyzed. At the same time, despite the
efficiency decrease, the overall performance of the program increases by 160%.

To clarify the reasons behind the efficiency decrease, we need to analyze the
averaged system monitoring data. When the benchmark with a fixed matrix
size is executed over the period in question, the number of cache misses per
second goes down steadily (see Fig. 5). This indicates a positive impact from
data decomposition — the data now fits in the cache memory more efficiently.
It is also noteworthy that the number of L3 cache misses (A), which are the
most costly in terms of performance, decreases by almost 15% on average over

all computing nodes. The number of L1 cache misses (B) doesn't decrease as quickly, which can likely be explained by the increase in program performance: the rate of cache misses drops, but the overall number increases as the total number of operations per second grows faster.

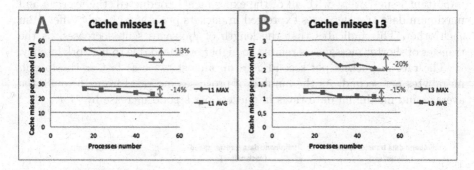

Fig. 5. Changes in the maximum and average (for all nodes) number of L1 (A) and L3 (B) cache misses per second, when executing the Linpack benchmark with a matrix size of 15,000 and a variable number of processes.

Figure 6 shows the changes in RAM access intensity. As the number of processes increases over the given interval, system monitoring data shows that the number of memory read operations remains more or less constant.

The growth in the maximum and average memory write operations can be explained by the increase in performance. Definitely, the 25% increase in the maximum number of memory write operations per second is bound to result in higher overhead costs. However, the numeric values are far from the limits for the used hardware, so it is unlikely they were the main reason for the reduction in the program's overall efficiency.

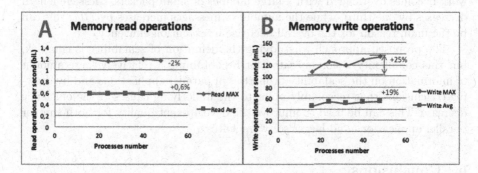

Fig. 6. Changes in the maximum and average (for all nodes) number of memory read (A) and write (B) operations per second, when executing the Linpack benchmark with a matrix size of 15,000 and a variable number of processes.

Figure 7 shows the changes in the maximum and average data transfer rates while executing the benchmark. This data shows that an increasing number of processes leads to a substantial increase in the intensity of data exchange over an Infiniband communication network. The average rate for all nodes in bytes per second goes up by 35%, while the maximum rate increases by 19%. Another important issue is that with all of the experiments conducted, the average and maximum data transfer rates expressed in packets per second barely differ from each other. This indicates that the length of messages sent decreases, as the transfer of shorter messages is related to higher overhead due to network latency.

The rate in packets per second goes up almost twice as fast as the rate in megabytes per second. As the number of processes increases from 16 to 48, the average and maximum data rates in packets per second increase by 77%.

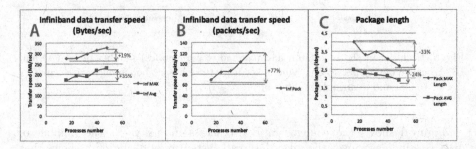

Fig. 7. Changes in the maximum and average (for all nodes) data transmission rate on an Infiniband network in bytes/sec (A) and packets/sec (B) and packet length (C) when executing the Linpack benchmark with a matrix size of 15,000 and a variable number of processes.

The graph showing the dependency on the packet length (C) supports the conclusion that as the number of processes increases, the communication network becomes overloaded with a large number of small packets. Message length decreases by one third, while the number of messages increases by 77%; this can be the main reason for the overall decrease in execution efficiency.

The proposed approach to studying the definition of scalability is complex, but this complexity is compensated for by obtaining a relatively large amount of information on the scalability properties of parallel applications and by drawing conclusions that reasonably point to the underlying causes of the efficiency decrease. This can be used to improve the development quality for both simpler parallel applications and larger software suites.

6   Conclusions

The practice of studying parallel programs requires the introduction of an expanded and generalized definition for the term "scalability". Scalability is a property that determines the nature of a multi-dimensional dependency between a program's dynamic characteristics and its startup parameters. The proposed approach to generalized scalability analysis is based on supercomputing co-design technologies and allows conclusions to be drawn about the program's quality, the reasons for reduced scalability and the most critical factors affecting its execution.

The proposed approach is universal and allows the same mechanism to be used to analyze any parallel applications. It also allows scalability studies by other authors to be generalized based on different definitions of this property. The approach can supplement the existing knowledge about an algorithm's features obtained from various studies. These properties of the proposed approach are particularly important for use in the AlgoWiki Open Encyclopedia of Parallel Algorithmic Features.

The data collected on the generalized scalability of an algorithm and its implementation can be used by parallel application developers to coordinate the hardware and software features within the supercomputing co-design concept. By analyzing the results, it is possible to provide recommendations on changes to be done in the hardware and software platform or to the software implementation of the algorithm, improving the overall efficiency of computing resource usage by parallel applications.

References

1. Voevodin, V., Antonov, A., Dongarra, J.: AlgoWiki: an open encyclopedia of parallel algorithmic features. Supercomputing Front. Innovations **2**(1), 4–18 (2015)
2. Frolov, A.V., Antonov, A.S., Voevodin, VI.V., Teplov, A.M.: One problem solving different methods' comparison according to the criteria of the Algowiki project. In: Proceedings of the 10th Annual International Scientific Conference on Parallel Computing Technologies, Arkhangelsk, Russia, pp. 347–360 (2016)
3. Gddeke, D., et al.: Exploring weak scalability for FEM calculations on a GPU-enhanced cluster. Parallel Comput. **33**(10), 685–699 (2007)
4. Bondi, A.B.: Characteristics of scalability and their impact on performance. In: Proceedings of the 2nd International Workshop on Software and Performance, pp. 195–203. ACM (2000)
5. Patil, R.V., George, B.: Tools and techniques to identify concurrency issues. MSDN Magazine (2008)
6. Levin, M.P.: Parallel Programming Using OpenMP. Binom, Moscow (2008)
7. Ivanov, D.E.: Scalable parallel genetic algorithm for generating the identifying sequences for modern multicore computing systems. Control Syst. Comput. (1), 25–32 (2011)
8. Gergel, V.P., Fursov, V.A.: Lectures on Parallel Computations, Samara (2009)
9. Alabdulkareem, M., Lakshmivarahan, S., Dhall, S.K.: Scalability analysis of large codes using factorial designs. J. Parallel Comput. **27**(9), 1145–1171 (2001)
10. Barnes, B., et al.: A regression-based approach to scalability prediction. In: Proceedings of the 22nd International Conference on Supercomputing, pp. 368–377 (2008)

11. Chi, C.C., Alvarez-Mesa, M., Juurlink, B., Clare, G., Henry, F., Pateux, S., Schierl, T.: Parallel scalability and efficiency of HEVC parallelization approaches. IEEE Trans. Circ. Syst. Video Technol. **22**(12), 1827–1838 (2012)
12. Grama, A.Y., Gupta, A., Kumar, V.: Isoefficiency: measuring the scalability of parallel algorithms and architectures. IEEE Parallel Distrib. Technol. **1**(3), 12–21 (1993)
13. Reed, D., Roth, P.C., Aydt, R., Shields, K., Tavera, L.F., Noe, R.J., Schwartz, B.W.: Scalable performance analysis: the Pablo performance analysis environment. In: Proceedings of the IEEE on Scalable Parallel Libraries Conference, pp. 104–113 (1993)
14. Teplov, A.M.: Analysis of scalability of parallel applications on the basis of super-computer co-design technologies. Ph.D. thesis, Moscow (2015)
15. Adinetz, A.V., Bryzgalov, P.A., Zhumatiy, S.A., Nikitenko, D.A., Stefanov, K.S.: Job Digest–approach to jobs dynamic properties investigation on supercomputer systems. Vestnik UGATU (Sci. J. Ufa State Aviat. Tech. Univ.) **17**(2), 131–188 (2013)
16. Antonov, A.S., Teplov, A.M.: Analysis of the parallel programs scalability based on supercomputer co-design technologies. In: Computer Technologies in Sciences. Methods of Simulations on Supercomputers. Part 2 Proceedings, Tarusa, pp. 18–28 (2015)
17. Antonov, A., Voevodin, V., Voevodin, V., Teplov, A.: A study of the dynamic characteristics of software implementation as an essential part for a universal description of algorithm properties. In: 24th Euromicro International Conference on Parallel, Distributed, and Network-Based Processing Proceedings, pp. 359–363 (2016)
18. Nikitenko, D., Voevodin, V., Zhumatiy, S., Stefanov, K., Teplov, A., Shvets, P., Voevodin, V.: Supercomputer application integral characteristics analysis for the whole queued job collection of large-scale hpc systems. In: Proceedings of the International Scientific Conference on Parallel Computational Technologies (PCT 2016), Chelyabinsk, pp. 20–30 (2016)
19. Antonov, A.S., Teplov, A.M.: Use of system monitoring data to determine factors reducing application scalability. Izvestiya SFedU. Eng. Sci. **12**(161), 90–101 (2014)
20. Teplov, A.M.: An approach to the comparison of parallel program scalability. Numer. Methods Program. **15**(4), 697–711 (2014)
21. Adinets, A.V., Bryzgalov, P.A., Voevodin, V.V., Zhumatii, S.A., Nikitenko, D.A., Stefanov, K.S.: Job digest: an approach to dynamic analysis of job characteristics on supercomputers. Numer. Methods Program. **13**, 160–166 (2012)
22. Sadovnichy, V., Tikhonravov, A., Voevodin, V., Opanasenko, V.: "Lomonosov": Supercomputing at Moscow State University. Contemporary High Performance Computing: From Petascale toward Exascale. Chapman & Hall/CRC Computational Science, Boca Raton (2013)

System Monitoring-Based Holistic Resource Utilization Analysis for Every User of a Large HPC Center

Dmitry Nikitenko[✉], Konstantin Stefanov, Sergey Zhumatiy, Vadim Voevodin, Alexey Teplov, and Pavel Shvets

Research Computing Center of Moscow State University, Moscow, Russia
{dan,cstef,serg,vadim}@parallel.ru, alex-teplov@yandex.ru,
pavel.shvets.srcc@gmail.com

Abstract. The problem of effective resource utilization is very challenging nowadays, especially for HPC centers running top-level supercomputing facilities with high energy consumption and significant number of workgroups. The weakness of many system monitoring based approaches to efficiency study is the basic orientation on professionals and analysis of specific jobs with low availability for regular users. The proposed all-round performance analysis approach, covering single application performance, project-level and overall system resource utilization based on system monitoring data that promises to be an effective and low cost technique aimed at all types of HPC center users. Every user of HPC center can access details on any of his executed jobs to better understand application behavior and sequences of job runs including scalability study, helping in turn to perform appropriate optimizations and implement co-design techniques. Taking into consideration all levels (user, project manager, administrator), the approach aids to improve output of HPC centers.

Keywords: Performance monitoring · Performance analysis tools · Dynamic job characteristics · Integral job characteristics · Job analysis · Job sequence analysis · Job queue analysis · Scalability study · HPC center efficiency

1 Introduction

Supercomputer systems have always been different from lower-performance computers in virtually all aspects: scale, number and variety of components, complexity of architecture, power consumption, higher requirements for general infrastructure etc. Because of this, much deeper understanding of the dynamics of everything that occurs around a high-performance computing system is required as early as at the system development stage. Many hardware system components already have built-in sensors which can be read in one way or another. Initially most of those sensors were implemented by the manufacturers for individual component debugging purposes. However, the user-accessible portion of the characteristics can be successfully used to evaluate not only the performance of the component itself, but also the behavior of the entire hardware and software suite under specific conditions. In addition, a lot of useful information about the current application execution status can be obtained from the operating system. As

© Springer International Publishing AG 2016
J. Carretero et al. (Eds.): ICA3PP 2016 Workshops, LNCS 10049, pp. 305–318, 2016.
DOI: 10.1007/978-3-319-49956-7_24

a result, a relatively large set consisting of dozens of characteristics describing the current status of hardware and software components (CPU, network interfaces, input/output systems, operating system etc.) is available for each node. Use of such data collected by means of a monitoring system allows generating a computer system activity profile and understanding what was going on with each component as well as the entire system or a certain set of nodes [1].

General approaches to application and computing system performance analysis based on system monitoring data differ in a number of key aspects: association with a certain monitoring system or data storage method, number and configuration of analyzed characteristics, their collection frequency, and analytical capabilities. Another important peculiarity of monitoring systems is the orientation on a certain type of user. For example, as a rule, one can configure the system to collect data from a specified set of nodes or to collect data regarding an exact job run. As soon as node number and number of jobs scale, implementation difficulties grow, leading to more and more highly-specialized analysis.

In this article we propose an approach based on system monitoring that provides means for performance analysis for most typical user roles: regular user, project manager and system administrator. The approach allows every regular user getting dynamic and integral characteristics of any of his jobs that were run. On the next level, project managers and system administrators have access to a wider range of jobs according to their permissions.

2   Background and Related Work

A reasonable trade-off must be made between the two key issues: what data needs to be stored in the database, and when should data be analyzed? The most of the challenges can be overcome by the following principles:

- on-the-fly analysis – all relevant information is extracted from the monitoring data before it's stored in the database;
- on-site analysis – monitoring data must be processed where it is obtained;
- dynamic reconfiguration of monitoring systems – the monitoring system must be capable of adjusting its configuration during the course of its work, depending on the load on the supercomputer and the specific analysis objectives.

A prototype monitoring system based on these principles is currently being tested at our supercomputing center [2]. The majority of existing monitoring systems process no data at the source computing nodes [3–9]. Usually this approach is explained by the need to reduce the agent's impact on the applications executed at this computing node. But nowadays one should remember that data movement is much and much more expensive than compute operations and even noticeable overhead on the nodes can be reasonable if we get rid of excessive data movement. Another option to reduce the data flow from monitoring system is to cut the sensor set and data polling frequency for generation of profiles that represent general application behavior. The simplest set designed for dynamics analysis of an application can be as short as: CPU_user, Load Average, Flop/s, Interconnect and I/O activity measured in packets and bytes per second, number of cache misses and memory access operations [10]. Such a set can be extended to match used SW/HW capability and analysis requirements. Many approaches to monitoring job performance have been proposed [11–18]. Their common feature is that they are intended for monitoring the performance of specific jobs. A significant portion of these systems [11–15, 18] start agents at the respective computing nodes whenever a job is launched. Data from the agents are collected into a database then reviewed after the job is completed. Some systems, such as [16, 17], constantly collect and save data from computing nodes. Data analysis is also performed by selecting part of the data related to a specific job. This approach is quite reasonable when analyzing individual jobs. However, if we want to analyze the entire flow of jobs being executed by the supercomputer at any given moment, this approach would result in too much overhead.

Obviously, highly detailed analysis of monitoring data is only required for certain specific jobs. This means that data for most jobs will be written to the database only once and read only once to calculate the respective integrated metrics which characterize the application in general. However, this mode of operation results in a strong degradation of the data storage system performance, or in unreasonable expense.

An interesting performance analysis toolkit based on system monitoring data was developed recently. The HOPSA (HOlistic Performance System Analysis) suite [19] was created as a result of a joint Russian – European project. The project aimed to create an integrated application performance analysis environment that would combine research on the system monitoring data analysis level and traditional in-depth analysis methods. The main idea was to provide information on dynamic characteristics of the running jobs over standard protocols based on continuous collection of system monitoring data. The system allowed accessing the data both in the raw data flow mode and upon completion of work through generation of special queries. It is important to note that the system was originally designed for flexible setup. In particular, provisions were made for use of a wide range of potential data sources, such as system monitoring tools (Ganglia, Clustrx, etc.), data storage systems (specialized Mongo and Cassandra databases or OTF2 [20] trace files), visualization tools (Google Charts, High Charts) and other modules. Based on the initial system monitoring data analysis, options for a more detailed research into the problem became available using traditional instrumentation and profiling tools (Scalasca, Vampir, ThreadSpotter, Paraver etc.) [21]. In addition to achievement of the project objectives, successful implementation of the project provided valuable insight into the capabilities and prospects of approaches that utilize system monitoring data. The achieved results inspired authors to develop and deploy a sufficiently extended comprehensive technique based on system monitoring data analysis.

3   The Proposed Approach Principles

The main goal of our approach is to provide easy and useful tool aimed at performance and resource utilization analysis based on system monitoring data for every job and for every user of HPC center starting from a regular user up to the level of system administrator or manager, so the following design principles were placed in command.

Key design feature - availability of sufficient information on every application run.

(1) General information on every finished job must be available, including data from resource manager and average rate of resource utilization (here and elsewhere integral job characteristics) obtained from the monitoring system (Fig. 1).

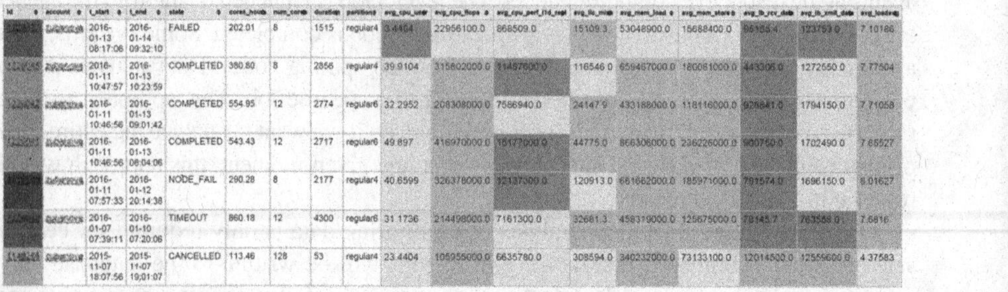

Fig. 1. Example of job list for a specific user

(2) The used monitoring system sensor set, polling frequency and saved data coarsening must be configured in a way to grant availability of job profiles based on dynamic characteristics for all finished jobs right after execution with no resource-intensive post mortem operations.

(3) There must be means for job marking and categorization based on certain job characteristics-based criteria or conjunction of such criteria in manual or automatic modes.

(4) Job information access restrictions must meet workflow regulations of certain HPC center, supporting various scopes of analysis: user (a project member), project manager, and administrator.

5) Portability and scalability with flexible configuration, supporting diverse data sources with no integration with system software. Open source components preferred.

3.1 General Information on Jobs

General information on jobs includes data that is obtained directly after job finishes, whether successfully or not. It includes such basic details like: id and owner; duration: submit, start and finish time; status (completed, canceled, failed, etc.) and partition; number of allocated cores; startup command line options, etc.

This type of info can be obtained from the resource manager directly or its log files as soon as the job ends. It doesn't depend on availability of monitoring system.

3.2 Average Rate of Resource Utilization

This group of data consists of averages, calculated on the base of dynamic characteristics obtained from the monitoring system. The set of metrics can be as wide as peculiarities of exact installation allow. If a monitoring system like DiMMon [2] is used, it becomes possible it calculate these types of values on-the-fly. Nevertheless, if there's no such monitoring system or there's a need for extending the list of averages with some other calculated values that require processing of whole system monitoring data related to the job with methods that require post-mortem analysis, of course, it is possible to enrich the set easily. We keep to the point that it is reasonable to use only those metrics that can be processed on-the-fly. If one needs post-mortem analysis methods, it might be reasonable to apply these methods to a certain set or sequence of jobs.

At present we use a set of averages and medians corresponding to the key set of dynamic characteristics described above. Some of dynamic characteristics are useful for fine analysis, but are not so good for study of their averages. So the averages set is a bit reduced, including now the following averages of: CPU_user, Flops, L1 cache replacement rate, LLC miss rate, memory load and store rate, interconnect sent/received data and packets, load average and for systems with HDDs, local storage usage intensity for reads and writes.

It's quite useful to highlight average values especially for similar jobs, e.g. jobs of a certain user, or consequent runs of same application with different options. It can be also a good option to specify some resource utilization rates as symptoms of anomalous node or system behavior. This can be managed by resilience systems [22].

3.3   Certain Job Analysis: Job Digests and Results of External Analyzers

Once any job was analyzed by an external analyzer, it's quite reasonable to keep the results or reports around. By default we find useful to provide links to Job Digest [23] reports built on coarse-grained system monitoring data - we use 5 min granularity at present for large jobs. The reports still represent major application behavior at this level of averaging.

At the same time, when the detailed Job Digest report is needed, it can be specified to the monitoring system or storing aggregator and the related collected data will be available for fine analysis. There's no need to keep fine-grained data for all the jobs.

3.4   Tags and Comments

The more the number of executed jobs is the more reasonable becomes analysis of the patterns and regularity. It can be done for a whole system, for a partition, for a project, for a software package, for a single user, or for a combination of the above. The processing of a number of Job Digests or just general info of multiple jobs can be done in different ways: something can be seen in on-the-fly mode, something requires post-mortem methods, and some analysis results are obtained manually.

The set of jobs' peculiarities that seem to be interesting and useful can't be fixed, we must be able to extend it whether it is done because of metrics list extension, because of new idea of performance degradation symptom, or just because of new and previously unseen type of unusual application behavior.

This drove us to implementation of different types of categories and tags as an extension for general application run info. The tags correspond to various clusters of jobs based on a number of criteria. For example, there are categories based on such application details on memory usage like ratio of total memory operations to L1 cache misses or ratio of L1 misses to L3 misses and so on.

It becomes possible to easily find intersections of such clusters, having in result a set of jobs that possess desired characteristics at the same time [24]. Besides tags, comments and analysis reports to every job run can be added. Important thing is that it allows not only to study a number of similar jobs, but to suggest methods of optimization to a number of similar applications if a solution is found for a single one.

3.5 Target User Groups

At present three target user groups are defined: regular users (project members), project managers and administrators. This follows from the logic of general organization of workflow in our HPC center. The resources (CPU hours, disk space, etc.) are granted for a certain project. Every project has a project manager, who is responsible for regular user activity in terms of the project and can ask administrator to adjust quotas for any project participant. Project members correspond to a UNIX group, every project member - to a single account. If a researcher participates in two different projects, he uses two different accounts, the access details for which are synchronized by user management system [25, 26]. It's quite reasonable to use authorization methods of such systems if available.

Regular users have access to the details of all jobs that were run under his accounts. This allows to focus on results of own work. As a rule users know the specifics of their applications, and unusual program behavior would most likely be recognized by the author. This means that this level of access is aimed at rising efficiency of specific user applications: user can notice low resource usage efficiency, crashed jobs, wasted CPU hours having access at the same time to detailed information for any of own jobs. At the same time the jobs run by the project co-members are available only to the project manager by default but can be made visible for all project members by request.

Project manager can access info on own jobs like a regular user, but at the same time he is given the permissions to see all the jobs of the supervised project. At this point project supervisor gains all means for observing the distribution of resource usage by project members having all necessary details on every job run. It allows making appropriate decisions regarding the project: resource distribution among project members, revealing low-efficient jobs that waste valuable resources, plan further requests for resources, project staff, optimization procedures, etc.

The level of administrator or system manager allows seeing the whole scope of jobs and their details. The main benefits for administrators are revealing users and projects with low-efficient jobs, analysis of overall queue of jobs for better planning of system tuning and adjusting of policies. System administrators can get rich knowledge on how do real applications use HPC resources. One can discover really resource-demanding applications or clusters of applications that do not exploit some particular capabilities or just cannot be run effectively on specific partitions, exact nodes, architecture, or software environment. Following co-design techniques such information can be used to rearrange the provision of resources to better fit the needs of applications or to recommend platform-specific optimizations for such user application. This information can be also of a value when an upgrade or a new HPC system is being planned.

4 Implementation Technologies Brief

The following software base is involved now:

- supported resource managers: Slurm [27], Cleo [28];
- tested monitoring systems: Ganglia, Collectd, tuned Clustrx [29] (in production mode), DiMMon [2] (in test mode, but most promising);
- data storage for coarsened system monitoring data and job info: PostgreSQL;
- coarsening system monitoring data before saving to DB: Python scripts;
- job info requests: JavaScript & jQuery (development purpose) and proprietary Ruby-on-Rails plug-in for user management systems with a standalone option (used in test mode);
- user management system with means of authentication and authorization: Octoshell [25].

For a 2.1 PFlops system with about 5K nodes the managed data is:

- metrics saved: 20+ , 5 min granularity;
- number of jobs: about a thousand per day;
- disk space used: about 1 Gbyte per day.

We kept in mind an idea of building a tool that might be deployed at any supercomputer center with minimal efforts. The basic scheme is presented at Fig. 2.

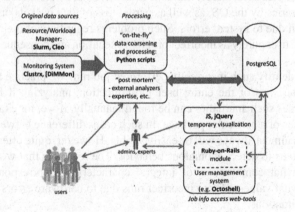

Fig. 2. General workflow scheme

5   Using of Integral Job Characteristics in Practice

When analyzing the performance of parallel applications it is very useful to have infor-mation on the application behavior and its overall resource utilization. The former can be based on system monitoring data and the latter on integral job characteristics built as averages and medians of corresponding dynamical characteristics. In this section we give a few typical use cases overview of how it is used in real everyday practice of our HPC Center.

5.1   Analysis Job Collections Searching for Anomalous Application Behavior

Many users of high-performance computer systems run applications that use standard models, sets of libraries, packages, and ready-to-use solvers. In these cases a typical proportion of required resources amount and the elapsed machine time usually can be found. Such a proportion is often considered as typical or even optimal, and users prac-tice the same startup program configuration to keep to it. The applications often use the same type of calculations organized in an iterative process. The main quality measure for this type of users is the correct execution and the correctness of the obtained results.

It is quite easy to distinguish the typical start-up in these cases because the same code is usually run, with the typical calculation sets by iterations. Therefore the analysis of dynamic characteristics shows similar patterns. Integral characteristics of these job runs also vary within a small deviation.

However there is the chance for application run to turn incorrect for some reason. This can happen either due to a user mistake, a problem of system software or a hardware problem. The user can incorrectly choose algorithm parameters, specify job start config-uration, the input data files, etc. At the same time there can be met access restrictions to the required libraries by the OS, as well as partial loss of data packets or node unavail-ability and so on due to system errors. Such problems regardless of their nature can be explained by the user purely as incorrect program execution and consequently unreliable obtained results.

In order to identify such incorrectly performed job runs we practice analysis of the integral characteristics of the entire user job collection, analyzing it for anomalous values. Sometimes such anomalies can be found manually, if we, for example, analyze multiple launches of a particular package. In such cases difference between normal and anomalous runs almost always will be easily visible. However, quite often manual anal-ysis cannot help us to detect anomalous behavior. The reason is that we need to know the criteria – what combination of integral characteristics corresponds to normal behavior, and what values refer to incorrect runs due to hardware errors or other types of emergency situations.

To solve this problem we are developing a software tool for supercomputer job flow analysis based on machine learning methods [30]. For classification purposes we currently use Random Forest method [31] as it shows the best accuracy in our case.

The classifier is trained on real jobs launched on Lomonosov supercomputer. Training set consists of 300 jobs that were manually classified as one of three classes – normal, anomalous or suspicious. Belonging to suspicious class means that we are not sure that this job is definitely anomalous, but it's surely worth analyzing it more accurately, using, for example, Job Digest report.

The input data for our classification method is integral characteristics aggregated from monitoring data. Each job is described using~20 features – median and oscillation ratio (maximum minus minimum divided by average) for each dynamic characteristic collected on Lomonosov supercomputer. In this case a job is called anomalous if the value of one or a combination of features noticeably differs of common values for most jobs. It should be noted that anomaly criteria will differ for different jobs flows, which means that our classifier should be retrained each time when used on a new supercomputer.

Currently our proposed method is being tested in the Supercomputing center of the Moscow State University. For the month our classifier detected~80 real anomalous jobs (we analyzed only jobs running for more than 1 h and not in test partitions). Next step

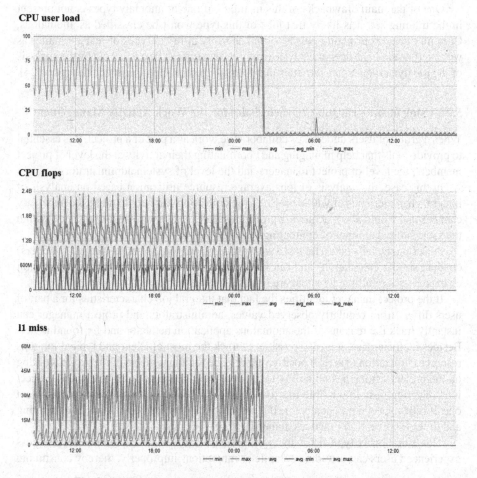

Fig. 3. Job Digest report: timeline graphs of dynamic characteristics.

we are currently working on – notify users about their running anomalous jobs, so they can quickly fix it.

The example of an anomalous job detected using our classification method is shown on Fig. 3 – a part of Job Digest report with timeline graphs of dynamic characteristics changing during job run. In this figure three characteristics are shown – CPU load, number of flops and number of misses to L1 cache per second. All other dynamic characteristics (memory or network usage, system load, etc.) are very similar.

These Job Digest graphs clearly show that this job is anomalous – nearly half of the time there were no computations or any other activity. But Job Digest report is usually used only when is it already known that something is wrong with a job. And in this case most of the time some intensive work was performed, which means that integral characteristics will have common values and won't arouse any suspicion during manual analysis. But such anomalous jobs have some distinctive combination of feature values. And since these jobs are present in the training set, our classifier has learned how to distinguish them, so it manage to automatically classify this job as definitely anomalous.

One of the main drawbacks of this method – if one of anomaly types is not present in the training set, it is likely that jobs of this type won't be classified as anomalous. Currently one of our main goals is to find as many different types of real anomalies as we can. If needed, the deeper analysis of any certain run can be carried out by the analysis of the job dynamical characteristics that form a job profile on resource utilization [24].

5.2 Using of Integral Job Characteristics for the Work Activity Management

When a group of users undertakes collaborative work as a part of a project, it is essential to provide tools that help managing and coordinating their activity at the level of project members, the level of project managers and the level of system administrators.

In this case, the analysis of jobs average resource utilization based on analysis of integral characteristics of whole project's job collection can help to make the necessary changes that would allow achieving project results faster or with better precision within the same limited amount of computing resources.

For example, let's take a look at a workgroup where some of users (project members) conduct similar calculations and run similar jobs and it is possible to analyze integral characteristics of all the jobs that are run as a part of the project.

If the project manager identifies the fact that integral job characteristics for a part of users differs from regularly observed values, administrators and project manager can instantly track the reasons of the anomalous application behavior and fix found issues. Besides inefficiencies, it is also possible to track the most efficient and typical job runs resources utilization to spread positive experience for all members of the group working on the project. If one has no ability to observe the characteristics of the whole project job collection, it is impossible to estimate any single run as an efficient or inefficient one. It is of a special practical value if a project has a very limited amount of computing and time resources and practices numerous short job runs.

This situation is typical for the workgroups with diverse experience levels. Less experienced users can use some compile or run options improperly, thereby consuming given resources less effectively. Also it happens frequently for geographically distributed research teams, conducting joint research.

Monitoring of the integral job characteristics for a certain project allows its project manager having clear understanding of resource utilization balance in the workgroup. This serves as a good base for further possible quota rearrangement, workload redistribution, and other changes, that would increase efficient outcome of the project and consequently increase output of an HPC center as a whole.

5.3   Enhancing Scalability of User Applications

The last, but definitely not the least example of a target is a challenging scalability topic. Parallel applications scalability analysis is an extremely resource-demanding task and often requires a large number of job runs and further analysis of large arrays of data collected on executed programs' characteristics.

The set of analyzed characteristics of the program includes such factors as job duration, performance, efficiency and other characteristics regarding the utilization of various resources and computing nodes components.

The majority of users create their applications trying to achieve minimum job duration for solving the problem and therefore reaching high performance of a computer system. This is sensible only if the allocation of computing resources is available at no cost and in any desired quantity. If so, scalability analysis focuses on search for such start configuration that would require minimum time for the solution of the problem with no care for any resource utilization rate. For example, when analyzing the scalability of Linpack benchmark with two parameters (size of the matrix and the number of used cores) a significant growth of the performance and a strong decrease in the efficiency in the same area can be observed (Fig. 3).

In the real world computing resources are limited and rarely free, CPU time and all other resources must be paid for and/or given an account of their utilization. The criteria for optimization and optimal program startup configuration becomes also dependable on many factors that represent computing cost: utilized CPU hours, number of nodes engaged, job duration, storage usage, etc. So the ability to provide scalability analysis and search for reasons of scalability decrease is essential when optimizing application performance.

Integral job characteristics appear to be an extremely informative source of data on program scalability. Using this source, one can find a correlation of values in changes of certain resource utilization characteristics (CPU, memory access and cache misses, interconnect, etc.) and generalized indicators of the overall performance, efficiency and execution time. Thus, comparing the obtained values of the certain characteristics and its general indicators makes possible to draw conclusions about the reasons for the overall efficiency degradation of the parallel program. The integral characteristics for a job collection (Fig. 1) can be exported and used to built and analyze dependencies of these integral characteristics from any startup parameters. For every integral characteristic one can perform stand alone analysis, or search for correlations between some of them (Fig. 4). After analyzing the shown correlations between the integral characteristics for this experiment series, one can conclude that the main reason for the efficiency degradation is increasing InfiniBand activity - the increase in the number of transmitted packets per second at a disproportionately low growth of transmitted amount of data per second. This indicates that the network is transmitting large number of packets of short length. And that's why the overall efficiency of communication is significantly reduced driving to overall efficiency degradation.

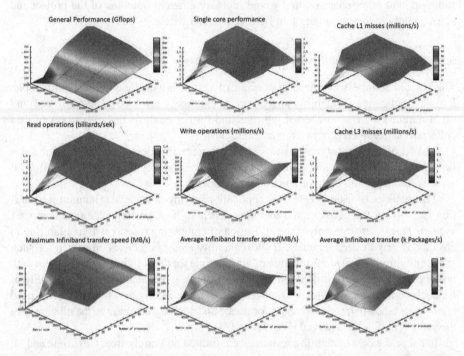

Fig. 4. Scalability of Linpack benchmark. Startup parameters: size of the matrix and the number of processes; characteristics: various resource utilization integral job characteristics available for all executed jobs.

Carrying out this type of analysis of integral characteristics is challenging because the data collection for a large series of experiments should be provided for a large number of characteristics and all relevant dependencies should be performed.

However, the result of such an analysis allows estimating the contribution of the certain components of a computer system in the overall performance of the application, its scalability and most critical resources for a certain application.

6   Conclusion and Acknowledgments

The main advantage of the proposed approach is in covering the whole scope of jobs that were run and providing various methods of giving access to this data to every user of supercomputing center according to user status and permissions.

At present the basic infrastructure of the approach is already implemented, arousing great interest among users that were invited for testing purposes. Current basic functionality already provides tons of valuable data for every user, but we have a wide range of enhancements that just are to be done in close future.

First, it's a finalizing development of Ruby-On-Rails module instead of JavaScript-controlled web tool. This is critical both for performance and security reasons.

Second, but very important issue is interactive tools for general job info analysis. Methods of selecting and grouping various jobs, visualization of results (histograms, charts, etc.), basic methods of prediction of user activity and resource utilization for regular users and project supervisors. This functionality will be available with moving to Ruby-On-Rails as well as availability to regular users.

This work was funded in part by the Russian Found for Basic Research, grants №16-07-01003A, № 16-07-01121, Russian Presidential study grant (SP-1981.2016.5) and by the Ministry of Education and Science of the Russian Federation, Agreement No. 14.607.21.0006 (unique identifier RFMEFI60714X0006).

References

1. Voevodin, V., Stefanov, K.: Supercomputers at exascale: bigdata and extreme computing of the total monitoring. In: BDEC Workshop, Barcelona, 29-30 January (2015)
2. Stefanov, K., Voevodin, V.: Distributed modular monitoring (DiMMon) approach to supercomputer monitoring. In: Proceedings of the 2015 IEEE International Conference on Cluster Computing, pp. 502–503. IEEE (2015)
3. Zenoss. http://www.zenoss.org
4. Zabbix. http://www.zabbix.com
5. Cacti®. http://www.cacti.net
6. Massie, M.L., et al.: The ganglia distributed monitoring system: design, implementation, and experience. Parallel Comput. 30(7), 817–840 (2004)
7. The OpenNMS project. http://www.opennms.org
8. Nagios - the industry standard in IT infrastructure monitoring. http://www.nagios.org
9. Collectd – The system statistics collection daemon. https://collectd.org
10. Nikitenko, D.: Complex approach to performance analysis of supercomputer systems based on system monitoring data. In: Numerical Methods and Programming vol. 15, pp. 85–97 (2014)
11. Gunter, D., Tierney, B., Jackson, K., Lee, J., Stoufer, M.: Dynamic monitoring of high-performance distributed applications. In: Proceedings 11th IEEE International Symposium on High Performance Distributed Computing, pp. 163–170 (2002)
12. Mellor-Crummey, J., Fowler, R.J., Marin, G., Tallent, N.: HPCVIEW: a tool for top-down analysis of node performance. J. Supercomput. 23(1), 81–104 (2002)
13. Jagode, H., Dongarra, J., Alam, S., Vetter, J., Spear, W., Malony, A.D.: A holistic approach for performance measurement and analysis for petascale applications. In: Allen, G., Nabrzyski, J., Seidel, E., van Albada, G.D., Dongarra, J., Sloot, P.M. (eds.) ICCS 2009, Part II. LNCS, vol. 5545, pp. 686–695. Springer, Heidelberg (2009)
14. Adhianto, L., Banerjee, S., Fagan, M., Krentel, M., Marin, G., Mellor-Crummey, J., Tallent, N.R.: HPCTOOLKIT: tools for performance analysis of optimized parallel programs. Concurrency Comput. Pract. Exp. 22(6), 685–701 (2010)

15. Eisenhauer, G., Kraemer, E., Schwan, K., Stasko, J., Vetter, J., Mallavarupu, N.: Falcon: online monitoring and steering of large-scale parallel programs. In: Proceedings of the Fifth Symposium on the Frontiers of Massively Parallel Computation, pp. 422–429 (1995)

16. Kluge, M., Hackenberg, D., Nagel, W.E.: Collecting distributed performance data with dataheap: generating and exploiting a holistic system view. Procedia Comput. Sci. **9**, 1969–1978 (2012)

17. Mooney, R., Schmidt, K.P., Studham, R.S.: NWPerf: a system wide performance monitoring tool for large Linux clusters. In: 2004 IEEE International Conference on Cluster Computing (IEEE Cat. No. 04EX935), pp. 379–389 (2004)

18. Ries, B., et al.: The paragon performance monitoring environment. In: Supercomputing 1993, Proceedings, pp. 850–859 (1993)

19. Joint RF-EU HOPSA Project. http://www.vi-hps.org/projects/hopsa/overview

20. Open Trace Format (OTF2). https://silc.zih.tu-dresden.de/otf2-current/html

21. Mohr, B., Hagersten, E., Giménez, J., Knüpfer, A., Nikitenko, D., Nilsson, M., Servat, H., Shah, A., Voevodin, V., Winkler, F., Wolf, F., Zhukov, I.: The HOPSA workflow and tools. In: Proceedings of the 6th International Parallel Tools Workshop, Stuttgart, September 2012

22. Antonov, A., Nikitenko, D., Shvets, P., Sobolev, S., Stefanov, K., Voevodin, V., Voevodin, V., Zhumatiy, S.: An approach for ensuring reliable functioning of a supercomputer based on a formal model. In: Wyrzykowski, R., Deelman, E., Dongarra, J., Karczewski, K., Kitowski, J., Wiatr, K. (eds.) PPAM 2015. LNCS, vol. 9573, pp. 12–22. Springer, Heidelberg (2016). doi:10.1007/978-3-319-32149-3_2

23. Adinets, A., Bryzgalov, P., Nikitenko, D., Stefanov, K., Voevodin, V., Zhumatiy, S.: Job digest: an approach to dynamic analysis of job characteristics on supercomputers. In: Numerical Methods and Programming: Advanced Computing, vol. 13. Sect. 2, pp. 160–166 (2012)

24. Nikitenko, D., Voevodin, V., Zhumatiy, S., Stefanov, K., Teplov, A., Shvets, P., Voevodin, V.: Supercomputer application integral characteristics analysis for the whole queued job collection of large-scale HPC systems. In: Parallel Computational Technologies (PCT 2016): Proceedings of the International Scientific Conference. Chelyabinsk, Publishing of the South Ural State University, pp. 20–30 (2016)

25. Nikitenko, D., Voevodin, V., Zhumatiy, S.: Octoshell: large supercomputer complex administration system. In: proceedings of Russian Supercomputing Days International Conference, Moscow, Russia, 28-29 September 2015, Proceedings, CEUR Workshop Proceedings, vol. 1482, pp. 69–83 (2015)

26. Nikitenko, D., et al.: Resolving frontier problems of mastering large-scale supercomputer complexes. In: Proceedings of the ACM International Conference on Computing Frontiers (CF 2016), pp. 349–352. ACM, New York (2016)

27. Slurm Workload Manager. http://slurm.schedmd.com

28. Cleo cluster batch system. http://sourceforge.net/projects/cleo-bs

29. Clustrx. http://t-platforms.ru/products/software/clustrxproductfamily/clustrxwatch.html

30. Voevodin, V., Voevodin, V., Shaikhislamov, D., Nikitenko, D.: Data mining method for anomaly detection in the supercomputer task flow. In: proceedings of Numerical Computations: Theory and Algorithms, The 2nd International Conference and Summer School, 20-24 June 2016, Pizzo calabro, Italy (2016)

31. Description of random forest algorithm and its realization. http://scikit-learn.org/stable/modules/ensemble.html#random-forests

Co-design of a Particle-in-Cell Plasma Simulation Code for Intel Xeon Phi: A First Look at Knights Landing

Igor Surmin[1], Sergey Bastrakov[1], Zakhar Matveev[2], Evgeny Efimenko[1,3], Arkady Gonoskov[1,3,4], and Iosif Meyerov[1(✉)]

[1] Lobachevsky State University of Nizhni Novgorod, Nizhni Novgorod, Russia
meerov@vmk.unn.ru
[2] Intel Corporation, Nizhni Novgorod, Russia
[3] Institute of Applied Physics of the Russian Academy of Sciences, Nizhni Novgorod, Russia
[4] Chalmers University of Technology, Gothenburg, Sweden

Abstract. Three dimensional particle-in-cell laser-plasma simulation is an important area of computational physics. Solving state-of-the-art problems requires large-scale simulation on a supercomputer using specialized codes. A growing demand in computational resources inspires research in improving efficiency and co-design for supercomputers based on many-core architectures. This paper presents first performance results of the particle-in-cell plasma simulation code PICADOR on the recently introduced Knights Landing generation of Intel Xeon Phi. A straightforward rebuilding of the code yields a 2.43 x speedup compared to the previous Knights Corner generation. Further code optimization results in an additional 1.89 x speedup. The optimization performed is beneficial not only for Knights Landing, but also for high-end CPUs and Knights Corner. The optimized version achieves 100 GFLOPS double precision performance on a Knights Landing device with the speedups of 2.35 x compared to a 14-core Haswell CPU and 3.47 x compared to a 61-core Knights Corner Xeon Phi.

1 Introduction

The first supercomputer to pass the 100 PFLOPS mark (according to the TOP500 list, https://www.top500.org/) opens a new stage in the road to exascale systems. Such systems are expected to solve important problems of computational science, such as climate modeling, improving efficiency of energy sources, human brain simulation at neural level, and others. Making progress in assembling and efficient utilization of large supercomputers requires an interdisciplinary collaboration of software developers with engineers, mathematicians, physicists, chemists, and experts in other areas. The interdisciplinary principle is an

This study was supported by the RFBR, project No. 15-37-21015. I. Surmin, S. Bastrakov and I. Meyerov are grateful to Intel Corporation for access to the system used for performing computational experiments presented in this paper.

© Springer International Publishing AG 2016
J. Carretero et al. (Eds.): ICA3PP 2016 Workshops, LNCS 10049, pp. 319–329, 2016.
DOI: 10.1007/978-3-319-49956-7_25

important part of co-design in supercomputing. Currently, a significant share of supercomputers is based on many-core architectures, most notably GPUs and, more recently, Intel Xeon Phi. Thus, it is important to co-design codes for such architectures.

In June 2016, during the ISC High Performance, the first performance results of the new Intel Xeon Phi of Knights Landing (KNL) generation for solving several problems have been presented [1,2]. New Xeon Phi devices are many-core CPUs with 60+ cores and 4 hardware threads per core, 512-bit SIMD, and 16 GB high-bandwidth MCDRAM. Compared to the previous Knights Corner (KNC) generation, the new Xeon Phi devices not only bring about 3 x improvement in the single-core performance, but also eliminate the need for a PCI Express connection, which might have been an issue for some applications on KNC coprocessors. Taking into account binary compatibility of the code between regular and KNL-generation CPUs, it is interesting to research performance of existing parallel codes on KNL as well as develop approaches to code optimization for KNL.

The studies presented in this paper are motivated with growing needs for carrying out large-scale 3D particle-in-cell simulations in several research directions of plasma physics. Performing such simulations is possible on supercomputers with specialized parallel codes. The particle-in-cell method inherently allows massively parallel processing and thus can be efficiently implemented for supercomputers. The growth of computational power accompanied with multi-level parallelization and optimization leads to gradual extension of capabilities of particle-in-cell codes, such as [3–7], giving access to fascinating studies that have been previously impossible.

Techniques of implementation and optimization of particle-in-cell codes for many-core architectures are rather well studied. There are several highly efficient implementations of the particle-in-cell method for GPUs, including [7–10]. Intel Xeon Phi is a newer platform with some specific features. Our previous work [11,12] was among the first attempts of implementation of the method for Xeon Phi of KNC generation, along with another study [13]. The previous work showed that the KNC generation of Xeon Phi allows relatively easy porting of existing parallel codes with reasonable performance, but obtaining significant speedups over multi-core CPUs could require some additional work, most importantly in terms of vectorization.

This paper presents the first performance results of PICADOR particle-in-cell laser-plasma simulation code [12,14] on Intel KNL. The code is developed by an interdisciplinary group of physicists, mathematicians, and software developers. The main contribution of this paper is performance evaluation of a plasma simulation code on high-end CPUs and Xeon Phi of KNC and KNL generations. We measure performance for a baseline, previously optimized, version of the code and show results of applying further optimization steps on CPUs and Xeon Phi.

The paper is organized as follows. Section 2 briefly describes the particle-in-cell method for laser-plasma simulation. Section 3 gives performance results for the baseline version of the code without additional modification on KNL. Section 4 presents results of optimization of the code with some KNL-specific methods and some methods that yield benefit on other platforms as well. Section 5 concludes the paper.

2 Particle-in-Cell Method Overview

The progress in utilization of supercomputers for particle-in-cell plasma simulation is of a special interest in the context of the rapid advancement of technologies of producing high-intensity laser pulses. Nowadays, high-intensity laser systems are reaching unprecedented densities of electromagnetic energy among all controllable sources available in a laboratory. Interaction of such laser pulses with various targets provides a possibility to access extreme conditions and new regimes that open up new ways towards solving important technological problems and carrying out fundamental studies, ranging from compact sources for hadron therapy to probing nonlinear properties of vacuum. Particle-in-cell simulations are known to play a key role in a wide range of related studies, because the methodology of the particle-in-cell method allows natural account for various phenomena, from target ionization at low intensities to the processes due to quantum electrodynamics at ultra-high intensities [15].

However, the basic stages of plasma simulation with the particle-in-cell method typically remain the most computationally demanding and challenging for optimization. The particle-in-cell method [16–18] implies representing real particles of plasma with a smaller number of so-called macro-particles. Just as for real particles, the dynamics of macro-particles is governed by the relativistic equations of motion. For the sake of shortness, hereafter we write particles instead of macro-particles.

Apart from the motion under the effect of external electromagnetic fields, the particles interact with each other through the self-generated electromagnetic field, which evolves according to the Maxwell's equations. In such a way, the electromagnetic field is affected by the particles through the current density, while the particles experience the Lorentz force due to the electromagnetic field. Both electromagnetic field and current density are defined on a discreet grid. Thus, the field is interpolated to the position of particles, while the contribution of each particle to the current density is distributed among the nearest grid nodes. The core of the particle-in-cell method consists of the following stages [18]: numerical integration of Maxwell's equations, field interpolation, solving particles' equations of motion, and computing the current density created by the particles. For the rest of the paper we refer to field interpolation and solving equations of motion together as particle push, computation of current density as current deposition.

From a computational point of view, the procedures of field interpolation and current deposition concern accessing and changing two differently arranged sets of data, for the particles and for the electromagnetic field and current density values at the grid nodes. Arranging efficient calculations becomes even more complicated because of migration of particles between the grid cells. Thus, because of both high demands of the modern studies and the method inherent complexity, efficient implementation of the particle-in-cell method remains challenging.

3   Baseline Version

PICADOR [11,12,14] is a C++ code for plasma simulation based on the particle-in-cell method. The code is currently used in several research projects concerning simulation of laser-plasma interaction [15,19–21]. Here we briefly describe the organization of parallel processing in PICADOR, more implementation and optimization details (improving memory locality and scaling efficiency, vectorization) are given in [12]. The code exploits parallelism on all levels available at modern cluster systems. Distributed memory parallelism is achieved by means of spatial domain decomposition and load balancing using MPI [22]. On the shared memory level particles are stored separately for each cell; OpenMP threads process particles in different cells in parallel. SIMD instructions are used by means of partial vectorization of loops over particles in a cell as well as manual coding of intrinsic-based implementation of some stages of the method.

Throughout this paper we use a frozen plasma benchmark problem with a $40 \times 40 \times 40$ grid, 50 particles per cell and 1000 time steps, that can be solved on a single CPU or Xeon Phi. Apart from the single-device performance, an important aspect for utilizing supercomputers is scalability on distributed memory. These two aspects are somewhat orthogonal for the particle-in-cell method, as it allows spatial domain decomposition with communications only between neighbor domains. Scaling results of PICADOR are presented in [11,12,22], including 90% strong scaling efficiency on a system with 64 KNC Xeon Phi coprocessors [12].

The simulations were performed in double precision using the standard cloud-in-cell particle form factor [18] and the charge-conserving Villasenor – Buneman current deposition scheme [23]. The computational experiments were performed at a node of Intel Endeavor system[1] with Intel Xeon E5-2697 v3 (Haswell, 14 cores, 2.6 GHz, 36 MB cache), Intel Xeon Phi 7120 (KNC, 61 cores, 1.2 GHz, 30.5 MB cache), and Intel Xeon Phi 7250 (KNL, 68 cores, 1.4 GHz, 34 MB cache, 16 GB MCDRAM). Intel Xeon Phi 7250 was used in Quadrant cluster mode, all data placed in MCDRAM.

We recompiled the code, which had been previously optimized for the KNC generation of Xeon Phi, to run on KNL. Since the optimal run configuration on KNC was a single MPI process and 4 OpenMP threads per core [12], first we tried running a single MPI process on KNL as well, with 1, 2, 3, and 4 threads per core. The comparison of these configurations is presented at Table 1. Same as for KNC, increasing the number of threads per core is beneficial for PICADOR on KNL. For the rest of the paper we only consider configurations with 4 threads per core.

Table 2 presents the run time of the baseline version running a single MPI process per device with 1 OpenMP thread per core on CPU and 4 OpenMP threads per core on Xeon Phi. The KNL device outperforms both 14-core Haswell CPU and 61-core KNC, the corresponding speedups are 1.51 x and 2.43 x. Thus, just rebuilding the code for KNL with no additional optimization results in a

---

[1] Not to be confused with Endeavor Supercomputer at NASA Ames Research Center.

Table 1. Run time of the baseline version on KNL with a single MPI process and different number of OpenMP threads per core. Time is given in seconds.

Stage	# threads per core			
	1	2	3	4
Particle push	13.41	11.69	9.51	10.92
Current deposition	12.72	9.84	10.95	8.91
Other	0.38	0.41	0.51	0.44
Overall	26.51	21.94	20.97	20.27

significant speedup compared to KNC. This is not a surprising result, since the theoretical performance on KNL is about 3 x of that of KNC. In the next section we demonstrate how additional optimization of the code and choosing a better configuration of processes and threads can further improve performance on KNL.

Table 2. Run time of the baseline version on CPU and Xeon Phi with a single MPI process on each device. Time is given in seconds.

Stage	Intel Xeon E5-2697 v3	Intel Xeon Phi	
		7120 (KNC)	7250 (KNL)
Particle push	18.30	22.69	10.92
Current deposition	12.02	25.64	8.91
Other	0.25	0.98	0.44
Overall	30.57	49.31	20.27

4   Performance Analysis and Optimization on Knights Landing

4.1   Choosing the Optimal Run Configuration

A run configuration of processes and threads can significantly influence the performance of an MPI + OpenMP code and the optimal configuration is often non-obvious [2]. Thus, our first step towards increasing performance is comparison of different configurations of processes and threads. Table 3 presents comparison of different configurations of processes and threads, each running 4 threads per core. Increasing the number of processes up to 8 while keeping the overall number of threads constant yields an increase in performance, up to 1.31 x compared to the single-process configuration. A possible explanation is that in this case data layout better fits the application. However, further increasing the number of processes results in performance degradation. For the rest of the paper we use the configuration with 8 MPI processes and 34 OpenMP threads per process on KNL.

Table 3. Run time of several process-thread configurations on KNL for the baseline version of the code. Time is given in seconds.

Stage	#processes × #threads per process			
	1×272	2×136	4×68	8×34
Particle push	10.92	9.16	8.51	8.07
Current deposition	8.91	7.68	7.60	7.15
Other	0.44	0.35	0.30	0.26
Overall	20.27	17.19	16.41	15.48

4.2 Auto-vectorization of Field Interpolation

Efficient vectorization of some stages of the particle-in-cell method is not easy, particularly for field interpolation that results in an intricate memory access pattern with indirect indexing [12,24]. For the version of the code for CPUs and KNC we explicitly disabled compiler auto-vectorization of the corresponding loops as it resulted in some slowdown due to inefficient operations with memory. However, new instructions in AVX-512 allow some speedup on KNL due to auto-vectorization of these loops. Table 4 presents comparison of the baseline version and a version with auto-vectorization of field interpolation, which is a part of the particle push stage, on KNL. The speedup of this stage due to vectorization is 1.19 x.

Table 4. Run time of the baseline version and a version with auto-vectorization of field interpolation on KNL. Time is given in seconds.

Stage	Baseline version	Auto-vectorization of field interpolation
Particle push	8.07	6.81
Current deposition	7.15	7.15
Other	0.26	0.26
Overall	15.48	14.22

4.3 Supercells

A promising approach to improve performance of the particle-in-cell method on many-core architectures is grouping and processing particles by supercells, formed by several nearby cells. First introduced for GPUs [7], it has been recently reported to be advantageous for CPUs as well [24]. The size of supercells is chosen so that particle and grid data processed during the particle push and current deposition stages fit L1 cache.

The exact amount of data processed is implementation-specific. For PICADOR with supercells of size $S \times S \times S$ cells, the size of data used for

Villasenor – Buneman current deposition on a single core can be estimated as

$$CurrentDepositionDataSize(S) = (4 \text{ threads per core}) \times$$
$$\left((S+1)^3 \text{ grid values}\right) \times (3 \text{ current components}) \times (8 \text{ Bytes per value}).$$

Particles are processed in chunks, for each chunk results of field interpolation and some auxiliary coefficients are stored in a local array. For field interpolation and particle push with cloud-in-cell formfactor the approximate size of data is

$$ParticlePushDataSize(S) = (4 \text{ threads per core}) \times$$
$$\left(\left((S+2)^3 \text{ grid values}\right) \times (6 \text{ field components}) \times (8 \text{ Bytes per value}) +\right.$$
$$(64 \text{ Bytes per particle} + 56 \text{ Bytes of auxiliary data per particle})$$
$$\left. \times (16 \text{ particles per chunk})\right).$$

Table 5 presents results for a single-core on KNL running 4 threads. For the sake of simplicity we consider only cubical supercells with equal number of cells for each dimension.

Table 5. Results for different supercell sizes on the single-core of KNL running 4 threads depending on the supercell size. Estimated size of data actively used while processing a supercell combined for 4 threads and run time are given.

Stage		Supercell size for each dimension					
		1	2	3	4	5	6
Particle push	Data size, KB	12.86	19.97	31.68	49.15	73.54	105.98
	Time, sec	34.28	31.23	32.35	30.95	32.12	34.10
Current deposition	Data size, KB	0.77	2.59	6.14	12.00	20.74	32.93
	Time, sec	40.44	30.69	30.25	28.85	28.77	28.00

As follows from Table 5, in the single-core case the most efficient supercell size for particle push is 4. For the current deposition stage, increasing the size up to 6 leads to a steady increase in performance. However, using larger supercells results in decreasing the number of independent subproblems solved in parallel using OpenMP, which could hinder the overall performance. For example, taking into account chessboard supercell processing scheme used in PICADOR, for grid size $40 \times 40 \times 40$ of the benchmark problem and supercell size $S = 6$ there are at most (depending on implementation details, usage of ghost cells, etc.) 64 independent subproblems, that is not enough to fully saturate Xeon Phi. Thus, taking into account multi-threading, the optimal supercell size is smaller than for the single-core case. For our code the empirically best supercell size on KNL was 2, on KNC and Haswell CPU it was 2 for particle push and 4 for current deposition. Table 6 presents results of the supercell version on each device and

Table 6. Run time of the version with supercells on CPU and Xeon Phi. For each device the empirically chosen best process-thread configuration was used. Time is given in seconds.

Stage	Intel Xeon E5-2697 v3	Intel Xeon Phi	
		7120 (KNC)	7250 (KNL)
Particle push	16.78	20.93	5.73
Current deposition	8.22	15.44	4.77
Other	0.27	0.95	0.25
Overall	25.27	37.32	10.75

the speedups compared to the baseline. Supercells are beneficial for all three platforms in question, with 1.21 x speedup on the Haswell CPU and 1.32 x speedup on Xeon Phi, both KNC and KNL.

4.4   Roofline Model

Finally, we measured performance of the optimized version using Intel VTune Amplifier. The resulting overall performance is 42.5 GFLOPS on the CPU and 100 GFLOPS on the KNL device in double precision. The obtained performance is much lower than the theoretical peak performance of the hardware used. Thus, on KNL we achieved only about 3% of the peak. However, particle-in-cell codes tend to have a rather low amount of arithmetic operations per amount of data loaded from memory, which could be a serious performance-hindering factor. To investigate it, we applied the roofline model [25], which is a tool that represents the attainable upper bound performance.

We used the roofline model based on data traffic through RAM and L1 cache. Data traffic was collected using Roofline Analysis of Intel Advisor. The

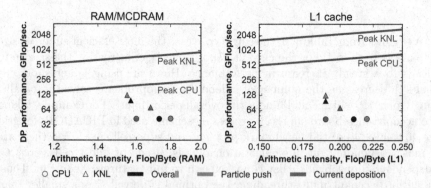

Fig. 1. Roofline model for the optimized version of the code on CPU and KNL. Left: roofline using RAM data traffic (MCDRAM on KNL). Right: roofline using L1 data traffic.

results for the main stages of the computational loop and overall are presented at Fig. 1. To compute arithmetic intensity, we divided the number of floating-point operations by data traffic through the corresponding type of memory (RAM and L1 for CPU, MCDRAM and L1 for KNL). The roofs were calculated as a product of arithmetic intensity and theoretical peak memory bandwidth. As follows from the constructed roofline, the attainable upper bound performance is much lower than the peak performance. Still, the code achieves only about 26% of the upper bound on CPU and 14% on KNL. Therefore, there is a large room for improvement, mainly in terms of efficient vectorization.

5 Conclusions and Future Work

This paper presents a first look at Intel Xeon Phi CPUs of Knights Landing generation for particle-in-cell plasma simulation. We use the plasma simulation code PICADOR, which has been previously ported and optimized for KNC. A simple rebuilding of the code for KNL yields a 2.43 x speedup compared to KNC in the same configuration. Choosing the optimal configuration of processes and threads for KNL and applying several techniques to improve performance leads to a 1.89 x speedup on KNL compared to the baseline version. Auto-vectorization of the field interpolation loop, which led to a slowdown on KNC, gives some benefit on KNL due to AVX-512 instruction set. Utilization of supercells gives speedup on CPU as well as on Xeon Phi. The speedup of the optimized version on a Knights Landing device is 2.35 x compared to a 14-core Haswell CPU and 3.47 x compared to a 61-core Knights Corner Xeon Phi coprocessor. The code achieves 100 GFLOPS double precision performance on KNL.

Overall, the obtained results show that KNL is a promising platform for particle-in-cell plasma simulation. Compared to the previous-generation KNC, it opens new prospects for performance improvement. Same as for KNC, approaches to optimization are mostly shared with CPUs. It allows maintaining a single version of the code for CPUs and Xeon Phi, probably with some minor changes. Our future work includes further performance improvement, especially in terms of vectorization, for benchmark and up-to-date physical problems.

References

1. Kunkel, J.M., Balaji, P., Dongarra, J. (eds.): ISC High Performance 2016. LNCS, vol. 9697. Springer, Heidelberg (2016)
2. Jeffers, J., Reinders, J., Sodani, A.: Intel Xeon Phi Processor High Performance Programming: Knights Landing Edition. Morgan Kaufmann, New York (2016)
3. Fonseca, R.A., Vieira, J., Fiuza, F., Davidson, A., Tsung, F.S., Mori, W.B., Silva, L.O.: Exploiting multi-scale parallelism for large scale numerical modelling of laser wakefield accelerators. Plasma Phys. Control. Fusion. 55(12), 124011 (2013)
4. Bowers, K.J., Albright, B.J., Yin, L., Bergen, B., Kwan, T.J.T.: Ultrahigh performance three-dimensional electromagnetic relativistic kinetic plasma simulation. Phys. Plasmas 15(5), 055703 (2008)

5. Pukhov, A.: Three-dimensional electromagnetic relativistic particle-in-cell code VLPL (Virtual Laser Plasma Lab). J. Plasma Phys. **61**(3), 425–433 (1999)
6. Vay, J.-L., Bruhwiler, D.L., Geddes, C.G.R., Fawley, W.M., Martins, S.F., Cary, J.R., Cormier-Michel, E., Cowan, B., Fonseca, R.A., Furman, M.A., Lu, W., Mori, W.B., Silva, L.O.: Simulating relativistic beam and plasma systems using an optimal boosted frame. J. Phys. Conf. Ser. **180**(1), 012006 (2009)
7. Burau, H., Widera, R., Honig, W., Juckeland, G., Debus, A., Kluge, T., Schramm, U., Cowan, T.E., Sauerbrey, R., Bussmann, M.: PIConGPU: a fully relativistic particle-in-cell code for a GPU cluster. IEEE Trans. Plasma Sci. **38**(10), 2831–2839 (2010)
8. Kong, X., Huang, M.C., Ren, C., Decyk, V.K.: Particle-in-cell simulations with charge-conserving current deposition on graphic processing units. J. Comput. Phys. **230**(4), 1676–1685 (2011)
9. Decyk, V.K., Singh, T.V.: Particle-in-cell algorithms for emerging computer architectures. Comput. Phys. Commun. **185**(3), 708–719 (2014)
10. Glinsky, B.M., Kulikov, I.M., Snytnikov, A.V., Romanenko, A.A., Chernykh, I.G., Vshivkov, V.A.: Co-design of parallel numerical methods for plasma physics and astrophysics. Supercomput. Front. Innov. **1**(3), 88–98 (2014)
11. Bastrakov, S., Meyerov, I., Surmin, I., Efimenko, E., Gonoskov, A., Malyshev, A., Shiryaev, M.: Particle-in-cell plasma simulation on CPUs, GPUs and Xeon Phi coprocessors. In: Kunkel, J.M., Ludwig, T., Meuer, H.W. (eds.) ISC 2014. LNCS, vol. 8488, pp. 513–514. Springer, Heidelberg (2014)
12. Surmin, I.A., Bastrakov, S.I., Efimenko, E.S., Gonoskov, A.A., Korzhimanov, A.V., Meyerov, I.B.: Particle-in-cell laser-plasma simulation on xeon phi coprocessors. Comput. Phys. Commun. **202**, 204–210 (2016)
13. Nakashima, H.: Manycore challenge in particle-in-cell simulation: how to exploit 1 TFlops peak performance for simulation codes with irregular computation. Comput. Electr. Eng. **46**, 81–94 (2015)
14. Bastrakov, S., Donchenko, R., Gonoskov, A., Efimenko, E., Malyshev, A., Meyerov, I., Surmin, I.: Particle-in-cell plasma simulation on heterogeneous cluster systems. J. Comput. Sci. **3**, 474–479 (2013)
15. Gonoskov, A., Bastrakov, S., Efimenko, E., Ilderton, A., Marklund, M., Meyerov, I., Muraviev, A., Sergeev, A., Surmin, I., Wallin, E.: Extended particle-in-cell schemes for physics in ultrastrong laser fields: review and developments. Phys. Rev. E **92**(2), 023305 (2015)
16. Hockney, R.W., Eastwood, J.W.: Computer Simulation Using Particles. McGraw-Hill, New York (1981)
17. Dawson, J.M.: Particle simulation of plasmas. Rev. Modern Phys. **55**(2), 403–447 (1983)
18. Birdsal, C.K.: Plasma Physics via Computer Simulation. CRC Press, Boca Raton (2004)
19. Muraviev, A.A., Bastrakov, S.I., Bashinov, A.V., Gonoskov, A.A., Efimenko, E.S., Kim, A.V., Meyerov, I.B., Sergeev, A.M.: Generation of current sheets and giant quasistatic magnetic fields at the ionization of vacuum in extremely strong light fields. JETP Lett. **102**(3), 148–153 (2015)
20. Mackenroth, F., Gonoskov, A., Marklund, M.: Chirped-standing-wave acceleration of ions with intense lasers. Phys. Rev. Lett. **117**(10), 104801 (2016)
21. Mackenroth, F., Gonoskov, A., Marklund, M.: Theoretical benchmarking of laser-accelerated ion fluxes by 2D-PIC simulations (to appear). http://arxiv.org/abs/1607.00776

22. Surmin, I., Bashinov, A., Bastrakov, S., Efimenko, E., Gonoskov, A., Meyerov, I.: Dynamic load balancing based on rectilinear partitioning in particle-in-cell plasma simulation. In: Malyshkin, V. (ed.) PaCT 2015. LNCS, vol. 9251, pp. 107–119. Springer, Heidelberg (2015). doi:10.1007/978-3-319-21909-7_12
23. Villasenor, J., Buneman, O.: Rigorous charge conservation for local electromagnetic field solvers. Comput. Phys. Commun. **69**, 306–316 (1992)
24. Vincenti, H., Lehe, R., Sasanka, R., Vay, J.-L.: An efficient and portable SIMD algorithm for charge/current deposition in Particle-In-Cell codes (to appear). http://arxiv.org/abs/1601.02056
25. Williams, S., Waterman, A., Patterson, D.: Roofline: an insightful visual performance model for multicore architectures. Commun. ACM **52**(4), 65–76 (2009)

Efficient Distributed Computations with DIRAC

Viktor Gergel[1], Vladimir Korenkov[2,3], Andrei Tsaregorodtsev[3,4(✉)],
and Alexey Svistunov[1]

[1] Lobachevsky State University of Nizhni Novgorod, Nizhni Novgorod, Russia
gergel@unn.ru, alexey.svistunov@itmm.unn.ru
[2] Joint Institute for Nuclear Research, Dubna, Russia
korenkov@jinr.ru
[3] Plekhanov Russian University of Economics, Moscow, Russia
[4] CPPM, Aix Marseille Université, CNRS/IN2P3, Marseille, France
atsareg@cppm.in2p3.fr

Abstract. High Energy Physics (HEP) experiments at the LHC collider at CERN
were among the first scientific communities with very high computing requirements. Nowadays, researchers in other scientific domains are in need of similar
computational power and storage capacity. Solution for the HEP experiments was
found in the form of computational grid - distributed computing infrastructure
integrating large number of computing centers based on commodity hardware.
These infrastructures are very well suited for High Throughput applications used
for analysis of large volumes of data with trivial parallelization in multiple independent execution threads. More advanced applications in HEP and other scientific domains can exploit complex parallelization techniques using multiple interacting execution threads. A growing number of High Performance Computing
(HPC) centers, or supercomputers, support this mode of operation. One of the
software toolkits developed for building distributed computing systems is the
DIRAC Interware. It allows seamless integration of computing and storage
resources based on different technologies into a single coherent system. This
product was very successful to solve problems of large HEP experiments and was
upgraded in order to offer a general-purpose solution. The DIRAC Interware can
help including also HPC centers into a common federation to achieve similar
goals as for computational grids. However, integration of HPC centers imposes
certain requirements on their internal organization and external connectivity
presenting a complex co-design problem. A distributed infrastructure including
supercomputers is planned for construction. It will be applied for inter-disciplinary large-scale problems of modern science and technology.

Keywords: Distributed computing · High-performance computations · Cloud
services · Grid systems · Workflow management · Big data management

1 Introduction

The number of scientific domains with highly intensive computational applications is
rapidly increasing. The High Energy Physics (HEP) experiments at the LHC collider,

© Springer International Publishing AG 2016
J. Carretero et al. (Eds.): ICA3PP 2016 Workshops, LNCS 10049, pp. 330–341, 2016.
DOI: 10.1007/978-3-319-49956-7_26

CERN, have pioneered the new era of highly data intensive studies. However, other disciplines are quickly increasing their data volume requirements. Applications dealing with Exabyte-level data volumes are already on the horizon. New scientific communities need urgently tools to work with large datasets and massively parallel applications adapted to their specific tasks and suitable to the expertise level of their scientists. The scientific collaborations nowadays are often international with many groups coming from different laboratories and universities. As a result, the available computing and storage resources of a given collaboration are usually distributed as each group is coming up with its own contribution. Therefore, there is a strong necessity of building computing systems that cope with large volumes of distributed data and distributed computing resources that can be used for these data analysis.

The DIRAC Project was started to solve the data intensive analysis problem for one of the LHC experiments, LHCb, in 2003 [1, 2]. It was started as a Workload Management System (WMS) in order to operate multiple computing centers in Europe to produce modeling data for the experiment optimization. However, the need in an efficient Data Management System coping with many millions of files with distributed replicas and having a close coupling with the WMS was quickly understood. As a result, the DIRAC allows performing all the data analysis tasks of LHCb and other HEP experiments [4–6].

After multiple years of successful usage in the HEP domain, the DIRAC software was generalized to be suitable for other applications requiring large data volumes and computing power. It provides a development framework and many ready-to-use services to build distributed computing systems adapted to particular scientific communities. These tools serve to interconnect technologically heterogeneous computing and storage resources into a coherent system seen by the users as a single large computer with a friendly interface and consistent computational and storage subsystems. Therefore, we speak about DIRAC Interware – technology to aggregate multiple computing resources and services. This toolkit can be also used to integrate computing centers of the HPC type supporting massively parallel applications along with the traditional grid sites. This requires development of several new components and also a model of an HPC center, which is rich enough for a large number of applications that can run in such HPC federations.

In this article we will overview the DIRAC Interware, its base architecture and implementation. We will describe the base Workload Management and Data Management systems of DIRAC as well as computing and storage resources accessible with these services. We will discuss specific features of HPC centers and possible ways to integrate them into a comment distributed infrastructure. We will present also plans for integration of several HPC centers into a federation dedicated to actual scientific problems.

2   DIRAC Overview

DIRAC Project provides all the necessary components to create and maintain distributed computing systems. It is forming a layer on top of third party computing infrastructures, which isolates users from the direct access to the computing resources and provides them with an abstract interface hiding the complexity of dealing with multiple heterogeneous services. This pattern is applied to both computing and storage resources. In both cases, abstract interfaces are defined and implementations for all the common computing service and storage technologies are provided. Therefore, the users see only logical computing and storage elements, which simplifies dramatically their usage. In this section we will describe in more details the DIRAC systems for workload and data management.

2.1 Workload Management

The DIRAC Workload Management System is based on the concept of pilot jobs [3]. In this scheduling architecture (Fig. 1), the user tasks are submitted to the central Task Queue service. At the same time the so-called pilot jobs are submitted to the computing resources by specialized components called Directors. Directors use the job scheduling mechanism suitable for their respective computing infrastructure: grid resource brokers or computing elements, batch system schedulers, cloud managers, etc. The pilot jobs start execution on the worker nodes, check the execution environment, collect the worker node characteristics and present them to the Matcher service. The Matcher service chooses the most appropriate user job waiting in the Task Queue and hands it over to the pilot for execution. Once the user task is executed and its outputs are delivered to the DIRAC central services, the pilot job can take another user task if the remaining time of the worker node reservation is sufficient.

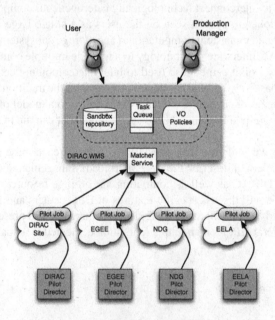

Fig. 1. WMS with pilot jobs

There are many advantages of the pilot job concept. The pilots are not only increasing the visible efficiency of the user jobs but also help managing heterogeneous computing resources presenting them to the central services in a uniform coherent way. Large user communities can benefit also from the ability of applying the community policies that are not easy, if at all possible, with the standard grid middleware. Furthermore executing several user tasks in the same pilot largely reduces the stress on the batch systems no matter if they are accessed directly or via grid mechanisms, especially if users subdivide their payload in many short tasks trying to reduce the response time.

The pilot job based scheduling system allows easy aggregation of computing resources of different technologies. Currently the following resources are available for DIRAC users:

- Computing grid infrastructures based on the gLite/EMI grid middleware. The submission is possible both through the gLite Workload Management System and directly to the computing element services exposing the CREAM interface. Examples of such grid infrastructures are WLCG and EGI grids.
- Open Science Grid (OSG) infrastructure based on the VDT (Virtual Data Toolkit) suite of middleware [7].
- Grids based on the ARC middleware which was developed in the framework of the Nordugrid project [8].
- Standalone computing clusters with common batch system schedulers, for example, PBS/Torque, Grid Engine, Condor, SLURM, OAR, and others. Those clusters can be accessed by configuring an SSH tunnel that will be used by DIRAC directors to submit pilot jobs to the local batch systems.
- Sites providing resources via most widely used cloud managers, for example Open-Stack, OpenNebula, Amazon and others. Both commercial and public clouds can be accessed through DIRAC.
- Volunteer resources provided with the help of BOINC software. There are several realizations of access to this kind of resources all based on the same pilot job framework.

As it was explained above, a new kind of computing resource can be integrated into the DIRAC Workload Management System by providing a corresponding Director using an appropriate job submission protocol. This is the plugin mechanism that allows connecting easily new computing facilities as needed by the DIRAC users.

2.2 Data Management

The DIRAC Data Management System (DMS) is based on similar design principles as the WMS [9]. An abstract interface is defined to describe access to a storage system and there are multiple implementations for various storage access protocols. Similarly, there is a concept of a FileCatalog service, which provides information about the physical locations of file copies. As for storage services there are several implementations for different catalog service technologies all following the same abstract interface.

A storage system can be accessible via different interfaces with different access protocols. But for the users this stays logically a single service providing access to the same physical storage space. Similar situation can happen also for the file catalog services. To simplify access to this kind of services, DIRAC defines aggregators that allow working with multiple services as if with a single one from the client perspective. All the plug-ins and aggregators are hidden behind the DataManager API which have methods to perform all the basic operations needing access to both storage and catalog services.

DIRAC is also providing a number of auxiliary and higher level services to support higher-level operations as well as to help administrators to run the system:

- Support for bulk asynchronous operations is provided by the Request Management System (RMS);
- Transformation System (TS) provides means to automate recurrent massive data operations driven by the data registration or file status change events;
- Staging service to manage bringing data on-line into a disk cache in the SEs with tertiary storage architecture. These operations are usually triggered automatically by the WMS before the jobs using these data as input can be submitted for execution to the worker nodes.
- FTS Manager service to submit and manage data transfer requests to an external File Transfer Service.
- Data Logging service to log all the operations on a predefined subset of data mostly for debugging purposes.
- Data Integrity service to record failures of the data management operations in order to spot malfunctioning components and resolve issues.
- The general DIRAC Accounting service is used to store the historical data of all the data transfers, success rates of the transfer operations, etc.

DIRAC provides plug-ins for a number of storage access protocols most commonly used in the distributed storage services:

- SRM, XRootd, RFIO, etc.;
- gfal2 library based access protocols (DCAP, HTTP-based protocols, S3, WebDAV, etc.) [10].

If some DIRAC user community would need access to a storage system not yet supported by the DIRAC Interware, it will be easy to incorporate it by providing a new plug-in to the system.

In addition DIRAC provides its own implementation of a Storage Element service and the corresponding plug-in using the custom DIPS protocol. This is the protocol used to exchange data between the DIRAC components. The DIRAC StorageElement service allows exposing data stored on file servers with POSIX compliant file systems, for example NFS or Lustre. This service helps to quickly incorporate data accumulated by scientific communities in any ad hoc way into any distributed system under the DIRAC Interware control.

2.3   DIRAC Development Framework

All the DIRAC components are written in a well-defined software framework with a clear architecture and development conventions. A large part of the functionality is implemented as plugins implementing predefined abstract interfaces. There are several core services to orchestrate the work of the whole DIRAC distributed system, the most important ones are the following:

- Configuration service used for discovery of the DIRAC components and providing a single source of configuration information;
- Monitoring service to follow the system load and activities;
- Accounting service to keep track of the resources consumption by different communities, groups and individual users;
- System Logging service to accumulate error reports in one place to be able to quickly react to problems.

Modular architecture and the use of core services allow developers to easily write new extensions concentrating on their specific functionality and avoiding recurrent tasks.

All the communications between distributed DIRAC components are secure following the standards introduced by computational grids, which is extremely important in the distributed computing environment.

Users are provided with a number of different interfaces to interact with the system. This includes a rich set of command-line tools for Unix environment, Python language API to write one's own scripts and applications. DIRAC functionality is available also through a flexible and secure Web Portal which follows the user interface paradigm of a desktop computer.

3   DIRAC Usage Examples

DIRAC based infrastructures are used by multiple scientific communities having to integrate heterogeneous resources at their disposal. Many of the common requirements are already satisfied by the core DIRAC components. However, each community can have its own specific workflows and data models. Therefore it is quite usual that large experiments are introducing new services implementing their particular management logic.

3.1   Physics Applications

DIRAC was originally developed for the LHCb experiments at the LHC collider at CERN, Geneva. Among the High Energy Physics experiments, LHCb stays the most intensive user of the DIRAC Interware using it as the basis for its data production system [12]. Figure 2 illustrates the scale of the computing resources usage by LHCb.

The plot is produced by the DIRAC Accounting system and shows that on average the LHCb data production system is controlling about 50 thousands of simultaneous jobs running at more than 100 distributed computing centers. This is equivalent to running a virtual distributed computing center of up to 100 thousands CPU cores. The LHCb data volume reaches about 40 PBytes spread over more than 20 data centers in Europe and Russia. LHCb is using mostly resources provided by the WLCG computing

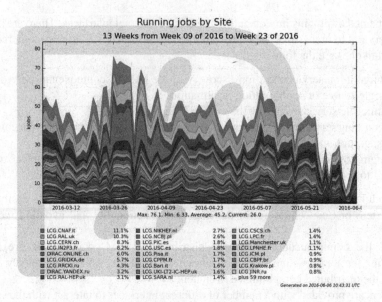

Fig. 2. Simultaneously running distributed LHCb jobs

grid infrastructure [13]. However, it also incorporates several large non-grid centers, such as Ohio Supercomputing Center in USA or Yandex computing farm in Russia. Those centers are incorporated seamlessly using the DIRAC Interware. LHCb is using all the DIRAC core services for managing workflows and data but it has also developed several specific ones, like for example, Bookkeeping service for storing all the data provenance information, or Production service for managing large numbers of tasks and files in am automated way. All the LHCb specific services are developed within the DIRAC Framework as extensions and thus reuse multiple core APIs.

Another example is the Belle II experiment at KEK, Tsukuba, Japan. This was the first experiment to start using DIRAC outside LHCb [5]. The initial requirement of the Belle Collaboration was the possibility to incorporate commercial cloud resources provided by the Amazon Company. The VMDIRAC subsystem was initiated as a DIRAC extension to manage computing resources coming from various cloud providers. Now it is making part of the DIRAC core services and other user communities can benefit from it.

The BES III experiment at IHEP, Beijing, China is one more HEP experiment using DIRAC for its production system [14]. In particular, IHEP developers contributed several modules to the DIRAC File Catalog service, for example, Dataset modules for managing large collections of files as a single entity. The DIRAC service installation for the BES III experiment in IHEP was recently upgraded to support multiple user communities, like the Juno experiment or the CEPC project [15].

3.2 Multi-domain DIRAC Services

The success of DIRAC for supporting large scientific user communities suggested the idea that DIRAC services can be also offered to smaller research groups without the need to install and maintain complicated software and hardware systems. Indeed many small groups, often without deep knowledge of the distributed computing matters, still need access to large computing infrastructures for their application. Therefore, DIRAC services were offered as part of several distributed computing infrastructure projects [16]. The first such service was provided by the France-Grilles National Grid Infrastructure (NGI) project in 2012. Now it serves about 20 different grid Virtual Organizations. For example, users from the international biomed Virtual Organization submit more than a half of their payloads through the FG-DIRAC service in France.

Since 2014, the DIRAC4EGI service is offered by the European Grid Infrastructure (EGI) Project. Several communities representing various scientific domains like life sciences, climatology and others use this service. The service is also intensively used for dissemination purposes, for example for tutorials on using distributed grid and cloud computing resources.

4 Federation of HPC Centers

Several examples of successful incorporation of HPC centers dedicated to massively parallel applications into a common distributed infrastructure including grid, cloud and stand-alone centers showed that it is possible to create a dedicated system to federate multiple HPC sites based on the DIRAC Interware technology. This will offer a full potential of these centers to large scientific communities that require more and more this kind of resources for their applications.

It is important to mention that combining grid computing centers together with the HPC centers can be very useful for communities with very complex workflows where some steps can be executed on a cheaper grid computing elements and others on HPC ones. Such optimization can reduce the time and the cost of the overall workflow execution.

4.1 Open Distributed Supercomputer Infrastructure Project

A project for construction of an Open Distributed Supercomputer Infrastructure (ODSI) will have to carry out several tasks. First of all, the concept of the ODSI must be formulated, which includes several aspects:

- Develop a model of an HPC center that will be as much in common for all the involved sites as possible. For each site, this model will be described in the system configuration with the site-specific parameters. As a result this will allow to present all the HPC centers as logical resources for the users that can be used in a transparent interchangeable manner;

- Develop efficient algorithms for managing large numbers of tasks executed in heterogeneous computing environment including HPC centers, which optimize the usage of computing and storage resources and minimize the overall execution time;
- Develop the necessary new DIRAC components to support the HPC specific workflows and reuse as much as possible the already existing tools. This will allow seamless migration for the DIRAC users to the new type of resources;
- Formulate common policies of usage of the HPC centers by large distributed user communities and implement tools to support those policies.

Building the ODSI infrastructure will need going through a number of prototypes involving an increasing number of HPC centers first on the national and then on the international levels. Several research laboratories and universities in Russia (JINR, Dubna, University of Nizhni Novgorod, and others) are planning to undertake such project. As a result it will create the infrastructure for solving a number of inter-disciplinary large-scale problems of the modern science and technology, which are already selected as the project pilot applications [17–19].

4.2   Co-design of a Federated HPC Supercomputer

In order to be included into the ODSI infrastructure an HPC center must follow several design requirements to ensure homogeneous access and security rules. Integration of traditional computing centers is relatively simple, especially those that participate in grid infrastructures. The HPC centers are in most cases designed and deployed without plans for eventual participation in any federation project. Therefore, their organization has little in common, which makes their integration difficult. The pilot job based WMS offers opportunities that can be very helpful in such projects because it does not require running complicated services on sites.

Interaction with the DIRAC Central Services. WMS with pilot jobs assumes outbound connectivity from the worker nodes. This is necessary to let pilots interact with the central services to report their status and request user payloads. If a computing center allows worker node outbound connectivity, then its connection to a DIRAC infrastructure is similar to traditional centers and requires minimal effort from the site administrators. However, a majority of HPC centers forbid such outbound connectivity for various reasons. In this case, DIRAC proposes a special service – Gateway – that can run on a HPC site gatekeeper host and serve as a proxy to pass messages from pilot jobs to the central services. Using this service requires a minor change in the pilot configuration on such sites while fully preserving the overall architecture and logic. The HPC center in this case must provide the gatekeeper host with appropriate dual external/local network connectivity. The host throughput capacity should be sufficient to support the possibly rather intensive traffic of data being produced or analyzed in the center. The security requirements to this host are very strict, as its certificate will be trusted by the DIRAC services as representing users whose jobs are running in the center.

Another problem of running jobs in the HPC centers with limited worker node connectivity is exporting the resulting data. If the data cannot be sent out directly from the worker nodes, this can be achieved by means of the Storage Element Proxy service.

This service allows access to any Storage Element from the machines not having the necessary software for corresponding plug-ins or other limitations. In this case, the client is accessing the Storage Element Proxy service with the DIRAC native DIPS protocol and the service transmits the access request to the destination SE with the suitable protocol. The client credentials are checked and used to access the destination service by delegation. In the case of running user jobs in computing centers where worker nodes do not have access to the WAN and therefore can not upload the resulting data directly, running the Storage Element Proxy service in the Gateway host of the computing center can help to export data from the worker nodes without a need to use some intermediate buffer storage and transfer data asynchronously by some additional agent or a *cron* job. Putting this all together, Fig. 3 illustrates the general scheme of connecting an HPC center to a DIRAC-based infrastructure.

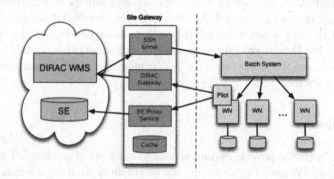

Fig. 3. Pilot job interaction with DIRAC central services in case of no outbound connectivity in the worker nodes

Multiple CPU Slot Reservation. Applications running at HPC centers usually use multiple processors or even multiple worker nodes together. The reservation of multi-host computing slots is a complicates task and can be done by means of the local batch system scheduler, for example SLURM, OAR, or others. The pilot based WMS can exploit the tools offered by the target batch system but it can also offer other interesting opportunities here.

Computing slots reserved by the pilots can be orchestrated by a central DIRAC MPI service [11]. This service keeps track of all the groups of pilots that can work together to run parallel applications. These groups are combining pilots that are running on worker nodes on the same high performance local network, which allows exchanges using some variation of the MPI protocol. Accumulation of such pilot groups that can eventually constitute an MPI ring is a rather complicated and time-consuming process. The computing slots that are freed by previously running jobs are blocked by the work-load management system in order to satisfy requirements of the jobs in its waiting queue and accumulate the necessary capacity. While the multi-processor slot is being accu-mulated, the constituent processors stay idle decreasing the overall efficiency. Therefore, the accumulated group of slots is a very valuable asset that should be used as much efficiently as possible. With the pilot jobs coordinated by the DIRAC MPI service such multi-worker reservations can be reused for multiple user payloads without the need to redo the multi-slot reservations. As a result, this can increase dramatically the efficiency of the usage of the HPC resources.

In a batch system, the computing slot is reserved for a limited amount of time in order to ensure a fair sharing of resources among different tasks and users. However, worker nodes reserved by the DIRAC WMS can execute multiple jobs coming from different users and ensuring fair sharing on the meta-scheduler level. This mode of operation has many advantages. It puts less load on the local batch system scheduler and increases the efficiency of resources usage. However, administration of the batch system may require stopping the worker nodes from time to time to perform maintenance tasks, e.g. software or hardware upgrades. In this case, the DIRAC pilots occupying the worker nodes should receive signals from the batch system ordering the node liberation. The signals should be well specified and the corresponding handlers should be included into the DIRAC pilots. The handlers will then ensure graceful finalization of the running user applications avoiding losses of the job results that can happen in case of abrupt killing of the batch jobs. The design of the batch system signals and of the pilot signal handlers requires a close cooperation between the HPC centers administrators and developers of the DIRAC software.

5   Conclusions

The DIRAC Interware provides a framework and a rich set of services to build distributed computing systems. Such systems are successfully used for a number of High Energy Physics and AstroPhysics experiments, but also for other applications in different scientific domains. The Workload Management System with pilot jobs proved to be very efficient to control user tasks in a High Throughput environment. However, it can be also applied for aggregation of the HPC computing resources. The pilot job scheduling paradigm can increase significantly the scheduling efficiency for parallel applications requiring multi-processor computing slots. Combining traditional, cloud and HPC computing centers in a single distributed infrastructure can allow execution of complex workflows needing different types of resources on different subsequent steps. As a result, this can increase the overall efficiency of the usage of otherwise heterogeneous computing resources.

Building an Open Distributed Supercomputer Infrastructure aggregating multiple HPC centers in Russia and abroad can bring the support for massively parallel applications to a new level. This will make the supercomputer resources elastic from the user perspective, which means that much more power can be provided momentarily for a given application when it is actually needed. On the other hand it will dramatically increase the usage efficiency of multiple HPC centers.

References

1. Tsaregorodtsev, A., et al.: DIRAC3: the new generation of the LHCb grid software. J. Phys. Conf. Ser. **219**, 062029 (2010)

2. DIRAC Project. http://diracgrid.org
3. Casajus, A., Graciani, R., Tsaregorodtsev, A.: DIRAC pilot framework and the DIRAC Workload Management System. J. Phys. Conf. Ser. **219**, 062049 (2010)
4. BES III Collaboration. http://bes.ihep.ac.cn/bes3
5. Kuhr, T., Hara, T.: Computing at Belle II. In: Proceedings of the CHEP 2012 International Conference, New-York, May 2012
6. Arrabito, L., et al.: Application of the DIRAC framework in CTA: first evaluation. In: Proceedings of the CHEP 2012 International Conference, New-York, May 2012
7. OpenScience Grid. https://www.opensciencegrid.org/
8. ARC project. http://www.nordugrid.org/arc/
9. Smith, A., Tsaregorodtsev, A.: DIRAC: data production management. J. Phys. Conf. Ser. **119**, 062046 (2008)
10. Gfal2 Project. https://dmc.web.cern.ch/projects-tags/gfal-2
11. Tsaregorodtsev, A., Hamar, V.: MPI support in the DIRAC Pilot Job Workload Management System. J. Phys. Conf. Ser. **396**, 032109 (2012)
12. Stagni, F., Charpentier, P.: The LHCb DIRAC-based production and data management operations systems. J. Phys.: Conf. Ser. **368**, 012010 (2012)
13. WLCG Computing Grid Infrastructure. http://wlcg.web.cern.ch
14. Zhang, X.M., Pelevanyuk, I., Korenkov, V., et al.: Design and operation of the BES-III distributed computing system. Procedia Comput. Sci. **66**, 619–624 (2015)
15. Yan, T., Suo, B., et al.: Multi-VO support in IHEP's distributed computing environment. J. Phys. Conf. Ser. **664**, 062068 (2015)
16. Tsaregorodtsev, A.: DIRAC Distributed Computing Services. J. Phys. Conf. Ser. **513**, 03209 (2014)
17. Barkalov, K., Gergel, V.: Multilevel scheme of dimensionality reduction for parallel global search algorithms. In: OPT-i 2014. An International Conference on Engineering and Applied Sciences Optimization, Kos Island, Greece, 4–6 June 2014, pp. 2111–2124 (2014)
18. Gergel, V.P., Strongin, R.G.: Parallel computing for globally optimal decision making on cluster systems. Future Gener. Computer Systems **21**(5), 673–678 (2005)
19. Bastrakov, S., Meyerov, I., Gergel, V., et al.: High performance computing in biomedical applications. Procedia Comput. Sci. **18**, 10–19 (2013)

The Co-design of Astrophysical Code
for Massively Parallel Supercomputers

Boris Glinsky[1], Igor Kulikov[1], Igor Chernykh[1(✉)], Dmitry Weins[1],
Alexey Snytnikov[1], Vladislav Nenashev[2], Andrey Andreev[3],
Vitaly Egunov[3], and Egor Kharkov[3]

[1] Institute of Computational Mathematics and Mathematical Geophysics
SB RAS, Lavrentjeva Ave. 6, 630090 Novosibirsk, Russia
chernykh@ssd.sscc.ru
[2] Novosibirsk State Technical University,
Prospekt K. Marksa, 630073 Novosibirsk, Russia
[3] Volgograd State Technical University,
Lenin Avenue, 28, 400005 Volgograd, Russia

Abstract. The rapid growth of supercomputer technologies became a driver for
the development of natural sciences. Most of the discoveries in astronomy, in
physics of elementary particles, in the design of new materials in the DNA
research are connected with numerical simulation and with supercomputers.
Supercomputer simulation became an important tool for the processing of the
great volume of the observation and experimental data accumulated by the
mankind. Modern scientific challenges put the actuality of the works in computer systems and in the scientific software design to the highest level. The
architecture of the future exascale systems is still being discussed. Nevertheless,
it is necessary to develop the algorithms and software for such systems right
now. It is necessary to develop software that is capable of using tens and
hundreds of thousands of processors and of transmitting and storing of large
volumes of data. In the present work the technology for the development of such
algorithms and software is proposed. As an example of the use of the technology, the process of the software development is considered for some problems of astrophysics.

Keywords: Exascale systems · Co-design · High performance computing ·
Computational astrophysics · Physics of plasmas

1 Introduction

Recently the scientific community is widely discussing the transition to exascale
supercomputers. The main global challenges that the computer science specialists are
facing are the following. First, it is the problem of the development of algorithms that

This work was partially supported by RFBR grants 15-31-20150, 15-01-00508, 16-01-00564,
14-01-00392, 16-07-00534, 16-29-15120 and by Grant of the President of Russian Federation for the
support of young scientists number MK 6648.2015.9.

J. Carretero et al. (Eds.): ICA3PP 2016 Workshops, LNCS 10049, pp. 342–353, 2016.
DOI: 10.1007/978-3-319-49956-7_27

can consider the massive exascale level parallelism. Second, it is also the high-energy consumption of high performance computers. Third, it is the necessity to store and to process of exadata. Finally, it is the possible deviation from the classical paradigms of parallel programming. It is very important to research and development of next generation algorithms, software, and applications as an investment in hardware [1]. During the recent 7–8 years, a huge number of papers on the above listed questions appeared. In [1–5] a review is given and various approaches to exascale scientific software design are given. Most of these papers are based on co-design approach and also on the presumption that exascale systems will be built as massively parallel computers with the use of computational accelerators. In [6–8] the intrinsic problems of exascale systems are listed, such as insufficient concurrent work available to maintain high utilization of all resources, time-distance delay intrinsic to parallel actions and resources on the critical execution path, which is not necessary in a sequential variant, delay due to the lack of availability of oversubscribed shared resources. Also in [6–8] various methods for overcoming the intrinsic problems are given. In [9] the performance analysis is given for splitter-based parallel sorting algorithm on one of the most interesting supercomputers, namely the TSUBAME 2.5, which has 4000 NVIDIA K20x GPUs. Detailed analysis, however, reveals that the limitation is almost entirely due to the bottleneck in CPU-GPU host-to-device bandwidth. One of the main questions is the energy efficiency of programs [10, 11]. The analysis of the energy efficiency of the programs using computation accelerators may be conducted with both Nvidia nvprof utility [12] and Intel micsmc [13]. The most powerful computer from Top500 list consume over 15 MW. That is why the efficient workload distribution for the exascale system is one of the most important questions. Due to this reason, the design of the algorithms and programs for the systems based on mobile processors is highly actual [14, 15]. Considering the above listed papers, we propose our approach to the design of algorithms and software for massively parallel supercomputers:

1. The co-design: co-design here is the adaptation of the computational algorithm as well as the mathematical method to the architecture of the supercomputer at every stage of the problem solution.
2. Simulation modeling with AGNES: development of the preemptive algorithms and software for the most promising exascale computers on the basis of simulation modeling
3. Estimation of the energy efficiency of the algorithm: efficiency of memory utilization, of the resources of the processor and computation accelerators and of the network resources, analysis of energy consumption.

The advantage of our approach is the use of the AGNES package for the simulation modeling of the program execution. The AGNES package [16] enables to make the prediction of the scalability of the program basing on the statistics accumulated from program runs on various architectures [16, 17]. This is the difference of the AGNES package from the work in papers [18, 19] and that is why it enables to get an exact enough prediction of the scalability based on the real execution data.

2 The Co-design Approach

The development of scientific software without considering the target architecture may result in scalability [20]. We propose the following four stages for the design of the scientific software:

1. The choice of the physical model according to the problem statement and the possibility of the implementation of the target supercomputer architecture.
2. The choice of the mathematical model for the accurate description of the physical processes under study. The mathematical model must take the details of the exascale system into account.
3. The choice of computational methods considering the details of the exascale system
4. The implementation of the parallel code for massively parallel supercomputers.

As it was already mentioned in the Introduction, the development of code for petascale and especially for exascale systems is a complex scientific problem that requires the co-design approach. In such a way, the peculiarities of the problems of astrophysics are considered while keeping in mind the four above listed stages of co-design. Thus in each stage the different though interrelated problems are solved. Let us further describe each stage in detail.

At the stage of the construction of the physical model, the specification of the problem under study is being done. In addition, the sub-grid physical processes are defined. Moreover, at this stage, it is possible to make a reserve for further stages. In the problems of astrophysics, there are two physically different components. They are the gas component and the collisionless component. The gas component is employed for the description of the intergalactic and galactic gas, and for the simulation of stars (for example, the collapse of stars). The collisionless component is used for the description of stars and of dark matter in the galaxies and sometimes of the interstellar dust. The simulation of the interstellar component implies many difficulties. In the N-body model, which is traditionally employed for the description of the collisionless component there is the hard restriction for the number of particles. There is also the problems of the spurious entropy, of the numerical noise and of the particle form-factor choice in Particle-Mesh methods. Moreover, particle methods require load balancing which is a complex procedure for Peta- and Exascale supercomputers. A powerful option for the N-body model is the model based on the first moments of the collisionless Boltzmann equation [21, 22]. This model was successfully tested on the problems of the evolution of galaxies and the collision of galaxies.

While the mathematical formulation of the gas component model involved no big difficulties, for the collisionless component it is another way. The mathematical formulation of the first moments of the collisionless Boltzmann equation may be written in different forms. The specificity of the astrophysical problems is that the thermal conductivity terms have no crucial meaning. All the dynamics is defined by the distribution of density and velocity and by the entropy function. The entropy function for the gas component is the pressure and for the collisionless component, it is the velocity dispersion tensor.

The original numerical method based on the combination of the Godunov method, operator splitting approach and piecewise-parabolic method on local stencil was used for numerical solution of the hyperbolic equations [23]. The piecewise-parabolic method on local stencil provides the high precision order. The equation system is solved in two stages: at the Eulerian stage, the equations are solved without advective terms and at the Lagrangian stage, the advection transport is being performed. At the Eulerian stage, the hydrodynamic equations for both components are written in the non-conservative form and the advection terms are excluded. As the result, such a system has an analytical solution on the two-cell interface. This analytical solution is used to evaluate the flux through the two-cell interface. In order to improve the precision order, the piecewise-parabolic method on the local stencil (PPML) is used. The method is the construction of local parabolas inside the cells for each hydrodynamic quantity. The main difference of the PPML from the classical PPM method is the use of the local stencil for computation. It facilitates the parallel implementation by using only one layer for subdomain overlapping. It simplifies the implementation of the boundary conditions and decreases the number of communications thus improving the scalability. The detailed description of this method can be find in [24]. The same approach is used for the Lagrangian stage. Now the Poisson equation solution is based on Fast Fourier Transform method. This is because the Poisson equation solution takes several percents of the total computation time. After the Poisson equation solution, the hydrodynamic equation system solution is corrected. It should be noticed here that the system is overdefined. The correction is performed by means of the original procedure for the full energy conservation and the guaranteed entropy nondecrease. The procedure includes the renormalization of the velocity vector length, its direction remaining the same (on boundary gas-vacuum) and the entropy (or internal energy) and dispersion velocity tensor correction. Such a modification of the method keeps the detailed energy balance and guaranteed non-decrease of entropy.

The limitation of the astrophysical codes based on the SPH [25] and AMR [26] methods is the limited scalability. It is stipulated by the use of the tree-based procedure in these methods. It is well known that the tree-based procedures have strict limitations on scalability resulting in the limitations of the AMR and SPH parallel implementations. In addition, the AMR method has many difficulties in the transition from one mesh to another. This may result in the distortion of the solution. In the original approach presented in the paper employs regular meshes. The usage of regular meshes does not cause new mesh problems and at the same time gives a possibility to use various Cartesian topologies of communication for supercomputers and for accelerators.

In this work, the attention is focused on three architectures: the classical multiprocessor architecture, the hybrid architecture equipped with NVIDIA Tesla/Kepler the graphical accelerators and the hybrid architecture equipped with Intel Xeon Phi accelerators. The main characteristic of the supercomputer is the topology of the connections between computational cores. For the classical architecture, the topology might be arbitrary, but in most cases, the multidimensional Cartesian topology is used.

If the graphical accelerators are being used, then the multilevel Cartesian topology of the GPU plays the major role. With Intel Xeon Phi accelerators, the topology has the shape of a ring, which is also a sort of Cartesian topology. In such a way, the focus must be on arbitrary multidimensional Cartesian topologies.

The MPI library was used as the main tool for the development of the parallel code. Nvidia's CUDA technology was used for computations with graphical accelerators. This technology was used despite its complexity because provides full control over the computational process. Moreover, CUDA provides the low-level means for data movement between CPU and GPU. It also enables to define the topology of computational threads explicitly and to control their resources.

OpenMP technology was used for the computations with Intel Xeon Phi accelerators in the native mode. It was performed by means of the decomposition of the outer computational loops along the subdomain cells. In the offload mode, the extension of the OpenMP technology was used with the explicit specification of the memory domain transmitted to the accelerator and the procedures executed by the accelerator.

3   The Essentials to Gain Performance on Intel Xeon Phi Accelerators

There are many papers and success stories about transferring codes from CPU to Intel Xeon Phi (KNC) accelerator. The most of them are dedicated to bottlenecks of Intel Xeon Phi architecture and problems of software design [27, 28]. The key stages of code optimization for Intel Xeon Phi accelerator are algorithm optimization, optimization of arithmetic operations, optimization of memory operations, reducing the number of memory load operations, FMA instructions usage. In case of our astrophysics code, we achieve 6.5x speed-up due to the next optimizations:

1. Vectorization (changing scalar data type to vector data type).

Initial code:

```
vppp = dmedium(Vx, i + 1, k + 1, l + 1, i, k, l, NX, NY,
NZ);
rvppp = a[i*NZ*NY + k*NZ + l];
 if (vppp < 0.0) rvppp = a[(i + 1)*NZ*NY + k*NZ + l];
```

Vectorized code:

```
vppp = dmediumVectPhi(Vx, i + 1, k + 1, l + 1, i, k, l,
NX, NY, NZ);
rvppp = _mm512_load_pd(a + i*NZ*NY + k*NZ + l);
__m512d next = _mm512_load_pd(a + (i + 1)*NZ*NY + k*NZ +
l);
__m512d zero = _mm512_set1_pd(0);
rvppp = _mm512_mask_blend_pd(_mm512_cmp_pd_mask(vppp, ze-
ro, _CMP_LT_OS), rvppp, next);
```

2. Optimization of arithmetic operations (changing slow data operations to fast data operations with vector data types).

Initial code:

```
__m512d four = _mm512_set1_pd(4.0);
FXP =
_mm512_div_pd(_mm512_add_pd(_mm512_add_pd(_mm512_mul_pd(v
ppp, rvppp), _mm512_mul_pd(vppm, rvppm)),
_mm512_add_pd(_mm512_mul_pd(vpmp, rvpmp),
_mm512_mul_pd(vpmm, rvpmm))), four);
```

Optimized code:

```
__m512d quoter = _mm512_set1_pd(0.25);
FXP =
_mm512_div_pd(_mm512_add_pd(_mm512_add_pd(_mm512_mul_pd(v
ppp, rvppp), _mm512_mul_pd(vppm, rvppm)),
_mm512_add_pd(_mm512_mul_pd(vpmp, rvpmp),
_mm512_mul_pd(vpmm, rvpmm))), quoter);
```

3. Memory aligning (alignment data in memory for optimal memory usage)

Initial code:

```
R    = new real[NX*NY*NZ];
inline __m512d _mm512_loadu_pd(double* a)
{
    __m512d v_temp = _mm512_setzero_pd();
    v_temp = _mm512_loadunpacklo_pd(v_temp, a);
    v_temp = _mm512_loadunpackhi_pd(v_temp, a + 8);
    return v_temp;
}
__m512d next = _mm512_loadu_pd(a + (i + 1)*NZ*NY + k*NZ +
1);
_mm512_storeu_pd(anext + i*NZ*NY + k*NZ + 1, result);
```

Optimized code:

```
R = (real*)_mm_malloc((NX*NY*NZ + 8) * 8, 64);
R+=7;
__m512d next = _mm512_loadu_pd(a + (i + 1)*NZ*NY + k*NZ +
1);
_mm512_storeu_pd(anext + i*NZ*NY + k*NZ + 1, result);
```

4. FMA instructions usage. The FMA instruction set is an extension to the 128 and
   256-bit Streaming SIMD Extensions instructions in the x86 microprocessor
   instruction set to perform fused multiply–add (FMA) operations [29].

Initial code:

```
FXM=_mm512_mul_pd(_mm512_add_pd(_mm512_add_pd(
_mm512_mul_pd(vmpp, rvmpp), _mm512_mul_pd(vmpm, rvmpm)),
_mm512_add_pd(_mm512_mul_pd(vmmp, rvmmp),
_mm512_mul_pd(vmmm, rvmmm))), quoter);
```

Optimized code:

```
FXM=_mm512_mul_pd(vmpp, rvmpp);
FXM=_mm512_fmadd_pd(vmpm, rvmpm,FXM);
FXM=_mm512_fmadd_pd(vmmp, rvmmp,FXM);
FXM=_mm512_fmadd_pd(vmmm, rvmmm,FXM);
FXM=_mm512_mul_pd(FXM, quoter);
```

4 Simulation Modeling for an Astrophysics Problem

Supercomputers of the exascale level will appear approximately in 2018–2020.
Nevertheless, the scalability of an algorithm may be studied now by means of the
simulation modeling. It is known that simulation modeling is applied for the study of
the behavior of the complex systems.

One of the kinds of such complex systems are the exascale computers since they
contain tens or hundreds of millions of computational cores. The simulation model
enables to find the bottlenecks in the algorithms and to find out the need for
improvement. It provides the information on parameters that impact scalability. In the
present work, the peculiarities of the behavior of computational algorithms on various
clusters are considered. The estimation of their scalability is performed by the
multi-agent modeling system called AGNES (AGent NEtwork Simulator) [16]. Special
agents were created in the AGNES system for the astrophysics algorithms under study.
The agents simulate the behavior of computational nodes in the course of execution of
the corresponding algorithms (AstroGrid). These agents simulate the behavior of
computational nodes by the modeling of computations for each of the problems and by
the modeling of sending data to neighbor nodes. The AstroGrid agent sends messages
to a couple of neighbors and waits for the messages from them. Only after that, the
computation loop continues. The modeled delay time intervals are gathered and
compared with the delay time intervals taken from the real launches of the astrophysics
code under study. Simulation modeling results are compared to the parameters of the
program run. This is done in order to check the simulation model of the astrophysical
code execution. The real run was performed with the supercomputer called the
Polytechnic in the Saint-Petersburg Polytechnic University. The computer is essentially
the RSC PetaStream architecture [30] machine equipped with Intel Xeon Phi 5120D
(KNC) accelerators. Each node of Polytechnic has 8x Intel Xeon Phi accelerators with
their own interconnect (only native mode can be used for calculations). Users cannot

use CPUs in this architecture. This installation has Intel Parallel Studio XE 2016 software tool with Intel C ++ compiler 16 and Intel MPI 5.3.3. This system has 256x Intel Xeon Phi accelerators (more than 60000 cores). The results of the checking of the simulation model are given in Fig. 1. It is possible to say that the simulation model is similar to the real run. Unfortunately, we cannot use 100 % of KNC performance. We got from 30 to 100 GFLOPS performance on each accelerator for astrophysical code due to memory size restrictions (it is not possible to put enough data to 16 GB of internal accelerator memory). We hope that next Intel Xeon Phi series (KNL archi-tecture) accelerators with hybrid memory mode will speed up our code better.

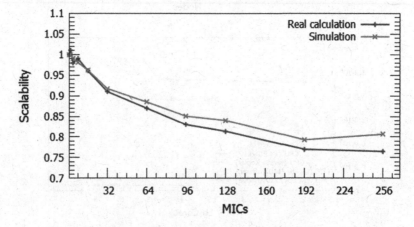

Fig. 1. Simulation for the astrophysical code.

The source data for the scalability study were obtained from the NKS-30T cluster in the Siberian Supercomputer Centre and in the Joint Supercomputer Centre RAS. The simulation modeling was done for a large number of cores. The simulation results are given in Fig. 2.

It follows from the Fig. 2 that the execution time slightly (about 20%) grows for 5120 computational nodes and the best scalability results are shown for the compu-tational nodes with Nvidia Kepler K40 and Intel Xeon Phi (native mode).

5 Energy Efficiency

At the moment energy, efficiency is actual mostly for commercial platforms [3]. However, with the age of exascale coming closer, the importance of HPC will increase greatly. The inefficient use of tens of megawatts may bring to naught the very idea to create exascale computers.

The term «energy efficiency for scientific HPC applications» in the present work means the most efficient use of each core, processor or computational accelerator; the minimization of communication between computational nodes; good workload bal-ancing of the program. The minimization of communications enables to decrease the

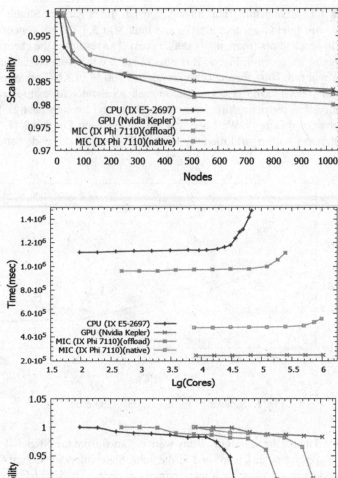

Fig. 2. Scalability research of the astrophysical code.

idle standing time for processors and accelerators. Good workload balancing enables to load the computational system uniformly. In the case of good workload balancing and stable node balancing we can make a set of the program runs that shows the relation between power consumption and usage of cores. The most energy efficient algorithm gave the best FLOPS per Watts (Joules/sec) value. For our astrophysical code, we reduced the time for MPI operations to 7–8% of the total time and to achieve the level of imbalance of 2–3% through all the process threads. These parameters provided the weak scalability of 75% for 224x Intel Xeon Phi accelerators (more than 50 K cores). We achieved 3 GFLOPS per Watt for our astrophysical code.

6 Conclusion

In this work, an approach is presented for the development of algorithms and software for massively parallel supercomputers. The approach consists of the three interrelated stages. The stage is the co-design, the simulation of scalability and the improvement of the energy efficiency. Co-design here is the adaptation of the computational algorithm as well as the mathematical method to the architecture of the supercomputer at every stage of the problem solution. In our case, the key stages of code optimization are algorithm optimization, optimization of arithmetic operations, optimization of memory operations, reducing the number of memory load operations, FMA instructions usage. The simulation of the scalability by means of the AGNES package is an important stage in the development of algorithms and software. At this stage, the proposed architecture of the exascale system is set and the scalability is studied with this architecture. The stage of the improvement of energy efficiency stage consists of the analysis of the possible code improvements such as the increase of the computational load of CPUs and GPUs, making better load balancing and reducing the number of MPI operations.

References

1. Reed, D.A., Dongarra, J.: Exascale computing and big data. Comm. ACM **58**(7), 56–68 (2015)
2. Dongarra, J.J., et al.: The international exascale software project roadmap. Int. J. High Perf. Comp. App. **25**(1), 3–60 (2011)
3. Keyes, D.E.: Exaflop/s: the why and the how. C.R. Mechanique **339**, 70–77 (2011)
4. Hsu, C-H., Kremer, U.: The design, implementation, and evaluation of a compiler algorithm for CPU energy reduction. In: Programming Languages, Design, and Implementation (2003)
5. Asanovic, K., Bodik, R., Demmel, J., Keaveny, T., Keutzer, K., Kubiatowicz, J., Morgan, N., Patterson, D., Sen, K., Wawrzynek, J., Wessel, D., Yelick, K.: A view of the parallel computing landscape. Comm. ACM **52**, 56–67 (2009)
6. Sterling, T.: Achieving scalability in the presence of asynchrony for exascale computing. Adv. Parall. Comp. **24**, 104–117 (2013)
7. Gao, G., Sterling, T., Stevens R., Hereld, M., Zhuparallex, W.: A study of a new parallel computation model. In: Proceedings of IEEE International Parallel and Distributed Processing Symposium, pp. 1–6 (2007)
8. Tabbal, A., Anderson, M., Brodowicz, M., Kaiser, H., Sterling, T.: Preliminary design examination of the parallex system from a software and hardware perspective. Sigmetrics Perform. Eval. Rev. **38**(4), 81–87 (2011)

9. Shamoto, H., Shirahata, K., Drozd, A., Sato, H., Matsuoka, S.: Large-scale distributed sorting for GPU-based heterogeneous supercomputers. In: Proceedings 2014 IEEE International Conference on Big Data, IEEE Big Data 2014, pp. 510–518 (2014)

10. Springer, R., Lowenthal, D.K., Rountree, B., Freeh, V.W.: Minimizing execution time in MPI programs on an energy-constrained, power scalable cluster. In: Proceedings of the Eleventh ACM SIGPLAN Symposium on Principles and Practice of Parallel Programming, pp. 230–238 (2006)

11. Freeh, V.W., Pan, F., Lowenthal, D.K., Kappiah, N., Springer, R., Rountree, B., Femal, M. E.: Analyzing the energy-time tradeoff in high-performance computing applications. IEEE Trans. Parall. Distr. Sys. **18**(6), 835–848 (2007)

12. NVIDIA profiler. http://docs.nvidia.com/cuda/profiler-users-guide/

13. Intel micsmc utility. https://software.intel.com/en-us/articles/measuring-power-on-intel-xeon-phi-product-family-devices

14. Nikolskiy, V., Stegailov, V.: Floating-point performance of ARM cores and their efficiency in classical molecular dynamics. J. Phys.: Conf. Ser. 681, Conf. **1**, 1–7 (2015)

15. Keller, V., Gruber, R.: One joule per GFlop for BLAS2 now!. In: AIP Conference Proceedings, vol. 1281, pp. 1321–1324 (2010)

16. Podkorytov, D., Rodionov, A., Sokolova, O., Yurgenson, A.: Using agent-oriented simulation system agnes for evaluation of sensor networks. In: Vinel, A., Bellalta, B., Sacchi, C., Lyakhov, A., Telek, M., Oliver, M. (eds.) MACOM 2010. LNCS, vol. 6235, pp. 247–250. Springer, Heidelberg (2010). doi:10.1007/978-3-642-15428-7_24

17. Bellifemine, F.L., Caire, G., Greenwood, D.: Developing Multi-Agent Systems with JADE. Wiley, Chichester (2007)

18. Glinsky, B., Rodionov, A., Marchenko, M., Podkorytov, D., Weins, D.: Scaling the distributed stochastic simulation to exaflop supercomputers. In: Proceedings of IEEE High Performance Computing and Communication and 2012 IEEE 9th International Conference on Embedded Software and Systems, pp. 1131–1136 (2012)

19. Chavarría-Miranda, D., Manzano, J., Krishnamoorthy, S., Vishnu, A., Barker, K., Hoisie, A.: SCaLeM: a framework for characterizing and analyzing execution models. In: Proceedings of 20 Years of Beowulf Workshop, ACM International Conference Proceeding Series, pp. 34–43 (2015)

20. Kulkarni, A., Lang, M., Lumsdaine, A.: GoDEL: A multidirectional dataflow execution model for large-scale computing. In: Proceedings of the First Workshop on Data-Flow Execution Models for Extreme Scale Computing, pp. 10–18 (2011)

21. Kulikov, I.: GPUPEGAS: a new GPU-accelerated hydrodynamic code for numerical simulations of interacting galaxies. Astrophys. J. Suppl. Ser. **214**(12), 1–12 (2014)

22. Kulikov, I.M., Chernykh, I.G., Snytnikov, A.V., Glinskiy, B.M., Tutukov, A.V.: AstroPhi: a code for complex simulation of dynamics of astrophysical objects using hybrid supercomputers. Comp. Phys. Comm. **186**, 71–80 (2015)

23. Godunov, S.K., Kulikov, I.M.: Computation of discontinuous solutions of fluid dynamics equations with entropy nondecrease guarantee. Comput. Math. Math. Phys. **54**, 1012–1024 (2014)

24. Kulikov, I., Vorobyov, E.: Using the PPML approach for constructing a low-dissipation, operator-splitting scheme for numerical simulations of hydrodynamic flows. J. Comput. Phys. **317**, 316–346 (2016)

25. Gingold, R.A., Monaghan, J.J.: Smoothed particle hydrodynamics: theory and application to non-spherical stars. Mon. Not. R. Astron. Soc. **181**, 375–389 (1977)

26. Berger, M.J., Colella, P.: Local adaptive mesh refinement for shock hydrodynamics. J. Comput. Phys. **82**, 64–84 (1989)

27. Pennycook, S.J., Hughes, C. J., Smelyanskiy, M., Jarvis, S.A.: Exploring SIMD for molecular dynamics, using intel xeon processors and intel xeon phi coprocessors. In: 2013 IEEE 27th International Symposium on Parallel and Distributed Processing (IPDPS) 2013, pp. 1085–1097. IEEE (2013)
28. Kim, S., Han, H.: Efficient SIMD code generation for irregular kernels. In: Proceedings of the Symposium on Principles and Practice of Parallel Programming, New Orleans, LA, 25–29 February 2012, pp. 55–64 (2012)
29. Intel® Architecture Instruction Set Extensions Programming Reference. https://software. intel.com/sites/default/files/m/9/2/3/41604
30. RSC PetaStream – 1PFLOPS per cabinet massively parallel supercomputer. http://www. rscgroup.ru/sites/default/files/rsc_petastream_en_print.pdf

Hardware-Specific Selection the Most Fast-Running Software Components

Alexey Sidnev[✉]

Lobachevsky State University of Nizhni Novgorod,
Nizhny Novgorod, Russia
alexey.sidnev@itmm.unn.ru

Abstract. Software development problems include, in particular, selection of the most fast-running software components among the available ones. In the paper it is proposed to develop a prediction model that can estimate software component runtime to solve this problem. Such a model is built as a function of algorithm parameters and computational system characteristics. It also has been studied which of those features are the most representative ones. As a result of these studies a two-stage scheme of prediction model development based on linear and non-linear machine learning algorithms has been formulated. The paper presents a comparative analysis of runtime prediction results for solving several linear algebra problems on 84 personal computers and servers. The use of the proposed approach shows an error of less than 22% for computational systems represented in the training data set.

Keywords: Software development · Software component selection · Runtime prediction · Computational system characteristics · Machine learning

1 Introduction

High performance and distributed computing has been being a relevant field in recent years. At present, we have a deeper understanding of the necessity of the algorithm optimization for core computational problems with respect to specific architecture and problem parameters. As a result, there are plenty of high performance libraries specially optimized for various hardware architectures (such as Intel MKL, AMD ACML, NVIDIA CUDA SDK, Sun Performance Library, etc.) at present. Some of these libraries allow automatic selecting efficient algorithm implementations and the parameters of these ones, which would be optimal for specific architectures and problem features. ATLAS is one of the most known examples of such libraries, which provides portably efficient BLAS implementation.

Currently, the prediction of runtime and, consequently, selecting the optimal algorithms for specific problems is one of the most important fields of distributed and

This research was supported by Russian Science Foundation, Project No 16-11-10150 "Novel efficient methods and software tools for the time consuming decision making problems with using supercomputers of superior performance".

J. Carretero et al. (Eds.): ICA3PP 2016 Workshops, LNCS 10049, pp. 354–364, 2016.
DOI: 10.1007/978-3-319-49956-7_28

high performance computing applications. Some research has been carried out in this area. J.R. Rice has stated the problem of algorithm selection for the first time [1] and has reduced this one to the approximation problem. One of the main approaches to the best algorithm selection consists in the runtime prediction and the selection of the fastest algorithm.

One of the possible ways to predict the algorithm runtime can be based on the results of the test runs. Brewer [2] has described the supercomputer runtime prediction by means of linear modeling based on the results of numerical experiments. However executing the experiments for all possible values of studied parameters can be time-consuming too much. Yang et al. [3] suggested analysis of an algorithm efficiency based on the information obtained in the course of its partial execution. In the same way, it is possible to predict the runtime for small dimensions and to extrapolate the results onto greater ones. However, the execution efficiencies for small and greater dimensions may differ. Since mid-1990s, machine learning algorithms have been used to solve the runtime prediction problem. The methods used the most extensively include the linear regression and its modifications (namely, the ridge and lasso regressions), the ensembles of decision trees, the support vector machines, the neural networks (see [4] for example), and the stochastic Gaussian processes [5]. Kotthoff et al. [6] have compared the results of several machine learning methods used for solving the algorithm selection problem. According to these results, the linear regression and the decision trees have been proven to be the most efficient in most cases.

In [7–9] the issue of algorithm selection efficiency has been discussed to consider a scheduling problem as an example (e.g. calculating foodstuffs transportation routes through a city). Howe et al. [8] have stated that depending on problem parameters, the majority of such algorithms either find an appropriate solution quickly or take a long time to find it (in the latter case, the algorithm is stopped because of preset runtime limit is exhausted). Therefore, it makes sense to use appropriate algorithms for specific classes of problem parameters only while the efficient planners enabling selection of suitable algorithm are demanded strongly. Xu et al. [10] have analyzed well-known the SAT solving planner. Gagliolo and Schmidhuber [11] have compared 28 planners using 4,726 test data sets. As can be seen from the above, the issue of automatic choice of the efficient algorithm selection has been studied extensively to date [12].

All authors referred to above use the run history for runtime prediction assuming the same computational system to be used to execute the algorithm. In the present paper, more generalized problem statement is considered, which enables the prediction without experiments involving the target computational systems.

2 Runtime Prediction Problems

We assume that $r, r > 1$, implementations of an algorithm are available and all of them solve the same problem and have the same set of parameters. For example, for matrix multiplication problem these parameters are the matrix dimensions. Let

$$P = (p_1, p_2, \ldots, p_m)$$

is the problem parameter vector and

$$X = (x_1, x_2, \ldots, x_k)$$

to be the characteristics vector of a computational system, so the ith implementation runtime y_i with the parameters P and the characteristics X will be

$$y_i = f_i(P, X),$$

where f_i is an unknown functional dependence, $i = \overline{1, r}$.

The most efficient implementation of algorithm i^* minimizes the time required to solve specific problem:

$$i^* = \underset{i=1..r}{\arg\min} f_i(P, X). \tag{1}$$

In order to solve problem (1), one needs to solve the runtime prediction problem, which consists in constructing a function $g_i(P, X)$ approximating f_i with a sufficient accuracy. The usual approaches produce the runtime predictions for particular algorithm implementation using the history of runs on the same computational system, i.e. function f_i depends on the algorithm parameters P only. Such an approach requires testing the algorithm implementation on every computational system that might take a lot of time. This paper proposes an alternative approach that allows predicting without testing on the target computational systems.

We choose the prediction quality to be the subject to the next loss function:

$$Q(g_i) = \sum_{(P, X) \in T} (g_i(P, X) - f_i(P, X))^2, \tag{2}$$

where T is the test data set, which values $f_i(P, X)$ are known in advance. So far, the runtime prediction problem for the specific computational system involves the construction of a function g_i^*, which minimizes the loss function:

$$g_i^* = \underset{g_i}{\arg\min} \sum_{(P, X) \in T} (g_i(P, X) - f_i(P, X))^2. \tag{3}$$

In order to construct g_i^*, let us use the runtime data for n computational systems. The set

$$T = \left(X_i, \left(y_{i,j}, P_{i,j} \right)_{j=1}^{e_i} \right)_{i=1}^{n} \tag{4}$$

contains the results of all executed runs (the training set), where e_i is the number of experiments involving the ith computational system.

3   Approach to Solving Runtime Prediction Problems

Runtime prediction problem (3) can be considered as a special case of the regression problem, which can be solved by a wide range of machine learning methods. In order to use any of these methods, we need to define a parametric set of mappings $g(P, X, \theta)$, where $\theta \in \Theta$ is some undefined parameters and $g : P \times X \times \Theta \to R^+$ is a function, which can be used to approximate the exact prediction dependencies f_i, $i = \overline{1, r}$. Problem (3) has several non-trivial features, which make it difficult to construct such a parametric set:

1. The algorithm implementation runtime depends on the parameters of the computational systems in a non-trivial way, so this dependency can be hardly represented as an analytical function with sufficient accuracy.
2. The extrapolation is necessary, e.g. a runtime prediction is to be done for larger problem dimensions then it is available in the training set.

To overcome these difficulties the proposed approach combines the linear regression methods with the non-linear ones.

Let us assume that for each implementation of the algorithm, an asymptotic complexity estimate is given in the next unified form:

$$h(P, C) = c_0 + \sum_{i=1}^{l} c_i \varphi_i(P),$$
(5)

where φ_i is a function that depends on the algorithm parameters. Then, the runtime of algorithm implementation y_i can be represented as a function $h(P, C)$ with the adjusted coefficients $C = (c_0, c_1, \ldots, c_l)$. Note that the coefficients C depend on the problem parameters P because different implementations of the same algorithm may be optimized differently for different problem parameters.

There are two stages in the learning algorithm (Fig. 1):

1. For each computational system with the characteristic X and for each value of P from the training set, the coefficients C of function $h(P, C)$ are being found with a preset threshold value W for the coefficient of determination. The regression of the coefficients C is applied for each computational system $i = \overline{1, n}$ separately:
   (a) Initialize the training set $T_i = (y_{i,j}, P_{i,j})_{j=1}^{e_i}$, $s = 1$.
   (b) If $s > e_i$, then all samples were processed, go to step (f); else use the linear least squares algorithm to estimate the coefficients $C = (c_0, c_1, \ldots, c_l)$ of the function $h(P, C)$ for the data set T_i.
   (c) Calculate the adjusted coefficient of determination for the linear model from previous step and the data set T_i considering the number of model parameters

$$\overline{R^2} = R^2 - \left(1 - R^2\right) \frac{l}{e_i - l - 1'}$$
(6)

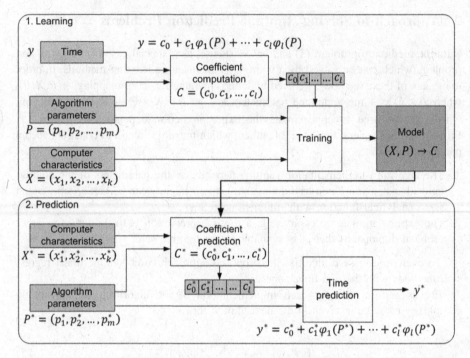

Fig. 1. Algorithms of learning and prediction

where R^2 is the coefficient of determination.

(d) If the value of $\overline{R^2}$ is larger than the preset threshold value W, then $PC_s = C$, $s = s + 1$, go to step (b); else go to step (e).

(e) If $h(P_{i,s}, C) > y_{i,s}$, then exclude $\arg\max\limits_{j=1..e_i} (h(P_{i,j}, C) - y_{i,j})$ from T_i, else exclude $\arg\min\limits_{j=1..e_i} (h(P_{i,j}, C) - y_{i,j})$ from T_i. $e_i = e_i - 1$, go to step (b).

(f) For computational system i perform clustering of coefficients $PC_{j=1}^{e_i}$ using DBSCAN [13] in order to eliminate the outliers.

2. Form the training set using the coefficients obtained at the previous step and corresponding characteristics of computational system and algorithm parameters $(X, P) \rightarrow C$, perform training of non-linear model on the obtained data (using the Random Forest method [14]).

The prediction algorithm has two stages also (Fig. 1):

1. The computational system characteristics X^* and the algorithm parameters P^* are used to predict the coefficients $C^* = (c_0^*, c_1^*, \ldots, c_l^*)$ from (5).
2. The algorithm parameters P^* and the calculated coefficients C^* are used to calculate the runtime prediction

$$y^* = c_0^* + c_1^* \varphi_1(P^*) + \cdots + c_1^* \varphi_l(P^*) \tag{7}$$

So far, the proposed solution of problem (3) consists of the prediction coefficients of asymptotic complexity function instead of the actual runtime values. The obtained solution provides extrapolating and successful analysis of a complex dependence of the algorithm runtime on the system parameters.

4 Features

4.1 Parameters of Algorithms

To predict the algorithm implementation runtime for a specific computational system, the linear regression method was used (i.e. linear least squares). For each algorithm, an asymptotic complexity estimate was available, so function $h(P, C)$ was known. The algorithms, their parameters, and the functions $h(P, C)$ are given in Table 1.

Table 1. Algorithm, parameters, the asymptotic complexity function and the conditions of the numerical experiments

Algorithm	Parameters P	Function $h(P, C)$	Experiments on every computational system
Matrix multiplication $C = A \cdot B$, $A \in R^{m \times k}$, $B \in R^{k \times n}$	Matrix size: m, k, n	$T = C_1 mkn + C_0$	200 random matrixes from 100×100 to 5000×5000
Sorting	Array size: n	$T = C_1 n log(n) + C_0$	49 random arrays from 10^5 to $4 \cdot 10^7$ elements
Direct method for solving system of linear equations	Computational grid size: n	$T = C_1 n^3 + C_0$	46 random computational grid from 100×100 to 10000×10000
Fast Fourier transform	Array size: n	$T = C_1 n log(n) + C_0$	30 random arrays from 10^4 to $25 \cdot 10^6$ elements

4.2 Static Characteristics of Computational Systems

The static characteristics of the computational systems are the parameters, which remain unchanged during the computations and may be obtained from the respective system information (e.g. from the processor registers [15]). Some parameters of the systems used are listed below.

1. Theoretical peak performance of the computational system for double-precision floating point computations (the calculations were subject to the number of vector instructions the processor is capable to handle per cycle [16]).

2. The information for each level of the processor cache:
   (a) Cache size.
   (b) Whether the cache is shared by multiple cores or belongs to a single core.
   (c) The number of cache access ports.
3. CPU clock speed in normal and turbo modes, the front side bus speed.
4. Memory subsystem information:
   (a) Number of channels.
   (b) Memory timing: CAS Latency, RAS to CAS Delay, RAS Precharge, Cycle Time.
5. The number of cores, the number of processors.
6. Hyper Threading availability.
7. Processor type: mobile, desktop, or server.
8. Processor manufacturer: Intel, AMD.
9. Core type: Ivy Bridge, Sandy Bridge, Conroe, Haswell, Wolfdale, Arrandale,. Brisbane, Yorfield, Pineview, Penryn, Lynnfield.
10. Supported instruction set: AVX, FMA4, SSE5, SSE4a, SSE4.2, etc.

In all, 77 static characteristics were used. All of them are either numerical or binary numbers.

4.3   Measurable Characteristics of Computational Systems

The static characteristics of the computational systems provide a sufficient description of the computational system performance. However, the description of the memory subsystems (both cache and RAM) requires some additional parameters. One of these parameters is the memory bandwidth.

The memory bandwidth is measured during the writing and reading operations. To execute these operations the data block size is taken to the power of two within the range from 8 KB to 64 MB (total 14 cases). This range enables the evaluation of all memory hierarchy elements. Access to memory elements may be either sequential or random. Thus, the memory bandwidth is measured for 4 different access types:

1. Sequential writing.
2. Sequential reading.
3. Random writing.
4. Random reading.

In all, 56 measurable parameters are used.

4.4   Feature Selection of Computational Systems

133 characteristics of the computational system are redundant for the data set with only 84 samples. Using such a large amount of features decreases the generalization ability of the model, so one needs to select the relevant features only. For example, for the matrix multiplication problem, the next four features were experimentally found to be the most relevant: the theoretical computer performance peak, the sequential write

speed for 2 MB memory block, the random write speed for 2 MB memory block, and the random read speed for 2 MB memory block. For all further experiments, these 4 features of the computational systems were used.

5 Results of Numerical Experiments

For each computational system, the experiments were carried out using MKL [17], OpenBLAS [18], TBB [19], and FFTW [20] libraries to estimate the algorithm runtimes depending on the problem parameters. Detailed information about the experiments is presented in Table 1. Total, 84 computational systems with shared memory were used (mobile, desktop, and server). Note that the performance of the computational systems used in the experiments varied within very wide range. Thus, solving the systems of linear equations with 10,000 variables using MKL library took from few seconds (for Intel Core i5-4570) up to 1,500 s (for Intel Atom N475).

5.1 Runtime Prediction

Figure 2 presents the boxplots of the runtime prediction errors for each computational system using the proposed approach for matrix multiplication from Intel MKL library. Training was performed on the small matrices (up to 1,000 × 1,000; total 36

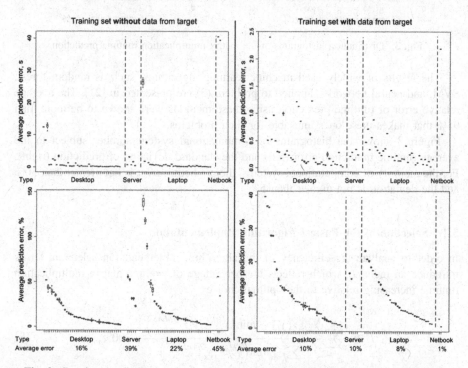

Fig. 2. Runtime prediction results for matrix multiplication using the proposed approach

experiments for each computational system) only, and the predictions were performed for the matrices up to $5,000 \times 5,000$ in size. Each computational system was used for generating a test set while the others were used as the training ones thus ensuring leave-one-out cross-validation. The results for the training set without the samples from the target computational system are presented as well as the results for the training set containing 5 samples from the target computational system.

The estimates obtained with proposed approach had the average error less than 22% for the systems, which are represented in the training set widely (desktops and laptops). The presence of data from the target computational system allows decreasing the average error down to 10% for these systems.

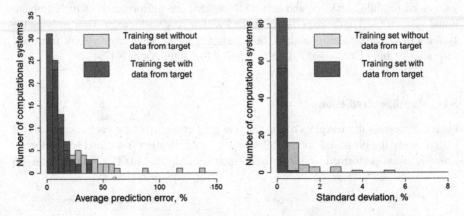

Fig. 3. Distribution histograms of the matrix multiplication runtime prediction

The results of widely used machine learning algorithms, such as random forest, SVM, and neural networks, applied to problem (3) are presented in [21]. The average relative error of runtime prediction using these methods were shown to be more than 95% that makes these ones unusable for such problems.

Figure 3 shows the histograms of computational system number subject to the average runtime prediction error (left) and the standard deviation of prediction (right). For the majority of computational systems, the prediction error is not greater than 30% and the deviation is not greater than 5%.

5.2 Selection of the Fastest Algorithm Implementation

In order to analyze the efficiency of the algorithm implementation selection, let us introduce an index L, which reflects the percentage of average matrix multiplication runtime increasing relative to the optimal choice

$$L = \frac{1}{n} \sum_{i=1}^{n} \frac{\sum_{j=1}^{e_i} \left(\overline{y_{i,j}} - \min\left(y_{i,j}^{MKL}, y_{i,j}^{OpenBLAS} \right) \right)}{\sum_{j=1}^{e_i} \min\left(y_{i,j}^{MKL}, y_{i,j}^{OpenBLAS} \right)} \cdot 100\%, \tag{8}$$

where $\overline{y_{i,j}}$ is the runtime of the selected implementation.

The following widely used strategies lead to a significant increasing of matrix multiplication runtime relative to the optimal choice:

- using OpenBLAS on all systems lead to 32% runtime increasing,
- using Intel MKL on all systems lead to 13% runtime increasing,
- using Intel MKL on Intel systems and OpenBLAS on AMD systems lead to 11% runtime increasing.

The proposed approach allows achieving 2% runtime increasing only relative to the optimal implementation choice for the matrix multiplication algorithm. For the experiments with other algorithms, this value is shown to be not greater than 6%.

6 Conclusions

This paper formulates the algorithm implementation selection problem subject to a computational system based on the experimental results obtained from the other computational systems. The proposed approach provides a runtime prediction model in the form of the runtime function of algorithm parameters and computational system characteristics. Four parameters from total 133 ones were found to be the most relevant: the theoretical computer performance peak, the sequential write speed for 2 MB memory block, the random write speed for 2 MB memory block, and random read speed for 2 MB memory block. Learning was based on the combination of the linear least squares method and the non-linear machine learning techniques (the random forest method). Such an approach combines the extrapolation ability and minor prediction error for the systems represented in the training data set widely.

The results may be used for the selection of the most efficient algorithm implementation in the target computer system without running the actual experiments. Besides, such data may be used for the evaluation of efficiency of the algorithm implementations as well as of the one of the computational system for the purposes of solving the problems mentioned above.

The results demonstrate the effectiveness of the proposed approach. The experiments with proposed approach on 84 computational systems and 4 libraries have shown the average increasing of problem solving time to be not greater than 6 % relative to the optimal choice.

The proposed approach for the runtime prediction and the most efficient implementation selection was applied to the global optimization algorithms as well [22–24].

References

1. Rice, J.R.: The algorithm selection problem. Adv. Comput. **15**, 65–118 (1976)
2. Brewer, E.A.: High-level optimization via automated statistical modeling. In: Proceedings of the 5th ACM SIGPLAN Symposium on Principles and Practice of Parallel Programming (PPOPP 1995), pp. 80–91 (1995)

3. Yang, T., Ma, X., Mueller, F.: Cross-platform performance prediction of parallel applications using partial execution. In: Proceedings of IEEE/ACM Supercomputing: International Conference on High-Performance Networking and Computing (2005)
4. Hastie, T., Tibshirani, R., Friedman, J.: The Elements of Statistical Learning: Data Mining, Inference, and Prediction. Springer Series in Statistics. Springer, Heidelberg (2009)
5. Rasmussen, C.E., Williams, C.K.I.: Gaussian Processes for Machine Learning. The MIT Press, Cambridge (2006)
6. Kotthoff, L., Gent, I.P., Miguel, I.: An evaluation of machine learning in algorithm selection for search problems. AI Commun. **25**(3), 257–270 (2012)
7. Fink, E.: How to solve it automatically: selection among problem-solving methods. In: Proceedings of the Fourth International Conference on AI Planning Systems, pp. 128–136. AAAI Press (1998)
8. Howe, A.E., Dahlman, E., Hansen, C., Scheetz, M., Mayrhauser, A.: Exploiting competitive planner performance. In: Biundo, S., Fox, M. (eds.) Recent Advances in AI Planning (ECP 1999). Lecture Notes in Computer Science, vol. 1809, pp. 62–72. Springer, Berlin Heidelberg (2000)
9. Roberts, M., Howe, A.: Learned models of performance for many planners. In: ICAPS 2007 Workshop AI Planning and Learning (2007)
10. Xu, L., Hutter, F., Hoos, H., Leyton-Brown, K.: SATzilla2009: an automatic algorithm portfolio for SAT. Solver description, SAT competition 2009 (2009)
11. Gagliolo, M., Schmidhuber, J.: Dynamic algorithm portfolios. In: International Symposium on Artificial Intelligence and Mathematics (ISAIM 2006) (2006)
12. Hutter, F., Xu, L., Hoos, H.H., Leyton-Brown, K.: Algorithm Runtime Prediction: Methods & Evaluation. Artif. Intell. **206**, 79–111 (2014)
13. Ester, M., Kriegel, H.-P., Sander, J., Xu, X.: A density-based algorithm for discovering clusters in large spatial databases with noise, pp. 226–231. AAAI Press (1996)
14. Breiman, L.: Random forests. Mach. Learn. **45**(1), 5–32 (2001)
15. Intel Processor Identification and CPUID Instruction. Application Note 485, May 2012
16. Fog, A.: Instruction tables: Lists of instruction latencies, throughputs and micro-operation breakdowns for Intel, AMD and VIA CPUs. http://www.agner.org/optimize/instruction_tables.pdf. Accessed 4 June 2014
17. Intel Math Kernel Library 11.1. https://software.intel.com/en-us/intel-mkl. Accessed 6 Apr 2014
18. OpenBLAS 0.2.9. http://www.openblas.net/. Accessed 6 Apr 2014
19. Intel Threading Building Blocks 4.2. https://www.threadingbuildingblocks.org/. Accessed 6 Apr 2014
20. FFTW 3.3.4. http://www.fftw.org/. Accessed 6 Apr 2014
21. Sidnev, A.: Runtime prediction on new architectures. In: Proceedings of the 10th Central and Eastern European Software Engineering Conference in Russia (CEE-SECR 2014), p. 7, Article 17. ACM, New York (2014)
22. Barkalov, K., Gergel, V.: Multilevel scheme of dimensionality reduction for parallel global search algorithms. In: An International Conference on Engineering and Applied Sciences Optimization (OPT-i 2014), Kos Island, Greece, 4–6 June 2014, pp. 2111–2124 (2014)
23. Bastrakov, S., Meyerov, I., Gergel, V., et al.: High performance computing in biomedical applications. Procedia Comput. Sci. **18**, 10–19 (2013)
24. Lebedev, I., Gergel, V.: Heterogeneous parallel computations for solving global optimization problems. Procedia Comput. Sci. **66**, 53–62 (2015)

Automated Parallel Simulation of Heart Electrical Activity Using Finite Element Method

Andrey Sozykin[1,2,3]([✉]), Timofei Epanchintsev[1,2,3], Vladimir Zverev[1,3],
Svyatoslav Khamzin[2,3], and Aleksandr Bersenev[1,3]

[1] Krasovskii Institute of Mathematics and Mechanics, Ekaterinburg, Russia
[2] Institute of Immunology and Physiology UrB RAS, Ekaterinburg, Russia
[3] Ural Federal University, Ekaterinburg, Russia
Andrey.Sozykin@urfu.ru

Abstract. In this paper we present an approach to the parallel simulation of the heart electrical activity using the finite element method with the help of the FEniCS automated scientific computing framework. FEniCS allows scientific software development using the near-mathematical notation and provides automatic parallelization on MPI clusters. We implemented the ten Tusscher–Panfilov (TP06) cell model of cardiac electrical activity. The scalability testing of the implementation was performed using up to 240 CPU cores and the 95 times speedup was achieved. We evaluated various combinations of the Krylov parallel linear solvers and the preconditioners available in FEniCS. The best performance was provided by the conjugate gradient method and the biconjugate gradient stabilized method solvers with the successive over-relaxation preconditioner. Since the FEniCS-based implementation of TP06 model uses notation close to the mathematical one, it can be utilized by computational mathematicians, biophysicists, and other researchers without extensive parallel computing skills.

Keywords: Heart simulation · Finite element method · Scalability · Krylov subspace methods · FEniCS · Parallel computing

1 Introduction

The mechanical contraction of a heart, which pumps the blood throughout the entire body, is caused by its electrical activity. In order to understand how the heart works, it is important to be able to simulate cardiac electrical processes. However, heart simulation is a complex multilevel (cell-tissue-organ) modeling task [9] that is very computationally intensive. Therefore, for a fast and accurate heart simulation, parallel computing is required.

The work is supported by the RAS Presidium grant I.33P "Fundamental problems of mathematical modeling," project no. 0401-2015-0025. Our study was performed using the *Uran* supercomputer of the Krasovskii Institute of Mathematics and Mechanics and computational cluster of the Ural Federal University.

J. Carretero et al. (Eds.): ICA3PP 2016 Workshops, LNCS 10049, pp. 365–372, 2016.
DOI: 10.1007/978-3-319-49956-7_29

However, the parallel heart simulation is impeded by the two obstacles. First, it requires a deep knowledge in a number of modern computational architectures and parallel programming technologies, which most of biophysicists do not possess. Secondly, sophisticated multilevel models are hard to implement in code, especially when the complex optimization for modern computational architectures is required. As a result, multilevel simulation software is very hard to support, while models and computational architectures are changing constantly.

Nowadays, automated scientific computing frameworks that allow software development using near-mathematical notation are becoming popular. Recently, the performance of such frameworks was significantly improved by the use of just-in-time compilers, highly efficient mathematical libraries, parallel computing, etc.

We propose an approach to simulation of the heart electrical activity using the scientific computing framework FEniCS [6], which provides the ability to automatically solve partial differential equations (PDE) using the finite element method (FEM) on MPI clusters. We use the FEniCS framework to study the space propagation of the membrane potential alternation over the left ventricle (LV) of a human heart using the *ten Tusscher–Panfilov* (TP06) cell model [10].

Due to the fact that FEM produces sparse matrices, computations heavily depend on the degree of sparsity because it allows to use various optimization techniques such as the *compressed row storage*, the *sparse matrix-vector multiplication*, or custom approaches [3]. Various models produce matrices with different degrees of sparsity. Hence, linear solvers and appropriate preconditioners demonstrate different results on parallel systems for various models. We evaluated which combination of the linear solver and the preconditioner is the most suitable for the simulation of a cardiac electrical activity using the *TP06 model*.

2   Model of the Heart Electrical Activity

There are many mathematical models of cardiac electrical activity. However, all of them contain the description of the *action potential* (AP), which is the difference of the potential between the intra- and extracellular space. We adopted the TP06 model [10,11] for the simulation of the electrical activity in the LV of a human heart. This model uses the reaction-diffusion equations to describe the space and time evolution of the action potential (V):

$$C_m \cdot \frac{dV}{dt} = \nabla \cdot (D\nabla V) - I_{ions}, \tag{1}$$

$$\frac{dS}{dt} = g(V, S), \tag{2}$$

where C_m is the capacitance of a cell membrane, D is the 3×3 diffusion matrix, I_{ions} is the sum of the ionic currents, S is the vector of the model variables that govern the ion currents, and g is the vector-valued function that describes the time evolution of each variable. The boundary conditions provide the LV electrical isolation.

On the intracellular level, the electrical potential arises from a very complicated interaction among ionic currents and cell organelles (organized structures
in cells). The *TP06* model contains the equations that describe how does the
state of ion channels change with time and the kinetics of intracellular concentra-
tions of calcium, sodium and potassium, extracellular potassium, the kinetics of
calcium complexes, and calcium kinetics in the organelles. All of this processes
are described by 18 phase variables. System (1)–(2) is defined at each point
of the heart tissue, and, consequently, we should solve it for each node of the
computational mesh.

Thus, the *TP06* model is a nonlinear system of partial and ordinary differential equations (ODE) that cannot be solved analytically and, hence, must be
solved on a computer using numerical techniques. This task is highly computationally intensive due to the big number of equations in the 3D domain and the
stiffness of the *TP06* model.

3 FEniCS and the Finite Element Method

FEM provides a powerful methodology for discretizing differential equations,
however, it produces algebraic systems the solution of which is also a challenge.
Linear solvers must handle sparsity and possible ill-conditioning of the algebraic
systems. In addition, modern solvers should also be able to use parallel computing systems efficiently. The FEM implementation in FEniCS is intended to
automate a PDE solution. In particular, FEniCS relies on the automation of discretization, discrete solution, and error control. FEniCS provides two approaches
for a PDE solution: direct and iterative. Iterative solution is more efficient
because it uses less memory and is easier to parallelize [6].

The FEniCS framework is a collection of software components for the formulation of variational forms (UFL [1]), the discretization of variational forms
(FIAT, FFC [4]), and the assembly of the corresponding discrete operators (UFC,
DOLFIN [7]). To solve a problem, FEniCS uses several highly efficient parallel
algebra backends, such as PETSc and Hypre. UFL is a domain-specific language
designed for convenient and understandable formulation of variational forms
using the near-mathematical notation. The discretization of variational forms
is done by generation of arbitrary order instances of the Lagrange elements on
lines, triangles, and tetrahedra (FIAT), and compilation of efficient low-level
C++ code that can be used to assemble the corresponding discrete operator
(FFC). The assembly of the discrete operators (tensors) is crucial for acceleration on parallel computing systems. The idea is to split the mesh among processing units, compute the local matrix, and insert the values back into the global
matrix. The FEniCS team designed the local-to-global mapping algorithm [4] to
map values between the local and global matrices.

The most computationally intensive task is solving the local linear system.
Hence, optimization of this step by selecting appropriate linear solver and preconditioner can provide a significant computation speedup.

4   Model Implementation in FEniCS

In order to implement the *TP06* model in FEniCS, we transformed the nonlinear system (1)–(2) into a linear one, which let us use iterative solvers. The transformation was performed with the help of the first order operator splitting scheme (the Marchuk–Yanenko method) [5]. The scheme of computing $V(t_n)$ and $S(t_n)$ can be described as follows. Let us assume that we have already calculated the values of $V(t)$ and $S(t)$ for $t < t_n$. In order to find the values of $V(t_n)$ and $S(t_n)$, we solve Eq. (3),

$$\frac{dV^*}{dt} = D\nabla V^*, V^*(t = t_{n-1}) = V(t_{n-1}), t \in [t_{n-1}, t_n],$$

$$\frac{dV^{**}}{dt} = I_{ions}, V^{**}(t = t_{n-1}) = V^*(t_n), \tag{3}$$

$$\frac{dS^{**}}{dt} = g(V^*, S^{**}), S^{**}(t = t_{n-1}) = S(t_{n-1}).$$

First, we solve the diffusion PDE. After that we have to find the solution of the ODE system for cell ionic currents. We get the final values of $V(t_n)$ and $S(t_n)$ according to the rules $V(t_n) = V^{**}(t_n)$ and $S(t_n) = S^{**}(t_n)$. This method is also known as the method of splitting into physical processes. The disadvantage of the approach is the necessity to use a very small integration time step (0.0005 s) in order to capture the fast electrochemical processes.

The model was implemented in the Python language using UFL. The code fragment for the diffusion PDE problem formulation is presented in Listing 1.1. First, a finite element mesh is created and loaded from the file. After that the discrete function space for AP is defined. FEniCS uses the term *trial function* to specify the unknown function that should be approximated (the variable v contains a trial function and the $v0$ variable contains the initial values). The next step is to define the linear variational problem for the diffusion equation. Lastly, the PDE solver is created.

Listing 1.1. Formulation of the diffusion PDE variational problem

```
mesh = Mesh()
# Code for loading mesh from the file
# Building function space for action potential
Space_AP = FunctionSpace(mesh,"Lagrange", lagrange_order)
# Define the PDE Problem
v = TrialFunction(Space_AP)
v0 = Function(Space_AP)
PdePart = (1.0/dt)*inner(v - v0, q1)*dx \
        - (-inner(D*grad(v),grad(q1)))*dx
PDEproblem = LinearVariationalProblem(lhs(PdePart),
    rhs(PdePart), v, bcs=bcs)
# Creating the PDE solver
PDEsolver = LinearVariationalSolver(PDEproblem)
```

Listing 1.2 demonstrates the code fragment for solving differential equations. The first step in the *for* loop solves the diffusion PDE using the PDEsolver. After that, the values of the state variables and AP, which was computed on the previous step, are stored. Next, the ODE system describing the cell ion currents is solved using the ODEsolver. There is no need for explicit, manual parallelization because the parallelization is provided by FEniCS. In addition to parallel computation, FEniCS provides the parallel output, during which each process writes its part of the data to a single file.

Listing 1.2. Solving the differential equation systems

```
for t in time_range [1:]:
    # Solving diffusion equation
    assign(v0, v)
    PDEsolver.solve()
    # Solving cell equations
    assign(ode_vars0, ode_vars)
    assign(ode_vars0.sub(0), v)
    ODEsolver.solve()
    # Storing data if necessary
    if steps
        v_file << (v, t)
    steps += 1
```

5   Performance Evaluation

During the experiments, we simulated the electrical activity of the human heart LV using the asymmetric anatomical model that was previously developed in our group [8] (an example of LV 3D mesh is presented in Fig. 1). We used the tetrahedral mesh with the length of the tetrahedrons from 2 to 4 mm; the mesh contained 7178 points and 26156 tetrahedrons. The GMSH software [2] was used for the initial mesh generation. Next, the mesh was converted by the DOLFIN module to the HDF5 format in order to enable parallel I/O operations.

The initial simulation conditions were the activation of a small part of LV near the apex (the potential is greater than 40 millivolt). The simulation duration was 0.3 s of physical time, because after this period the electrical activity tends to the equilibrium state in absence of an external stimulus.

The experiments were carried out on the *Uran* supercomputer of the Krasovskii Institute of Mathematics and Mechanics with the following computational nodes configuration: 2 x Intel Xeon CPU X5675 CPU, 192 GB RAM, Infiniband DDR interconnect, CentOS 7 operating system. The FEniCS version 1.6.0 was used.

The *TP06* model implementation was executed on the *Uran* supercomputer in parallel using various numbers of CPU cores, from 1 to 240. We used Krylov parallel linear solvers and preconditioners available in FEniCS (Table 1). The

Table 1. Parallel Krylov solvers and preconditioners available in FEniCS

Solver	Preconditioner
Biconjugate Gradient Stabilized	Algebraic Multigrid (amg)
Method (bicgstab)	Default preconditioner (Block Jacobi)
Conjugate Gradient method (cg)	Hypre Algebraic Multigrid (hypre_amg)
	Successive Over-relaxation (sor)

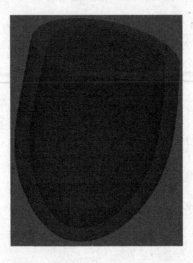

Fig. 1. An example of 3D mesh of the left ventricle (asymmetric model)

Table 2. The simulation time (minutes) using for various numbers of CPU cores

Solver and Preconditioner	Number of CPU cores									
	1	12	36	60	96	120	156	180	216	240
bicgstab + amg	1937	275	109	74	50	44	36	33	29	28
cg + amg	1930	242	96	65	44	39	35	32	29	27
bicgstab + default	1915	214	82	53	38	34	28	25	22	20
cg + default	1896	224	86	53	35	30	27	24	21	20
bicgstab + hypre_amg	1947	248	98	67	45	39	35	33	29	28
cg + hypre_amg	1925	268	106	71	49	43	35	32	29	27
bicgstab + none	2021	263	92	61	40	34	30	27	23	22
cg + none	1963	247	95	63	42	37	29	26	23	21
bicgstab + sor	1845	208	79	53	34	30	26	24	20	19
cg + sor	1839	220	85	55	36	32	26	23	20	19

simulation time with various combinations of solvers and preconditioners is presented in Table 2, the achieved speedup is demonstrated in Fig. 2.

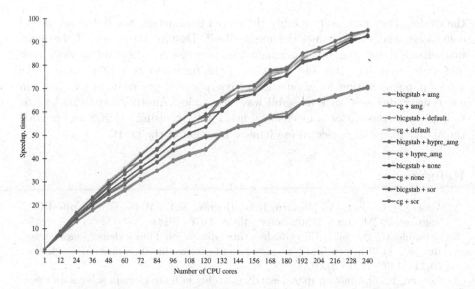

Fig. 2. Simulation speedup depending on the number of CPU cores

6   Discussion

The experiments demonstrated that the FEniCS-based *TP06* model implementation provides acceptable performance and good scalability. The best result was achieved using the *conjugate gradient method* and the *biconjugate gradient stabilized method* solvers with the *successive over-relaxation* preconditioner: 19 min of the simulation time, 95 times speedup using the 240 CPU cores.

Choosing the appropriate combination of the solver and the preconditioner is an important task. The best combination from our experiments (Table 1) provided 30% more performance on 240 CPU cores than the worst one (the *biconjugate gradient stabilized method* solver with the *algebraic multigrid* preconditioner). To save space, we presented in the paper only the best experiment results. FEniCS includes other solvers and preconditioners not listed in Table 1. Hence, in practice, the difference in performance of the best combination and other solvers and preconditioners available in FEniCS could be more than 30%.

As the number of CPU cores increases, the preconditioner's influence on performance becomes greater than the solver's. When we conducted the simulation on 132 CPU cores or more, there was no tangible difference in performance between different solvers working with the same preconditioner (Table 2).

7   Conclusion

The created implementation of the *TP06* model uses the near-mathematical notation provided by the FEniCS framework. As a result, computational mathematicians and biophysicists can use this implementation for experimenting with the model. They can easily modify the model parameters, the initial activation conditions, and even change the model itself. Despite the usage of the near-mathematical notation, our implementation provides an acceptable performance and scales well. The possible direction of the future work is to use the *TP06* model implementation for simulation of complicated processes in LV that can cause heart diseases, such as scroll wave dynamics. Another important task is to implement the model of mechanical heart activity using FEniCS and provide the ability to simulate electro-mechanical function of the heart.

References

1. Alnæs, M.S., Logg, A., Ølgaard, K.B., Rognes, M.E., Wells, G.N.: Unified form language. ACM Trans. Math. Softw. **40**(2), 1–37 (2014)
2. Geuzaine, C., Remacle, J.F.: Gmsh: a three-dimensional finite element mesh generator with built-in pre- and post-processing facilities. Int. J. Numer. Methods Eng. **79**(11), 1309–1331 (2009)
3. Jansson, N.: Optimizing sparse matrix assembly in finite element solvers with one-sided communication. In: Daydé, M., Marques, O., Nakajima, K. (eds.) VECPAR 2012. LNCS, vol. 7851, pp. 128–139. Springer, Heidelberg (2013). doi:10.1007/978-3-642-38718-0_15
4. Kirby, R.C., Logg, A.: A compiler for variational forms. ACM Trans. Math. Softw. **32**(3), 417–444 (2006)
5. Li, Y., Chen, C.: An efficient split-operator scheme for 2-D advection-diffusion simulations using finite elements and characteristics. Appl. Math. Model. **13**(4), 248–253 (1989)
6. Logg, A., Mardal, K.A., Wells, G.: Automated Solution of Differential Equations by the Finite Element Method: The FEniCS Book. Springer Science & Business Media, Heidelberg (2012)
7. Logg, A., Wells, G.N.: DOLFIN: automated finite element computing. ACM Trans. Math. Softw. (TOMS) **37**(2), 1–28 (2010)
8. Pravdin, S.F., Berdyshev, V.I., Panfilov, A.V., Katsnelson, L.B., Solovyova, O., Markhasin, V.S.: Mathematical model of the anatomy and fibre orientation field of the left ventricle of the heart. Biomed. Eng. Online **54**(12), 21 (2013)
9. Kerckhos, R.C.P., Healy, S.N., Usyk, T.P., McCulloch, A.D.: Computational methods for cardiac electromechanics. Proc. IEEE **94**, 769–783 (2006)
10. Ten Tusscher, K.H., Panfilov, A.V.: Alternans and spiral breakup in a human ventricular tissue model. Am. J. Physiol. Heart Circulatory Physiol. **291**(3), H1088–H1100 (2006)
11. Ten Tusscher, K.H., Panfilov, A.V., et al.: Organization of ventricular fibrillation in the human heart. Circulation Res. **100**(12), e87–e101 (2007)

Using hStreams Programming Library for Accelerating a Real-Life Application on Intel MIC

Lukasz Szustak[1], Kamil Halbiniak[1(✉)], Adam Kulawik[1],
Roman Wyrzykowski[1], Piotr Uminski[2], and Marcin Sasinowski[2]

[1] Czestochowa University of Technology, Częstochowa, Poland
{lszustak,khalbiniak,adam.kulawik,roman}@icis.pcz.pl
[2] Intel Corporation, Santa Clara, USA
{piotr.uminski,marcin.sasinowski}@intel.com

Abstract. The main goal of this paper is the suitability assessment of the hStreams programming library for porting a real-life scientific application to heterogeneous platforms with Intel Xeon Phi coprocessors. This emerging library offers a higher level of abstraction to provide effective concurrency among tasks, and control over the overall performance. In our study, we focus on applying the FIFO streaming model for a parallel application which implements the numerical model of alloy solidification. In the paper, we show how scientific applications can benefit from multiple streams. To take full advantages of hStreams, we propose a decomposition of the studied application that allows us to distribute tasks belonging to the computational core of the application among two logical streams within two logical/physical domains. Effective overlapping computations with data transfers is another goal achieved in this way. The proposed approach allows us to execute the whole application 3.5 times faster than the original parallel version running on two CPUs.

Keywords: Intel MIC · Hybrid architecture · Numerical modeling of solidification · Heterogeneous programming · Hstreams library · Task and data parallelism

1 Introduction

Efficient concurrency on the task level is difficult to achieve, especially on heterogeneous platforms. An emerging effort on the way to meet this challenge is the hStreams programming framework [1–3], a new heterogeneous streaming library. It is based on a simple FIFO streaming model, and supports concurrency across nodes, among tasks within a node, and between data transfers and computation.

This research was conducted with the financial support of National Science Centre grant no. UMO-2011/03/B/ST6/03500. The authors are grateful to the Czestochowa University of Technology for granting access to Intel Xeon Phi coprocessors provided by the MICLAB project no. POIG.02.03.00.24-093/13.

J. Carretero et al. (Eds.): ICA3PP 2016 Workshops, LNCS 10049, pp. 373–382, 2016.
DOI: 10.1007/978-3-319-49956-7_30

This framework is aimed at making it easier to port and tune task-parallel codes by offering such features as [1]: (i) separation of concerns, (ii) sequential semantics, (iii) task concurrency, (iv) pipeline parallelism, and (v) unified interface to heterogeneous platforms. In particular, the first feature addresses key programming productivity issues by allowing a separation of concerns between (1) the expression of functional semantics and disclosure of task parallelism, and (2) the performance tuning and control over mapping tasks onto a platform. As a result, while creators of scientific algorithms receive something simple and intuitive, code tuners may work long after them, having the freedom to control over the code execution without the need for application domain expertise. A detailed comparison of hStreams with other heterogeneous programming environments such as OpenMP, OmpSs, Offload Streams and CUDA Streams is presented in paper [1].

Heterogeneous platforms become increasingly popular in many application domains [2–4]. The combination of using a general-purpose CPUs combined with specialized computing devices (e.g., GPU, Intel Xeon Phi or FPGA) enabled in many cases for accelerating an application by significant amounts [4–6]. However, realizing these performance potentials remains a challenging issue.

The main goal of this paper is the suitability assessment of the hStreams framework for porting a real-life scientific application to heterogeneous platforms with Intel Xeon Phi coprocessors. We focus on utilizing the FIFO streaming model in a parallel application which implements a numerical model of alloy solidification. This application has been already studied in our previous work [7], where we developed an approach for porting and optimizing the application on computing platforms with a single Intel Xeon Phi accelerator [4]. The proposed scheme of parallelization and workload distribution was implemented using the offload interface [7], dedicated directly for the Intel MIC architecture.

The contribution of this paper to the area of co-design technologies are as follows: (1) demonstration of applicability of the hStreams programming framework for porting a complex application to a heterogeneous platform in a relative quick and easy way, which justifies the conclusion that using the hStreams framework increases the level of abstraction for the code development in hybrid hardware environments; (2) hardware-aware performance tuning of the resulting code with its experimental evaluation showing practically the same performance as in the case of the low-level offload interface.

The material of the paper is organized as follow. Section 2 provides an overview of the hStreams library, while Sect. 3 introduces the numerical model of solidification, and the idea of its parallelization on platforms containing Intel Xeon Phi coprocessors. The next section outlines the most important details of mapping the solidification application onto heterogeneous streams. Section 5 presents performance results achieved for the proposed approach, while Sect. 6 concludes the paper and addresses future works.

2   Introduction to Hetero Streams Library

2.1   Overview of hStreams

The hetero Streams library (hStreams) [1,2] allows stream programming in heterogeneous platforms consisting of Intel Xeon CPUs and Intel Xeon Phi coprocessors. Stream programming model assumes existence of one or more FIFOs abstractions, where computation jobs are submitted on the computing entities.

Before proceeding further, the introduction is needed for two key definitions that hStreams uses: **source** is a place where work is enqueued to be performed, and **sink** is a place where work is executed. Source and sink can either share resources of the same processor or reside on separate ones. In a typical scenario, source resides on an Intel Xeon CPU, while sinks are present on the same CPU, as well as on Intel coprocessors connected to the main processor over PCIe.

Memory resources shared between source and sinks are called **logical buffers**. Logical buffers are registered by the application on the source. Once the hStreams run-time is aware of the buffer, a pointer to a memory location anywhere inside that buffer is recognized as a handle, and can be used for performing data transfers or compute actions involving that buffer. A logical buffer created by the user may have instantiations in many **logical domains** beside the source. Those instantiations of the buffer are called **physical buffers**. A logical buffer must have a corresponding physical buffer on the logical domain where it is intended to be used (either as an operand of a data transfer or a compute action).

Actions are enqueued in a FIFO queue called **stream**. From the operating systems point of view, the stream is a subset of processor cores with access to the local memory. There are three categories of actions: **task computations**, **memory transfers** and **synchronization**. The task computation is performed entirely on the sink side. Memory transfers are performed between buffers on the source and their sink instantiations. Transfers are defined by the direction (source to sink or sink to source) and source-side buffer addresses. Synchronization actions involve the sink endpoint of a stream waiting on a collection of events, triggered by the completion of actions enqueued in any stream.

Streams are organized into **logical domains**. Memory buffers are shared by all streams inside a single logical domain, while being disjointed from other logical domains. One or more logical domains belong to a **physical domain**. The physical domain can be treated as physical device: an Intel Xeon Phi coprocessor or an Intel Xeon server. This approach allows us to have the same API for a coprocessor and server, while also sharing the same memory on server.

Internally, hStreams has implicit dependency management. By default a task enqueued in a stream depends on the previous task in this stream and on all buffers used by this task, but does not depend on memory transfers of buffers not related to the previous task. Dependencies can also be controlled explicitly by the application - for example, the application can wait for completion of one or more previously defined events. Such dependency management allows programmers to hide communication behind computation.

Two levels of API are exposed by hStreams - the higher level App API and lower level Core API. The former offers a subset of the hStreams functionality and is designed to allow a novice user to quickly start writing programs. Its productivity is boosted by helper functions and common building blocks. The Core API - on the other hand - exposes the full functionality of hStreams, and is targeted at a more advanced user. Currently, the hStreams library supports Intel Xeon CPUs and the first generation of Intel Xeon Phi coprocessors. Support for other configurations may be added in the future. The hStreams framework was created by Intel and is maintained on the public repository. Its latest version and source code is available at https://github.com/01org/hetero-streams.

2.2   Comparison of hStreams with OpenMP

In this section, we briefly compare hStreams with OpenMP as the most popular parallel programming standard, which offers support for heterogeneous computing [8]. The most obvious differences between them is that hStreams represents a library-based API, while OpenMP is a compiler-based language extension [1]. An important advantage of hStreams is independence from the compilers. In this case, the utilization of new features requires only updating the library, unlike OpenMP where new mechanisms are available only after updating the compiler to the latest version. For many programmers who prefer to change compilers rarely, the use of the library-based extensions seems to be most attractive.

Unlike OpenMP, the Hetero Streams library provides an uniform interface for heterogeneous platforms [1,2]. Both environments are based on the host-centric model, where one of the host threads transfers data and computation to the platform components. However, in hStreams all the resources of a platform are handled in uniform way, whie OpenMP separates constructs used to assign the application workload to host and remote devices. The current version of the hStreams library gives also the possibility for offloading computation to remote nodes over fabric. The great advantage of hStreams over OpenMP is the ability to subdividing a device, that allows executing multiple offload regions concurrently.

The differences between hStreams and OpenMP are noticeable also in data management. Both environments give the possibility to transfer data from memory of one device to another. In hStreams, buffers used for data movements have to be allocated before starting the transfer, while in OpenMP data allocations can be performed explicitly or implicitly. Opposite to OpenMP, the hStreams framework provides also an efficient support for memory allocations in different memory types [1].

3   Application: Numerical Model of Solidification and Parallelization on Platforms with Intel MIC

3.1   Numerical Model

The phase-field method is a powerful tool for solving interfacial problems in materials science [9]. It has mainly been applied to solidification dynamics [10], but it has also been used for other phenomena such as viscous fingering [11], fracture dynamics, [12], and vesicle dynamics [9]. The number of scientific papers related to the phase-field method grows since the 90 years of XX century, reaching for the last 7 years more than 400 positions (according to the SCOPUS database) [13].

In the numerical examples studied in this paper, a binary alloy of Ni-Cu is considered as a system of the ideal metal mixture in the liquid and solid phases. The numerical model [14] refers to the dendritic solidification process in the isothermal conditions with constant diffusivity coefficients for both phases. It allows us to use the field-phase model defined by Warren and Boettinger [14]. In this model, the growth of microstructure during the solidification process is determined by solving a system of two PDEs [14,15], which define the phase content ϕ and concentration c of the alloy dopant (one of the alloy components).

The resulting numerical scheme belongs to the group of forward-in-time iterative algorithms [7]. The application code consists of two main blocks of computation, which are responsible for determining either the phase content (Fig. 1) or the dopant concentration. In the model studied in the paper, values of ϕ and c are calculated for nodes uniformly distributed across a square domain. However, the presented approach, which is based on the generalized finite difference method, allows for solving PDEs not only for regular, but also irregular grids.

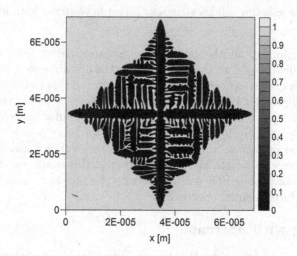

Fig. 1. Phase content for the simulated time $t = 2.75 \times 10^{-3} s$ (original code)

3.2 Idea of Parallelization for Platforms with MIC

In the studied application, computation are interleaved with writing partial results to a file. In the original version (Fig. 2a), parallel computations are executed for subsequent time steps, while writing results to the file is performed after the first time step, and then after every package of 2000 time steps. Figure 2b shows the idea of adapting the application to platforms with a single Intel Xeon Phi. In this approach, the coprocessor is employed to perform major parallel workloads, while the rest of application is assigned to CPU, as not requiring massively parallel resources. In consequence, writing data to the file is the responsibility of CPU, while the coprocessor provides execution of parallel regions of the code.

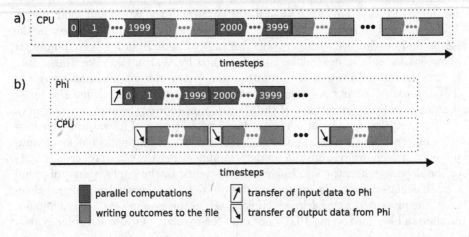

Fig. 2. Idea of adapting solidification application to platforms with Intel MIC [7]

At the beginning, all the input data are transferred from CPU to the coprocessor, which then starts computation for the first time step. After finishing it, all the results are transferred back to CPU. During this transfer, coprocessor starts computations for the next package of 2000 time steps. At the same time, CPU begins writing results to the file, immediately after receiving outcomes from the coprocessor. Such a scheme is repeated for every package of 2000 time steps. A critical performance challenge here is to overlap workload performed by the coprocessor with data movements. To meet this challenge, data transfers between CPU and Xeon Phi, writing data to the file, as well as computation have to be performed simultaneously.

4 Porting with hStreams

4.1 Mapping Application Workload onto Heterogeneous Streams

The hStreams library supports the task parallelism by creating multiple streams. This advantage can be efficiently applied for the proposed idea of adapting the solidification application to platforms with a single Intel MIC. Our approach distinguishes the two main tasks: (i) writing outcomes to the file, and (ii) running parallel computation. These tasks are mapped onto two logical streams created within two logical domains. This solution allows for executing streams on different computing resources, such as processor and coprocessor.

The idea of mapping the application on heterogeneous streams is illustrated in Fig. 3. While the first stream is responsible for parallel computation performed for subsequent packages of 2000 time steps, the second one has to provide transfers of outcomes from the first stream, in order to write them further to the file. These streams are assigned respectively to the coprocessor and CPU.

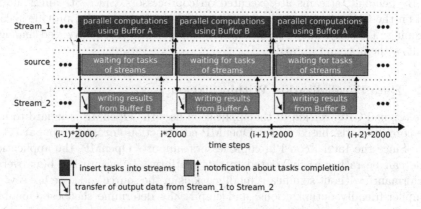

Fig. 3. Mapping solidification application onto heterogeneous streams

Because of mutual dependencies between the execution of streams, their synchronizations becomes a crucial issue. The hStreams library offers two scenarios for solving this issue that correspond to various ways of filling queues of streams. The first way requires to fill the FIFO queue before the stream execution, while the second one refill the FIFO queue during the execution of stream. In both cases, the source process is responsible for the management of queues. For the first way, the stream synchronization is based on the completion of events that have to be inserted into the streams before execution. The second way, called the active synchronization, employs the source process to provide the synchronization of streams during execution. In this scenario, the source process waits for the completion of tasks of a stream, in order to insert subsequent tasks to queues, and then run streams. In our approach, the second scenario is chosen (see Fig. 3) as more suitable for the proposed idea of parallelization. As a results, the synchronization points occur after every package of 2000 time steps.

Selecting an appropriate method for providing efficient data transfers is important for the overall performance. In the proposed approach, data are transferred excluding the source process. It allows us to reduce the communication path from the default scheme Stream_1 → source → Stream_2 to the shorter one, where data are transferred directly between streams: Stream_1 → Stream_2. The task of data movement that downloads outcomes from the logical domain of Stream_1 is inserted into queue of Stream_2.

To overlap computation with data transfers, the double buffering techniques is applied: the first buffer is used to provide computation while the second one is responsible for data movement of outcomes of the previous time steps (Fig. 3). However, a right policy of hStreams data dependencies has to be applied for enabling this optimization. The default police HSTR_DEP_POLICY_CONSERVATIVE prevents the simultaneous execution of tasks for data transfers and computation. To solve this problem, the policy HSTR_DEP_POLICY_BUFFERS has to be set in order to ensure the asynchronous execution of these tasks using different buffers.

By defauult, streams are executed on coprocessors. Since Stream_2 should run on the CPU site, the hStreams Core API has to be used to provide such a mapping. This API allows programmers to perform a more advanced management of the hStream library.

4.2 Data Parallelization Within Streams

The original CPU version of the application uses the OpenMP standard to utilize cores/threads, based on the OpenMP construction #pragma omp parallel for. Since the Intel Xeon Phi coprocessors supports OpenMP, the application code can be rather easily ported to this platform. To ensure the best overall performance without significant modifications in the source code, we use several compiler-friendly optimizations, and empirically determine the best OpenMP setup for the loop scheduling.

The utilization of vector processing is crucial for ensuring the best performance on Intel Xeon Phi. The quickest way to achieve this goal is the compiler-based automatic vectorization. However, in the studied case the innermost loop cannot be vectorized safely, mainly because of data dependencies. To solve this problem, we propose to change slightly the code by adding temporary vectors responsible for loading the necessary data from the irregular memory region, and than providing SIMD computations (see our previous work [5,7]).

5   Performance Results

In this study, we use the platform [16] equipped with two Intel Xeon E5-2699 v3 CPUs (Haswell-EP), and Intel Xeon Phi 7120P coprocessor (Knight Corner). The benchmarks are compiled using the Intel icpc compiler (v.15.0.2) with the same optimization flags. All tests are performed for modeling solidification application using the double precision floating-point format, 110000 time steps, and grid with 4000000 nodes (2000 nodes along each dimensions x and y).

Table 1 presents the comparison of the execution times obtained for: (i) original CPU parallel version of the solidification application, (ii) optimized parallel version based on the offload interface (see our previous work [7]), and (iii) new parallel code programmed with hStreams. Both the offload- and hStreams-based versions correspond to the proposed adaptation of the studied application to platforms with a single Intel Xeon Phi.

The total execution time of the original version (see Fig. 2a) includes the sum of execution times necessary for performing parallel computation and writing outcomes to the file. The proposed approach (see Fig. 2b) allows us to hide more than 99 % of computations behind data movements, for both the offload- and hStreams-based versions, and finally accelerate the whole application about 3.50x. Comparing the execution times of the hStreams- and offload-based codes, we can see that the difference is negligible, since it is equal to 0.28 %.

Table 1. Performance results for different versions of the solidification application

| Code version | Tasks | | Time | Speedup |
	data movements	parallel computation		
original	CPU	CPU	641 min 32 s	-
offload-based	CPU	MIC	183 min 08 s	3.50x
hStreams-based	CPU	MIC	183 min 39 s	3.49x

6   Conclusions and Future Works

The hStreams programming library is a promising solution for the exploration of emerging multi- and manycore architectures that become increasingly complex, hierarchical and heterogeneous. It is expected that the potential of using hStreams on current and future platforms will be manifested for a wide range of real-life applications. Our research allow us to conclude that the hStream library enables for porting such applications on modern architectures, including Intel MIC, in a relatively quick and easy way.

The streaming abstraction is one of advantages of this library which enables for mapping concurrent tasks onto computing resources. A rich functionality of hStreams, including synchronization scenarios and overlapping tasks, makes this library programmer-friendly, and increases the level of abstraction for the code development. The performed benchmark confirms that the hStreams library allows for achieving the performance results at the same level as the offload model, dedicated directly for the Intel MIC architecture. At the same time, it is worth to mention that the proposed adaptation of the solidification application to platforms with Intel MIC plays the main role in accelerating computations, while the hStreams library and offload interface are "only" tools that allows us to reach this goal.

The performance results achieved in this study provide the basis for further research on the development and optimization of code. The primary direction of our future work is to utilize hStreams for porting the studied application on heterogeneous platforms with more than one Intel Xeon Phi coprocessor, and taking advantage of all the computing resources to process together the application workload. Also, we plan to use our application as a valuable benchmark for comparing hStreams with other programming models and languages interfaces, and in particular, with the OpenMP 4.x support [17] for heterogeneous computing and task-parallelism.

References

1. Newburn, C.J., et al.: Heterogeneous streaming. In: IPDPSW, AsHES (2016)
2. Jeffers, J., Reinders, J.: Fast matrix computations on heterogeneous streams. In: Jeffers, J., Reinders, J. (eds.), High Performance Parallelism Pearls: Multicore and Many-core Programming Approaches, vol. 2, pp. 49–52. Morgan Kaufmann (2015)
3. Li, Z., et al.: Evaluating the Performance Impact of Multiple Streams on the MIC-based Heterogeneous Platform (2016). arXiv preprint arXiv:1603.08619
4. Szustak, L., Rojek, K., Olas, T., Kuczynski, L., Halbiniak, K., Gepner, P.: Adaptation of MPDATA heterogeneous stencil computation to Intel Xeon Phi coprocessor. Sci. Program. (2015). http://dx.doi.org/10.1155/2015/642705
5. Szustak, L., Halbiniak, K., Kuczynski, L., Wrobel, J., Kulawik, A.: Porting, optimization of solidification application for CPU-MIC hybrid platforms. Accepted to print: Int. J. High Perform. Comput. Appl., 13 (2016)
6. Rojek, K., et al.: Adaptation of fluid model EULAG to graphics processing unit architecture. Concurrency Computations Pract. Experience **27**(4), 937–957 (2015)
7. Szustak, L., Halbiniak, K., Kulawik, A., Wrobel, J., Gepner, P.: Toward parallel modeling of solidification based on the generalized finite difference method using intel xeon phi. In: Wyrzykowski, R., Deelman, E., Dongarra, J., Karczewski, K., Kitowski, J., Wiatr, K. (eds.) PPAM 2015. LNCS, vol. 9573, pp. 411–422. Springer, Heidelberg (2016). doi:10.1007/978-3-319-32149-3_39
8. OpenMP Application Programming Interface (2015)
9. Steinbach, I.: Phase-field models in materials science. Model. Simul. Mater. Sci. Eng. **17**(7), 73001 (2009)
10. Provatas, N., Elder, K.: Phase-Field Methods in Materials Science and Engineering. Wiley, New York (2010)
11. Folch, R., Casademunt, J., Hernandez-Machado, A., Ramirez-Piscina, L.: Phase-field model for Hele-Shaw flows with arbitrary viscosity contrast. II. Numer. Study. Phys. Rev. E **60**(2), 1734–1740 (1999)
12. Karma, A., Kessler, D., Levine, H.: Phase-field model of mode III dynamic fracture: Phys. Rev. Lett. **87**(4), 40401 (2001)
13. Takaki, T.: Phase-field modeling and simulations of dendrite growth. ISIJ Int. **54**(2), 437–444 (2014)
14. Warren, J.A., Boettinger, W.J.: Prediction of dendritic growth and microsegregation patterns in a binary alloy using the phase-field method. Acta Metall. et Mater. **43**(2), 689–703 (1995)
15. Longinova, T., Amberg, G., Ågren, J.: Phase-field simulations of non-isothermal binary alloy solidification. Acta Mater. **49**(4), 573–581 (2001)
16. Pilot Laboratory of Massively Parallel Systems (MICLab). http://miclab.pl
17. Michael Klemm. Heterogeneous Programming with OpenMP 4.5. https://www.scc.kit.edu/downloads/sca/Heterogeneous%20Programming%20with%20OpenMP%204.5.pdf

Author Index